THE EARLY STUARTS

The Early Stuarts

A political history of England 1603–1642

Roger Lockyer

Longman
London and New York

Longman Group UK Limited,
Longman House, Burnt Mill, Harlow,
Essex CM20 2JE, England
and Associated Companies throughout the world.

Published in the United States of America
by Longman Inc., New York

© Longman Group UK Limited 1989

First published 1989

British Library Cataloguing in Publication Data
Lockyer, Roger, 1927–
 The early Stuarts: a political history of England,
 1603–1642.
 1. England, 1603–1660
 I. Title
 942.06

ISBN 0-582-03294-6 CSD
ISBN 0-582-49338-2 PPR

Library of Congress Cataloging-in-Publication Data
Lockyer, Roger.
 The early Stuarts.

 Bibliography: p.
 Includes index.
 1. Great Britain – History – Early Stuarts,
 1603–1649. 2. Great Britain – Politics and government
 – 1603–1649. 3. England – Civilization – 17th
 century. 4. Stuart, House of. I. Title.
 DA390.L6 1988   941.06   88-2789
 ISBN 0-582-03294-6
 ISBN 0-582-49338-2 (pbk.)

Set in Linotron 202 10/11 pt Bembo

Produced by Longman Singapore Publishers (Pte) Ltd.
Printed in Singapore

Contents

List of Maps

Acknowledgements

The publishers are indebted to the following for permission to reproduce copyright material: The American Philosophical Society for extracts from *The Letters of John Chamberlain*, ed. N. E. McClure, Philadelphia 1939; and Yale University Press for extracts from *Proceedings in Parliament 1610* Vols 1 and 2 ed. Elizabeth Read Foster (New Haven 1966) and *Commons Debates 1628* Vols II, III and IV, ed. R. C. Johnson, Marja Jansson Cole, Mary Frear Keeler & W. B. Bidwell (New Haven 1977).

CHAPTER ONE

Early Stuart England: the economic background

AGRICULTURE AND RURAL SOCIETY

The reigns of James I and Charles I coincided with the final phase of a rapid increase in population which affected every aspect of English economic and social life. It had taken the country more than a century to recover from the effects of the Black Death, but by the time Henry VII came to the throne the long period of decline was over and the population was beginning to expand. In 1500 there may have been 2.5 million people in England; fifty years later there were around 3 million, and by the time James came to the throne this figure had risen to well over 4 million. There was no slackening in this rate of growth, and by the middle of the seventeenth century the population exceeded 5 million – in other words it had doubled during the course of the Tudor and early Stuart period. This put a great strain upon a society that was basically agricultural, for output could not be expanded at an equal rate, nor could a finite quantity of land provide a living for a rapidly increasing labour force. Yet food production did go up, and although a run of bad harvests might lead to near-starvation conditions in certain areas, England was spared the massive famines which affected countries such as Spain and Italy. The pressure on resources sent agricultural prices soaring – they rose by 300 per cent in 1550–1650 – but while this made life difficult for those at the bottom end of the social scale it acted as a stimulant to farmers, who responded by extending the area under cultivation, improving techniques to some extent, and orienting themselves towards a market economy.

Farming conditions were not uniform throughout England. Broadly speaking, there was a distinction between the north and

1

west, which had a high proportion of mountains and moorlands with thin soil best suited to pasture farming, and the lusher south and east where corn could be grown as well as grass, and 'mixed husbandry' was therefore the rule. The two zones were not mutually exclusive. There were 'highland' regions in the south and east, and 'lowland' ones in the north and west, but mixed farming, usually carried out on a communal basis in open fields, dominated the corn-growing areas of central and southern England. Communal farming was not necessarily inefficient, but it left limited scope for the man who wanted to go his own way and grow new crops or adopt new rotations without waiting for the approval of his neighbours. One or more such men would often enclose their fields, thereby removing them from the common stock and increasing the pressure on those lands that remained generally available. These included the wastes, on which villagers depended for their fuel supply, and the commons where they pastured their sheep and cattle. Waste land, however, was diminishing in availability, since it made better sense to take it into cultivation in order to provide food for the growing population. Commons were threatened by overstocking, since the demand for meat was rising and so too was that for wool. Sixteenth-century governments had fought in vain to prevent the conversion of arable to pasture, for fear that corn supplies would be insufficient, but by the beginning of the seventeenth century grain prices were going up, and the economic incentive to turn corn lands into sheep ranches was diminishing.

The process was still continuing, however, and in 1604 Sir Edward Montagu drew the attention of the House of Commons to 'the depopulation and daily excessive conversion of tillage into pasture' in his own county of Northamptonshire.[1] His fears about the possible consequences were fully justified, for in May 1607 a major revolt broke out in Northamptonshire and quickly spread to neighbouring counties. Upwards of a thousand self-styled 'levellers' tore down hedges, 'laying open enclosed grounds of late years taken in, to their damage, as they say', and ignoring orders to disperse.[2] In the end the local gentlemen, including Montagu, had to raise troops from among their own servants and followers and suppress the rebellion by force. They were authorised to do so by the King, who had been stung by the rebels' charge that he was indifferent to their sufferings, 'seeing it is manifest by Act of Parliament passed since our coming to this crown that we have been careful to prevent such enclosures and depopulations, and that it hath been an ordinary charge given by us to our justices of assizes, when they went to their circuits, to enquire of all unlawful depopulations and enclosures, and to take order to remedy the same, and to punish the offenders therein according to the due course of law'.[3]

James recognised that repression by itself was not a sufficient response to the revolt. In August he appointed commissioners to enquire into enclosures in the midland area, and their report showed that there had been a significant increase during the last four years of Elizabeth's reign and the first four of his own. Some of the chief offenders were brought before Star Chamber, and bound over to cease their activities. The court also ordered a number of enclosures to be pulled down, in order to demonstrate that lawful protest would be far more productive in the long run than riotous assembly. But Stuart governments were no more successful than their Tudor predecessors in holding up the course of economic change, and after a brief pause the process of enclosing commenced again.

Fears of a shortage of food declined in the 1620s, when harvests were good, and in 1624 the Elizabethan Act for the maintenance of tillage was repealed. The early 1630s, however, were marred by poor harvests, and as the price of corn rose, the government became alarmed at the prospect of renewed discontent. Magistrates and assize judges were instructed to order the removal of recent enclosures, and Star Chamber set an example by imposing heavy fines on those who had carried them out. Laud was particularly active in this sphere, for he confessed himself to be 'a great hater of depopulations in any kind, as being one of the greatest mischiefs in this kingdom'.[4] Indeed, Clarendon was of the opinion that Laud's opposition to 'enclosures and improvements of that nature' contributed to his unpopularity. Moreover, 'he did a little too much countenance the Commission for Depopulation, which brought much charge and trouble upon the people, which was likewise cast upon his account'.[5] Clarendon's comment reflects the shifting attitude on the part of the political nation towards the developments in agrarian techniques subsumed under the name of 'enclosure'. No longer were they regarded as socially unacceptable. On the contrary, the crown's attempt to pursue a conservative policy and moderate the forces of economic change brought it into disrepute with those sections of society which had a powerful influence upon the moulding of public opinion.

The Midland Revolt of 1607 had been prompted by enclosure of the open fields rather than commons or wastes. However, it was the enclosure of forests that led to a series of outbreaks of violence in the period 1628–31. Areas designated as forest, and subject to special laws, formed a significant part of the crown estates, but it had long been recognised that they were underexploited. Plans to disafforest and cultivate them, or even sell them off, had been drawn up under James, but they were only put into effect after his death, as war placed intolerable strains upon the crown's finances. In July 1626 Charles appointed commissioners who began the process of selling forests to courtiers and entrepreneurs who planned to enclose them and put the land under cultivation. In order to do so, they would secure the agreement of the property-owners in the affected areas but they rarely made provision for landless artisans and cottagers who found their entire livelihood threatened. In many places these took the law into their own hands. In the south-west they found a leader in John Williams, a miner who operated under the pseudonym of Lady Skimmington, and they had covert support from many of their social superiors, who resented the intrusion of outsiders into the forests and their wanton assault on customary attitudes and established ways of life. In some places the rioters achieved their object, and persuaded the enclosers to set aside land where they could pasture their animals. Elsewhere they were either put down or relapsed into sullen inertia, punctuated by occasional further rioting. A similar defence of local interests sparked off risings in eastern England in the 1630s against the projectors who were undertaking the drainage of the Fenlands.

THE CLOTH TRADE

Changes in the pattern of English agriculture were often made in response to the demands of England's major industry, the production of woollen cloth. Raw wool was bought up by clothiers who then distributed it, or 'put it out', to households located principally in the West Country, East Anglia, and the West Riding of Yorkshire, where it was woven into cloth. The same clothiers would subsequently collect the finished product and take it to London or a regional centre where it would be sold to merchants and shipped to the European market. The cloth trade accounted for some 90 per cent of all English exports. It was, in the words of one commentator in 1623, 'the axis of the commonwealth, whereon all the other trades . . . do seem to turn and have their revolution'. It was also, as a somewhat more poetic writer put it, 'the flower of the King's crown, the dowry of the kingdom, the chief revenue of the King . . . the gold of our Ophir, the milk and honey of our Canaan, the Indies of England'.[6] The export trade in 'white' or 'undressed' cloth was controlled by the Merchant Adventurers who had fixed their staple at Hamburg in 1611 and used it as the centre from which their goods were distributed to factories in Germany and the United Provinces. With the return of peace to western Europe soon after James I's accession, trade flourished, and the number of shortcloths exported from London increased from just over 100,000 in 1601 to more than 127,000 in 1614.

The 'white' cloths which the Merchant Adventurers shipped were dyed and dressed in continental factories and subsequently distributed throughout Europe and further afield. On the face of it, there was a strong case for those who argued that it would make better sense, and create more employment, to do the secondary manufacturing processes at home, rather than allow foreigners to cream off the profits. The Privy Council therefore gave a sympathetic hearing to Alderman Cockayne, who in 1614 proposed banning the export of undressed cloth. A royal proclamation put his suggestion into effect, and at the end of 1614 the Merchant Adventurers' charter was suspended and control of the cloth trade to northern Europe was transferred to Cockayne and his associates. They had promised to export 50,000 dressed cloths every year, but in practice they came nowhere near this figure. In fact the whole scheme was designed not to shift the emphasis of English clothmaking from undressed to dressed, but to take over the trade in white cloth and oust the Merchant Adventurers from their profitable monopoly. It turned out that Cockayne and his allies, who were established by charter as the New Company of the King's Merchant Adventurers, had insufficient capital, let alone expertise, to handle the business, and the only consequence of their intervention was a collapse of the cloth market. The Dutch forbade the importation of dressed cloths and looked to other sources, particularly Spain, for supplies of raw wool. Foreign competition had already been threatening the prosperity of the English cloth trade before Cockayne took a hand. The two years in which he dominated the scene merely provided foreign manufacturers with a breathing space in which to become even more competitive.

The Merchant Adventurers had their privileges restored in December 1616, and trade rapidly improved. In 1618 more than 100,000 shortcloths were exported from London, and it looked as though slump had given way to boom. The improvement was only temporary, however, for the outbreak of the Thirty Years War was accompanied in Germany by currency devaluations that made English imports increasingly expensive and therefore uncompetitive. By 1622 exports of English cloths were down by 40 per cent compared with 1614, and although the end of currency manipulations on the continent improved matters, there was no return to the former high levels. In 1632 fewer than 60,000 shortcloths were exported, and by 1640 this already low figure had dropped to 45,000. These changes were indicators of a fundamental shift in the English economy, as cloth gradually lost its dominant position. English woollen products had long been highly prized in Europe, but it looks as though the enclosure movement had had an unintended side effect in that by enabling sheep to be better fed it had lengthened and coarsened their wool. The shorter, more delicate Spanish wool now dominated the market, and the demand was for lighter fabrics rather than the heavy English broadcloths.

In short, fashion had changed, and the English cloth industry had no alternative but to change with it. A lead had already been given by Dutch and Huguenot refugees who had settled in England, particularly in East Anglia, during Elizabeth's reign, and brought with them the knowledge of how to manufacture lighter cloths such as bays, says and perpetuances, known collectively as the New Draperies. These were made from the coarser varieties of wool which were now plentifully available in England, and they were highly acceptable in the markets of southern Europe which catered for a warmer climate than the old broadcloth centres. While broadcloth sales slumped, the New Draperies went from strength to strength, and by the eve of the civil war they accounted for half the total exports of English cloth. They were also well placed to take advantage of the new markets that were opening up in America and the Orient.

Because the cloth industry was a major employer of labour, its health was a matter of great concern to the government. James I had given his backing to Cockayne's scheme because he believed it would strengthen the English economy, as well as increase the crown's receipts from Customs duties. When the scheme collapsed, and the subsequent recovery proved to be short-lived, the royal government again intervened, this time to mitigate the sufferings of the unemployed cloth workers. The Privy Council was alarmed by reports that 'they are much discouraged in the clothing counties for want of money. The trade of clothing is so much decayed for want of vent . . . that many poor people are ready to mutiny for want of work'.[7] It reacted to the crisis by trying to force the clothiers to keep manufacture going, on the grounds that 'whosoever had a part of the gain in profitable times . . . must now in the decay of trade (till that may be remedied) bear a part of the public loss'.[8] This argument cut little ice with the clothiers, who could not afford to manufacture cloth that the merchants were unwilling to buy, and although the Council put pressure on the merchants it could not force them to trade at a loss. In 1622, therefore, it set up a commission to enquire into the causes of the decay of trade, and it subsequently accepted the recommendation that the commission should be made permanent. For the first time the government had a standing body of experts to advise it on economic matters, and it was at the commission's suggestion that in 1624 the Council threw open the trade in New Draperies to all merchants. The Council was also reacting to pressure from Parliament, which was hostile to monopolists, including the trading companies, and believed that restrictions inhibited commerce. There was, however, the counter-argument that increasing competition and shrinking markets demanded concentration rather than dispersal of effort, and in the absence of Parliament in the 1630s this view prevailed. In 1634, therefore, the Merchant Adventurers were given a monopoly over the export of both Old and New Draperies to the Low Countries and Germany. This may have improved their fortunes in the short run, but it could not turn back the course of economic change, which was beyond the government's control.

LONDON

One of the main reasons for the Commons' dislike of the trading companies was that they were located in London and served not merely to perpetuate but to increase the dominance of the capital over the economic life of the country. London's importance was reflected in its expanding population. This rose from some 200,000 at the end of the sixteenth century to 375,000 by the middle of the seventeenth, and its growth was so remorseless that James I declared, with horror, that 'soon London will be all England'.[9] The increase in the city's population was caused entirely by immigration, for among the residents deaths outnumbered births, and even to maintain a stable level an inflow of 7,000 settlers was needed every year. People came to London for a variety of reasons. More than 2,500 were involved in the running of the Court, while at least as many were required to attend to the needs of the ninety peers and the several hundred gentlemen who were living in the city for a substantial part of the year by the 1630s. Sons of gentry came to acquire a knowledge of the law at the Inns of Court, the 'third university' of the kingdom, which were attracting students in increasing numbers. Their younger brothers were often apprenticed to a city merchant, which required several years' residence in the capital. It has been estimated that these two groups alone accounted for an annual influx of 750 young men from the upper sections of English society. The number of apprentices from lower down the social scale ran into several thousands, but they were absorbed largely by manufacturing. Much of this was small-scale, designed to meet the demands of the ever-expanding population, but long-established processes like ship-building and cloth-dyeing were labour intensive, and there were, in addition, new industries such as sugar refining, silk weaving, and the manufacture of pins, glass and paper. A great deal of this productive activity took place outside the city walls in the sprawling suburbs which were, in effect, a law unto themselves.

While boys and young men went to the city to further their careers, their fathers visited it, if at all, for a mixture of motives. If they were elected to Parliament, of course, they had no choice, but even as private individuals they might wish to put in an appearance at Court and ensure that their lines of communication with great patrons were kept open. Or they might be concerned either with pursuing a legal action or defending themselves against one, for this was an intensely litigious age. The capital contained the most prestigious doctors as well as lawyers, and medical treatment was a frequent reason for visiting London. So too was pleasure, for the early Stuart period saw the development of a London season, with visitors pouring in to enjoy each other's company, catch up on news from all parts of the world, go to the the theatre, sample the latest fashions, and do some shopping. The Duchess of Newcastle, writing after the Restoration, recalled the life of her sisters prior to the civil war. They spent half the year in London, where 'their customs were in wintertime to go sometimes to plays, or to ride in their coaches about the streets to see the concourse and recourse of people; and in the springtime to visit the Spring Garden, Hyde Park, and the like places; and sometimes they would have music, and sup in barges upon the water'.[10]

Because land was in short supply and the demand for it was never-ending, rents rose sharply, and the property owners, who were mainly aristocrats, were quick to seize their opportunity. In

1608 Robert Cecil, Earl of Salisbury and James I's chief minister, began the construction of the 'New Exchange' on the south side of the Strand. This was designed as a meeting place for men of business, but also included a number of shops designed to cater for the tastes of the fashionable world. From a financial point of view Cecil's venture was not a success, for the income from rents never justified his expenditure of some £12,000. The Earl of Bedford was more successful in developing the Covent Garden estate on the other side of the Strand. He employed Inigo Jones to build a magnificent square which quickly became one of the sights of London and attracted wealthy residents. Bedford's income from rents rose rapidly as a consequence; even so it never reached the levels attained by the Earl of Clare, who benefited from the inheritance of his great-grandfather, a successful London merchant. Clare developed his properties in the Drury Lane area to such effect that by the mid-1630s he was drawing £1,200 a year from them; ten years later this figure had more than doubled.[11]

While many aristocrats had houses alongside the Strand and took a major part in extending the urban area to the north and west, the government of the City proper was in the hands of the Lord Mayor and aldermen, elected from among its merchant oligarchs. These were wealthy men, worth, for the most part, at least £10,000. Some of them were enormously rich. Sir John Spencer, for instance, who served as Lord Mayor in the closing years of Elizabeth's reign, had accumulated a fortune of half a million pounds by the time of his death in 1610, while Baptist Hicks, a successful mercer who was knighted by James I and subsequently elevated to the peerage as Viscount Campden, was said to have given each of his two daughters £100,000.[12] About half the merchant oligarchs derived their wealth from domestic operations; the remainder were prominent figures in the great chartered companies that dominated foreign trade. Sir Thomas Smythe, who acted as one of James I's principal advisers on commercial matters, was a founder member of the East India Company, and served as its governor for fifteen years. He was also governor, at various times, of the Russia, the French, and the Levant Companies. Sir William Garway, another founder member of the East India Company and a prominent Levant merchant, joined the syndicate which farmed the Great Customs, a highly profitable operation and one which brought its members into the political arena. Garway's son, Sir Henry, succeeded his father as a Customs farmer, and was governor of the Levant, East India and Russia Companies.

The Garways may serve as a reminder that although the London merchant community acted as a magnet for the sons of rural land-owners – lesser gentry, yeomen and even husbandmen, rather than the greater gentry and aristocracy – it retained the services of native Londoners as well. It was not the custom for wealthy merchants to retire to the country and set themselves up as gentlemen. After a lifetime spent in business they could not easily give up the habit, and they usually stayed in or near the City, both to look after their own affairs and to keep an eye on their children who were following the same career.[13] Sir Henry Garway is also a reminder that 'the City' was not anti-royalist, for in the turbulence that marked the collapse of the Personal Rule he took the King's side and was subsequently imprisoned by Parliament. The oligarchs, particularly if they were Customs farmers, were closely connected with the royal govern-ment, and although they might resent specific actions on its part they recognised that their long-term interest, like that of the crown, consisted in the preservation of stability.

This was not the case, however, with those merchants whose attention was focussed primarily upon America and the West Indies, particularly the interlopers who resented the restraints imposed by the Virginia Company. These men had allies among the puritan peers and gentry who formed the Providence Island Company, and they approved of the buccaneering activities of the Earl of Warwick, who was to command Parliament's navy in the civil war. Although they might well be members of the chartered trading companies, they did not hold the top positions, nor were they prominent in the Court of Aldermen, which assisted the Lord Mayor, or the elected Common Council. They therefore had no vested interest in the maintenance of the *status quo*, and welcomed the political crisis of 1640–42 as a chance to destroy it. Their opportunity came in December 1641 when elections to the Common Council returned an anti-royalist majority and opened the way to the creation of a Committee of Safety which effectively took over the direction of affairs from the Lord Mayor and aldermen. From that point onwards the wealth and influence of the City were at the disposal of Parliament.

NOTES AND REFERENCES

(The place of publication is London, unless otherwise stated)
1. **Historical Manuscripts Commission** *Report on the Manuscripts of the Duke of Buccleuch & Queensbury*. Vol. III (1926), Part VI, *The Montagu Papers*, p. 81.
2. **James F. Larkin** & **Paul L. Hughes** (eds) *Stuart Royal Proclamations*. Vol. I, *Royal Proclamations of King James I* (Oxford 1973), pp. 152–3. (Hereafter Larkin & Hughes *Royal Proclamations*)
3. Larkin & Hughes *Royal Proclamations*, p. 153.
4. **H. R. Trevor-Roper** *Archbishop Laud 1573–1645* 2nd edn (1962), p. 169.
5. **Edward, Earl of Clarendon** *The History of the Rebellion and Civil Wars in England*, ed. W. Dunn Macray (Oxford 1888). Vol. I, p. 131.
6. **B. E. Supple** *Commercial Crisis and Change in England 1600–1642* (Cambridge 1959), p. 6 (Hereafter Supple *Commercial Crisis and Change*)
7. Supple *Commercial Crisis and Change*, p. 56.
8. Supple *Commercial Crisis and Change*, p. 65.
9. **F. J. Fisher** 'The Development of London as a Centre of Conspicuous Consumption in the Sixteenth and Seventeenth Centuries', *Transactions of the Royal Historical Society* (4th series). Vol. 30, 1948, p. 37.
10. **Margaret, Duchess of Newcastle** *The Life of William Cavendish, Duke of Newcastle*, ed. C. H. Firth (1886), p. 285.
11. **L. Stone** *The Crisis of the Aristocracy 1558–1641* (Oxford 1965), pp. 360–1.
12. **R. G. Lang** 'Social Origins and Social Aspirations of Jacobean London Merchants', *Economic History Review* (2nd series). Vol. 27, 1974, p. 30. (Hereafter Lang 'Social Origins')
13. Lang 'Social Origins', pp. 45–7.

CHAPTER TWO

England and Europe: the foreign policy of James I and Charles I

JAMES AS MEDIATOR

When James VI became James I, England was still at war with Spain. Scotland, however, had never been involved in this war, and the King did not share the rabidly anti-Spanish feelings which the long struggle against the Catholic Monarchy had generated in his English subjects. He was, by nature, a peacelover; furthermore, he saw no point in continuing a conflict which was a drain upon the public purse, an impediment to trade, and an incentive to privateering, which he regarded as little better than piracy. The Spaniards were also tired of the war, and since the death of Philip II in 1598 and the accession of his son, Philip III, they had lost much of the crusading fervour that had formerly animated them.

The major stumbling block to a settlement was the Dutch Revolt, for the Spaniards were unwilling to acknowledge the independence of the United Provinces, which the Dutch had made a precondition for peace. England was involved because she was the ally of the Dutch, and had provided them with both troops and money. James could not simply abandon the Dutch, even though he had little sympathy for republican rebels, but he was not prepared to allow them to dictate the parameters of his own policy. When the Spaniards suggested that he should act as mediator between them and the Dutch and thereby help bring about a general peace, James willingly accepted. Only after the Dutch made it plain that they intended to carry on their struggle for freedom and were not interested in conditional peace terms did the King authorise the opening of separate negotiations with Spain. These culminated in the Treaty of London, signed in August 1604, which brought the war between the two countries to a close. Under the terms of the treaty, English merchants were at liberty to pursue their business in Spain and the Spanish Netherlands, and were to be free from the Inquisition as long as they did not give 'occasion of public scandal'.[1] Nothing was said about trade with the Spanish possessions in the New World. This was still officially prohibited by the Spaniards, but in practice their writ ran only as far as they could enforce it. As for the Dutch, James gave some assurances couched in deliberately vague terms, but the Spaniards can have been under no illusion that the English troops serving there would be withdrawn, or that the flow of volunteers would be seriously impeded.

One significant omission from the Treaty of London was any provision relating to the English catholics. Philip II would have insisted on the need to guarantee them freedom of worship, but Philip III and his chief minister, the Duke of Lerma, recognised that any such insistence would be self-defeating since the English would break off negotiations rather than give way on this point. The English catholics felt abandoned, and one consequence of their mood of despair was the Gunpowder Plot. However, the Spanish government had not totally lost interest in their fate; it was merely changing its tactics. It now hoped to achieve by gradual means what it could not obtain at a single stroke, and for this reason the Constable of Castile, who signed the Treaty of London for Spain, welcomed (and may indeed have prompted) a suggestion from Queen Anne, James's Roman Catholic wife, that in due course her son, Prince Henry, should be married to a Spanish princess. Such a union would not only bind the two crowns together; it might also lead to the diminution of ill-feeling between the two religions which they represented and prepare the ground for toleration.

As far as the Spaniards were concerned this toleration would be distinctly one-sided, applying only to the catholics in England, for they would never under any circumstances have permitted protestants freedom of worship in Spain. They did not believe in toleration as such, but regarded it as a major step along the road that would lead England back to Rome. Supremely confident in the superiority of their own catholic faith, and convinced that it was bound to prevail in the long run, they would have agreed with the view expressed by Pym in 1621 that toleration would lead to equality, equality to superiority, and superiority to the eventual restoration of the old faith in England (see p. 291). Although James had declared that he would never tolerate the open exercise of the Roman Catholic religion within his kingdoms, the Spaniards intended to try and push him in this direction during the course of negotiations over a possible marriage. They also hoped to persuade him that Prince Henry should be given instruction in catholic doctrine, and to secure his agreement that the children of the marriage should be brought up as catholics. They worked on the assumption that the English Reformation had been an act of state, and that by clearing the ground for the accession at some future date of a catholic ruler they would ensure ultimate victory for Rome. As they saw it, what one monarch had done, another could easily undo. Cut off from England as they had been for close on half a century, they had no awareness of the extent to which anti-catholicism had woven itself into the very fabric of English life.

The suggestion of a Spanish match for Prince Henry was not immediately followed up. One reason for this was the youth of the parties concerned, for Henry himself was only ten in 1604, while the Infanta Anna was a mere three years old. Another was the relative stability of the international situation, which prompted a gradualist approach towards the formulation of foreign policy. In 1609 the long struggle between Spain and the United Provinces came to a halt, with the signing of a twelve-year truce, and for the first time for many decades Europe was free of major conflicts. There were, however, two factors which threatened the maintenance of peace. The first was the continuing tension within Germany between prot-estants and catholics, the Reformation and the Counter-Reformation. The second was the re-emergence of France as a major power under Henri IV and the consequent revival of Franco-Spanish rivalry. The two factors were linked, for although France and Spain were both catholic, Henri was quite prepared to make common cause with the German protestants. Religious tension led to the formation of the Protestant Union of German princes in 1608, under the leadership of Frederick IV, the Calvinist ruler of the Palatinate. This was count-ered, the following year, by the creation of the Catholic League, in which the driving spirit was Maximilian I of Bavaria. Both sides seemed to be heading for open collision in 1609 over the question of who should succeed to the Rhine principality of Julich-Cleve, and the protestants appealed for help to Henri IV. Henri welcomed their overtures, for he was planning an all-out attack upon Spain. He did not, of course, reveal this to James, who had agreed, along with the Dutch, to supply several thousand troops to support the Protestant Union. James assumed that these would be used for the preservation, not the destruction, of the *status quo*. However, he might have found himself dragged into a general war at the heels of France had it not been for the assassination of Henri IV in May 1610.

Henri's successor was his nine-year-old son, Louis XIII, but the direction of affairs passed to his widow, Marie de Médicis, who preferred the security of peace to the risks of war. She abandoned Henri's forward policy, and instead promoted the cause of Franco-Spanish friendship by arranging a marriage between Louis and the Infanta Anna. The new Queen of France, usually known as 'Anne of Austria', was the princess who had been spoken of, in 1604, as a possible bride for Prince Henry, and even as late as 1611 James was hoping to bring this match to fulfilment. He felt insulted and angry when he learned that the Spaniards had preferred a French husband for Anna, and initially rejected their offer of her younger sister, the Infanta Maria. But in fact the Spanish proposal fitted in with the overall policy which James was now developing. His concern for peace made him acutely aware that the major threat to it came from religious tensions. Spain and the House of Austria represented militant catholicism, the Dutch and the German Protestant Union an equally militant protestantism. James was unequivocally protestant, but he was no bigot. Far from glorying· in the religious division of Europe and embracing an apocalyptic interpretation of the struggle between protestantism and catholicism as one between God and the Devil, he longed to heal the rift. What was needed, as he saw it, was a mediator, someone who could talk to both sides and retain their confidence. Who better than himself to fill this crucial role?

Already, at the time of the Julich-Cleve crisis, James had shown his willingness to support the German protestants against what he regarded as an attempt on the part of the catholic Emperor to undermine their position. Now, in March 1612, he signed a treaty of mutual assistance with the princes of the Protestant Union. Furthermore, he agreed that its nominal head, the sixteen-year-old Frederick V, who had recently succeeded his father as Elector Palatine, should marry his daughter, Princess Elizabeth. Frederick was the embodiment of European protestantism, for his grandfather was William the Silent, the hero of Dutch resistance, and he was connected by marriage with the King of Sweden, the Elector of Brandenburg and the Huguenot Duc de Bouillon, all of them leading figures in the protestant world. James himself was linked to another major protestant power, Denmark, whose king, Christian IV, was his brother-in-law. Once the marriage between Elizabeth and Frederick had been concluded, therefore, James would be at the centre of the protestant network, ideally placed to make his views known and his influence felt. If he was to be an effective mediator he needed a similar *entrée* into the catholic world, and a Spanish match for his son, Prince Henry, would be a highly effective way of achieving this.

James was not willing, at this stage, to pin all his hopes on Spain. Savoy and Tuscany were also angling for a marriage alliance with England, and Marie de Médicis had dropped hints that she would be happy to see the Prince marry her seven-year-old daughter, Christina. Prince Henry himself had no wish for a catholic bride. He was far more in tune with English opinion than his father could ever be, and would far rather have led a protestant crusade against the Pope and his temporal supporters than tried to build bridges between the two halves of Christendom. He strongly approved of the match between his sister and the Elector Palatine and was apparently toying with the idea of going off to Germany himself and marrying into the Palatine's family.[2] But whatever plans he may have had, they came to nothing, for in November 1612 he succumbed to typhoid fever.

Prince Henry's death caused widespread and genuine grief in England, for he had become the symbol of protestant aspirations, and the prospect of his eventual succession had cheered all those who despaired of James's temporising policies and longed to see England re-emerge as the champion of the Reformed religion. They looked back nostalgically to Elizabeth's reign, when there had been open war against Spain, the greatest of all catholic powers, and open support for her enemies throughout Europe. As for Elizabeth herself, they venerated her as Gloriana, the embodiment of all that was best in English religious and political traditions. In this they were straying a long way from the truth, for Elizabeth's attitude towards foreign policy was very similar to James's. She was, like him, a *politique* by temperament, detesting bigotry in all its forms, and opposed to the reduction of international relations to crude categories of black and white. Insofar as his championship of the protestant cause was concerned, Prince Henry had been the heir not of Elizabeth but of those like the Earl of Leicester, Sir Philip Sidney, Sir Walter Ralegh, and the Earl of Essex, who chafed at her lack of resolution and complained, in Ralegh's words, that she 'did all by halves'.[3]

The marriage between Princess Elizabeth and Frederick V took place in February 1613, and for a time it seemed as though James was about to adopt the role of protestant champion. The Spaniards were sufficiently alarmed to send to England, as their ambassador, Diego Sarmiento de Acuña, better known by his later title of Count

of Gondomar, with instructions to undermine the continuing negotiations for a French marriage – now, of course, for Prince Charles
– and to revive the idea of a Spanish match. Gondomar very quickly
established good relations with James, and was subsequently credited
with an undue influence over him. But in the complex diplomatic
power game, James was as much the deceiver as the deceived, and
if he responded warmly to Gondomar's proposals for a Spanish
marriage for Prince Charles it was because they fitted in with his
overall plan to become the mediator of Europe. The question of
foreign policy polarised James's Court, for the Howards and their
allies were generally in favour of a Spanish alliance, while Archbishop Abbot and the Earl of Pembroke headed a 'protestant faction'
which wanted James to break with Spain and throw himself upon
the affections of his subjects. In the spring of 1614 it looked as
though the protestant interest was in the ascendant, for James
decided to summon Parliament. However, the failure of this 'addled'
assembly and the intemperate language used by some of its members
made James fear for his own security and encouraged him to seek
support and protection from Spain (see p. 185). In late 1614, therefore, he despatched Sir John Digby to Madrid with instructions to
open negotiations for a marriage between the Infanta Maria and
Prince Charles.

THE BOHEMIAN CRISIS

It was the apparent triumph of the Spanish faction which encouraged
Abbot and Pembroke to take the dangerous step of promoting
another favourite. They were successful, insofar as Buckingham
replaced Somerset and subsequently toppled the Howards. But a
new favourite did not mean a new policy, for James was his own
master in this respect and was now committed to the Spanish Match.
There was no obvious cause for haste, since Prince Charles was only
as old as the century and the Infanta five years younger. Admittedly,
the peace of Europe was threatened, as always, by religious tensions,
but these had so far been contained. However, the situation changed
dramatically for the worse in 1618, when the Bohemians, who had
earlier elected as their king the Archduke Ferdinand, heir-apparent
to the Holy Roman Emperor, renounced their allegiance to him and
offered the throne instead to the Elector Palatine, Frederick V.

Bohemia was one of the few examples of a religiously pluralist

17

state, and the protestant elements in it had been alarmed by Ferdinand's commitment to Counter-Reformation catholicism in its most uncompromising form. Since pluralism was no longer an option, they were forced to choose between a catholic and a protestant ruler, and they opted for the latter. There was nothing accidental or ill-considered about their choice of Frederick. His key position in the protestant world was a great strength in their eyes, for he would bring with him to Prague – or so they hoped and assumed – not simply the goodwill of his fellow protestants but their active support. The Bohemians, in other words, were working on the assumption that while the Habsburgs might challenge a new ruler who stood alone, they would think twice before taking on the united forces of European protestantism.

This assumption turned out to be unjustified, for Ferdinand was a catholic version of Prince Henry, a man who put religion first and all other considerations a long way behind. Moreover, the death of the Emperor Matthias in March 1619 opened the way for his own accession to the imperial throne and the headship of the Austrian branch of the House of Habsburg. In fact his election as Emperor in August 1619 came only two days after the Bohemian estates had made a formal offer of their crown to Frederick. The Bohemian crisis was already becoming internationalised, and Frederick would have to take this into account before he decided whether or not to accept. He turned for advice to his father-in-law, James I, who was strongly of the opinion that Frederick should reject this poisoned chalice. However, by the time his advice reached Heidelberg, Frederick had made up his mind and was already *en route* to Prague.

The new King of Bohemia and his English wife were immensely popular among James's subjects, as was shown in 1621 when Parliament imposed the most savage punishments upon an aged Roman Catholic lawyer, Edward Floyd, who had dared to criticise them. They did indeed carry with them to Prague the best wishes of the majority of James's subjects, but these were of no avail against the forces of the Catholic League, which Maximilian of Bavaria offered to use on the Emperor's behalf. In November 1620 the Bohemian army was crushed in the battle of the White Mountain, just outside Prague, and Frederick and Elizabeth had to flee from their newly acquired kingdom after just one brief winter. They could not return to their hereditary Palatinate on the Rhine, for half of this had been occupied by the Catholic League while the remainder was in the hands of a Spanish contingent under the command of the Marquis Spinola, one of Philip III's finest generals. The Spaniards had intervened for a mixture of motives. The 'family compact' was one, for Spanish ministers regarded the fortunes of the two branches of the House of Austria as being interdependent and accepted an obligation to support the Emperor now that he had called on them for help. They also hoped that in due course the Austrian Habsburgs would give reciprocal assistance to Spain in her struggle to regain all her provinces in the Netherlands. The war against the Dutch was the primary motive for Spanish intervention, for the twelve-year truce was due to expire in 1621, and Spain had to safeguard her supply route to the Netherlands, which ran from Milan across the Alps and along the Rhine. It passed through the middle of Frederick's territories, and it was in order to secure it that Spinola moved in his troops and occupied the left bank in the summer of 1620.

The direct intervention of Spain inflamed public opinion in England and made the Palatine's cause even more popular. James had been opposed to the Bohemian venture on the grounds that it would upset the *status quo*, but for the same reason he condemned the Spanish occupation of Frederick's hereditary territories. He allowed a volunteer force of some 4,000 men to be recruited and sent to the Palatinate, under the command of Sir Horace Vere. He also appointed a Council·of War, with instructions to prepare plans for raising an army of 25,000 infantry and 5,000 cavalry. It reported in February 1621, and gave its estimate that £200,000 would be needed to set out an army of this size, and £900,000 a year to keep it in the field.[4] Sums of this magnitude were far beyond the existing resources of the crown, and James had already summoned Parliament to meet in January 1621. In his opening speech he described how, at an early stage, and 'at the request of the King of Spain and the Emperor on the one side, and my son[-in-law] on the other side' he had attempted to defuse the crisis. 'But within three days, and while I was mediating between the Emperor and them [the Bohemians], they chose my son[-in-law] for their king. He wrote to me, to know my mind if he should take that crown; but within three days after, and before I could return answer, he put it on'.[5]

James's anger at what he regarded as Frederick's intemperate action was plain for all to see. It had cut away the foundation of James's position as mediator, which he had so carefully and laboriously constructed, and it now threatened to engulf him in a war which he did not want and could not afford. James rejected the claim that Frederick's cause was that of religion, 'for what hath religion to do to decrown a king? Leave that opinion to the Devil and to the Jesuits, authors of it and brands of sedition. For may subjects rebel

19

against their prince in quarrel of religion? Christ came into the world to teach subjects obedience to the king, and not rebellion'.[6] James may have had logic on his side, but his hearers were swayed by powerful emotions, and placed religion at the heart and centre of the conflict. As one member declared, 'if we think not that man of Rome and his son of Spain to be our enemies, we're deceived. For it's this country that drew the one from his spiritual monarchy and hindered the other from being that which he hath ever aspired unto, *viz.* to be Monarch of the West'.[7]

At the end of the first session of Parliament, in June 1621, the Commons pledged themselves to give the utmost support to the King if he was forced into war over the Palatinate (see p. 200), and as an earnest of their good intentions they voted two subsidies, which eventually brought in just under £150,000. There is no reason to doubt the members' sincerity, but the King had learnt from experience that even genuine professions were never translated into their equivalent in hard cash. Despite the clamour for war, therefore, he clung to his hopes of a negotiated settlement, and called on Spain to assist him. In this respect James and his subjects were at one, for they both assumed that Spain conducted the policies of catholic Europe. This was a false assumption, for the Emperor and his allies did not dance to the Spanish tune. In these early stages of the Thirty Years War it was Maximilian of Bavaria who exerted the greatest influence, for he directed the forces of the Catholic League, which he had placed at the Emperor's service. Maximilian had insisted on having the Palatinate transferred to him as his reward, and this ruled out a negotiated settlement of the sort that the Spaniards would have welcomed. They deceived James insofar as they encouraged him in his belief that they could restrain the Emperor, but they were the victims rather than the masters of a crisis which was rapidly spiralling out of control.

THE SPANISH MATCH

In the short term the Spaniards concentrated on preventing the war from spreading – which meant, in effect, persuading James not to intervene – in the hope that a swift victory on the battlefield would resolve matters in their favour. They therefore encouraged James to assume that the long-sought Spanish marriage for his son was gradually approaching fulfilment, and that once this was achieved it would give him the leverage in international diplomacy that he needed in order to act as an effective mediator. But as the months passed and negotiations dragged on indefinitely, it seemed to many of James's subjects that he was chasing a chimera and allowing his love of peace to subordinate both him and them to the strategy of the House of Austria. The end of this state of suspended animation came with startling suddenness in 1623, when Prince Charles, accompanied by Buckingham, rode incognito through France and Spain and arrived unannounced in Madrid, where he claimed his bride. It may be that Charles was inspired solely by love for the Infanta, but the effect of his unexpected arrival was to force the Spaniards to show their hand. They managed to spin out negotiations for a few more months, and also to secure a formal promise from Charles – acting in the name and with the authority of his father – that the penal laws against English catholics would be suspended, and that within the space of three years Parliament would be asked to repeal them. Only at this point did the Spaniards agree that the marriage should take place, but even then they insisted that the Infanta should remain in Spain until it became apparent that the provisions of the marriage treaty were being put into effect.

James had intended the marriage negotiations simply as the first step in the process of agreeing with the Spaniards a timetable for the restoration of the Palatinate to his son-in-law, Frederick. However, it became plain to Buckingham, who was charged with the conduct of these negotiations, that the Spaniards were not committed to restoration, except as a hypothetical possibility at some far-off date. Indeed, his months in the Spanish capital and his experience of negotiating with Spanish ministers had made him aware for the first time of the extent of their ambitions and the threat that this posed to all non-Habsburg states. If Spain recovered the Dutch provinces she would control the entire coastline of Flanders, from where she could point a pistol at England. And to the extent that Spain and the Emperor forged closer links they would be moving towards the re-creation of the Habsburg dominance of Europe and the western world that had ended some eighty years earlier with the abdication of Charles V. Buckingham became convinced that the continued existence of England as an independent power demanded the formation of an anti-Habsburg alliance. Even before he left Spain he had established unofficial contact with France, and no sooner had he returned to England than he began pressing the Dutch to make overtures to James.

ANGLO-DUTCH RELATIONS

Anglo-Dutch relations in James's reign had been characterised by an uneasy mixture of friendship and hostility. There was considerable fellow-feeling for the mainly Calvinist Dutch, particularly among those of puritan inclination in England, and widespread admiration for the way in which they had asserted their independence from Spain despite the heavy odds against them. Queen Elizabeth, however reluctantly, had supported the Dutch in their struggle, and they had pledged three of their towns to her as security for the repayment of her loans. English garrisons were stationed in these towns until 1615, when James agreed to the restoration of Dutch sovereignty, in return for the payment of £200,000 in settlement of the outstanding debt. James, like Elizabeth, disapproved· of rebels and found the whole idea of a republican state distasteful. He was also envious, as were many of his subjects, of the commercial success of the Dutch and the enormous wealth it was bringing to them. The Dutch had established themselves as the principal fishermen and the leading merchants of western Europe, but their domination was resented by the English, who aspired to play exactly these roles. There were simmering disputes about fishing rights in the North Sea and off Greenland, and about trading rights in the East Indies, all of which increased the general awareness of the extent to which the Dutch were 'usurping' the place of England, their original patron and protector. 1610 saw the appearance of *Observations touching Trade and Commerce with the Hollanders and Others, wherein is proved that our Sea and Land Commodities serve to enrich and strengthen other Countries than our own*, attributed to Sir Walter Ralegh, and ill feeling was increased by the hostile Dutch reaction to Alderman Cockayne's project for exporting finished rather than white cloth (see p. 5).

Sporadic attempts had been made to resolve outstanding issues between the two countries, but they met with little success. Even those who were predisposed in favour of the Dutch were offended at their apparent arrogance. In 1621, for example, John Chamberlain reported that they began 'every day to be descried and decried more and more; and their best friends, who, for the common consider-ations of religion and neighbourhood, always wished them well, cry out upon them for the continual injuries and insolencies we receive from them, so that the good affection [which] was borne them breaks out into indignation, that those of whom we have so many ways deserved so well should thus requite us'.[8] James would have shed no tears if the upstart republic had vanished from the map.

Indeed, he had instructed Charles, while he was in Spain, to discuss with Philip IV's ministers the possibility of a joint Anglo-Spanish operation to conquer the rebel provinces and split them between the two crowns. With the collapse of the Spanish marriage negotiations, however, the situation changed, and the Dutch were now regarded as potential allies. James therefore gave a favourable response to the feelers put out by the Dutch (at Buckingham's suggestion) in 1624, and in June he accepted an agreement which bound him to allow four additional regiments, each of 1,500 men, to be raised by the Dutch in England, and to meet their costs for two years.

The agreement came just in time, for reports were beginning to reach England of the torture and execution of English merchants at Amboyna, in the East Indies, carried out by their Dutch rivals in February of the previous year. The 'Amboyna massacre' created intense anger in England, and Chamberlain recorded in July 1624 that it 'hath so much alienated our affections that we cry out mainly [i.e. strongly] for revenge'. He thought the best response would be to intercept Dutch East Indiamen 'and hang up upon Dover cliffs as many as we should find faulty or actors in this business'. There was no other way, he added, in which to deal with 'such manner of men as neither regard law nor justice nor any other respect of equity or humanity, but only make gain their God'.[9]

James, for once, shared the public anger, but Buckingham was too aware of the advantages of Dutch co-operation to indulge in thoughts of revenge. He was instrumental in bringing about an offensive and defensive alliance with the United Provinces by the Treaty of Southampton in September 1625, and he persuaded the Dutch to contribute ships to the expedition against Cadiz. This set sail in October, and in the following month Buckingham went over to Holland to lay the foundations on which an anti-Habsburg league could be built. By the Treaty of the Hague, signed in December 1625, England, Denmark and the United Provinces bound themselves to work together for the containment of Habsburg power and the restoration of the Palatinate to Frederick V. The treaty was open-ended, in the sense that other states were free to join the Hague League as and when they wished. In particular it was hoped that France and Sweden would subsequently become members, for their adhesion would transform the embryonic League into a major force in European politics.

THE MANSFELD AND CADIZ EXPEDITIONS

Buckingham had already taken steps to associate France with England through a marriage alliance. This was concluded in December 1624, and under its provisions Prince Charles was to marry Louis XIII's sister, Henrietta Maria. The first fruits of this newly-forged relationship became immediately apparent when France agreed to contribute 3,000 cavalry to an English expeditionary force of 12,000 men, the whole to be commanded by an experienced mercenary leader, Count Mansfeld. The plan was that Mansfeld would take his infantry across to France where they would link up with the French horse and then fight their way into the Palatinate. Louis XIII, who held the title of 'Most Christian King' and was a conventional adherent of the Roman Catholic faith, was reluctant to publicise his military co-operation with a protestant state and felt he had gone quite far enough by agreeing to joint operations. James, however – who had long experience of what he regarded as French perfidy, and feared being led into a trap – insisted that Louis should give a written undertaking to support Mansfeld's expedition. The French king and his ministers interpreted this as a typical example of James's deviousness, believing that his principal aim was not to fight Spain but to come to an agreement with her, and that he would use Louis' undertaking as a means to this end.

It was on these rocks of mutual suspicion that Mansfeld's expedition foundered, for Louis withdrew his permission for the English force to land in France, and at the last moment, and in the depths of winter, Buckingham had to make other arrangements. The infantry were shipped to Holland, but the Dutch could offer only limited accommodation, and half the force had to remain on shipboard. This was nearly always fatal, for the soldiers, drawn as they were from the dregs of the population, had only the haziest ideas about hygiene, and infection rapidly set in. Things were not much better for those who went ashore, for the intense cold and lack of food left them prey to illness. As the men died like flies, or simply ran away, Mansfeld's force was reduced to an ineffective rump. It was an inauspicious opening to the anti–Habsburg campaign and cast a pall over the parliamentary session which began in June 1625.

Mansfeld's expedition had been designed to appeal to James, for although the King was opposed to all–out war against Spain he was prepared to sanction an operation to recover the Palatinate, which was, by right if not in fact, the property of his son-in-law. However, Buckingham was aware that public opinion, at least insofar as it was represented in the House of Commons, did not approve of what Chamberlain described as 'pottering and pelting in the Palatinate only to consume both our men and means'.[10] It would not be satisfied by anything less than a war of diversion – in other words direct action against Spain which would divert her attention and her resources from other theatres. Buckingham planned to provide just such diversionary pressure through an assault on Cadiz, and it became much easier to do so after the removal of James from the political scene and the accession of Charles I. In May 1625, therefore, he was able to inform Sir Edward Cecil, whom he had chosen as general, of the new King's decision 'that a fleet of ships may be employed, accompanied with ten thousand land soldiers, which may do some notable effects to move those that have dispossessed His Majesty's dear sister of her inheritance to loose that prize'.[11] As usual in such operations, the objectives were outlined only in general terms, for a great deal depended upon time and circumstance as interpreted by the commander on the spot. If Cadiz were taken, plundered and then evacuated, this would redound to England's credit and dishonour Spain. If it could be held, it would provide a base for a permanent English naval presence off the Spanish coast, as well as tying down many thousand Spanish troops. There was also the prospect of capturing the treasure fleet from the New World which constituted Spain's life blood and was headed for Cadiz.

Combined expeditions were always hazardous and much depended upon the speed with which they could be assembled and despatched, for salt beef, biscuit and beer, stored in barrels, began to deteriorate as soon as they were put on board. What Buckingham needed was not simply parliamentary supply but, even more important, the evidence of parliamentary commitment which would enable him to raise loans and get preparations under way immediately. This was why he regarded the vote of two subsidies as inadequate and persuaded the King to recall the 1625 Parliament for a second session (see p. 329). The failure of this session left him with the problem of setting out a fleet and army for which there were insufficient funds available; it was almost as if members of Parliament, having publicly doubted whether the expedition would ever set sail, had now ensured that it could not. In these circumstances, what is surprising is that the fleet did set sail, in October 1625, made its way to the Spanish coast, and actually landed the troops within striking distance of Cadiz. From this point onwards, however, the whole operation descended into farce, for the troops who were meant to be thrusting ahead towards the city came across some farmhouses containing great vats of wine, and in next to no time the army transformed itself into a drunken rabble. All Cecil could do was to usher it back on board the ships and head for home, narrowly missing the Plate Fleet as he did so. By now, some of the victuals had been stored for more than six months and were rotten. Shortage of food and drink, and poor standards of hygiene among the soldiers, produced the inevitable consequences, and it was only with difficulty that the ships managed to straggle back to English and Irish ports. The troops who landed at Plymouth were, according to an official report, in a 'miserable condition and state, in respect of their wants and sicknesses' and one eye-witness made the pithy observation that 'they stink as they go, and the poor rags they have are rotten and ready to fall off if they be touched'.[12]

The ignominious collapse of the Cadiz expedition, coming as it did on top of the failure of Mansfeld's campaign to recapture the Palatinate, created a mood of anger and despair in England. Buckingham was held responsible for both disasters, and it is possible – though by no means certain – that if he had been replaced by a minister more acceptable to Parliament and public opinion the English war effort might have been more successful. Charles, however, was unwilling to dismiss the man whom he had charged with the execution of a strategy that he believed to be in the best interests of his country. He knew that James, not Buckingham, had crippled Mansfeld's expedition, and he held Parliament responsible for the tardy and inadequate funding which had forced the Cadiz expedition to sail late in the year with its provisions already rotting. Charles and Buckingham were agreed that the appropriate response to defeat was not to throw in the sponge but to redouble England's commitment to war and to fight more efficiently. There had been no significant change in the European situation, no diminution of the threat from Habsburg expansionism. There was no occasion, therefore, to change English strategy. All that the failures had demonstrated was the need for England to find allies and act in concert with them. It was to achieve this that Buckingham, with Charles's full approval, bent his efforts towards securing the adhesion of France to the Hague League.

BUCKINGHAM AND RICHELIEU

When negotiations had first been opened with the French in 1624 they had gone smoothly, mainly because of the sympathetic attitude of Louis XIII's chief minister, the Marquis of La Vieuville. However, during the course of the negotiations La Vieuville had been toppled from power in a palace *coup* and replaced by Richelieu. This transformed the situation, for Richelieu was not simply a cardinal and therefore likely to be more resistant to the prospect of alliance with a protestant state; he had also made himself a spokesman for the *dévots*, the French catholic equivalent of the English puritans, who believed that religious considerations must be given priority in the formulation of policy and that the French crown should therefore hold out the hand of friendship to Spain. It was to become clear during the course of the next decade that Richelieu had simply used the *dévots* as a ladder up which he could climb to power, and that once securely established he would kick it away. But 1624 was only the opening stage of his rise to supremacy, and he could not afford openly to embrace a 'secular' policy of the sort that Buckingham advocated, even though his ultimate objectives were similar to the Duke's. Buckingham was therefore left with the problem of interpreting Richelieu's words by setting them against his actions, and it is hardly surprising that he found his suspicions increasing.

Buckingham was not the only person who 'misread' Richelieu. The French protestants, the Huguenots, did the same, for they assumed that the Cardinal intended not merely to curb their political independence but altogether to extirpate them, and that they must therefore look to their own defence. The first overt challenge came from the Huguenot Duke of Rohan and his brother, the Count of Soubise, who in January 1625 attacked and seized a number of ships that were being prepared for a blockade of the Huguenot stronghold of La Rochelle. Louis, whose naval resources were limited, appealed to his Dutch and English allies for assistance, on the grounds that France could not engage in war against the common enemy abroad unless and until she was sure of peace at home. The Huguenots had not so far come out in support of Rohan and Soubise, who seemed to be more concerned with self-advancement than leading a protestant crusade, so both England and the United Provinces agreed to lend ships to Louis. When it subsequently became apparent that La Rochelle would, in fact, follow the lead given by the rebel brothers, Buckingham delayed the transfer of the vessels until he was assured that Louis and the Huguenots had come to terms. In the summer of 1625 the English agent in France reported that this had happened and that Louis' forces would now 'be sent into Italy' where they would 'attack the Spaniard on his own dunghill'.[13] The English and Dutch ships were thereupon handed over, but it later emerged that the optimistic reports of agreement between Louis and the Huguenots had been inspired by Richelieu and had no substance. The French government was still committed to defeating the challenge from Rohan and Soubise, and in September 1625 it achieved this by wiping out the Huguenot fleet in an operation in which the English and Dutch ships took part.

Buckingham had now been made to appear responsible for aiding Richelieu – in English eyes an archetypal catholic aggressor – to suppress the French protestants, and this was one of the charges laid against him in the parliamentary impeachment of 1626. Buckingham believed that Richelieu, while professing friendship, had deliberately deceived him, but he would have been prepared to overlook this if, as a consequence of the Huguenot defeat, French forces had been turned against the Spaniards. However, La Rochelle was still in revolt, and not until January 1626 was a negotiated settlement achieved through the mediation of specially deputed English envoys. One of these reported to Buckingham that Richelieu had promised that 'all other things should follow according to our wish' and that Louis would 'enter – in effect if not in title – into our German league'.[14] Buckingham hoped that a French attack upon the Spanish duchy of Milan would draw off Spanish forces operating against the Dutch and in the Palatinate and give the allies a valuable breathing space. But his hopes were dissipated by the news that France and Spain had settled their differences and agreed to maintain peace in Italy. The Duke of Savoy, who had been planning joint operations with the French, was outraged at what he described as 'the perfidiousness of this treason' and so were other states on the periphery of France, such as Lorraine and Venice.[15]

Although Richelieu protested his continuing commitment to the cause of restoring the Palatinate and containing Habsburg power, the evidence persuaded Buckingham that the contrary was true. Since the success of the anti-Habsburg alliance depended in the final count upon French co-operation, and since this would apparently be unforthcoming while the Cardinal remained in power, Buckingham concerted a strategy for displacing him. Richelieu had many enemies among the princes of the blood in France, including Louis' brother Gaston, Duke of Orleans. He was also, of course, hated by the Huguenots. The Cardinal's opponents could achieve little while he had the King's confidence, but Louis XIII was a devious character and might well be persuaded to dispense with Richelieu's services if he turned out to be more of a liability than an asset. What Buckingham proposed, therefore, was a simultaneous rising by the

Huguenots and the princes of the blood, accompanied by military intervention from Savoy and Lorraine. Louis would be called upon to dismiss Richelieu or face the consequences – which could include his replacement on the throne by Gaston. The whole complex operation was to be set in motion by the landing of an English army on the island of Ré, just off La Rochelle.

Whereas the Cadiz expedition had suffered from a shortage of parliamentary funding, the Ré expedition had none at all. It had to be financed out of the proceeds of the Forced Loan (see p. 223), yet despite – or perhaps because of – this it sailed on time, in June 1627, and achieved the difficult feat of landing some 7,000 men on Ré in the face of repeated enemy attacks. This initial success turned out to be its last, however, for the French took refuge in the citadel at St Martin from which it proved impossible to dislodge them. Rohan was of the opinion that if the English had captured the citadel 'there was every possibility of a great change in the face of affairs' both within France and subsequently in Europe.[16] But the expeditionary force, which was commanded by Buckingham in person, was ill equipped for a long siege, and while the French were steadily building up their numbers on the mainland, in preparation for a counter-attack, reinforcements from England came only belatedly and in dribs and drabs. After sixteen weeks in the field, and with winter drawing on, Buckingham ordered an assault on the citadel in late October, but this was beaten off with heavy losses and the English had to fight their way back to their ships, harried by the French as they did so. The survivors returned safely to England, where they arrived in November, but this third defeat in a row made Buckingham even more unpopular, if such a thing was possible, than he had been before.

Although the inhabitants of La Rochelle had been reluctant and slow to commit themselves, they had eventually come out in support of the English. As a consequence, they were threatened by a blockade from both land and sea which Richelieu mounted with his accustomed thoroughness. Charles I could not ignore the appeals for assistance which arrived from the Huguenots. He had bound himself to uphold the terms of the peace which his envoys had helped to negotiate, and which the French government was now infringing. Furthermore, he had to take account of public opinion in England, which demanded action to save the beleagured protestant stronghold. Buckingham therefore prepared yet another expedition, equipping a number of ships as floating bombs so that they would be able to breach the palisade which Richelieu was constructing to block the

seaward approaches to La Rochelle. Had he been in charge of operations, as he intended, the assault would have been pushed hard and
might conceivably have succeeded. But in August 1628, while the
expedition was still at Portsmouth, Buckingham was assassinated.
Charles immediately appointed another commander, and the ships
duly set sail, but the attempt to breach the palisade was half-hearted
and merely served to convince the defenders that they had nothing
to hope for from England. In October 1628, therefore, while
Charles's fleet was still cruising off La Rochelle, the city surrendered.

FOREIGN POLICY DURING THE PERSONAL RULE

The death of Buckingham and the King's subsequent decision to rule
without Parliament marked the end of England's active involvement
in the Thirty Years War. In April 1629 the Peace of Susa terminated
hostilities between England and France on the basis of non-
interference by each state in the affairs of the other. This meant that
Louis abandoned his championship of the catholic cause in England
while Charles gave up his role as guarantor of Huguenot liberties. 1630
saw the opening of peace negotiations with Spain, which culminated
in the Treaty of Madrid, signed in November. Philip IV now gave
a formal promise that he would work for the restoration of the
Palatinate to the Elector Frederick, and Charles was content to accept
this, in the hope of achieving by co-operation with the Catholic
Monarchy what he had conspicuously failed to win by war. In the
following year Charles also agreed, in principle, to a plan for an
Anglo-Spanish partition of the Netherlands. No doubt he hoped that
this would be interpreted by Spain as evidence of his goodwill, but
in the prevailing circumstances it was merely a gesture.

Charles's problem was that he had little to offer any party in the
endless negotiations that marked the course of the Thirty Years War.
The future of Europe would be decided on the battlefield, but the
campaigns of the mid-1620s had demonstrated England's feebleness
as a military power. Nor could she use money to compensate for
this, since where large sums were involved the King could do
nothing without Parliament, and his distaste for this institution
effectively limited his freedom of action. In 1631–32, for instance,
Charles put out feelers to Gustavus Adolphus, the King of Sweden,
who had assumed the championship of the protestant cause in
Germany. Gustavus demanded a force of 10,000 men to aid him in

recovering the Palatinate, and English naval assistance to safeguard his communications with the Baltic. A majority of the Privy Council favoured the acceptance of these terms, but they also advised the recall of Parliament in order to raise the quarter of a million pounds which would be required. Charles would not hear of this. Instead, he proposed a monthly subsidy to Sweden of £10,000, but Gustavus was all too aware that a similar commitment to Denmark had never been honoured and that reliance upon English promises was an invitation to disaster. Gustavus therefore went ahead without Charles's aid, and although he extended his protection to the exiled Elector Palatine, he did so for his own purposes. In the spring of 1632 he invaded and laid waste Bavaria, the heartland of German catholicism, and when, in May, he made his triumphal entry into its capital, Munich, he invited Frederick to ride by his side. Frederick did not have long to savour the taste of revenge, however, for he died later that year without ever regaining his hereditary Palatinate.

Sweden's emergence as a major power owed a great deal to the financial support of France, and this was a direct result of Richelieu's dominance of affairs. November 1630 saw the Day of the Dupes, which marked the eclipse of his rivals and enemies at home and the confirmation of his position as Louis XIII's political *alter ego*. Now at last he could jettison the *dévots* and pursue what he regarded as the best interests of France without having to give primacy to religious considerations. He acted as paymaster to the Dutch as well as the Swedes, and he disposed of sums of money far greater than anything Charles could ever have contemplated. Charles was apprehensive about the growth of French power and turned his attention once again towards Spain. Philip IV's ministers gave renewed assurances about their desire to see the Palatinate restored, and in the summer of 1636 Charles despatched the Earl of Arundel to Vienna to see what terms the Emperor would consider. Ferdinand was prepared to offer little except vague promises, for he had already committed himself to the transfer of the electoral title and most of Frederick's possessions to Maximilian of Bavaria. Charles, when he realised this, swung back towards France, which promised to employ its best endeavours for the restoration of the Palatinate to Frederick's heir. This francophil policy was supported by an influential group of peers, including the Earls of Holland and Warwick, who had close links with the Queen, Henrietta Maria. They pressed Charles to recall Parliament, and assured him that if he did so, and announced his firm intention to make war against Spain, the two Houses would supply his needs.[17]

Whether or not Charles was really considering a French alliance and the renewal of war against Spain remains an open question. The eruption of the Scottish crisis in the summer of 1637 put an end to the possibility, for Charles could not risk foreign ventures when his position at home was under threat. Moreover, he was inclined to believe that Richelieu had fomented trouble in Scotland as part of a campaign to force him into the arms of France, and that he had more to hope for from Philip IV than from Louis XIII where his own security was concerned. Now that the advance of French armies towards the Rhine was threatening the passage of Spanish troops and supplies along that route, the sealane through the Channel was of increasing importance to Spain, and English ships could be extremely useful in guarding it. Charles at last had a bargaining counter, but it was of limited value, for in October 1639 he could not stop the Dutch from attacking and destroying a large Spanish fleet which had taken refuge in the Downs. He had demanded £150,000 from Spain as the price for his protection, but he had also offered to abandon the ships to the Dutch if they put pressure upon France to restore the Elector Palatine. In other words, in his foreign as in his domestic policy, Charles was overplaying a weak hand and managed to win only the distrust of all the other participants. As the Scottish crisis became more acute he looked to Spain to provide him with money and, if necessary, armed support, but in the summer of 1640 the outbreak of revolt in Catalonia brought Philip IV's government under exactly the same sort of strain that Charles was experiencing. Spain was in no position to help Charles now, even if she wanted to, and he had to accept that his foreign policy must henceforth be governed by domestic considerations. Since he had been accused of showing undue favour to catholics, he demonstrated his commitment to protestantism by giving his consent, in December 1640, to a marriage between his daughter, Mary, and William, Prince of Orange, the Calvinist *stadtholder* of the United Provinces.

There was a consistent thread in Charles I's foreign policy – namely the desire to secure the restoration of the Palatinate to his sister and brother-in-law and their children. In the opening years of his reign Buckingham sought to expand this somewhat narrow and specific objective into the much broader one of the containment of Habsburg power through a secular alliance of protestant and catholic states. But the English gentlemen who made up the political nation and dominated the House of Commons, which alone could provide the financial underpinning for English participation in the Thirty

Years War, never understood – and insofar as they did understand, deeply disapproved of – a secular foreign policy. They were prisoners of the Elizabethan legend, and wanted Charles to do what they believed his elder brother, Prince Henry, would have done – namely, place himself at the head of a protestant crusade against the powers of darkness represented by the Pope and the King of Spain. They assumed that with God on their side, all other considerations, including financial ones, were as nothing. This belief did credit to the depth of their protestant faith, but it took no account of the realities of war and of the fact that England, after a quarter of a century of peace, was unprepared for it. They blamed Buckingham for failures for which they themselves were in large part responsible, and after his death they blamed Charles for refusing to support the protestant cause, despite the fact that when he had done so, with their avowed approval, at the beginning of his reign, they had washed their hands of the whole business. They were still strong on rhetoric, however, and when, in 1640–41, they acquired a public forum once again, they openly condemned the King for having made peace with Spain, 'whereby the Palatine's cause was deserted and left to chargeable and hopeless treaties'. They also called on him to appoint ministers firmly committed to the defence of religion abroad as well as at home, who would take the lead in giving 'such assistance to the protestant party beyond the sea as is desired'.[18]

Foreign policy was not a peripheral concern in Charles's reign. The desire for news of the Thirty Years War was intense and led to the circulation of *corantoes*, the first English newspapers. The death of Gustavus Adolphus caused widespread grief in England, and Sir Simonds D'Ewes recorded in his journal that it cast a blight over what would otherwise have been a 'happy and blessed' year. D'Ewes confessed that from a secular point of view it could be argued that Germany would have been better off had Gustavus never entered the war, 'but to speak as a Christian, and much more as a pious protestant, all ages have to bless God that the king's arms were God's just scourge for the space of about two years and three months, to avenge Him on the bloody and lustful soldiers of the Emperor's army, to abate their pride, and to save England, France, the Low Countries and all from ruin'.[19] Charles's refusal to embrace the protestant cause in the 1630s accentuated the divergence between him and a significant section of his subjects. Rubens described the English people during the Personal Rule as 'rich and happy in the lap of peace',[20] but in fact the prevailing mood among many of them was one of discontent. Given the choice between an ignoble peace and a holy war they would have had no doubt where their duty and their preference lay.

NOTES AND REFERENCES

(*The place of publication is London, unless otherwise stated*)
1. **S. R. Gardiner** *History of England from the Accession of James I to the Outbreak of the Civil War 1603–1642* (1884). Vol. I, p. 213.
2. 'Correspondencia Oficial de Don Diego Sarmiento de Acuña, Conde de Gondomar' in *Documentos Ineditos para la Historia de España*. Vol. I (Madrid 1936), p. 347.
3. **David Norbrook** *Poetry and Politics in the English Renaissance* (1984), p. 117.
4. **Public Record Office** SP 14, 119,93 (Hereafter *PRO*).
5. **Wallace Notestein, Frances Helen Relf** & **Hartley Simpson** (eds) *Commons Debates 1621* (New Haven 1935). Vol. II, p. 9; Vol. VI, p. 370. (Hereafter *Commons Debates 1621*)
6. *Commons Debates 1621.* Vol. VI, p. 370.
7. *Commons Debates 1621.* Vol. II, p. 408.
8. **The Letters of John Chamberlain**, ed. N. E. McClure (Philadelphia 1939). Vol. II, p. 346. (Hereafter Chamberlain *Letters*)
9. Chamberlain *Letters.* Vol. II, pp. 569–70.
10. Chamberlain *Letters.* Vol II, p. 412.
11. PRO *SP 84.* 127,22.
12. PRO *SP 16.* 12, 35; Charles Dalton *The Life and Times of General Sir Edward Cecil, Viscount Wimbledon* (1885). Vol. II, p. 236.
13. PRO *SP 78.* 75,189.
14. PRO *SP 78.* 77,95.
15. PRO *SP 92.* 12,58.
16. *Mémoires du Duc de Rohan* (Paris 1975), pp. 207–8.
17. **R. M. Smuts** 'The Puritan Followers of Henrietta Maria in the 1630s', *English Historical Review*, Vol. 93, 1978.
18. **S. R. Gardiner (ed.)** *The Constitutional Documents of the Puritan Revolution 1625–1660* (Oxford 1906), pp. 208–9, 231.
19. **The Autobiography and Correspondence of Sir Simonds D'Ewes**, ed. J. O. Halliwell (1845), Vol. II, p. 84.
20. **The Letters of Peter Paul Rubens**, ed. R. S. Magum (Cambridge, Mass. 1955), p. 320.

CHAPTER THREE

James I and the Constitution: liberties, authority, and law

POLITICAL IDEAS AND ASSUMPTIONS

In the realm of political ideas the Middle Ages bequeathed a mixed inheritance to the early modern period. During the course of their long dispute with the Emperors the Popes had asserted a right to act as absolute monarchs over the temporal world of Christendom, and had used their jurists to provide a legal foundation for their claim. This provoked first the Emperors and subsequently the rulers of other major western European states to put forward the counter claim that they derived their authority directly from God and could not be called to account by the Pope or any human institution. While the Popes had relied for legal support principally upon canonists – experts in the canon law of the Church – the secular rulers made use of the 'civilians' who were skilled in the study of the *lex civile* of ancient Rome, particularly in the form in which it had been codified in the *Institutes* and *Digest* commissioned by the Emperor Justinian in the sixth century. In view of the fact that the principal collections of civil law derived from imperial and not republican Rome it is hardly surprising that they put great emphasis upon the authority of the ruler: indeed one of the most frequently quoted maxims affirmed that *quod principi placuit legis vigorem habet* ['the ruler's will has the force of law']. This meant that when the secular princes of late medieval Europe asserted an 'imperial' authority coeval with that of the Popes they were simultaneously claiming to be the source of law within their own states. This appeared to leave little room for alternative concepts of law, such as those which derived it from immemorial custom or the will of the people as expressed through representative assemblies.

By the end of the Middle Ages the rulers of the major European states had successfully established their freedom from papal control, and the initial stages of the protestant Reformation in the sixteenth century saw their power enormously strengthened. When Luther took the dangerous step of challenging the right of the papacy to lay down doctrine he called to his aid the secular rulers of Christendom to whom he attributed the God-given task of organising the Church within their dominions. Many rulers were swift to respond, not simply because they shared Luther's beliefs but also because they saw the advantage of extending their authority over the religious as well as the secular sphere. Criticism of the ruler now came close to blasphemy, for as St Paul had informed the Romans 'the powers that be are ordained of God'. Subjects were bound to obey their ruler unless he ordered them to act in a way that ran counter to God's will, but even in this case they only had the right to resist passively, not to offer open opposition and certainly not to take up arms.

Calvin maintained this position until nearly the end of his life, but Calvinists, like the Lutherans before them, had to face up to the dilemma posed by princes who acted in an 'ungodly' manner – by espousing the catholic cause, for instance, and persecuting protestants. When the German Lutherans were confronted by a catholic counter-attack led by the Emperor Charles V in the 1530s they quickly developed a theoretical justification for their determination to resist him. They based their case upon a principle derived from Roman private law that asserted the right of any individual to oppose the decisions of an unjust judge. This justification for rebellion proved to be of great value to the French Calvinists, the Huguenots, during the wars of religion that convulsed France from the early 1560s until nearly the end of the century. One of the most lucid statements of the Huguenot case was that put forward by Philippe Duplessis-Mornay in *The Defence of Liberty against Tyrants*, published in 1579. Mornay argued that men were born free but agreed to limit their freedom by setting up a political community in order to preserve their natural rights of life, liberty and property. The original delegation of authority from the people to the ruler was made by their elected representatives, and it was these, according to Mornay, who retained the ultimate right to decide whether the ruler was fulfilling the terms of the original contract. If they decided that, far from protecting the rights of his people, the ruler was threatening them, then it was incumbent upon the representatives to lead resistance to him.

Among those who developed this theory of the justification of resistance to a tyrannical ruler was the Scotsman George Buchanan. He went beyond the Huguenot position by arguing that the right of resistance belonged not merely to the magistrates or elected representatives but to the people as a whole. Moreover, when the people agreed to hand over power to a ruler they did not thereby grant away their ultimate sovereignty. They laid down how the ruler should behave and thereafter regarded him as 'a guardian of the public accounts' who could be dismissed from office for misbehaviour.[1] Buchanan was to be of direct relevance not only to Scottish but also, ultimately, to English history, for he was appointed tutor to the three-year-old James VI. Buchanan himself was over sixty, suffered from ill health, and was arrogant and short-tempered. Although James later praised him as a teacher he disliked him intensely as a man and lived in awe and fear of him. No sooner did the King come of age than he rejected Buchanan and his doctrines, which he persuaded the Scottish Parliament formally to condemn in 1584. The need to assert his independence against this overbearing advocate of popular sovereignty was one of the major impulses driving James to develop his own political theory and ensuring that he would move in a very different direction. His speech to the English Parliament in March 1610 was not simply a statement of his beliefs but also an emphatic refutation of Buchanan's:

Kings are justly called gods for that they exercise a manner or resemblance of divine power upon earth. For if you will consider the attributes to God, you shall see how they agree in the person of a king . . . They make and unmake their subjects, they have power of raising and casting down, of life and death, judges over all their subjects in all causes, and yet accountable to none but God only . . . And to the King is due both the affection of the soul and the service of the body of his subjects.[2]

It was not only the radical puritans who had challenged James's authority in Scotland. Another threat, and one which became even more menacing after his accession to the English throne, came from Roman Catholic controversialists. These used arguments which were virtually identical to those of the radical puritans, but the right of resistance which they asserted was directed against *protestant* sovereigns. James responded to this by taking over the position developed by the imperial jurists in the late Middle Ages and emphasising that, like all secular rulers, he held his authority by direct grant from God and was not accountable to the Pope or to any merely human institution. James's insistence upon his 'divine right' to rule was not, therefore, prompted by vainglory or an exaggerated sense of his own importance. In a world in which religious passions were calling into question the legitimacy of secular authority James had good reason for buttressing the theoretical foundations of his own throne. Otherwise victory in this incessant propaganda war which was being waged all over Christendom might have gone to those such as the Jesuit Francisco Suarez who, in a series of works published from 1612 onwards, claimed that 'if the king converts his just power into tyranny' by ruling in such a way that he becomes 'manifestly pernicious to the entire commonwealth' then it is lawful 'for the community to make use of its natural power to defend itself'.[3] This could be taken as a retrospective justification for the Gunpowder Plot, and given these circumstances it is hardly surprising that the special service prescribed for the annual commemoration of that event emphasised the divine origin of kingly power (and, by implication, the sinfulness of resisting it). In the words of the appointed lesson, taken from the Old Testament and recording the exultation of King David as he triumphed over his enemies, 'it is God that avengeth me, and that bringeth down the people under me. . . He is the tower of salvation for His king: and showeth mercy to His anointed, unto David, and to his seed for evermore'.

MAGNA CARTA AND THE ORIGINS OF THE COMMON LAW

James's long apprenticeship in polemics had taught him not simply how to state a case but also how to develop it to its maximum potential. Since he was fighting to preserve his life and his throne against those who threatened both, he deployed his full arsenal of verbal rapiers and philosophical muskets, and in pursuit of immediate victory he was not over-concerned about the possible long-term implications of what he wrote. This was to prove a major disadvantage when he acceded to the throne of England, for his works, such as *The Trew Law of Free Monarchies: Or The Reciprock and Mutuall Dutie Betwixt a Free King and his Naturall Subjects*, had preceded him and had given rise to the fear that the first Stuart king would not be so observant of those constraints upon royal power which many Englishmen regarded as a unique and priceless characteristic of their system of government. These constraints were embodied in the common law, for as one of its practitioners, Nicholas Fuller, told the House of Commons in 1610, 'the common laws of England do measure the King's prerogative, as it shall not tend to take away or prejudice the inheritance of the subject'.[4]

In his speech Fuller made two significant references, one to Fortescue, the other to Magna Carta. Sir John Fortescue sat in the House of Commons in the early fifteenth century, served as Chief Justice of the King's Bench under Henry VI, and was the author of a number of politico-legal treatises, of which the two most famous and influential were *De Laudibus Legum Angliae* ('In Praise of the Laws of England') and *On the Governance of the Kingdom of England*. In these works Fortescue drew a distinction between two types of polity. One he described as *dominium regale* or 'kingly rule', and the other as *dominium politicum et regale*, which may be translated as 'kingly and constitutional rule'. In the former the king ruled his people 'by such laws as he maketh himself. And therefore he may set upon them *tailles* and other impositions, such as he will himself, without their assent'. France, according to Fortescue, was a *dominium regale*. England, on the other hand, was a *dominium politicum et regale*, in which the king 'may not rule his people by other laws than such as they assent unto. And therefore he may set upon them no impositions without their own assent'.[5] Fortescue's work was well known and widely circulated in Tudor and early Stuart England. *De Laudibus* went through four editions in Elizabeth's reign and two in James I's, the last of these being an annotated version drawn up by John Selden.

Magna Carta was familiar to lawyers in the statutory version issued by Henry III in the ninth year of his reign. Its Latin text was in print, in collections of statutes, from 1508 onwards, and in 1524 George Ferrers – better known for his subsequent involvement in a case concerning the privileges of the House of Commons – produced an English translation. Until the 1580s Magna Carta was simply a statute, albeit an important one, but the appointment of Whitgift as Archbishop of Canterbury in 1583 led to a significant change in its status. Whitgift set about enforcing conformity by requiring all ministers to subscribe to a statement that the Prayer Book contained nothing contrary to the word of God, and those who refused to do so risked deprivation. Furthermore, he instructed the High Commission to proceed against suspects by means of the *ex officio* oath, whereby they could be legally compelled to give information about the nature of their beliefs.

Ministers of puritan inclination deeply resented this, and they found allies among some of the common lawyers who were already doubtful about the validity of the jurisdiction exercised by the High Commission. These included Sir James Morice, who acted as one of the counsel for Robert Cawdrey, a puritan minister whose deprivation by High Commission on the grounds of non-conformity led to a test case before the Queen's Bench in 1591. Cawdrey lost his case, but Morice drew up a treatise in which he declared that 'those general citations which bishops make to cite men to appear before them . . . without expressing any cause especial, are against the law . . . for by the statute of Magna Charta (containing many excellent laws of the liberties and free customs of this kingdom) it is ordained that no free man be apprehended, imprisoned, distrained or impeached but by the law of the land'.[6] In the session of 1593 Morice put forward a Bill in the House of Commons against unlawful imprisonment and restraint of liberty, but the Queen ordered the Speaker to prevent any debate on this thorny topic which threatened to involve discussion of her prerogative. The Speaker was Edward Coke, who was subsequently to become the great parliamentary champion of Magna Carta and its liberties, but on this occasion he did as he was told. The Bill disappeared from sight, but what may be a surviving draft contains the clause 'that the provisions and prohibitions of the said Great Charter . . . be duly and inviolately observed, and that no person or persons be hereafter committed to prison but it be by sufficient warrant and authority and by due course and proceeding in law'.[7]

Another defender of the puritans against what he regarded as the abitrary actions of the bishops and their courts was Robert Beale, a member of Parliament and Clerk of the Privy Council. In 1583 he wrote a tract 'against oaths ministered in the courts of ecclesiastical commission' which brought him into confrontation with Archbishop Whitgift. In a later tract he described Magna Carta as 'the law of laws' and expressed the hope that 'neither any common or ecclesiastical lawyer will make any exception at all' against it.[8] Beale was a member of the Elizabethan Society of Antiquaries which was founded in the 1580s to promote the study of English institutions, customs and topography. Among his fellow members was William Lambarde who made a name for himself as the historian of English law.

There was a sense in which all common lawyers were historians, since the importance which they attached to precedents meant that they were constantly delving into the records. Yet the very assumptions which led them in this direction were a barrier to historical understanding, for they regarded the past as being, in a legal sense, ever-present, so that medieval judgments or statutes could be applied to their own day without any awareness of the differences between

earlier societies and the one in which they lived. This ran counter
to the humanist approach of continental scholars, who had begun,
under the influence of the Renaissance, by attempting to recover the
lost world of antiquity, and had then gone on, in many cases, to
investigate the history of their own countries.

It was no coincidence that in England one of the pioneers of this
sort of research was Elizabeth's first Archbishop, Matthew Parker,
for he was concerned to place the newly created Church of England
firmly in its historical context, so that, in his own words, 'that most
holy and godly form of discipline which was commonly used in the
primitive Church might be called home again'.[9] He was appalled by
the way in which the monastic libraries, which contained the written
evidence of the history of the Church in England, were being
dispersed as a consequence of the Dissolution, and he made it his
self-appointed task to buy up and thereby preserve for posterity as
many manuscripts and books as he could obtain. His companions
in this task included Laurence Nowell, who made an intensive study
of Anglo-Saxon manuscripts and thereby acquired a detailed knowledge not merely of the language but also of the customs and institutions of the early English. It was Nowell who taught Lambarde
Anglo-Saxon, and it was at his request that Lambarde undertook the
mammoth task of preparing an English version of Anglo-Saxon laws
which he published in 1568 as the *Archaionomia*.

The effect of Lambarde's work was to push the origins of
common law back beyond the Conquest – so far back in fact that
it seemed to be as old as civil society itself. This made it possible
for Sir Edward Coke later to claim that 'it doth appear most plain
by successive authority in history what I have positively affirmed
out of record, that the grounds of our common laws at this day were
beyond the memory or register of any beginning, and the same
which the Norman Conqueror then found within this realm of
England'.[10] Coke also asserted that the fundamental principles of the
common law were immutable and should remain so, 'for that which
hath been refined and perfected by all the wisest men in former
succession of ages, and proved and approved by continual experience
to be good and profitable for the commonwealth, cannot without
great danger and hazard be altered or changed'.[11] What Coke and
those who thought like him were arguing in effect was that the
common law provided the 'frame of government' or constitution
within which the life of the community was to be carried on.

The insistence upon the primacy and antiquity of law, based as
it was upon immemorial custom, ran counter to James's assertions,

made in the *Trew Law*, that 'kings were the authors and makers of law, and not the laws of the king' and that 'the king is above the law, as both the author and giver of strength thereto'.[12] There was clearly a substantial gap between these two views of the nature of law and the origins of secular authority, but it should not be assumed that Coke had all the common lawyers on his side. Lambarde, for instance, argued that monarchical power was a natural phenomenon, deriving from the authority which, from the very earliest times, fathers had exercised over their families. The same argument was employed by Bacon when he claimed, in Calvin's Case, that submission to a monarch was 'natural and more ancient' than submission to law.[13] Another distinguished common lawyer, Lord Chancellor Ellesmere, had no doubts that God 'hath authorised and given power to kings to give laws to their subjects; and so kings did first make laws, and then ruled by their laws, and altered and changed their laws from time to time as they saw occasion, for the good of themselves and their subjects'. Moving from the general to the particular, he showed his confidence in James by adding that if any case of great complexity arose which the lawyers were unable to resolve, it should be decided 'by sentence of the most religious, learned and judicious king that ever this kingdom or island had'.[14]

It was in many ways unfortunate for James that he succeeded to the English throne at a time when, in the words of a modern historian, 'the concept of the State – its nature, its powers, its right to command obedience – had come to be regarded as the most important object of analysis in European political thought'.[15] During the last decade of Elizabeth's reign the financial demands of the war with Spain had driven the crown into the increasing use of expedients such as monopolies which made it seem the oppressor rather than the protector of its subjects. This had focussed attention upon the relationship between authority and the individual, the royal government on the one hand and free-born Englishmen on the other. In 'Darcy v Allen', 1602, the judges were called upon to decide whether a monopoly grant of the manufacture of playing-cards was legal, and decided that it was not, on the grounds that no man could be 'restrained from exercising any trade but by Parliament'.[16] Three years later, in 'The Case of Penal Statutes', they resolved that 'when a statute is made *pro bono publico* ['for the public good'] and the King . . . is by the whole realm trusted with it, this confidence and trust is so inseparably joined and annexed to the royal power of the King in so high a point of sovereignty that he cannot transfer it to the disposition or power of any private person or to any private use'.[17]

Another case which came before the courts, in 1591, concerned the issue which was to raise such a furore in 1627–28 of whether the crown had the right to imprison without showing cause. It was decided that it did indeed have such a right where the security of the state was involved, but that the Privy Council should privately inform the judges of the cause, so that they could be satisfied that it fell within the prescribed category.[18]

It seems as certain as any hypothesis can be that if Elizabeth had been succeeded by another Tudor sovereign the debate over the nature and extent of royal power would have continued and intensified, for governments throughout Europe were facing similar problems of how to maintain their authority at a time when population growth, poverty and vagrancy, religious divisions, outbreaks of plague, fluctuations in the economy, and the ever-present threat of war were making their task increasingly difficult. Elizabeth managed to contain the pressures that were mounting on her own government during the last decade or so of her reign, but there is no reason to doubt the statement made in the *Form of Apology* of 1604 'that in regard of her sex and age, which we had great cause to tender, and much more upon care to avoid all trouble which . . . might have been drawn to impeach the quiet of Your Majesty's right in the succession, those actions were then passed over which we hoped, in succeeding times of freer access to Your Highness of renowned grace and justice, to redress, restore and rectify'.[19] In other words, the Commons and the political nation which they represented had accepted that there was no point in trying to resolve disputed constitutional issues or to draw a clearer boundary line between the royal prerogative and the liberties of the subject until after the Queen's death.

THE KING, THE COMMONS, AND THE JUDGES

The accession of a new sovereign was traditionally a time for stock-taking and redefinition, and in James's case this was bound to be a difficult and controversial task. James was a foreigner, with firm convictions about the role and authority of an English monarch but no first-hand knowledge of English institutions. Had James been an Englishman he might well have been given the benefit of any doubts, but as a stranger, and one, moreover, who was the author of the *Trew Law of Free Monarchies*, James seemed to embody a threat to this traditional framework which could not simply be ignored or allowed to pass unheeded in the general atmosphere of goodwill that greeted his arrival. His newly acquired English subjects were sufficiently aware of events on the European continent to know that, in the words of the *Apology*, 'the prerogatives of princes may easily and do daily grow; the privileges of the subject are for the most part at an everlasting stand'. They also knew that rights which are not asserted go by default, that 'they may be by good providence and care preserved, but being once lost are not recovered but with much disquiet'. It was true that God 'in His great mercy hath given us a wise King and religious', but it was equally true that 'the same God . . . doth also sometimes permit hypocrites and tyrants in his displeasure'.[20]

It was in order to safeguard themselves against such a contingency that some members of the political nation became hyper-sensitive about the protection of their privileges. It was not so much that they distrusted James as that the accession of an alien after more than a hundred years under a native dynasty cast everything into doubt, opening the door to all sorts of possibilities, many of them highly undesirable. James was still a relatively young man at his accession, not yet forty, and this made it all the more important to establish, as it were, an agreed ground-plan for his rule. If he lived to be as old as Elizabeth he would reign in England for over thirty years, and during that long space of time any rights which had not been firmly asserted at the beginning would sink without trace. Conversely, if James were to be struck down by illness or an assassin's dagger – neither of which could be ruled out in the circumstances of the early seventeenth century – his heir would be a ten-year-old boy, and nobody could be sure what a minority might mean in terms of the preservation, or loss, of liberties. For all these reasons the members of James's first Parliament – or at least a determined minority who could usually carry the majority with them – put the conservation of the rights of the subject at the very top of their order of priorities. This involved keeping a watchful eye on the common law and its guardians, the judges, who were responsible for upholding these rights. It also involved the maintenance of parliamentary privileges, for only a 'free' Parliament could ensure that these rights would not be eroded.

James opened this Parliament on 19 March 1604, but a mere ten days later he was caught up in the dispute over the Buckinghamshire election (see p. 158). James proposed, as a way out of the impasse, that the judges should be called upon to decide which of the two members, if any, had been validly elected. This was, on the face of it, a sensible suggestion, but it raised the sensitive issue of whether or not the Commons' privileges – among which they included the right to decide disputed elections – were a matter for judicial review. Henry Yelverton, himself a lawyer, and a future judge, asserted that the judges 'cannot take notice of private customs or privileges . . . The judges informed the King of the law, but not of the case of privilege . . . Let us be constant, and resolve to control it by Parliament'. Bacon, in contrast, argued that somebody must determine the validity of returns before Parliament assembled, otherwise it could never meet. 'That must be judged by law,' he added, whereas the Commons, when they eventually assembled and considered the matter, 'judge it by discretion. The King ought to judge according to the positive laws of the realm'.[21]

It may be that the judges were themselves unwilling to become involved in a privilege case, where they were uncertain of their jurisdiction, for although they were present at the conference which resolved the election issue they seem to have kept a low profile. They played a more prominent part in the debate over the proposed Union, however, since this had profound implications for the law which they administered. They began with a rebuff to James in 1604 over the question of changing the name of his newly united state to *Great Britain* (see p. 162), but they were on his side when it came to declaring the status of the *post-nati*. In February 1607, when the Lords were preparing for a conference with the Commons on this matter, they called on the judges to advise them. All but one of the eleven judges who were present were of the opinion that 'such of the Scottish as have been or shall be born in Scotland since His Majesty's coming to the [English] crown are not aliens but are inheritable in this realm by the law (as it now stands in force) as native English'.[22]

James assumed that this was the end of the matter, but as had already been shown in the Buckinghamshire election case, the attitude of the Commons towards the judges was ambiguous. In matters of private law, which concerned disputes between individuals, they were prepared to accept the judges' decision as final, but in issues of public law, which revolved round the relationship between the individual citizen and the royal government, they were increasingly determined to assert their own competence. After all, this was a sphere in which the precedents were often conflicting and the law unclear. Moreover it fell within the area of 'discretion' rather than 'positive laws', and this, as Bacon had acknowledged, was a legitimate concern of the Commons. There was the further point that whereas a wrong judgment in a private law case would affect at the most a few individuals, a decision in public law could be regarded as universally applicable.

Although the Commons determined to reject the judges' opinion over the *post-nati* they recognised the dangers of undermining judicial authority and therefore defined their position with great care. In the words of Sir Edwin Sandys, reporting from the committee set up to consider the Commons' response in March 1607,

first, that point is not by the judges themselves clearly agreed, for one of them dissenteth. Secondly, though the judges are always and in all places reverend, yet are not their words so weighty when they are but assistants to the Lords in Parliament as when they sit judicially in courts of justice, for in the latter case they have an oath to tie them. Thirdly, in all demurrers, before the judges speak they hear counsel on both sides argue, and afterwards, upon study themselves, argue and deliver the law. But here they delivered their opinions before they heard our reasons.[23]

The Lords stood by the judges, but Sandys, and those many members of the Commons who thought like him, were clearly hoping, in Salisbury's words, 'to get some such definite sentence pass in the House of the invalidity of the judges' resolution as may make them dainty hereafter to judge the question, or make the judgment less acceptable'.[24] With the two Houses at loggerheads and the King determined to uphold the judges' decision, the *post-nati* might have remained in a state of legal limbo. In order to resolve this situation a test case concerning a certain Robert Calvin was brought before all the judges assembled in Exchequer Chamber. Lord Chancellor Ellesmere, when he announced their verdict confirming the previous opinion of the judges expressed in the House of Lords, went out of his way to reject the Commons' assertion 'that there is not like regard to be had of judges' opinions given in Parliament as ought to be of their judgments in their proper courts and seats of justice; for in those places their oath bindeth them, but not so in the other'. On the contrary, he asserted, 'the reverence and worthiness of the men is such as is not to be quarrelled and doubted of if there were no oath at all' and in point of fact 'their oath doth bind them as much in the court of Parliament as in their proper courts; for that is the supreme court of all'. Ellesmere resented the implied slur upon his brethren and made a plea for traditional attitudes to be upheld: 'it becomes us to esteem of judges now as our forefathers esteemed them in times past; for as they succeed them in time and place . . . so they succeed them and are not inferior to them in wisdom, learning, integrity and all other judicious and religious virtues'.[25]

The *post-nati* issue was not the only one on which the judges and the Commons were in disagreement. A major difference of opinion had emerged over the important question of Impositions (see p. 77) after the judgment in favour of their legality given by the Court of the Exchequer in 1606. Chief Baron Fleming, who was presiding, chose his words carefully when he explained how he had arrived at his judgment. There was no question, he said, of giving the King authority to 'impose upon the subject or his goods', for that was not the issue under consideration. The disputed Imposition was on currants, which were foreign commodities, and if any English merchant bought them he did so in the knowledge that they were liable to tax, and therefore, by implication, voluntarily accepted the obligation to pay. It was not as if currants were a staple commodity which people *had* to buy. They were, on the contrary, 'rather delicacy or medicine than a victual' and they came from the Venetians, whose Duke had taxed English imports into his own dominions. Was it right, asked Fleming, 'that so many of our good and staple commodities should be exported to Venice for such a slight delicacy, and that all the impost shall be paid to the Venetians for them, and the King should have none for their commodity'? The King was responsible for the general well-being of his subjects and was obliged to relieve them 'if they are oppressed by foreign princes'. He was therefore justified in maintaining this levy.[26]

If Fleming had said no more than this his judgment might well have won general acceptance, for Sir Edward Coke and a fellow judge, when they considered the matter shortly afterwards, came to a similar conclusion, namely that 'if in foreign parts any Imposition is put upon the merchandises of our merchants . . . the King may put an Imposition upon their merchandises . . . for the end of all such restraints is *salus populi* ['the good of the community']. And so, in the case of currants . . . such Impositions were lawful'.[27] However, Fleming also drew a distinction between two aspects of the royal prerogative. The first or 'ordinary' prerogative gave the King certain privileges by virtue of his office, was defined and limited by common law and statute, and could not be changed except through Parliament. The second or 'absolute' prerogative was not 'guided by the rules which direct only at the common law' and was best described as 'policy and government'. Into this category came 'all commerce and affairs with foreigners; all wars and peace; all acceptance and admitting for current foreign coin; all parties and treaties whatsoever'.[28]

Fleming acknowledged that his judgment might imply an unfettered right on the part of the King to levy Impositions at will, but he was only concerned in this case with Impositions upon foreign commodities, not upon Englishmen or their goods. Moreover, as he pointed out, the King had to be trusted not to abuse his discretionary powers. 'The King may pardon any felon; but it may be objected that if he pardon one felon he may pardon all, to the damage of the commonwealth, and yet none will doubt but that is left in his wisdom'. Similarly with Impositions: 'whereas it is said that if the King may impose, he may impose any quantity what he pleases, true it is that this is to be referred to the wisdom of the King, who guideth all under God by his wisdom, and this is not to be disputed by a subject; and many things are left to his wisdom for the ordering of his power, rather than his power shall be restrained'.[29]

In a sense Fleming was merely stating the obvious, for every government must have discretionary powers which it can use in an emergency or for the public good, the *salus populi*, and since the King was entrusted with the responsibility for governing England this discretionary power was vested in him. But in 1606 there was no emergency, merely a crisis in the royal finances which many members of the political nation blamed on James's extravagance. Nor was it blindingly obvious that Impositions were for the general good: since one effect of them was to force merchants to raise their prices, it could be argued that they were harmful rather than beneficial. While a technical case might be made out for their lawfulness, the real reason for their use, as everyone knew, was the crown's shortage of money.

The royal commission which authorised the new Impositions of 1608 referred to 'the care imposed upon princes to provide for the safety and welfare of their subjects', but added that the cost of this was so great that it had long been accepted by 'men of understanding in all ages, and by the laws of all nations' that rulers had the right to 'raise to themselves such fit and competent means by levying of Customs and Impositions upon merchandises . . . as to their wisdoms and discretions may seem convenient'.[30] This could be taken as implying a prerogative power of taxing trade which went far beyond the limits laid down in Fleming's judgment. Indeed it seemed to strike at the principle that no taxation should be levied without the consent of the representatives of the people assembled in Parliament – a principle which was generally assumed to be so fundamental that it could not be challenged, let alone changed.

When the Commons complained about Impositions in 1606, James pointed to his 'extraordinary and gracious dealing herein, in suffering a case which so nearly toucheth his ancient prerogative in this nature to be disputed in the common form of law'.[31] Four years later, however, when the Commons again took up the matter, there were clear indications of that distrust of the judges which was now becoming a significant element in the formation of opinion in the Lower House. One member expressed this bluntly when he declared that 'judges are but men, and their places doth not so sanctify their persons but that sometimes there happens evil as well as good. Judges and judgments may sometimes savour of partiality, sometime of human infirmity . . . Therefore [there is] no reason that a judgment should be so sacred or firm that it may not be touched or changed'.[32]

When the Commons drew up their petition against Impositions in May 1610 they refrained from impugning the judgment in Bate's Case, but they denied that it was of general application. On the contrary, 'being only in one case and against one man, it can bind in law no other but that person, and is also reversible by writ of error'.[33] A writ of error was the accepted way of appealing against a judgment in a common-law court, and it worked by transferring the case to the House of Lords for a final decision. In practice the Lords always consulted the judges and followed their advice, but the advantage of such a procedure was that it brought the whole weight of the judiciary to bear upon a specific issue, instead of leaving it, as in Bate's Case, to the judges of one court only. Admittedly the Lords could call upon the judges to give their opinions upon a matter in dispute without waiting for it to be brought before them by writ of error. They had done so in the case of the *post-nati*, but in this instance the Commons had refused to accept the judges' ruling on the grounds that they had been acting in a political rather than a judicial capacity.

It was probably for this reason that when, in 1614, the Lords asked the judges for advice on the validity of Impositions they declined to give it. Sir Edward Coke, acting as their spokesman, explained that 'if your lordships will undertake to dispute the matter, we will, upon the hearing of it argued on both sides, deliver our opinions'.[34] In other words, the judges would only act in a strictly judicial capacity, which would require the issue of a writ of error. James followed this up by informing the Commons in May 1614 that 'if a writ of error should be brought' to test the validity of the judgment in Bate's Case, he would 'stand to the opinions of the judges'.[35]

Some years before he had been poised to allow the question of the *post-nati* to be resolved in the same way, but nothing had come of it. Nor was his new offer taken up. There was little reason to suppose that the entire judicial bench would differ from its constituent parts when it formulated its judgment on disputed issues, and by 1614 many, if not most, members of the Commons had come to believe that in the resolution of such issues the judges had no role to play.

This attitude emerged very clearly in the debates on Impositions which dominated the Addled Parliament. Sir Edwin Sandys, reporting from committee in May 1614, declared that when the Barons of the Exchequer gave their judgment in Bate's Case they had not 'proceeded *more maiorum* [i.e. according to custom]. That they should in this case have asked the advice of Parliament. Precedents that, when done otherwise, the Barons have been censured in Parliament. Some points above the judges' commission or power. Not the title to the crown, nor the subjects their liberties'.[36] Sandys was not, of course, asserting that the judges had no role to play in protecting the liberties of the individual; this indeed was one of their essential functions. His point was a more subtle one, that in cases where matters of principle were involved, where the issue concerned the fundamental laws upon which all individual liberties were founded, the ultimate decision must rest with the High Court of Parliament of which the Commons were an integral part. To make an analogy with modern American practice, constitutional issues were to be dealt with by a supreme court, and in the context of early Stuart England that could only mean Parliament.

Impositions were not the only subject which brought the judges into disfavour with the Lower House. Purveyance (see pp. 168–173) was another. In 1606 the House of Lords, at Salisbury's suggestion, asked the judges for their opinion on the King's right to purveyance. Nicholas Fuller was present when they gave their reply, and subsequently reported to the Commons how 'I lately heard the chief not in place only but in judgment [Sir John Popham, Chief Justice of the King's Bench] say that the statutes for purveyors do not bind the King. And it is not my opinion or any of yours, but the judgment is theirs in whose mouths judgment is put'.[37] A few weeks later the judges were again consulted on the extent to which statutes could bind the prerogative, and, in the words of Dudley Carleton, himself a member of the Commons, they 'overruled all on prerogative side . . . and delivered one judgment in all men's opinions of dangerous consequence, that the prerogative was not subject to law, but that it was transcendent above the reach of Parliament'.[38]

The judges came under further criticism in the Parliament of 1621 for failing to provide adequate protection for the individual against the activities of unscrupulous patentees and their agents. A Bill 'for better securing of the subjects from wrongful imprisonment and deprivation of their trades and occupations, contrary to the 29th chapter of the statute of Magna Charta', which passed through all its stages in the Commons, laid down that 'if judges do wrongfully commit any to prison' they were 'to be censured by [the] Lords of the next Parliament'.[39] Another indication of the critical attitude of at least some members of the Commons towards the judiciary was given by Edward Alford's response to the announcement in June 1621 that the judges had advised James that if he adjourned Parliament by commission this would not put an end to the session. 'Let judges take heed of trenshing into the liberties of Parliament', said Alford. 'They are not judges of Parliament. When they have exceeded too far, they have been taken off by a Parliament'. He added that it was 'dangerous that the judges – a few persons, dependent and timorous some of them – should judge between the King and the state of their liberties. If this be suffered, what will become of us?'.[40]

SIR EDWARD COKE

Were the judges 'dependent and timorous'? Arthur Wilson, who lived through James's reign and subsequently wrote a highly critical history of it, made a disparaging reference to the judges when he dealt with Calvin's Case. 'Such power is in the breath of kings', he observed, 'and such soft stuff are judges made of, that they can vary their precedents and model them into as many shapes as they please'. One judge in particular 'was fit metal for any stamp royal' – in other words, ready to do whatever James told him, or so at least Wilson believed.[41] His verdict is surprising, for the judge in question was Sir Edward Coke, of whom James Whitelocke, who eventually became himself a member of the judicial bench, wrote: 'never man was so just, so upright, free from corruption, solicitations of great men or friends, as he was'.[42] James was far from finding Coke subservient. On the contrary, he regarded him as a thorn in his side, a source of irritation that he was not able or willing to endure indefinitely.

During the second half of the sixteenth century law had become *par excellence* the career for ambitious and talented young men. Coke was one of these and like all successful lawyers he did very well out of his profession: while serving as Attorney General he was said to have made £12,000 a year, which compared favourably with the income of many nobles, and it is unlikely that he earned less as a judge. Coke was not unique by any means: Blickling Hall in Norfolk survives to this day as a symbol of the wealth of its builder, Sir Henry Hobart, who succeeded Coke as Attorney General and later took his place as Chief Justice of the Common Pleas. Nor was wealth the only reward of a successful career in the law; office was another. Coke was at one time spoken of as a possible Lord Treasurer and in 1620 this great office was conferred on Sir Henry Montagu, who succeeded Sir Edward as Chief Justice of the King's Bench. Another former Chief Justice, Sir James Ley, became Lord Treasurer in 1624.

The prospect of political advancement was no doubt one of the factors which determined the attitudes of judges towards the crown and its prerogatives. Bacon showed his awareness of this when he advised James in 1613 to shift Coke from the Common Pleas to the King's Bench: this nominal advancement, suggested Bacon, would make Coke 'think himself near a Privy Councillor's place and thereupon turn obsequious'.[43] However, it would be a mistake to assume that all the judges, or even a majority, were motivated by self interest when they upheld the interests of the crown. Their training, their position, and in many cases their temperament combined to make them respecters of authority. Moreover, they had no reason to believe, in James's reign at any rate, that the crown threatened their independence or integrity. James prided himself, with some cause, on his record with regard to the judiciary, informing Parliament in 1621 that 'I have made the best judges that I knew, judges of learning and integrity, and . . . I did neither move them either directly or indirectly to do otherwise than was agreeable to right and equity . . . He is not fit to be a king that hath not a care to have the judges under him like unto himself, just and faithful'.[44] In these circumstances it is hardly surprising that the great majority of judges regarded themselves as defenders of the rights of the crown as well as the lawful liberties of the subject. They would have agreed with Bacon when he told them, in 1617, that

it is proper for you by all means with your wisdom and fortitude to maintain the laws of the realm. Wherein, nevertheless, I would not have you head-strong, but heart-strong; and to weigh and remember with yourself that the twelve judges of the realm are as the twelve lions under Solomon's throne. They must be lions, but yet lions under the throne. They must show their stoutness in elevating and building up the throne.[45]

The judges' role in the early Stuart period, as earlier, went beyond the strictly judicial. When they toured the country on their assizes, for instance, they acted as the agents of the crown, reviewing the functioning of local government and reporting back to the King. Bacon gave his opinion, in 1615, that there had never been a ruler 'that did consult so oft with his judges' as did James. 'The judges are a kind of council of the King's, by oath and ancient institution, but he useth them so indeed. He confers regularly with them upon their returns from their visitations and circuits. He gives them liberty both to inform him and to debate matters with him, and in the fall and conclusion commonly relieth on their opinions'.[46] The judges were also consulted before a meeting of Parliament, in order, as Bacon put it, 'to engage and assure [them] for any points of law or right which may be foreseen as likely to come in question'.[47] In 1620 Bacon, as Lord Chancellor, carried out the consultation himself. As it happened the two Chief Justices were both former members of the House of Commons, and in the forthcoming Parliament they would join their fellow judges as advisers to the House of Lords, so there was no question of involving them against their will in a political process with which they were not familiar.

Frequent consultation had its dangers, of course, the most obvious being that the judges would come to regard themselves as part of the royal government and act, in cases where the interests of the crown were involved, in what might appear to be a partisan manner. Yet relations between James and the judicial bench were not always harmonious. One major source of disagreement came over the use by King's Bench and Common Pleas of writs of prohibition. These were designed to transfer cases from inferior courts on the grounds that the latter were exceeding their jurisdiction. Because of the number of courts in early Stuart England, and the problems of over-lapping, it made sense that the two greatest courts should attempt to maintain some sort of order and coherence. They also upheld the principle that cases affecting property were for the common law alone and not for the church courts or prerogative ones.

This created problems, however, where tithes were concerned, for they involved both property rights and the rights of the Church. Many an impoverished minister would sue his patron or parishioners in a church court for a more equitable tithe payment, and might well be on the point of winning when he found his case abruptly transferred to Westminster Hall, where Common Pleas and King's Bench held their sessions. The clergy had complained about the increasing (and, they believed, unjustified) number of prohibitions directed against ecclesiastical courts in the latter part of Elizabeth's reign, and in 1605 Archbishop Bancroft appealed to James to resolve the problem. James was nothing loth. He was genuinely concerned with the well-being of the Church and its ministers; he was aware of complaints that prohibitions were also being used excessively against his prerogative courts in the north and the marches of Wales; and he welcomed the opportunity to put into practice his claim to be the judge of judges, the ultimate resolver of problems of disputed jurisdictions. Bancroft's list of grievances, which Coke christened *Articuli Cleri*, was presented to the King in 1605, but the judges, led by Coke, refused to acknowledge the validity of the complaints. They accepted that both the secular and the ecclesiastical courts derived their authority from the King, 'and that if any abuses be, they ought to be reformed'; but they insisted that 'what the law doth warrant in cases of prohibitions, to keep every jurisdiction in his true limits, is not to be said an abuse, nor can be altered but by Parliament'.[48]

Bancroft was far from satisfied. He asserted that 570 prohibitions had been issued since James's accession, and even though the judges argued that the actual number was 314, this could still be regarded as excessive. The Archbishop therefore appealed once again to the King, and attempted to win his support by arguing that James, as the fount of justice, could withdraw cases from any court and determine them himself. This was in accordance with James's own view of his role, but as he was a stranger to common law he turned to the judges for advice. Coke, acting as their spokesman, delivered the opinion 'that the King in his own person cannot adjudge any case, either criminal . . . or betwixt party and party . . . but this ought to be determined and judged in some court of justice according to the law and custom of England'. James made the pertinent observation that law was founded upon reason, and that the exercise of this faculty was not confined to judges. Coke acknowledged 'that God had endowed His Majesty with excellent science and great endowments of nature' but added that James 'was not learned in the laws of his realm of England' and that cases affecting 'the life or inheritance or goods or fortunes of his subjects are not to be decided by natural reason but by the artificial reason and judgment of law'. Coke concluded (if his account is to be believed) by reminding James that the law not only provided a 'golden metewand and measure to try the causes of the subjects' but also 'protected His Majesty in safety and peace'. This deeply offended James, who believed that as the ultimate source and sanction of law he must be above it, but Coke quoted the great thirteenth-century legist, Bracton, to the effect that while the King was not subject to any human authority he was under God and the law.[49]

This exchange, in which James's philosophy of kingship came up against Coke's common-law version of the English constitution, added further strength to James's growing conviction that the Chief Justice of the Common Pleas was an impediment to the royal will rather than a means of enforcing it. Moreover, it did nothing to resolve the problem of prohibitions, and in November of the following year, 1608, John Chamberlain reported that 'the King hath had two or three conferences of late with the judges about prohibitions, as well touching the clergy and High Commission as the [prerogative] courts of York and Wales; which prohibitions he would fain cut off, and stretch his prerogative to the uttermost'.[50]

James presumably became aware that his actions were being unfavourably interpreted, for when he addressed Parliament in 1610 he expounded his attitude at some length. He told members:

I am not ignorant that I have been thought to be an enemy to all prohibitions and an utter stayer of them . . . It is true that in respect of divers honourable courts and jurisdictions planted in this kingdom I have often wished that every court had his own true limit and jurisdiction clearly set down and certainly known; which if it be exceeded by any of them, or that any of them encroach one upon another, then I grant that a prohibition in that case is to go out of the King's Bench, but chiefliest out of the Chancery: for other benches I am not yet so well resolved of their jurisdiction in that point. And for my part I was never against prohibitions of this nature, nor the true use of them, which is indeed to keep every river within his own banks and channels. But when I saw the swelling and overflowing of prohibitions in a far greater abundance than ever before . . . then dealt I with this cause . . . Therefore I gave admonitions to both sides. To the other courts, that they should be careful hereafter, every of them, to contain themselves within the bounds of their own jurisdictions; and to the courts of common law, that they should not be so forward and prodigal in multiplying their prohibitions . . . Otherwise, if prohibitions should rashly and headily be granted, then no man is the more secure of his own, though he hath gotten a sentence . . . A poor minister, with much labour and expense having exhausted his poor means . . . obtains a sentence, and then, when he looks to enjoy the fruits thereof, he is defrauded of all by a prohibition . . . So to conclude this point, I put a difference between the true use of prohibitions and the super-abounding abuse thereof. For as a thing which is good ought not therefore be abused, so ought not the lawful use of a good thing be forborne because of the abuse thereof.[51]

There is little doubt that Coke, especially during his time as Chief Justice of the Common Pleas, was the driving force behind the issue of prohibitions. His aim was to assert the supremacy of the common law over all other jurisdictions and to give the regulatory role to the central courts at Westminster. His vision of the law as a self-contained and autonomous system also led him to question the crown's right to intervene even when issues of security or preroga-tive were involved. In early 1615, for example, when a clergyman called Edmond Peacham was accused of inciting sedition, the Council asked the judges for their opinion whether the evidence against him was sufficient. There was nothing unusual about such a procedure except that the King, fearing that Coke would marshal the judges against him, gave orders that they were to be consulted separately. Coke protested 'that such particular and (as he called it) auricular taking of opinions was not according to the custom of this realm, and seemed to divine that his brethren would never do it'. On this occasion, however, – and not for the first time – Coke was odd man out. The prevailing view was put by Sir John Dodderidge, who said 'that every judge was bound expressly by his oath to give Your Majesty counsel when he was called; and whether he should do it jointly or severally, that rested in Your Majesty's good pleasure, as you would require it; and though the ordinary course was to assemble them, yet there might intervene cases wherein the other course was more convenient'.[52]

The following year saw another case which involved the crown. This time it concerned the King's right to grant a clergyman an additional benefice or *commendam*. James instructed his Attorney General, Bacon, to write to Coke asking the judges to delay any decision until they had been fully informed of the King's view of the matter. Coke regarded this as a threat to the independence of the judicial bench and persuaded his colleagues to make a joint statement that the oath which they swore upon taking office committed them to do justice without any delay and that therefore they could not agree to the King's request. James promptly reminded the judges that

if ye list to remember what princely care we have ever had since our coming to this crown to see justice administered to our subjects with all possible expedition, and how far we have ever been from urging the delay thereof in any sort, ye may easily persuade yourselves that it was no small reason that moved us to send you that direction . . . We are far from crossing or delaying anything which may belong to the interest of any private parties in this case, but we cannot be contented to suffer the prerogative royal of our crown to be wounded through the sides of a private person.[53]

James followed this up by summoning the judges to appear before him so that he could state his case in person. He did so forcefully and at length, whereupon 'all the judges fell down upon their knees and acknowledged their error for matter of form, humbly craving His Majesty's gracious favour and pardon for the same'.[54]

Chief Justice Coke, however, even though he remained in a kneeling posture, kept up his insistence that the action demanded of the judges was against their oath. James dismissed this as 'mere sophistry' and called upon Lord Chancellor Ellesmere to resolve the point of law. Ellesmere 'delivered his opinion clearly and plainly that the stay that had been by His Majesty required was not against law, or any breach of a judge's oath'. James then instructed the judges, one by one, to say 'whether if at any time in a case depending before the judges which His Majesty conceived to concern him either in power or profit, and thereupon required to consult with them, and that they should stay proceedings in the meantime, they ought not to stay accordingly?' Eleven of the judges 'acknowledged it to be their duty so to do'. The single exception was Coke, who gave the grudging and enigmatic reply 'that when that case should be, he would do that should be fit for a judge to do'.[55]

James was a short-tempered man, given to explosive outbursts. In 1607, when Nicholas Fuller – who had already roused James's anger by his conduct in the Commons – tried to invoke the authority of King's Bench to protect him against a prosecution before the High Commission, the judges refused to support him. James welcomed their decision, but told his Secretary that they 'had done well for themselves . . . for that he was resolved, if they had done otherwise . . . he would have committed them'.[56] Whether in practice James would have taken the portentous step of imprisoning judges, with all that that implied for the rule of law and the maintenance of social harmony, may be doubted. After all, he put up with the overbearing Coke for many years, and was only driven to part with him after Coke had displayed a degree of independence that was indistinguishable, in James's eyes at any rate, from wilful obstruction. Not only had he directly opposed the King's commands in the Case of Commendams; he had also been involved – whether directly or not is unclear – in a challenge to the authority of the Court of Chancery.

Many common lawyers disliked and distrusted Chancery as a threat to the autonomy of their own system, and although the Lord Chancellor who headed the court was usually chosen from among their ranks he suffered from being too closely identified with its operations. James Whitelocke, for instance, a lawyer and future judge, described Lord Chancellor Ellesmere as 'the greatest enemy to the common law that did ever bear office of state in this kingdom'.[57] However, Chancery had a long history as a court, and the Lord Chancellor, as the head of the royal administration, could count on the King's backing. It was therefore either unwise or deliberately provocative of the King's Bench to threaten, in 1616, to bring an action for *praemunire* against the Chancery for giving judicial consideration to a case that had already been decided at common law. James was outraged. 'How can the King grant a *praemunire* against himself?' he demanded, with some logic. The bringing of such an action was 'a foolish, inept and presumptuous attempt, and fitter for the time of some unworthy king'. If there were grounds for complaint that a certain court had exceeded its lawful bounds, then these should be notified to the King, so that he could take the appropriate action. Otherwise the whole process of law would be called into question, and 'what greater misery can there be to the law than contempt of the law? And what readier way to contempt than when questions come "What shall be determined in this court, and what in that?"'.[58]

A Chief Justice bore a greater responsibility than other men for ensuring that the authority of the law was maintained, but by the middle of 1616 James had become convinced that Coke had abandoned this responsibility in pursuit of his own wayward and idiosyncratic objectives, whatever they might be. In June 1616, therefore, Coke was summoned before the Privy Council to answer a number of charges arising out of his conduct, and when he failed to answer these to the King's satisfaction he was suspended from office. In the following November he was formally dismissed. Under his successor, Sir Henry Montagu, things returned to normal as the judges adopted a lower profile; for Montagu, as he announced at his installation, had no intention of being 'a heady judge . . . busy in stirring questions, especially of jurisdictions'.[59]

JAMES I AND THE COMMON LAW

Coke's career as a judge was now over, but he was already ensuring his posthumous reputation as one of the most learned of all common lawyers by publishing the series of *Reports* of judicial decisions which was designed to summarise and define the state of the law as it existed at the beginning of the seventeenth century. The first volume appeared in 1600 and was followed by ten more during Coke's lifetime. Volume nine, as its title page declared, was published 'in the tenth year of the most high and most illustrious James, King of England' whom Coke described as 'the fountain of all piety and justice, and the life of the law'. Although Coke, in common with the majority of his contemporaries, knew how to flatter, his tribute was justified, for James took his responsibilities as the guardian of law with the utmost seriousness, and made it his primary objective to maintain the balance between the powers of the crown and the rights of individual subjects that was the defining characteristic of the English system of government.

There had been fears when James came to the English throne that he would attempt to undermine the common law, which enshrined constitutional conventions, and try to replace it with a more authoritarian system, perhaps based on Roman law. Indeed, one of the major reasons for the widespread opposition to James's project of a statutory union between England and Scotland was the fear that the new state of *Great Britain* would have to be provided with a new set of laws. It may well be that if James had arrived in a primitive country in 1603 instead of in England he would have provided a code of law for his subjects much more authoritarian than anything he had left behind him. But, as he told the 1610 Parliament, he drew a distinction between communities in the first stage of their creation as political entities and those which were 'settled in civility and policy'. In the former the King's will would be law, but in the latter the King would be *lex loquens*, the voice of an already existing law.[60] James had committed himself, in the first Parliament of his reign, 'never hereafter to alter or innovate the fundamental laws, privileges and good customs of this kingdom',[61] and he had also solemnly sworn at his coronation 'to hold and keep the laws and rightful customs which the commonalty of your kingdom have'.[62] Whatever his beliefs about his theoretical powers, then, James was in practice an upholder of the common law. Indeed, as he himself said in 1610, 'as a king, I have least cause of any man to dislike the common law, for no law can be more favourable and advantageous for a king and extendeth further his prerogative than it doth. And for a King of England to despise the common law, it is to neglect his own crown'.[63]

It was not by coincidence that James made this public declaration of his commitment to the common law in 1610, for the parliamentary session of that year had seen an attack upon Cowell's *Interpreter* for implying quite the contrary. Dr John Cowell was professor of civil law at Cambridge and also served as Vicar-General to Arch-bishop Bancroft, for whom he was said to have drafted the *Articuli Cleri*. This connexion would have made him an object of some suspicion to the many puritan sympathisers in the House of Commons, and he courted further displeasure from that direction by producing, in 1605, the *Institutiones Juris Anglicani*, which was designed to promote the Union by demonstrating the similarities between the civil and common laws. In preparing this work Cowell had been forced to reflect on the meaning of certain legal terms, and this prompted him, two years later, to compile a law dictionary, which he entitled the *Interpreter*. It was a valuable work of reference, aimed primarily at law students, but in 1610, in the middle of the negotiations on the Great Contract, it was made the subject of a complaint in the House of Commons.

Cowell's offence, if such it was, consisted in his attempts to define the powers of the King and the role of Parliament in relationship to law. Under the heading 'King', for example, he wrote:

he is above the law by his absolute power; and though for the better and equal course in making laws he do admit the three estates – that is, Lords spiritual, Lords temporal, and the Commons – unto council, yet this . . . is not of constraint, but of his own benignity, or by reason of his promise made upon oath at the time of his coronation . . . And though at his coronation he take an oath not to alter the laws of the land, yet this oath notwithstanding, he may alter or suspend any particular law that seemeth hurtful to the public estate'.[64]

There was nothing wilful or eccentric about such a definition. Indeed it accorded closely with James's own views of the nature of his authority. But the King did not wish the negotiations over the Contract to be blown off course by this secondary issue, and he therefore issued a proclamation ordering the suppression of the *Interpreter*. Yet although James had managed to give the impression that he rejected Cowell's views, he never formally did so; the nominal reason given for Cowell's condemnation was that he had engaged in public discussion of matters far beyond his reach. It was an essential element in James's political philosophy that the powers of the crown should not be too closely defined, for he wished to retain in widest possible measure his freedom of action. Yet he accepted that in ordinary circumstances the prerogative should flow in its accustomed channels, and for this reason he was sensitive to the complaints voiced by the Commons in 1610 about the unpre-cedented use of royal proclamations. James had indeed begun his reign by issuing proclamations at a greater rate than his predecessors, and in 1609 he had ordered them to be gathered together and published in book form. The aim of this, as Salisbury explained, was to ensure that there was no clash between them and the law, but the Commons drew up a petition in which they referred to 'a general fear amongst Your Majesty's people that proclamations will by degrees grow up and increase to the strength and nature of laws [and] in process of time bring a new form of arbitrary government upon the realm'.

James, in his reply, accepted that 'proclamations are not of equal force and in like degree as laws' but insisted that they had to be used to restrain 'such mischiefs and inconveniences as we see growing in the commonweal, against which no certain law is extant, and which may tend to the great grief and prejudice of our subjects if there should be no remedy provided until a Parliament'. However, he thanked the Commons for calling to his attention the fact that proclamations had been used more extensively than before, and had dealt with matters affecting freehold which were beyond their legitimate range. He announced his intention of conferring with the judges, so that any existing proclamations found to be at fault could be amended, while all future ones should 'stand with the former laws or statutes of the kingdom'.[65]

James did consult the judges, and Coke reported them as saying that 'the King by his proclamation cannot create any offence which was not an offence before'. This was somewhat misleading, since they in fact ruled that the King did have the right, in case of necessity, to define an offence by proclamation and provide for its punishment.[66] James had already revoked all but one of the specific proclamations which Parliament had complained of in 1610, and during the next four years he used such measures sparingly. After the collapse of the Addled Parliament, however, the rate increased, and in many cases it was specifically provided that breach of the proclamation should be punishable in the prerogative court of Star Chamber. Chamberlain complained in July 1620 that 'the world is now much terrified with the Star Chamber, there being not so little an offence against any proclamation but is liable and subject to the censure of that court',[67] but although the issue was raised in subsequent parliaments it did not inflame tempers as it had done in 1610, nor was the King's prerogative power in this respect ever openly challenged. It was, as so often, the fear of innovation that had led the Commons to complain in 1610, but James's subsequent conduct showed that he had no intention of going beyond the limits of what 'our progenitors have by their prerogative royal used, in times of the best and happiest government of this kingdom'.[68]

61

Because James, at his accession, was a stranger to common law, he could take a clear-sighted view of it, and he recognised not only its strengths but also its weaknesses. In 1610 Salisbury reported him as being 'not so enamoured on this law that he thinks nothing therein could be amended. Experience, and the daily making new statutes to supply . . . the defects of the law, showeth the contrary'.[69] A few weeks later James explained what he had in mind:

I could wish some three things specially to be purged and cleared in the common law, (but always by the advice of Parliament) . . . First, I could wish that it were written in our vulgar language; for now it is in an old, mixt and corrupt language [i.e. 'law-French'], only understood by lawyers, whereas every subject ought to understand the law under which he lives . . . Next, our common law hath not a settled text in all cases, being chiefly grounded either upon old customs or else upon the Reports and cases of judges . . . It were good that upon a mature deliberation the exposition of the law were set down by Act of Parliament, and such Reports therein confirmed as were thought fit to serve for law in all times hereafter . . . And lastly, there be in the common law divers contrary Reports and precedents, and this corruption doth likewise concern the statutes and Acts of Parliament, in respect there are divers cross and cuffing statutes, and some so penned as they may be taken in divers, yea contrary, senses. And therefore would I wish both those statutes and Reports . . . to be once maturely reviewed and reconciled . . . And this reformation might, methinks, be made a worthy work, and well deserves a Parliament to be set of purpose for it.[70]

James was probably influenced in his desire for law reform by Bacon, who had long advocated it. One of the reasons why Bacon supported the project of Union between England and Scotland was that 'the review of our laws and theirs might work a better digest of our laws',[71] and in 1608 he set himself the task of reducing the laws of the two countries into one code. Pressure of other business left him insufficient time to concentrate on this, but in 1616–17 he drew up a detailed proposal for law reform which he presented to James. Bacon was no friend of Coke, but in his proposal he acknowledged the value of Coke's *Reports* 'which, though they may have errors and some peremptory and extrajudicial resolutions more than are warranted, yet they contain infinite good decisions and rulings-over of cases'. Indeed, had it not been for Coke's work in reinterpreting past decisions in order to make them relevant to his own day 'the law by this time had been almost like a ship without ballast, for that the cases of modern experience are fled from those that are adjudged and ruled in former time'.[72] Coke himself seems to have thought that his *Reports* provided the common law and its practitioners with all that they required, but he recognised the need to do something about the multiplicity and confusion of statutes, 'to make one plain and perspicuous law, divided into articles, so as every subject may know what Acts be in force, and what repealed, either . . . in part or in the whole'.[73]

James appointed commissioners to survey the statutes with a view to rationalising and consolidating them, and when the 1621 Parliament assembled it responded to the pressures from Bacon, now Lord Chancellor, and Sir Henry Hobart, Chief Justice of the Common Pleas, by co-operating in the process. In February William Hakewill told the Commons that he and his fellow commissioners, Heneage Finch and William Noy, had taken 'much pains in surveying the statutes . . . They found almost four hundred statutes fit to be repealed, as being snares to us. In the last statute for repeals [they had discovered] such defects as marvel they should pass an House of Parliament'. The House responded by appointing seven of its members, including Sir Edward Coke, to join with the royal commissioners 'to survey all the statutes and to draw all the statutes concerning one matter into one or more plain and perfect law; and to consider which are fit to be repealed, which expired, which in force, and which fit to be continued'.[74] This was a promising beginning, but the following month saw the revelations about Bacon's involvement in corrupt practices which led to his disgrace, and with his fall the impetus went out of law reform. A thorough review of the statutes, particularly if it was combined with reform of the common law, would have required a Parliament to itself, as James had foreseen, but by 1621 there were more urgent and more divisive matters to occupy the attention of the Houses. Like so many of James's enlightened projects, therefore, law reform came to nothing, and at his death the common and statute laws were in essence the same as they had been at his accession.

However, common law and statutes did not constitute the only forms of law in England. The church courts, or 'courts Christian', administered canon law, as defined in 1604, but since the study of canon law at university had been forbidden by Henry VIII in 1535 the practitioners in the courts Christian were drawn from the ranks of the 'civilians', usually clerics, who had qualified in Roman, or 'civil' law. The principal church courts were those held by the archdeacons, but above them, in every diocese, came the consistory court of the bishop. General supervision was exercised within each of the two provinces by the High Commission, set up by virtue of the regulatory powers inherent in the crown but also based in part upon the authority granted to Elizabeth I by the Act of Supremacy in

1559. In theory the High Commission for Canterbury was confined to that province, but in practice, by the early seventeenth century, it was acting in some respects as the principal church court for the whole kingdom.

As well as the courts Christian, there were the prerogative courts, of which the most famous was Star Chamber. This consisted of Privy Councillors with the addition of the two Chief Justices, and although it was obviously strongly influenced by common-law assumptions it was was not bound by precedent in the way that common-law courts were. Proceedings in Star Chamber were initiated by a bill of complaint written in English, as contrasted with the Latin writs required by the ordinary courts, and the Star Chamber judges, many of whom were not professional lawyers, used common sense rather than common law to decide on the issues before them. Star Chamber dealt with those offences, such as riot, which were not adequately covered by the ordinary courts and which needed prompt attention because they threatened state security. In theory Star Chamber could not deal with property matters, but plaintiffs were adept at disguising these as riots in order to get their case brought before it, for proceedings were swifter there than in the common-law courts, and judgment, once given, was not easily overthrown. Although Star Chamber was a popular court, in the sense that litigants made frequent use of it, the number of cases brought by individuals was declining in James's reign. At his accession it was dealing with some 400 such cases a year, but by the time he died this figure had dropped to 250. Part of the reason for this was the increase in the number of government prosecutions. These were brought by the Attorney General and instituted by a verbal procedure known as *ore tenus*, based upon the defendant's admission of guilt.

Lesser prerogative courts existed to strengthen the royal government in those parts of the kingdom which were remote from the capital. York was the seat of the Council of the North, under a President directly appointed by the King, while another royal President guided the proceedings of the Council in the Marches of Wales, which had its headquarters at Ludlow. There were also three other courts at Westminster which derived their authority from the royal prerogative. The first was Chancery, which, under the direction of whoever held the office of Lord Chancellor or Lord Keeper, tempered the rigidity of the common-law courts by administering fairness or 'equity'. The Lord Chancellor had originally been 'the keeper of the King's conscience', and 'equity' derived from the royal responsibility to provide justice even if this involved interference with judgments given in the ordinary course of the common law. However, since Lord Chancellors were almost invariably common lawyers by training and profession, the law which they administered was heavily influenced by common-law assumptions.

In its procedures Chancery showed the influence of civil law practices, and the same was true of the second of the three lesser prerogative courts, namely Requests. This had emerged from the general juris-diction exercised by the Council in the early Tudor period, in much the same way as Star Chamber, and was concerned with the complaints of men who could not afford the costs of a writ or of employing counsel and were therefore effectively barred from suing in a common-law court. These poor men's complaints were dealt with by four specially-appointed Masters of Requests, who invari-ably included two or three clerics trained in the civil law. The only prerogative court which was purely and simply a court of civil law was the Admiralty. The disputes arising out of shipping were, by the nature of commerce, likely to involve more than one country, and civil law was the nearest equivalent in seventeenth-century Europe to international law.

THE ROYAL PREROGATIVE AND THE LAW

Was the royal prerogative part of English law? Bacon had no doubt that it was. Speaking as Lord Keeper in 1617, he affirmed that 'the King's prerogative and the law are not two things, but the King's prerogative is law, and the principal part of the law . . . and there-fore in conserving and maintaining that, you conserve and maintain the law'.[75] James, likewise, saw no incompatibility between his determination to uphold his prerogative and his commitment to the common law: 'the marriage between law and prerogative is inse-parable, and, like twins, they must joy and mourn together, live and die together. The separation of the one is the ruin of the other'.[76]

According to Chief Baron Fleming, however, the prerogative had two aspects, and therefore two differing perspectives towards the law. James accepted this distinction, for he informed the judges in 1616 that he had 'a double prerogative, whereof the one was ordi-nary and had relation to his private interest, which might be, and was every day, disputed in [the courts in] Westminster Hall. The other was of an higher nature, referring to his supreme and imperial power and sovereignty, which ought not to be disputed or handled in vulgar argument'.[77] It did not follow, however, that because the absolute prerogative was above the common law it was therefore unlawful. James Whitelocke had implied this when he asserted, in 1613, that 'due process of law', as defined by Magna Carta, referred solely to common-law procedures. The King's learned counsel, on the other hand, insisted that 'the *Lex Terrae* ["law of the land"] mentioned in the said statute is not to be understood only of proceedings in the ordinary courts of justice, but that His Majesty's prerogative and his absolute power incident to his sovereignty is also *Lex Terrae*, and is invested and exercised by the law of the land, and is part thereof'.[78]

The Commons had been suspicious of the absolute prerogative ever since it was given shape and definition by Fleming's judgment. When, in the 1610 Parliament, Henry Yelverton acknowledged that the King had a limited right to levy Impositions, Richard Martin accused him of upholding 'an arbitrary, irregular, unlimited and transcendent power'. Martin went on to give his own definition of the dual capacity of the King: 'in his Parliament' he was 'the most absolute King', but when he acted outside this context 'his power is limited by law'.[79] This argument was subsequently developed by James Whitelocke, who began with the premise that in every state there were 'some rights of sovereignty, *jura majestatis*, which regularly and of common right do belong to the sovereign power of that state . . . which sovereign power is *potestas suprema*, a power that can control all other powers and cannot be controlled but by itself'. He agreed that the sovereign power was in the King, but drew the same distinction as Martin between the King's twin capacities:

in the King is a twofold power – the one in Parliament, as he is assisted with the consent of the whole state; the other out of Parliament, as he is sole and singular, guided merely by his own will. And if, of these two powers in the King, one is greater than the other and can direct and control the other, that is *suprema potestas*, the sovereign power, and the other is *subordinata*. It will then be easily proved that the power of the King in Parliament is greater than his power out of Parliament and doth rule and control it.[80]

The problem with this definition of the royal authority, which located sovereignty in the King in Parliament, was that Parliament was merely an occasional body which met at the King's pleasure: as Lord Keeper Williams reminded the Houses in November 1621 'when he bids us go, we must go; when he bids us come, we must come'.[81] Some members of the Commons had already concluded that the only way in which to prevent abuses of power was by making Parliament a regular part of the political system. A tract entitled *Motives to Induce an Annual Parliament* was in circulation in the period 1614–21,[82] and in the 1621 Parliament Sir Edward Coke laid emphasis upon a precedent from the fourth year of Edward III's reign when, 'for the redress of many mischiefs and grievances which daily increase in the commonwealth, it was ordained that a Parliament be held every year. In those days parliaments were accounted necessary every year. And is there not the same necessity still?'.[83]

However, even assuming that Coke was right and that annual parliaments were required by law, how could the King be persuaded to call them? The history of the laws against purveyance had shown how ineffective statutes could be when it came to restraining the King's prerogative. Even if the judges gave a decision against him he could ignore it, as James had done when he assumed the title of *King of Great Britain*, and the experience of his reign, and even more of Charles's, suggested that the judges were far likelier to uphold the royal prerogative than to restrain it. The King had the big advantage over Parliament that he *was* the government. Moreover he was, so to speak, in permanent session. In the last resort the power of the state was concentrated in his hands, and though he might choose to accept the prevailing conventions by ruling according to law and in co-operation with Parliament, he could not be *forced* to do so, except by means that implied the total breakdown of constitutional government. To this extent James's assertion that he was above the law was simply a statement of fact. For him – as for Charles (see p. 228) – the solution to all the difficulties that had arisen over differing views of the prerogative was a simple one. If only the King's subjects, and particularly their representatives in Parliament, were to trust the King and co-operate with him, he would not need to employ his absolute prerogative powers. As James reminded the 1607 session of Parliament, which was considering his offer to guarantee that the rights of his English subjects would not be infringed by a statutory Union,

it is objected, what security shall we have of these restrictions? For, say you, we can have none, by reason of the King's prerogative. Herein I am not able to resolve you, for first I am no common lawyer. Next, you will not believe the judges. But if I can give you no security, why seek it you? For then you were better take the honour of a prince than to leave the matter to the course of law.[84]

NOTES AND REFERENCES

(*The place of publication is London, unless otherwise stated*)

1. **Quentin Skinner** *The Foundations of Modern Political Thought*. Vol. 2, *The Age of Reformation* (Cambridge 1978), p. 342. (Hereafter Skinner *The Age of Reformation*)
2. *The Political Works of James I*, ed. C. H. McIlwain (Cambridge, Mass 1918), pp. 307–8. (Hereafter James I *Political Works*)
3. Skinner *The Age of Reformation*, p. 178.
4. **E. R. Foster** (ed.) *Proceedings in Parliament 1610* (New Haven 1966). Vol. 2, p. 158. (Hereafter Foster *Proceedings 1610*)
5. **Sir John Fortescue** *The Governance of England*, ed. Charles Plummer (Oxford 1885), p. 109.
6. **Faith Thompson** *Magna Carta: Its Role in the Making of the English Constitution 1300–1629* (Oxford 1948), p. 220. (Hereafter Thompson *Magna Carta*)
7. Thompson *Magna Carta*, p. 225.
8. Thompson *Magna Carta*, p. 219.
9. *Dictionary of National Biography* sub Parker.
10. *The Reports of Sir Edward Coke, Kt*. (1738). Part VIII, Preface, p. iv. (Hereafter Coke *Reports*)
11. Coke *Reports*. Part IV, Preface, p. v.
12. James I *Political Works*, pp. 62–3.
13. *The Works of Francis Bacon*, ed. James Spedding (1874). Vol. XV, p. 200. (Hereafter Bacon *Works*)
14. **L. A. Knafla** *Law and Politics in Jacobean England: The Tracts of Lord Chancellor Ellesmere* (Cambridge 1977), pp. 248–9. (Hereafter Knafla *Law and Politics*)
15. Skinner *The Age of Reformation*, p. 349.
16. Coke *Reports*. Part XI, p. 87v.
17. **W. S. Holdsworth** *A History of English Law* (1924). Vol. IV, pp. 358–9.
18. Holdsworth *History of English Law*. Vol. V, pp. 496–7.
19. **J. R. Tanner.** (ed.) *Constitutional Documents of the Reign of James I* (Cambridge 1930), p. 222. (Hereafter Tanner *Constitutional Documents*)
20. Tanner *Constitutional Documents*, pp. 222–3.
21. *Journals of the House of Commons 1547–1714* (1742). Vol. I, pp. 939–40. (Hereafter *Commons Journals*).
22. **E. R. Foster** *The House of Lords 1603–1649* (Chapel Hill 1983), p. 77. (Hereafter Foster *House of Lords*)
23. *The Parliamentary Diary of Robert Bowyer 1606–1607*, ed, D. H. Willson (Minneapolis 1931), p. 218. (Hereafter Bowyer *Parliamentary Diary*)
24. Bowyer *Parliamentary Diary*, p. 240, n. 1.
25. Knafla *Law and Politics*, pp. 209–10.
26. *A Complete Collection of State Trials*, ed. T. B. Howell (1816). Vol. II, pp. 390–1. (Hereafter *State Trials*)
27. Coke *Reports*. Part XII, pp. 33–4.
28. **J. P. Kenyon** (ed.) *The Stuart Constitution 1603–1688* 2nd edn (Cambridge 1986), p. 55. (Hereafter Kenyon *Stuart Constitution*)

29. Kenyon *Stuart Constitution*, p. 55.
30. **G. W. Prothero** (ed.) *Select Statutes and other Constitutional Documents illustrative of the Reigns of Elizabeth and James I* (Oxford 1913), p. 354. (Hereafter Prothero *Select Statutes*)
31. *Commons Journals.* Vol. I, p. 317.
32. Foster *Proceedings 1610.* Vol. 2, pp. 178–9.
33. Tanner *Constitutional Documents*, p. 247.
34. Foster *House of Lords*, p. 79.
35. **Wallace Notestein, Frances Helen Relf** & **Hartley Simpson** (eds.) *Commons Debates 1621* (New Haven 1935). Vol. VII. 632–33. (Hereafter *Commons Debates 1621*)
36. *Commons Journals.* Vol. I, p. 482.
37. Bowyer *Parliamentary Diary*, p. 60.
38. Bowyer *Parliamentary Diary* p. 134 n. 1.
39. *Commons Journals.* Vol. I, p. 653; *Commons Debates 1621.* Vol. II, p. 478.
40. *Commons Debates 1621.* Vol. III, p. 402; Vol. V, p. 195.
41. **Bruce Galloway** *The Union of England and Scotland 1603–08* (1986), p. 149.
42. **James Whitelocke** *Liber Famelicus*, ed. J. Bruce, Camden Society (1858), p. 50. (Hereafter Whitelocke *Liber Famelicus*)
43. Bacon *Works.* Vol. XI, p. 381.
44. *Commons Debates 1621.* Vol. II, p. 11.
45. Bacon *Works.* Vol. XIII, p. 201–2.
46. Bacon *Works.* Vol. XII, p. 143.
47. Bacon *Works.* Vol. XI, p. 367.
48. *State Trials.* Vol. II, p. 134.
49. Coke *Reports.* Part XII, p. 63–5.
50. ***The Letters of John Chamberlain*** ed. N. E. McClure (Philadelphia 1939). Vol. I, p. 269. (Hereafter Chamberlain *Letters*)
51. James I *Political Works*, pp. 312–13.
52. Bacon *Works.* Vol. XII, pp. 100–1.
53. Bacon *Works.* Vol. XII, p. 361.
54. Bacon *Works.* Vol. XII, p. 365.
55. Bacon *Works.* Vol. XII, pp. 365–7.
56. **R. G. Usher**, 'Nicholas Fuller: A Forgotten Exponent of English Liberty' *American Historical Review.* Vol. 12, 1906–7, p. 756.
57. Whitelocke *Liber Famelicus*, p. 53.
58. Bacon *Works.* Vol. XII, p. 384.
59. **J. P. Dawson** 'Coke and Ellesmere Disinterred: The Attack on the Chancery in 1616', *Illinois Law Review.* Vol. 36, 1941, p. 138.
60. James I *Political Works*, p. 309.
61. *Commons Journals.* Vol. I, p. 180.
62. Prothero *Select Statutes*, p. 392.
63. James I *Political Works*, p. 310.
64. Prothero *Select Statutes*, pp. 409–10.
65. **R. W. Heinze** 'Proclamations and Parliamentary Protest 1539–1610', in D. J. Guth & J. W. McKenna (eds) *Tudor Rule and Revolution* (Cambridge 1983), pp. 254–5. (Hereafter Heinze 'Proclamations')
66. Heinze 'Proclamations', p. 255.
67. Chamberlain *Letters.* Vol. II, p. 310.

68. Heinze 'Proclamations', p. 255.
69. Foster *Proceedings 1610*. Vol. 2, p. 50.
70. James I *Political Works*, pp. 311–12.
71. *Commons Journals*. Vol. I, p. 1034.
72. Bacon *Works*. Vol. XIII. p. 65.
73. Coke *Reports*. Part IV. Preface. pp. ix–x.
74. *Commons Journals*. Vol. I. pp. 519–20.
75. Bacon *Works*. Vol. XIII. p. 203.
76. Foster *Proceedings 1610*. Vol. 2. pp. 50–1.
77. Bacon *Works*. Vol. XII. p. 363.
78. Bacon *Works*. Vol. XI. p. 350.
79. **S. R. Gardiner** (ed.) *Parliamentary Debates in 1610*. Camden Society (1862), pp. 88–9.
80. Tanner *Constitutional Documents*. p. 260.
81. *Commons Debates 1621*. Vol. II, p. 434.
82. **Pauline Croft** 'Annual Parliaments and the Long Parliament', *Bulletin of the Institute of Historical Research*. Vol. 59, 1986.
83. *Commons Debates 1621*. Vol. II, pp. 197–8. For an earlier statement by Coke to the same effect, *c.* 1615, c.f. Bacon *Works*. Vol. XII, p. 203.
84. Bowyer *Parliamentary Diary*, pp. 287–8.

CHAPTER FOUR

James I and the Royal Finances

AN EXTRAVAGANT KING?

When James I ascended the throne of England in 1603 he described himself as being 'like a poor man wandering about forty years in a wilderness and barren soil, and now arrived at the land of promise'.[1] On his way south he was entertained by the leaders of English society, who displayed both in their houses and their style of living a degree of wealth that far surpassed anything in Scotland, and it is hardly surprising that James assumed that his days of penury were over and that as King of England he would be able to give free rein to his natural inclination for lavish display and unrestrained generosity. James was a typical Renaissance sovereign, taking it for granted that kings were bound to cultivate majesty and munificence, and that the resources of the state must be made to yield whatever was necessary for this transcendent purpose. It was unfortunate for his reputation that he came immediately after Elizabeth, who had been an exception to the general rule. She had learnt from bitter experience that the English crown was in fact under-endowed, and that she needed to keep a sharp eye on her expenditure in order to avoid falling more and more heavily into debt. Her 'nearness' or niggardliness was not appreciated by her subjects, and at first they welcomed James's open-handedness. However, when this led to demands for taxation they had second thoughts and began to complain of their new King's extravagance.

The rapid increase in royal expenditure under James was not attributable solely to the King's 'liberality'. James was a married man and, unlike his predecessor, had to maintain his wife, Queen Anne, and his eldest son, Prince Henry, in due state. The setting up of a separate establishment for Prince Henry cost £25,000 a year and items such as this were in large part responsible for the increase in overall expenditure on the royal households from £64,000 at James's accession to £114,000 by 1610. James also needed to re-equip himself and his (male) servants with appropriate robes and costumes after half a century of female rule: hence the increase in wardrobe expenditure from under £10,000 to more than £36,000 during the same period. But James's carefree attitude undoubtedly made matters worse. He found it difficult to say 'No', and he lacked that detailed knowledge of and interest in financial matters which had enabled Henry VII and Elizabeth to keep their expenditure in check. He positively enjoyed being generous to those he loved, and it was typical of him that in 1607, at a time when both the accumulated debt and the annual deficit were rising to new and alarming heights, James paid off not his own debts but those of three former favourites, Viscount Haddington, Lord Hay, and the Earl of Montgomery, at the cost of £44,000. 'Meantime', as John Chamberlain, the London letter-writer, laconically recorded, 'his own debts are stalled, to be paid the one half in May come two years, the residue in May following'.[2]

James Hay, the cadet of a noble Scots family, had been educated in France, which appealed to James, whose first favourite, Esmé d'Aubigny, was a native of that country. Hay, who became Viscount Doncaster and eventually Earl of Carlisle, was clearly an affable and convivial gentleman, but his extravagance was notorious. Clarendon described him as

a man of the greatest expense in his own person of any in the age [in which] he lived, and introduced more of that expense in the excess of clothes and diet than any other man; and was indeed the original of all those inventions from which others did but transcribe copies . . . After having spent, in a very jovial life, above £400,000 – which, upon a strict computation, he received from the crown – he left not a house or acre of land to be remembered by.[3]

Hay was not James's principal favourite. This position was filled by another Scot, Robert Carr, who had been a page to James in Scotland and made his way to London as a member of Hay's household. Although Carr came from a distinguished Scottish family he had little money and few possessions of his own. This, however, was a situation which James quickly changed. His first priority was to endow Carr with land, but this was difficult in view of the fact that James had just agreed to entail the crown estates. It appears that at one stage he proposed making Carr a gift of £20,000, to enable him to purchase property for himself, but Salisbury was appalled by this suggestion and persuaded the King instead to grant his favourite the manor of Sherborne, forfeited by Sir Walter Ralegh upon his attainder. Ralegh had transferred the property to trustees, to hold on behalf of his wife and son, but the deed of trust had a legal flaw in it, and James took advantage of this to seize the estate for his own use, since it enabled him to endow Carr without formally breaching the entail on crown lands. James was duly grateful to his chief minister and assured him that 'the more I think of your remembrance of Robert Carr for yon manor of Sherborne, the more cause have I to conclude that your mind ever watcheth to seek out all advantages for my honour and contentment'.[4]

The fact that Hay and Carr were both Scots was of more than passing significance, for it was James's generosity to his fellow-countrymen that caused particular resentment in England. By 1610 the Scots who followed James south had garnered nearly £90,000 in outright gifts, £133,000 in old crown debts (which were not necessarily recoverable), and more than £10,000 a year in pensions. If this is averaged out, it shows that they were gaining well over £40,000 a year from James's generosity compared with £10,000 for English beneficiaries. It is often said that James, as a newcomer to the English throne, needed to 'buy' support, but his grants to his Scottish followers served rather to alienate his English subjects.

Yet James's generosity was not entirely misplaced. The union of the two crowns was designed to put Scots and English on an equal footing, but James took the wise decision to reserve all major posts in government and administration for Englishmen. In order to avoid complaints from his Scottish subjects that they had been unfairly discriminated against, he gave them the lion's share of gratuities and pensions. Furthermore, as he reminded members of Parliament in 1610, kings had a moral obligation to reward those who served them. 'It may be', he confessed, 'that I have given much amongst Scottishmen, [but] if I had not been liberal in rewarding some of my old servants of that nation, ye could never have had reason to expect my thankfulness towards any of you that are more lately become my subjects'. In any case, he insisted, 'ye will find that I have dealt twice as much amongst Englishmen as I have done to Scottishmen' – a point that he also made to Salisbury in the same year, assuring him 'that the English have tasted as much, and more, of my liberality than the Scots have done'.[5] If the grant of offices and titles is put into the balance alongside pensions and gratuities, James's defence of his actions has a good deal of justification. But this argument cut no ice with the members who sat at Westminster, and it was not so much the facts of the case as the prevailing impression which had an unfavourable effect upon relations between the first Stuart sovereign and his newly-acquired subjects south of the border.

In 1610, when James looked back on the opening years of his reign in England, he acknowledged that he had been improvident, though he pointed out that 'a King's liberality must never be dried up altogether, for then he can never maintain nor oblige his servants and well-deserving subjects'. However, he reassured the members of Parliament whom he was addressing that 'the vastness of my expenditure is past which I used in the first two or three years after my coming hither . . . That Christmas and open-tide is ended. For at my first coming here, partly ignorance of this state – which no man can acquire but by time and experience – and partly the form of my coming, being so honourable and miraculous, enforced me to extend my liberality so much the more'.[6] James's reign had indeed opened with a period of euphoria, but already by October 1605 he was telling Salisbury 'that it is a horror to me to think upon the height of my place, the greatness of my debts, and the smallness of my means'.[7] He emphasised that he was now fully conscious of 'that needless and unseasonable profusion of expenses' of which the minister had complained, and was determined to mend his ways. 'I have promised, and I will perform it', he assured Salisbury, 'that there shall be no default in me'.[8]

James was undoubtedly sincere in his frequently expressed desire to staunch 'this continual haemorrhage of outletting'. In October 1607 he reminded his Councillors that where this 'eating canker of want' was concerned 'I am the patient and ye have promised to be the physicians and to use the best cure upon me that your wits, faithfulness, and diligence can reach unto. As for my part, ye may assure yourselves that I shall facilitate your cure by all the means possible for a poor patient, both by observing as strait a diet as ye can in honour and reason prescribe unto me, as also by using seasonably and in the right form such remedies and antidotes as ye are to apply unto my disease'. He charged them to do all that they could, not only to increase his revenue but to cut down on his charges by removing 'needless superfluities (the honour, greatness, and safety of the King and kingdom being always respected)'.[9]

The qualification is significant, for the honour and greatness of the King involved expenditure, and James, like any other monarch, was expected to be 'bounteous'. Yet at the same time he was expected to restrain his bounty within reasonable limits, and there

were no objective standards by which to judge what was 'reasonable'. Salisbury took up this theme in 1610 when he reminded
Parliament that 'bounty' was

a disease that few complained of in Queen Elizabeth's days: which I speak
not to cast any aspersion on her, for there are many (in which number I am
one) that have tasted of her bounty; but true it is, she was the grandchild
of a frugal father, daughter of a loose-handed father, which made her study
more a mediocrity therein than some others did before her. For as it is true
that bounty is inseparable from this King, who, as he is a man, cannot live
without desires (though never so moderate as they concern himself), so, as
he is a King, if he did not give, I should think his subjects lived in a miserable climate.[10]

THE CUSTOMS FARM

Salisbury was sufficient of a realist to perceive that while a reduction
in the King's expenditure was an essential part of any reform
package, it could not be achieved overnight. Nor would it, by itself,
solve the crown's financial problems, for the erosion of royal
revenues brought about by half a century of inflation had to be
remedied. There was a good prospect of doing this, for Elizabeth
and Lord Burghley, her conservative Lord Treasurer, had failed to
increase the income from crown lands, Customs and feudal rights
in line with inflation. The Book of Rates, for instance, which set
down the values of dutiable commodities, had not been revised since
Mary Tudor's reign, fifty years earlier. One of the first actions of
James's Lord Treasurer, the Earl of Dorset, was to issue a new Book,
in 1604. He also decided to lease the administration of the Customs
duties to private individuals, in order to produce a certain instead
of a fluctuating revenue. The wealthy merchants and financiers who
bid for the Customs farm sought out Court patrons, and it was a
group associated with Salisbury that won the contract, with a seven-
year lease at an annual rent of £112,400. The farmers would never
have agreed to pay this rent unless they had felt confident that they
would make a substantial profit. The end of the war with Spain
offered the prospect of expanding trade, and in fact the farmers did
so well that in 1607, even though their lease had four years to run,
they agreed to increase their annual payments to £120,000 rather than
risk having it cancelled. When the lease eventually expired, in 1611,
it was renewed for several years at £136,000, and in 1614, when
another seven-year lease was issued, the rent was fixed at £140,000.

This compares very favourably with an average yield of just under £100,000 in the closing years of Elizabeth.

It goes without saying that the Customs farmers did well out of their position. At the time of expiry of the first lease Lionel Cranfield, a City businessman and financial adviser to the crown, estimated that they had made a clear profit of more than £200,000, and he added that 'divers of them who before were but mean officers in that place have raised themselves to great estates'.[11] If the crown could have administered the Customs as efficiently, this profit would have gone into the royal Exchequer instead of the farmers' pockets, but early Stuart governments, like their Tudor predecessors, were not well equipped for financial administration of this sort. They lacked the men, the money, and even, perhaps, the will. Salisbury – a hard-working and committed administrator if ever there was one – found that his efforts to increase the yield from crown lands became bogged down in technical objections, legal delays, and endemic corruption, and although Cranfield, his eventual successor as Lord Treasurer, kept up the pressure to reform the royal finances, the limited degree of success he achieved was offset by the resentment of the vested interests whom he threatened – resentment which opened the way to his fall from power in 1624.

In these circumstances the crown was probably well advised to opt for Customs farming. At least it provided a regular revenue, and there was the further advantage that the farmers, in order to retain royal goodwill, were prepared to act as the crown's bankers. They subsidised it by allowing their rent payments to run ahead of receipts, which meant that the King was benefitting from interest-free loans averaging some £20,000 a year – though in 1614–15 this figure rose temporarily to £90,000. They were also prepared to make formal advance payments, on which they charged interest. In 1618–19 the crown received £40,000 by this means, and in the last four years of James's reign the average annual figure was not far short of £30,000. Furthermore, in 1607 the farmers organised a syndicate to raise the enormous sum of £120,000 which they loaned to the crown, thereby enabling the Exchequer to reduce its backlog of long-term debts to more manageable proportions.

IMPOSITIONS

The remorseless increase in royal expenditure made the task of successive Lord Treasurers extremely difficult. While the existing sources of revenue could be made to yield more, they could not cope with all the demands made upon them. What was needed was a new source, and this was found in Impositions. These were duties on trade, additional to the Customs duties, or Tonnage and Poundage, granted to James for life by the first Parliament of his reign. Impositions had first been levied, by prerogative action, under Mary Tudor, and Elizabeth kept them in being, though on a small scale. The Elizabethan Impositions included one on imported currants, but in 1606 its legality was challenged by a merchant called John Bate, who refused to pay on the grounds that it had never been sanctioned by Parliament. Bate's case came before the Court of the Exchequer, where Chief Baron Fleming found in favour of the crown. 'No exportation or importation can be but at the King's ports', he stated in giving judgment. 'They are the gates of the King, and he hath absolute power by them to include or exclude whom he shall please; and ports to merchants are their harbours and repose, and for their better security he is compelled to provide bulwarks and fortresses, and to maintain for the collection of his Customs and duties collectors and customers [i.e. Customs officers]; and for that charge it is reason that he should have this benefit'.[12]

Salisbury, as the King's chief minister, and Lord Treasurer Dorset had welcomed the opportunity provided by Bate to put Impositions on a stronger legal basis. Dorset, as nominal head of the Exchequer Court, conferred with Fleming and the other barons before they passed judgment and was pleased to find that their opinion concurred with his own. He had some reservations about the need for a detailed statement of the reasoning behind the judgment, but accepted the barons' view that only by publishing this could they hope to pre-empt further challenges and thereby ensure that the verdict in Bate's Case would be, in Dorset's words, 'an assured foundation for the King's Impositions for ever'. James, when he was informed of these proceedings, expressed his approval, for he was now fully persuaded that 'Customs or Impositions' were 'almost the only sure hope that is left for increase of my rent'.[13]

According to Salisbury, Dorset would have liked to take immediate advantage of the judgment by extending the range of Impositions, but the Council 'thought fit by a general concurrence of opinion to defer that course and to supply the present wants by borrowing some great sums upon interest, rather than to put the same in execution – except some further cause should afterwards appear'. It was not long before such a cause did appear, in the shape of O'Dogherty's rebellion in Ireland, which turned the 'wants in His

Majesty's estate . . . into so violent necessities . . . as it was then thought no ill counsel to prefer the former project of Impositions as the best temporary remedy for those charges'. Nevertheless, before new duties were imposed, Salisbury held consultations with a representative body of merchants and agreed that these duties should be levied only 'upon such commodities as in the use of them were grown to great excess: as spices, silks, cloth of gold, and such other things as we are desirous should be made at home'.[14]

CROWN LANDS AND WARDSHIP

The new Impositions, levied from 1608 onwards, brought in some £70,000 a year. This was a welcome addition to the King's revenues, but although it diminished the annual deficit it did not eradicate it, nor did it have any significant effect upon the accumulated debt. To deal with this, Salisbury had recourse to the sale of crown lands. He did so reluctantly, for he appreciated that such sales weakened the crown's position in the long term. Indeed, in 1609 he persuaded James to agree that the principal crown estates should be entailed in order to make them inalienable, but by this time he had already sold off properties to the value of more than £400,000. With the addition of £100,000 from increased rents and entry fines on the remaining lands, and £200,000 from the collection of outstanding debts, the royal finances showed a marked improvement. There were also smaller sums to be taken into account, such as the £20,000 raised in 1609 by way of a feudal aid for the knighting of Prince Henry (even though this had taken place six years earlier).

However, Salisbury was not deceived by the scale of his success into believing that the crown's financial problems could be solved without radical changes. On the contrary, many of the measures he had put into effect, such as land sales, could not – or at least ought not to – be repeated. He had already decided to appeal to Parliament to re-endow the crown, but before he did so he wanted to demonstrate that the King was able and willing to set his finances in order. Salisbury may have hoped to eliminate the debt entirely, but despite herculean efforts he was unable to do so. At the beginning of 1610 there was still £160,000 outstanding, and Salisbury reckoned that this would be increased during the current year by a deficit of £50,000. He was being uncharacteristically optimistic, for as it happened the deficit turned out to be not far short of £80,000.

Salisbury had become Lord Treasurer in 1608 after the death of Richard Sackville, Earl of Dorset, who had been appointed to this post by Queen Elizabeth. He was already Master of the Court of Wards, however, having succeeded his father, Lord Burghley, in 1599, and he was therefore well placed, once James had come to the throne, to increase the royal revenue from this source. Wardship applied to those landowners who held their estates on a feudal tenure from the crown. In theory they were bound to give the King military service when he called on them to do so, but this obligation had all but disappeared and feudalism survived only as an irritating element of prerogative taxation. When a tenant-in-chief died leaving an under-age male heir, the unfortunate boy became a ward of the crown. The sovereign was supposed to look after him and protect his interests, but in practice the wardship was normally sold to the highest bidder, who recouped his outlay and added a substantial bonus by exploiting the ward's lands. The crown made a double profit, for as well as selling the wardship it also charged the heir for his 'Livery' or freedom to assume control of his despoiled property when he eventually came of age. The losses in this system of prerogative taxation were borne by the landowners who had the misfortune to be caught within its toils, and a series of wardships could ruin an estate.

Lord Burghley, who realised that wardship was an irritant, inflaming relations between the crown and the political nation which was its natural supporter, made no attempt to increase the yield from this source in line with inflation. He did not even maintain its nominal value, with the result that by the end of Elizabeth's reign wardship was bringing in only some £14,000 a year compared with well over £20,000 at the beginning. Salisbury, on the contrary, insisted on a realistic valuation of properties and trebled the selling price for wardships. As a consequence the income from this source rose steadily. In 1607 it was £17,000; by the time of Salisbury's death in 1612 it was over £23,000; and by the end of James's reign it was approaching £40,000. However, Salisbury was careful not to alienate the landowners by too reckless a disregard of the wards' interests, and when, in 1611, he issued new instructions for the conduct of the Court of Wards he laid down that members of a ward's family were to be given preference when the guardianship was put up for sale.

Following the death of Burghley in 1598 there had been suggestions that wardship should be commuted into an increase in the crown's permanent revenue, but these came to nothing. Shortly after James's accession, however, Robert Cecil revived the idea of having

79

'wards turned to a certain annual rent to be propounded in Parliament', and no sooner did the first session begin than Sir Robert Wroth, presumably with Salisbury's connivance, proposed to the Commons that 'the King might have a composition [for wardship], and the subject freed from that tenure'.[15] The Commons gave a positive response to this suggestion, but Salisbury apparently had second thoughts, and the project therefore came to nothing. By 1610, however, the financial position of the crown was becoming so desperate that Salisbury felt compelled to reconsider the whole question. He explained to the two Houses that by September 1608 the accumulated debt had risen to the alarming figure of £1,400,000 and was increasing at the rate of £140,000 a year. By sale of lands and other measures he had reduced the debt to £300,000 and the annual deficit to £46,000, but he could do no more. Hence his appeal to Parliament, which resulted in the negotiations for the Great Contract (see p. 173).

PARLIAMENTARY SUPPLY

The failure of the Great Contract was not simply a personal blow to Salisbury. It was also a blow to the royal finances, and, indirectly, to the English state, since it meant that the existing antiquated system, with its inbuilt arbitrariness and inefficiency and its tendency to provoke resentment rather than win support, seemed set to continue indefinitely. Elizabeth had managed to make ends meet, but only on a hand-to-mouth basis. In the first part of her reign she had even managed to accumulate a small surplus, but war with Spain and subsidies to the Dutch and the French quickly consumed this. She turned to her subjects for help, and because both she and the war were popular Parliament responded by voting supply in every session. James brought the war to a close with the Treaty of London, signed in August 1604, but this removed the major justification for the crown's requests for financial aid from Parliament. Admittedly the situation in Ireland was still threatening, and matters took a distinct turn for the worse when O'Dogherty's rebellion broke out. In the first five years of his reign in England James had to spend nearly £600,000 on the army in Ireland. He also continued to maintain English garrisons in a number of Dutch towns, which cost him some £25,000 a year. In other words, the end of the war with Spain did not mean the end of military expenditure, yet the prevailing mood in the country was one of war-weariness and a desire for an end to taxation.

James's ministers had hoped for a parliamentary grant in 1604, but this was hardly likely in view of the fact that the last Parliament of Elizabeth's reign had voted the impressive total of four subsidies and eight fifteenths, which were still being collected. Fifteenths and tenths were survivals from the late-medieval system of taxation and had steadily decreased in value until, by the time of James's accession, one fifteenth and tenth brought in less than £30,000. The subsidy was an early Tudor device, largely the work of Wolsey, and at the time of its inception it represented a realistic attempt to tap the wealth of the subject in both lands and goods. During Henry VIII's reign one subsidy could produce as much as £120,000, but the tax began to suffer from the same process of ossification that had crippled the fifteenth and tenth.

Until early in Elizabeth's reign those who were liable to the subsidy (which excluded the poor) were assessed on oath; thereafter they were merely required to declare their wealth, and such is human nature that their declarations frequently failed to reflect the true value of it. Sir Walter Ralegh, speaking in the closing years of Elizabeth's reign, confessed that 'our estates that be £30 or £40 in the Queen's books are not the hundredth part of our wealth',[16] and matters did not improve under the early Stuarts. Lionel Cranfield, Earl of Middlesex, was rated at £150 in 1622, yet his total wealth was probably closer to £90,000, while the Duke of Buckingham, who had an income approaching £20,000 a year, was assessed at £400. As men dropped out of the subsidy books through death or impoverishment they were not fully replaced by those who were increasing in wealth or rising in society, and although the Privy Council repeatedly reprimanded the assessors, who were local gentlemen, for under-valuing both themselves and their neighbours, these reproaches fell on deaf ears. As a consequence the yield of the subsidy steadily declined. In the first year of Elizabeth one subsidy had been worth over £137,000, but by 1621 this figure had dropped to £72,500. The decline continued, for the subsidies voted to Charles I in 1628 brought in only £55,000 each.

Neither James nor his subjects talked of 'the constitution', much less of constitutional conventions, but these existed nevertheless, and one of the most basic was that Parliament should supply the King's 'extraordinary occasions'. The most obvious of these was war, but if, more generally, it could be shown that the crown's financial difficulties were not of its own making, there was a presumption that the Commons would be prepared to consider assistance. This is what the King's ministers attempted to prove when they pressed Parliament for supply in 1606. Lord Treasurer Dorset explained that Elizabeth had died owing £400,000. 'These be the fruits and effects of the war [against Spain]', he reminded members, 'and this hath brought upon the King this great debt'. Although, as Treasurer, he had managed to reduce the debt to £250,000, his efforts to eliminate it altogether had been frustrated by the addition of 'divers extraordinary but yet most necessary expenses' which James had incurred. These included the cost of moving the royal family from Scotland (£10,000), of Elizabeth's funeral (£20,000), of the King's formal entry into London (£10,000), of the entertaining of 'foreign ambassadors and other great personages coming to His Majesty' (£40,000), and of 'new buildings and alterations for the King and Queen and the Prince' (a mere £2,000).[17]

Dorset admitted that other items were not so obviously 'necessary'. There were, for example, the 'sundry gifts and grants made and passed by His Majesty since his coming to the crown', which he described as 'the hard and knotty difficulty and exception that troubleth the minds of some'. Yet many of these were 'such as even in justice were to be granted; others such as in equity could not be denied'. This left those which had been 'won from His Majesty by incessant importunity, straining the gentleness and bounty of his most benign nature and taking advantage of his lack of knowledge, at his first coming, of the state and course of his affairs'. Yet now, Dorset assured the assembled members, James was beginning 'to have a feeling understanding of the lack of his own means' and was determined to put an end to this self-imposed drain on his resources.[18]

Not all members of the Commons were convinced by Dorset's arguments. One member, described as a 'plain fellow', said that 'whereas it is moved we should fill the King's coffers, it would be likewise understood whether they *will* be filled; for if the bottoms be out, then can they not be filled'. Another argued that 'the King's debts [are] no cause of subsidies', and added that a grant under these circumstances would create a dangerous precedent. Mr Holt expressed the general view about parliamentary supply when he declared 'that a subsidy is a public contribution, not to be employed to private use, bounties, expenses [and] ceremonies'.[19] Nevertheless, the House not only agreed to vote two subsidies and four fifteenths, but, in response to pressure from Salisbury, added a further subsidy and two fifteenths. James had good reason to be pleased, for the parliamentary grant eventually brought in to the Exchequer just under £400,000. But the relative ease with which it had been obtained may have misled him into assuming that the Commons would always help him out of his financial difficulties. In fact the circumstances of early 1606 were uniquely favourable, for the King was still basking in the popular esteem aroused by the reaction against the Gunpowder Plot in the previous November. The prevailing mood was indicated by the concern caused by a rumour, in late March 1606, that James had been murdered. Chamberlain describes how

at his coming to town . . . the whole Court went to meet him; the Parliament sent Sir Maurice Berkeley, with four knights more, to welcome him; the Speaker, with his mace, went beyond the Park corner to bring him in . . . to all which he made several harangues, as likewise to the people's acclamations the next day when he went to the sermon, telling them that he took these demonstrations more kindly than if they had won a battle for him: that a better King they might have, but a more loving and careful for their good they could not, and that these signs were the more welcome to him for that foreign ambassadors might see the vanity of those reports that were spread abroad in other countries of mislikes and distastes twixt him and his people.[20]

The final session of James's first Parliament, in 1610, was dominated by the Great Contract, but it ended with the grant of only one subsidy and one fifteenth which between them yielded less than £100,000. By the time of Salisbury's death two years later the financial position of the crown was almost as bad as it been when he took office as Lord Treasurer in 1608. The accumulated debt once again stood at half a million pounds and was increasing at an annual rate of £160,000. The short-term needs of the crown had been met by raising a loan of £100,000 from the City in 1610, but this carried interest payments at ten per cent, and although in theory it was to be repaid within a year, the collapse of the Contract meant that it remained outstanding until 1614. The only other major addition to the crown's revenue came through the sale of baronetcies. These newly-created hereditary titles were made available, at a price, to the possessors of lands worth at least £1,000 a year, and by 1614 they had netted the King £90,000.

James did not immediately replace Salisbury with another Lord Treasurer. Instead, he put the office into commission, but the Treasury commissioners were faced with the same problems which had defeated Salisbury and were no more successful in dealing with them than he had been. In April 1614, therefore, James turned to

Parliament once again for help in resolving his financial difficulties. To sweeten the pill, he assured members that

although his urgent necessity moved him to desire relief of his subjects, yet he hoped this should be the last time, for hereafter he would call a Parliament either to make good laws or else to execute those that are already enacted; that he would not, like a merchant, contract nor demand any sum of his subjects, but did refer himself to their loves, and although he had done heretofore for private men, yet hereafter his whole endeavour should be for the good of the commonwealth.[21]

Sir Julius Caesar, the Chancellor of the Exchequer, urging the Commons to make a generous response to the King's request, emphasised that it was the pressing needs of the state which had caused James's problems – 'not of private expenses, or of household, but of navy, forts'. Dover Castle, he said, was in such ruinous condition that it was near to collapse, as were a number of castles in the Isle of Wight. Money was desperately needed to pay the forces in Ireland and also the garrisons in the Dutch towns, for although the King had given pledges for £700,000 there were insufficient funds to honour them.[22]

Unfortunately for James the Commons were not impressed either by his promises of reform or by Caesar's insistence that any money they granted would be used solely for public purposes. Sir James Perrott declared that James had given away £70,000 a year in pensions, which was more than the yield of crown lands or Impositions, and there was no guarantee that supply, if it were granted, would not be dissipated in the same manner. His opinion was shared by Nicholas Hyde, a future Chief Justice, who pointed out that in 1606 the debt stood at £700,000, yet two years later, despite the collection of the subsidies voted in that session, it had not diminished; on the contrary, it had risen to £1,400,000.[23]

Given time, the Commons might eventually have voted supply in 1614, but only in return for the abolition of Impositions, which they deeply resented. Members were lavish in their assurances that once the King had remedied this grievance they would relieve his wants, but James, bearing in mind the scant yield of the 1610 session, could not afford to take the risk. Impositions were now bringing in the equivalent of one subsidy every year. Why should he abandon this certain revenue and throw himself upon the uncertain charity of the Commons? Rather than do so he dissolved this 'addled' Parliament before it had completed any business, including supply.

LORD TREASURER SUFFOLK

Shortly after the dissolution, Chamberlain gave it as his opinion that 'it is more than time we had a Treasurer, if that would any way mend the matter, for we are at a very low ebb for money'.[24] James had obviously come to the same conclusion, for in the following month he appointed Thomas Howard, Earl of Suffolk, to this office. He also called on the City to lend him £100,000, but the City's opinion of the crown's creditworthiness was shown in their response, for they declined to make a loan but offered a free gift of £10,000 instead. It may have been this which inspired Suffolk to send out letters calling on the King's subjects to demonstrate their good-will by making similar gifts. This Benevolence eventually produced some £65,000, in addition to London's contribution, but it made no appreciable difference to the crown's financial position. James was still desperately short of money, and it was this which persuaded him to give credence to a London alderman, William Cockayne, who proposed to enrich him to the tune of £300,000 a year by shifting the emphasis in English cloth exports from the unfinished to the finished product (see p. 5). The collapse of Cockayne's scheme left the King in a worse state than before, since the disruption of trade threatened to diminish the yield from duties on it. Another device, the sale of peerages, which began in 1615, was more rewarding financially, but the King had to pay a price all the same, for in the long term it brought him into disrepute with his more important subjects.

The most profitable of all the projects which were considered in the period following the Addled Parliament was the withdrawal of the English garrisons from the 'cautionary towns' in the United Provinces. These were held as a 'caution' or security for repayment of the subsidies given to the Dutch by Elizabeth to assist them in their struggle against Spain. The nominal amount outstanding was in excess of £600,000, but James agreed to accept a once-and-for-all payment of £200,000. No sooner did this reach the Exchequer, however, than it went out again. The Treasurer of the Navy was owed £50,000, the Irish army needed £10,000, the King's chamber and wardrobe ate up £16,000, while the royal households, including that recently established for Prince Charles, now heir to the throne, consumed a further £15,000. Soon there was little left, but James chose this moment to revisit his native kingdom. The formal progress to Scotland and back could only be paid for by raising another loan, of just under £100,000, from the City. By the time James returned, there was a deficit on the current account of £140,000, and the accumulated debt had risen to nearly three quarters of a million pounds.

James had appointed Suffolk as Lord Treasurer because the experiment of putting the office into commission had not succeeded, 'proving . . . grievous to the subject, who could not be despatched with that expedition as before'. When the King announced his intention of 'resuming the wonted custom of this kingdom, in putting the employment into one man's hands' he also took the opportunity to make a number of disparaging remarks about Salisbury, 'the late Lord Treasurer deceased, who, in lieu of supplying his [the King's] wants, was wont to entertain him with epigrams, fine discourses and learned epistles and other such tricks and devices, which yet he saw would pay no debts'.[25] Whether or not these comments on Salisbury were justified, there is no doubt about the contrast between him and his successor, Suffolk, for the latter had no intellectual pretensions, and had first made his mark in the world by the skill and courage he displayed in naval operations against the Spaniards in Elizabeth's reign. James described him as 'a plain honest gentleman',[26] but Suffolk did not display any marked commitment to honesty during his four years in office. His most notable achievement was the construction of a vast palace for himself at Audley End in Essex, the cost of which could not possibly have been met either from his official salary or his limited private resources. Like all office-holders he benefited from innumerable gratuities and other perquisites which fell into the twilight zone between legality and illegality, but it seems highly likely that he also pocketed large sums of money which rightly belonged to the state.

There was nothing novel about this. William Cecil, Lord Burghley, had used his profits as Treasurer to build Theobalds, which despite the fact that he referred to it as one of his 'poor cottages' was the largest house in England at the time of its construction. He later described it, more accurately, as a 'monument to Her Majesty's bountifulness to a faithful servant',[27] and this description could have been applied, with equal justice, to Audley End. The essential difference between Burghley and Suffolk is not that one was honest and the other was corrupt; it is that Burghley kept the ordinary account in balance and stopped the Queen from falling heavily into debt even at the height of the struggle against Spain, while Suffolk seemed powerless to prevent both the deficit and the debt from going steadily and inexorably upwards.

Suffolk was not a catholic, and always denied that he advised the

King to pursue a pro-Spanish policy. But as Lord Treasurer he was acutely aware of the fragile condition of the royal finances. An active foreign policy which might lead to war was, quite simply, something that the King could not afford. Rapprochement with Spain, on the other hand, would diminish international tension and, if it culminated in a marriage alliance, result in the payment by Spain of a dowry which would eliminate the greater part of James's debt. Financial considerations, then, inclined Suffolk to support the hispanophil policy which James was pursuing, but this earned him the enmity of the 'protestant faction' (see p. 17) and led to his downfall. He was caught up in the power struggle which led to the overthrow of Robert Carr, Earl of Somerset – who had become the patron of the Howards after his marriage to Suffolk's daughter – and his replacement by George Villiers. In the autumn of 1618 Suffolk was suspended from office, and in the following year he was brought before Star Chamber and found guilty of corruption.

LIONEL CRANFIELD, EARL OF MIDDLESEX

The emergence of a new favourite was the occasion for further lavish displays of generosity on James's part. Villiers was not only advanced in honour – being made Marquis of Buckingham in January 1618 – but also in wealth, of which he had little before he met the King. James immediately granted him an annual pension of £1,000, and planned to endow him with the Sherborne estate confiscated from the fallen Somerset. Buckingham, however, refused to profit from his predecessor's misfortunes, so the King offered him royal lands in lieu. Sherborne was valued at just over £25,000, but the Attorney General, Francis Bacon, who was anxious to ingratiate himself with the new favourite, managed to increase the valuation to well over £30,000, and crown lands equivalent to this amount were duly transferred to Buckingham. It soon became apparent that the King's favour extended to Buckingham's kindred, no matter how remote, and his generosity was unrestrained.

From the financial point of view, therefore, Buckingham's emergence was a setback to hopes of reform. But in his determination to show his gratitude to his royal benefactor, Buckingham made himself the champion of the reformers. He had already become acquainted with Lionel Cranfield, who not only acted as his financial adviser but also made a significant addition to his income by persuading the syndicate that farmed the Irish Customs to surrender their lease to the King, who promptly granted it to Buckingham. Cranfield, with the favourite's support, began investigations into the royal household, where he uncovered evidence of waste on a huge scale. His relentless probing brought him up against powerful vested interests who would normally have been able to block his progress. With the favourite behind him, however, Cranfield was able to press home his attack, and as a consequence the expenditure of the household was at long last brought under control. There was no dramatic improvement but a steady reduction from an average figure of more than £80,000 a year, prior to Cranfield's intervention, to less than £65,000 by 1620.

Encouraged by his success, Cranfield went on to investigate another big spending department, the navy. An earlier commission of enquiry into the state of the navy, which reported in 1608, had been ineffective because James was unwilling to act on its recommendations. But James was ready to listen to Buckingham, particularly as he proposed to appoint him Lord Admiral. When the commissioners put forward a scheme to reduce annual expenditure on the navy from £53,000 to £30,000, with no decline in ship construction, repairs, or general efficiency, Buckingham not only accepted it but persuaded the King to suspend the officers who were officially responsible for running the navy and to transfer control to the commission, which was now constituted on a permanent basis. Further reforms involved the ordnance office, which had its costs reduced from £34,000 to £14,000 a year, and the royal wardrobe, which suffered a fifty per cent cut in its annual expenditure of £40,000 after Cranfield was appointed its Master in September 1618.

In 1619 Cranfield was added to the commission which James had nominated to run the Treasury after Suffolk's dismissal. The reforms already carried out in the spending departments meant a reduction in the deficit on the ordinary account, and the death of Queen Anne in the summer of 1619 promised further savings: Chamberlain reported that 'for yearly income the King shall have £60,000 that her household, her servants and stable stood him in, besides £24,000 that was her jointure and allowed for her own person'.[28] There were also increases in the Impositions upon a number of items, and a new tax, the pretermitted customs, upon exports of woollen cloth. Surplus gold- and silver-plate, much of it the Queen's, was disposed of, and further amounts were raised through the continuing sale of titles of honour. Admittedly the profits from this last source went to the favourite and other intermediaries rather than to the King, but this lessened the demands they would otherwise have made on James's purse. In May 1619 the commissioners informed the King that his ordinary income and his ordinary expenditure were now in balance. The King professed a certain scepticism and asked for this to be set down in writing, but it was indeed true that the long 'Christmas and open-tide', of which James had spoken earlier, was at last drawing towards its close. James continued to display the liberality that was expected of a monarch, but it was no longer the case that 'extra-ordinary' sources of revenue, such as parliamentary subsidies, were eaten up by the deficit on the ordinary account.

By the time the commissioners made their optimistic report a new threat to financial stability was emerging in the shape of the political crisis sparked off in Europe by the action of James's son-in-law, the Elector Palatine, in accepting the crown of Bohemia (see p. 18). James called for voluntary contributions from his richer subjects to assist Frederick and Elizabeth, but this 'Palatine Benevolence' brought in only £40,000. James made his personal contribution by borrowing £7,500 from his brother-in-law, the King of Denmark, and adding £2,500 of his own money to bring the total up to £10,000. Another £10,000 was sent to the princes of the German Protestant Union to persuade them to take up arms, and ambassadors were despatched, at great expense, to the major European capitals to try to negotiate a peaceful settlement to the crisis. James estimated his expenditure on diplomacy at £200,000, but he also needed money for military preparations in case his efforts met with no success. The Council of War which he had appointed to advise him on this matter estimated that the cost of maintaining a force of 30,000 men for one year would be £900,000.

The provision of sums on this scale could only be made by Parliament, and this was why James summoned the two Houses to meet in January 1621. In his opening speech he admitted that some people might feel that 'his own expenses were so profuse that they were not to be supplied'. However, he rebutted this by listing the reductions made in the running costs of the household and other departments, and promised members that 'they should not put their money into a broken purse, but might be right well assured to have it well and husbandly disposed'.[29] When the debate opened in the Commons, Cranfield confirmed that the King's 'ordinary revenue was able to discharge his ordinary expense'. What was now required was supply to meet extraordinary charges, 'and the extraordinary of a King hath ever been borne by his subjects'.[30] Cranfield was supported by other Councillors, and there was a general disposition on the part of the House to vote supply. The only question was how much, and here members were swayed by their awareness of the continuing economic depression. As one of them put it, 'though we are all ready to give, yet let us consider the state of the country. That which yielded £100 yearly is come to £60. Therefore let us not make too bold with our countrymen's purses'.[31]

This concern for their constituents led the Commons to make a grant of two subsidies without the usual fifteenths, since these were held to bear down too heavily on the poorer sections of the population. The two subsidies, which the House described as a 'gift', were clearly insufficient to meet the King's extraordinary needs, and when Parliament reassembled at the close of 1621 further supply was requested to maintain the English volunteer force in the Palatinate. The Commons voted a single subsidy, but this was never paid, because of the abrupt ending to the session (see p. 140). The King therefore had recourse to a Benevolence, which eventually brought in £87,000 – considerably more than the aborted subsidy would have done.

Shortly before the 1621 Parliament opened, James appointed Sir Henry Montagu, whom he created Viscount Mandeville, as his new Lord Treasurer. Montagu was a distinguished lawyer, who had succeeded Sir Edward Coke as Chief Justice of King's Bench, and the main reason for his appointment was that he was prepared to pay £20,000 for the privilege. However, he spent less than a year in office, for as the likelihood of war grew ever greater and it became apparent that Parliament could not be relied on for more than token assistance, James was forced to accept the fact that he needed a financial expert and a man of strong character at the Treasury. Mandeville was therefore eased out, and his place was taken by Lionel Cranfield, who was made a baron in July 1621 and Earl of Middlesex in the following year. At his installation as Treasurer, in September 1621, the Lord Keeper effectively summarised the reasons for his appointment: 'if any man living can improve the King's revenue, you are that good husband[man]'.[32]

By the time Cranfield took office the debt was standing at over £900,000, which was double the annual revenue of £465,000. There was no obvious way of raising capital, since Cranfield was determined not to resort to further property sales. Moreover, the monies received from subsidies and the Benevolence did not cover the crown's extraordinary expenditure; on the contrary, the ordinary revenue had to subsidise the extraordinary to the tune of nearly £100,000 a year. Since revenue-raising was apparently out of the question, Cranfield concentrated on cost cutting, and this meant restraining the King's liberality. Where Salisbury had been perhaps over-sensitive to the King's wishes, Cranfield, who had the blunt assertiveness of a self-made man, was more outspoken: his friend, Bishop Goodman, was to say of him that 'no man did more boldly tax the prodigality of King James than he did'.[33] Cranfield managed to persuade James to order that all pension payments should be stopped and that no new grants of any sort should be made without the Treasurer's express authorisation. It was at this time that Buckingham once again demonstrated his support for Cranfield's reform measures by telling him that when he received letters from the favourite asking him to show consideration for a particular suppliant he was to 'do no more than you shall think fit in your own judgment, knowing that nothing is more dear to me than what may best stand with His Majesty's service'.[34]

Buckingham probably meant what he said, but in fact he was not a free agent. Like his royal master he was the prisoner of a patronage system that was built upon the distribution of gifts and perquisites of one sort and another. Patrons were valued because they could obtain a share of the spoils for their clients, and the less successful they were in this key function, the less support they attracted. If, as Salisbury had stated, 'bounty is an essential virtue of the King',[35] it was also an essential attribute of patrons. Asking them to stop giving was the seventeenth-century equivalent of asking capitalists to stop accumulating capital. Given the fact that the system was tilted against him, it is hardly surprising that Cranfield had only temporary and limited success in this field. Indeed, this may have been all that he expected. The fact remains, however, that when he took office as Treasurer, pensions were costing the crown some £75,000 a year; by the time of his dismissal in 1624 this figure had risen to £90,000.

Although Cranfield managed to keep the ordinary expenditure more or less in line with income, he could not control the extra-ordinary. He estimated that the Palatinate crisis cost the crown £600,000 in the period 1619–24, of which £120,000 was spent on the journey to Spain by Prince Charles and Buckingham in 1623. £600,000 was the amount provisionally agreed on for the dowry of the Spanish Infanta if and when she became Charles's bride, and it is hardly surprising, therefore, that Cranfield was a firm advocate of the Spanish match. He shared James's love of peace, though for different reasons, and was appalled at reports from Spain in 1623 that Buckingham was becoming increasingly bellicose. English involvement in hostilities with Spain would mean the end of everything that Cranfield had done, or tried to do, to improve the royal finances, and in order to prevent such a catastrophe from occurring he took the highly dangerous step of promoting his nephew, Arthur Brett, as a rival favourite to Buckingham. This was a threat that the Duke dared not ignore, and in any case the sacrifice of the Treasurer – whose low birth, rasping manner, and attack upon the rapacity of courtiers and other intermediaries, had made him many enemies – would signal Buckingham's change of course to more populist policies. In 1624, therefore, Buckingham brought about the end of Cranfield's political career by organising his impeachment (see p. 212). James pronounced the appropriate epitaph on the fallen minister when he commented that 'all Treasurers, if they do good service to their master, must be generally hated'.[36]

The 1624 Parliament was dominated by the war party, led by Prince Charles and Buckingham, and all the King could do was to try to delay the inevitable as long as possible, or at least ensure that if war came the royal finances would not collapse under the strain. His initial request for five subsidies and ten fifteenths for war purposes and an annual grant of one subsidy and two fifteenths to eliminate the accumulated debt (see p. 208) was based on a realistic appraisal of the likely costs. In the end, James reluctantly agreed to accept three subsidies and three fifteenths, but he made it plain that he regarded this as sufficient only 'to make a good beginning of the war. For what the end will be, God knows'.[37] James's forebodings were justified, for he had been persuaded, against all his natural inclinations, to embark upon an active foreign policy involving military and naval operations that were certain to consume far greater sums of money than Parliament could or would provide. Fortunately for him he died before the catastrophic effects of this change of course became apparent.

Over the entire course of his reign James received £910,000 from parliamentary grants, which works out at £41,000 a year on average. He was also voted supply by the clergy who met in Convocation at the same time as Parliament. Clerical subsidies totalled £228,000, or £10,000 a year, a considerable sum in view of the despoliation of the Church and the decline in the value of livings during the Tudor period. Yet even when lay and clerical subsidies are added together they only produced £51,000 a year, which was far less than the yield of the new Impositions levied from 1608 onwards. Parliamentary supply had a propaganda value in that it symbolised harmony between the King and his people. It also reassured business interests and made them more willing to advance money to the crown. Yet in strictly financial terms it was relatively unimportant when compared to the King's ordinary revenue, which by the end of James's reign was edging up to half a million pounds a year and seemed capable of almost indefinite expansion. Insofar as constitutional conventions were based upon the assumption that parliamentary supply, although intermittent, was a substantial and significant element in the royal finances, there was an increasing gap between ideal and reality in the early Stuart period.

NOTES AND REFERENCES

(*The place of publication is London, unless otherwise stated*)
 1. **D. H. Willson** *King James VI and I* (1956), p. 17.
 2. **The Letters of John Chamberlain** ed. N. E. McClure (Philadelphia 1939). (Hereafter Chamberlain *Letters*)
 3. **Edward, Earl of Clarendon** *The History of the Rebellion and Civil Wars in England* ed. W. Dunn Macray (Oxford 1888). Vol. I, pp. 77–8.
 4. **S. R. Gardiner** *History of England from the Accession of James I to the Outbreak of the Civil War 1603–1642* (1884). Vol. II. 43–9.
 5. **The Political Works of James I** ed. C. H. McIlwain (Cambridge, Mass. 1918). p. 320 (Hereafter James I *Political Works*); **Letters of King James VI & I** ed. G. P. V. Akrigg (1984). p. 317. (Hereafter James I *Letters*)
 6. James I *Political Works*, p. 320.
 7. James I *Letters*, p. 261.
 8. James I *Letters*, pp. 269–70.
 9. James I *Letters*, pp. 291–92.
10. **E. R. Foster** (ed.) *Proceedings in Parliament 1610* (New Haven 1966). Vol. 2, p. 23.
11. **L. L. Peck** *Northampton: Patronage and Policy at the Court of James I* (1982), p. 134.
12. **J. P. Kenyon** (ed.) *The Stuart Constitution 1603–1688*, 2nd edn. (Cambridge 1986), p. 55.
13. **Pauline Croft** 'Fresh Light on Bate's Case', *Historical Journal*. Vol. 30, 1987.
14. **S. R. Gardiner** (ed.) *Parliamentary Debates in 1610*. Camden Society (1862). Appendix B, pp. 156–57. (Hereafter Gardiner *1610 Debates*)
15. **Pauline Croft** 'Wardship in the Parliament of 1604' *Parliamentary History* Vol. 2, 1983, p. 40.
16. **F. C. Dietz** *English Public Finance 1485–1641*. Vol. II. *English Public Finance 1558–1641* (New York 1932), p. 387.
17. **The Parliamentary Diary of Robert Bowyer 1606–1607** ed. D. H. Willson. (Minneapolis 1931). Appendix A, p. 372. (Hereafter Bowyer *Parliamentary Diary*)
18. Bowyer *Parliamentary Diary*, p. 373.

19. *Journals of the House of Commons* *1547–1714* (1742). Vol. I, pp. 282, 284. (Hereafter *Commons Journals*)
20. Chamberlain *Letters*. Vol. I, p. 223.
21. **Wallace Notestein, Frances Helen Relf** & **Hartley Simpson** (eds.) *Commons Debates 1621* (New Haven 1935). Vol. VII, pp. 632–33. (Hereafter *Commons Debates 1621*)
22. *Commons Journals*. Vol. I, p. 462.
23. *Commons Journals*. Vol. I, p. 506.
24. Chamberlain *Letters*. Vol. I, p. 542.
25. *The Court and Times of James the First . . . transcribed by Thomas Birch* ed. R. F. Williams (1849). Vol. I, pp. 335–36. (Hereafter *Court and Times James I*)
26. *Court and Times James I*. Vol. I, pp. 335–36.
27. **Menna Prestwich** *Cranfield: Politics and Profits under the Early Stuarts* (Oxford 1966), p. 3. (Hereafter Prestwich *Cranfield*)
28. Chamberlain *Letters*. Vol. II, p. 224.
29. *Commons Debates 1621*. Vol. V, pp. 427–28.
30. *Commons Debates 1621*. Vol. II. p. 23; Vol. V, p. 437.
31. *Commons Debates 1621*. Vol. II, p. 91.
32. Prestwich *Cranfield*, p. 328.
33. **Robert Ashton** 'Deficit Finance in the Reign of James I' *Economic History Review*, 2nd series. Vol. X. 1957–58, p. 20.
34. **Kent Archive Office**, *Sackville MSS*. ON 22.
35. Gardiner *1610 Debates*, p. 7.
36. Prestwich *Cranfield*, p. 448.
37. **John Rushworth** *Historical Collections* (1682). Vol. I, p. 138.

CHAPTER FIVE

James I and the Church of England

THE MILLENARY PETITION

At the time of Queen Elizabeth's death in 1603 the Church of England, as established by law in 1559, had almost half a century of continuous existence behind it. Although the doctrinal attitudes of its bishops and clergy had drifted 'leftwards' during her reign, moving closer towards a Calvinist theology, Elizabeth had ensured that in outward appearance it remained unchanged. It was still an episcopal church, despite the criticisms of the Presbyterian wing of the puritan movement, and the forms of service prescribed in the Prayer Book retained many traces of the pre-Reformation Roman Catholic church from which it was descended. Elizabeth, who was by temperament deeply conservative, had been responsible for blocking further reform and ensuring that the fledgling Church had a chance to grow and to establish itself in the affections of her people. So successful was she that the Church of England survived a prolonged Presbyterian assault and produced, in men like Whitgift, bishops who believed that with all its faults it was very close to the ideal model of a Christian community.

The increasing self-confidence of the episcopate was reflected in the assertion made by Richard Bancroft in 1588 that bishops held their spiritual powers *jure divino*, directly from God, and were only dependent upon the secular ruler for the exercise of their temporal authority. This was a rebuttal of the puritan insistence upon the parity of all ministers rather than a challenge to the royal supremacy, but it may be that the minority of bishops who advocated *jure divino* episcopacy under Elizabeth were hoping that it might help them to shield the Church from harm in the period of uncertainty that was

95

bound to follow the Queen's death. They knew little of James, apart from the fact that he ruled over a Presbyterian country, but they feared the worst. Bancroft, for instance, when he attacked the puritans in his Paul's Cross sermon of 1589, accused them of deliberately undermining the established Church and the royal supremacy in the hope of producing a situation similar to that in Scotland, where the Presbyterian ministers had 'established an ecclesiastical tyranny of an infinite jurisdiction, such as neither the law of God or man could tolerate'.[1]

James was understandably furious when he heard of these comments, for he prided himself on the way in which he had curbed the pretensions of the Presbyterian clergy in Scotland and reduced them to obedience, if not conformity. He set out his own views at length in the *Basilikon Doron* which he wrote for the instruction of his son in 1599 (though it was not published in England until 1603). He defined puritans as 'brainsick and heady preachers' who held civil authority in contempt; who dismissed as profane all those who refused to accept their 'fantasies'; who treated every ecclesiastical issue, no matter how minor, 'as if the article of the Trinity were called in controversy'; and who were prepared, rather than allow 'any of their grounds [to] be impugned', to 'let King, people, law and all be trod under foot'. These words must have sounded like music in the ears of Bancroft and those who shared his views, but there was less comfort for them in James's qualification that he did not apply the term 'puritan' to those who 'like better of the single form of policy in our Church than of the many ceremonies in the Church of England; that are persuaded that their bishops smell of a papal supremacy; that the surplice, the cornered cap, and such like, are the outward badges of popish errors'. On the contrary, said James, 'I am so far from being contentious in these things (which for my own part I ever esteemed as indifferent) as I do equally love and honour the learned and grave men of either of these opinions'.[2]

James's moderation was a reflection not only of his basic attitude but also of his awareness that among his future English subjects were many who were sincere in their commitment to the Church of England, rejected the 'puritan' label as implying separatism, but nevertheless hoped for a further purification of the authorised services through the elimination of a number of ceremonies. These low-churchmen were probably in a majority among the clergy and conceivably in the political nation as a whole, and although they had given up hope of any further change while Elizabeth was alive, they were determined to make their views known to her successor. They caught James while he was on his way south to take possession of his new kingdom and presented him with the Millenary Petition, so called because it was said to have been signed by a thousand ministers. This was a carefully worded document, designed to fit in with James's views as revealed in the *Basilikon Doron*. The signatories began by insisting that they were neither 'factious men affecting a popular parity in the Church' nor 'schismatics aiming at the dissolution of the state ecclesiastical': they were simply 'Your Majesty's subjects and ministers, all groaning as under a common burden of human rites and ceremonies' from which they begged to be 'eased and relieved'.

The ceremonies to which they objected included signing with the cross in baptism, confirmation, the administration of baptism by women, the use of the ring in marriage, and bowing at the name of Jesus. They also disliked popish terms such as 'priest' and 'absolution', and popish garments such as the square cap which clergy were obliged to wear and the surplice. They wanted better observance of the sabbath, and the provision of sermons on that and other days through the appointment as ministers of 'able and sufficient men' who should be resident in their parishes. They called for an end to pluralism – the holding of more than one benefice – and in order to make this possible they proposed that part of the revenue from impropriated tithes which had been diverted into secular hands should be used to endow a preaching ministry. As far as ecclesiastical discipline was concerned, they asked (in a phrase of studied ambiguity) that it should be 'administered according to Christ's own institution'; that the penalty of excommunication (which was virtually the only one available to church courts) should not be imposed by lay officials, nor 'for trifles and twelvepenny matters'; and that there should be greater restraint in the use of the *ex officio* oath, whereby men could be required to incriminate themselves. There was no hint in the Petition of any dissatisfaction with the royal supremacy. On the contrary, they professed their conviction that God had 'appointed Your Highness our physician to heal these diseases', and referred themselves 'with all dutiful submission' to James in the confident assurance that he would do 'that which we are persuaded shall be acceptable to God'.[3]

THE BISHOPS AND THE HAMPTON COURT CONFERENCE

The signatories of the Millenary Petition did not assume that they would achieve their objectives merely by presenting it to James. This was simply the first stage in their campaign, and they had indicated their hopes for the next stage by stating that the ceremonies of which they complained were not justified by scripture and that they would be happy to prove this either 'more at large by writing' or 'by conference among the learned'.[4] No doubt they were aware of James's relish for theological discussions and also of the need, at this outset of a new reign and a new dynasty, to define the direction in which the Church of England would henceforth be moving. Their suggestion met with a rapid and favourable response, for James announced his intention of calling a conference of bishops and puritan★ representatives at which the points raised in the Petition would be examined.

The puritan leaders followed up this initial success by distributing to their followers the *Advice tending to Reformation*. This recommended that puritan sympathisers should be encouraged to 'complain of corruptions, and desire reformation, in several petitions signed with as many hands of every sort as may be procured, and the same presented to His Majesty in the name of the rest. There must be sundry petitions of ministers of sundry parts, and yet but few [names] in a petition', to avoid the suspicion of conspiracy'.[5] The petitions were to vary in wording but to focus upon the same issues – namely those put forward in the Millenary Petition – and to eschew, as the Petition had done, any attack upon episcopacy. One of the framers of the *Advice* was a Northamptonshire gentleman called Lewis Pickering, and it is therefore hardly surprising that his county was at the forefront of the petitioning movement. In May 1603, shortly after the presentation of the Millenary Petition to James, the Northamptonshire puritans decided to draw up a detailed statement about the scandalous state of the ministry of their locality, and to appoint two of their number to act as advisers to Parliament when it met. Similar activities occurred in Oxfordshire, Suffolk and Sussex, and in July a general meeting of ministers took place in

---

★ The term 'puritan' is one that caused confusion at the time and has done so since. In this book it is used, unless otherwise indicated, to describe 'low-church' members of the Church of England, even though they themselves would probably have rejected such a label. For a detailed discussion of the meaning of the term, readers are referred to Nicholas Tyacke's *Anti-Calvinists* (1987).

London at which a standard form of petition was adopted. Henceforth the petitioners would formally request 'that the present state of the Church may be farther reformed in all things needful, according to the rule of God's holy word'. Meanwhile lawyer adherents of the movement were to be asked to draw up draft Bills for the reformation of ecclesiastical abuses in readiness for the assembly of Parliament early in 1604.[6]

James's ready acceptance of the Millenary Petition and his decision to allow the puritans to state their case at a conference confirmed the worst fears of the bishops. They were not blind to the weaknesses of the Church which they administered, but they feared that the puritans, under the guise of limited reform, were aiming at the destruction of episcopacy and therefore of the Church of England as it had been established by law. They were in a difficult position, for they had to convince James that they were not opposed to the principle of reform, but only to the specific demands of the puritans. They believed, with good reason, that many, if not most, of the abuses in the Church were caused by poverty, and that this was the direct consequence of the transfer of tithes into lay hands after the Dissolution of the Monasteries. Yet when James announced his intention, in July 1603, of using the impropriated tithes in the crown's possession for the improvement of livings, and called upon the two universities to follow his example, they were shocked. The crown might be able to survive the loss of income from impropriations, but the universities, which were the training ground for ordinands, would be seriously weakened. Moreover the royal initiative was most unlikely to be taken up by Parliament. The two Houses represented the landowners who were the major beneficiaries from impropriations, but they had never shown any willingness to pass legislation returning tithes to the Church. They regarded impropriate tithes as falling within the sacrosanct category of property rights, and they preferred to blame the hierarchy for the Church's deficiencies rather than re-endow it by parting with their property. James's generous gesture would merely provide members with the comforting assurance that something was being done, and that they therefore needed to do nothing themselves. Archbishop Whitgift managed to persuade James that the situation was more complex than he had realised, and not amenable to simple solutions, but the bishops could hardly be blamed for fearing that the projected conference might be yet another example of misdirected royal goodwill.

James had intended to hold the conference in November 1603, but an outbreak of plague forced him to postpone it until after Christmas. He announced this by proclamation in October and used the occasion to show his displeasure at the tactics of the puritans:

some using public invectives against the state ecclesiastical . . . some gathering subscriptions of multitudes of vulgar persons to supplications to be exhibited to us to crave that reformation which, if there be cause to make, is more in our heart than in theirs. All which courses it is apparent to all men are unlawful and do savour of tumult, sedition and violence, and not of such Christian modesty as beseemeth those who for piety's sake only desire redress of things they think to be amiss.[7]

It looks as though the puritan campaign had backfired, for the beginning of a new reign was always a testing time, and events in the Netherlands and in France had shown how Calvinist claims to freedom of worship tended to undermine the authority of the secular ruler. The signatories of the Millenary Petition had been careful to distance themselves from any suggestion of 'faction', but the organisers of the petitioning campaign, who had to appeal to public opinion, were less restrained in their approach. James declared his belief that their 'pretended zeal' was a cloak under which they planned to bring about 'novelty, and so confusion'. In order to prevent this, he now declared his intention 'to preserve the estate, as well ecclesiastical as politic, in such form as we have found it established by the laws here'. There were to be no structural changes; reform would be confined to 'abuses which we shall apparently [i.e. clearly] find proved'.[8]

In the conference which took place at Hampton Court Palace in January 1604 the hierarchy was represented by Archbishop Whitgift and eight bishops, of whom the most forceful was Richard Bancroft, at that time bishop of London but already spoken of as Whitgift's successor. They were assisted by eight deans and one archdeacon. The four or five Puritan spokesmen were all moderates and may have been chosen by the King in consultation with Whitgift: at any rate this seems to have been the view of Henry Jacob, a religious radical, who declared that 'the whole managing of it [the Conference] was underhand plotted and procured by the prelates themselves'.[9] The *de facto* leader of the puritan delegation was John Reynolds, President of Corpus Christi College, Oxford, who had long been an advocate of further reformation in the Church but had avoided controversy by outwardly conforming, and had done so with such success that Queen Elizabeth was said to have offered him a bishopric.

The Conference began with a meeting between the King and the bishops, which focussed on the particular complaints put forward by the puritans in the Millenary Petition. After a long discussion about absolution and confirmation, the King declared himself 'well satisfied . . . so that the manner might be changed and some things cleared'. Private baptism, especially by women, proved a more contentious issue, but the King eventually persuaded the bishops to agree 'that it should only be administered by ministers, yet in private houses if occasion required'. James then turned to the question of ecclesiastical discipline, and it was swiftly decided that the procedures of the commissaries' courts, which were a frequent object of puritan complaint, should be reviewed and amended by the Lord Chancellor and Lord Chief Justice. As for 'excommunication for trifles', this was to be 'utterly abolished'. There remained the puritan request that 'the discipline . . . may be administered according to Christ's own institution'.[10] This had already been considered by Francis Bacon when he drew up *Certain Considerations* for the King's enlightenment and he argued strongly that bishops should not exercise their authority unaided. 'There is no temporal court in England of the higher sort where the authority doth absolutely rest in one person', he declared, 'and it therefore seems to me a thing reasonable and religious, and according to the first institution, that bishops, in the greatest causes and those which require a spiritual discerning . . . should not proceed sole and unassisted'.[11] This was evidently James's view as well, for (in the words of James Montagu, a future bishop, but at this time one of the deans attendant at the Conference) 'he gained that of them [the bishops] that . . . in ordination, suspension and degradation, and such like, they shall ever have some grave men to be assistants with them in all censures'.[12]

James had good cause to feel pleased with this first day's proceedings, for he had secured agreement to many of the changes that had been requested in the Millenary Petition. On the second day James met the puritan representatives, who presented their requests under four headings: 'That the doctrine of the Church might be preserved in purity, according to God's word. That good pastors might be planted in all churches to preach the same. That the Church government might be sincerely ministered, according to God's word. [And] that the Book of Common Prayer might be fitted to more increase of piety'.[13] The first heading offered little difficulty, especially in view of the fact that James, in a proclamation issued in May 1603, had condemned the 'great neglect in this kingdom of keeping the sabbath day' and ordered that in future it should be more strictly observed.[14] As for Reynolds's suggestion that there should be a new translation of the Bible, because the existing ones were deficient, James welcomed this and declared that the task should be undertaken 'by the best learned in both the universities'.[15]

The second heading was also relatively uncontentious, since James had concluded his meeting with the bishops by propounding 'matters whereabout he hoped there would be no controversy, as to have a learned ministry, and maintenance for them as far as might be, and for pluralities and non-residencies to be taken away, or at least made so few as possibly might be'.[16] The third heading should not have required much discussion, since the King and the bishops had already agreed to make significant concessions. However, Reynolds suggested that any disputed issues should be ultimately resolved at an 'episcopal synod, where the bishop with his presbytery should determine all such points as before could not be decided'.[17] Bishop Barlow, who wrote the official account of the Conference, describes the King as being 'somewhat stirred' by this speech. On the face of it, James's reaction is surprising, for he had more or less forced the bishops to agree to just such a procedure. Perhaps he was stung by the mention of the word 'presbytery' with all its unhappy connotations for the past and alarming ones for the future. Or perhaps he decided to seize the occasion to reassure the bishops by stressing his fundamental orthodoxy. Whatever his reason, he immediately interrupted and announced that if the puritans were aiming at a Scottish presbytery they were wasting their time. Such a system, he declared, 'as well agreeth with a monarchy as God and the Devil . . . Stay, I pray you, for one seven years before you demand that of me, and if you then find me pursy and fat and my wind-pipes stuffed. I will perhaps hearken to you'.[18]

Despite the King's outburst, there was only a narrow gap between him and the puritan representatives over the question of discipline. Alterations to the ceremonies prescribed in the Prayer Book were, however, a different matter, for James refused to allow any unless it could be demonstrated that the ceremonies in question were unjustified. 'If they had no word of God against them, but all authority for them, being already in the Church, he would not take them away. For he came not to disturb the state, nor to make innovations, but to confirm whatever he found lawfully established and to amend and correct whatever was corrupted by time'.[19] According to Montagu, James took the lead in debate himself, submitting every one of the puritan proposals to examination by reference to the scriptures and the writings of the fathers. Montagu's opinion was that the King had the best of the argument and that 'they were answered fully in everything'.[20] He was hardly an impartial witness, but James was a formidable disputant, well versed in theology and well read in the Bible. He was also, of course, King, and it would not be surprising if the puritan representatives were overawed as much by his royal authority as by his forensic skills.

The third and final day of the Conference began with a meeting between the King and the bishops at which James, in Montagu's words, 'took order how to have these things executed which he had concluded; that it might not be (as the King said) as smoke out of a tunnel, but substantially done, to remain for ever. So they were debated to whom they might most fitly be referred and by them made fit to be hereafter enacted by Parliament; so all the bishops and all the Council have their parts given them'.[21] Montagu listed the reforms that had been agreed. There were to be changes in the description of absolution and confirmation, to make them more acceptable to puritans, while private baptism was to be administered only by clergy and not by midwives or any other women. The jurisdiction of bishops was to be limited by the provision that 'either the dean and chapter or some grave ministers' should be 'assistant to them in ordination, suspension, degrading, etc'. 'Excommunication, as it is now used, shall be taken away both in name and nature, and a writ out of Chancery shall be framed to punish contumacies'. Schools and preachers were to be provided for Ireland, Wales and the Scottish borderlands, while the shortage of learned ministers and the inadequacy of the endowments in many English parishes were to be remedied as men and money became available. The number of pluralists was to be reduced, and those who were suffered to remain would have to hold livings reasonably near to each other, and also to ensure that preaching was made available in the parish where they were non-resident. A new translation of the Bible was to be made; the Articles of Religion were to be 'explained and enlarged'; and a uniform catechism was to be issued. As for the enemies of the faith, a strict watch was to be maintained to prevent the importation of popish books, while at local level note was to be taken of all those who did not receive communion at least once a year. Finally, the Court of High Commission was 'to be reformed and to be reduced to higher causes and fewer persons, and those of more honour and better quality'.[22]

The puritans had not got all they wanted. In particular, they had not been able to persuade James, any more than Elizabeth, to do away with ceremonies such as using the ring in the marriage service and signing with the cross in baptism. Moreover, all ministers were still required to wear the square cap as their customary habit and the surplice when they were in church. Yet significant changes had been agreed upon, particularly in the area of ecclesiastical discipline, and James had committed himself to the ideal of a preaching ministry throughout his dominions, which was more than Elizabeth had ever done. But these changes could not be brought about overnight, or by the King alone. The Hampton Court Conference was merely the first stage in a long process, and one that would entail the co-operation of Parliament if it was to be successful. In the event, the hopes raised at Hampton Court were not fulfilled, but the main reason for this was Parliament's unwillingness to re-endow the Church by restoring to it at least part of the income from tithes of which it had been deprived.

Montagu may have been correct when he described Reynolds and his fellow representatives as being 'all exceedingly well satisfied' with the outcome of the Conference,[23] but this was certainly not the case with the religious radicals, who had regarded the Millenary Petition as merely a minimum statement of their demands and were looking for more sweeping changes. If James insisted that all ministers should wear the prescribed garments, carry out the prescribed ceremonies, and confine themselves strictly within the limits laid down in the Prayer Book, many puritan ministers would be worse off than they had been under Elizabeth, for while the Queen had been a tireless opponent of puritanism at the national level she had allowed a considerable degree of non-conformity to take root in the localities. In January 1605, to give but one example, the Mayor of Northampton asserted that the ceremonies now being enforced had not been practised at the town church for more than thirty years. In other words, the imposition of conformity, which James regarded as essential, would amount to innovation, and innovation of a particularly unpalatable sort, in those areas where puritanism had established itself.

James almost certainly did not realise this. The bishops who advised him on ecclesiastical matters were hardly likely to have told him, since this would have been, in effect, to avow their own negligence. Much the same was true of members of his Privy Council. They, like the bishops, had local connexions which made them aware of the contrast between ideal and reality, but James at this stage was still a stranger, inclined to take the formal pronouncements of his predecessor at their face value. In fact it was the chief puritan spokesman, John Reynolds, who, on the final day of the Hampton Court Conference, pointed out that there were a number of ministers who 'long had been exempted from the use of ceremonies', and asked that they might be given time 'to resolve themselves in using or not using them'.[24] James was perfectly willing to do this, no doubt assuming that the number of such non-conformists would be small. In July 1604 he issued a proclamation announcing that ministers would be given until the end of November to 'resolve either to conform themselves to the Church of England and obey the same, or else to dispose of themselves and their families some other ways'. Meanwhile the bishops were to use 'their uttermost endeavours, by conferences, arguments, persuasions, and by all other ways of love and gentleness, to reclaim all that be in the ministry to the obedience of our Church laws . . . to the end that, if it be possible, that unity which we desire may be wrought by clemency and by weight of reason, and not by rigour of law'.[25]

THE ENFORCEMENT OF CONFORMITY

One essential prerequisite to the imposition of conformity was a clear statement of what exactly was required, for ever since the Break with Rome under Henry VIII the canon law of the Church had been in a state of limbo. James determined to put an end to this, and in April 1604 instructed Convocation to prepare a definitive code of canons. This was done with great rapidity, and in September of that year James promulgated them by virtue of his authority as supreme governor. The 1604 Canons made it an offence punishable by excommunication for anyone to impugn the hierarchy of the Church of England, or its Articles, or its rites and ceremonies. Moreover, all ministers were required to subscribe to three articles. The first, affirming the royal supremacy, offered little difficulty. The third, acknowledging that all the Thirty-Nine Articles were 'agreeable to the Word of God', was more contentious. But the major sticking point for puritans came with the second article, whereby they had to commit themselves to the proposition 'that the Book of Common Prayer . . . containeth in it nothing contrary to the Word of God' and also to promise to use the authorised services and none other.[26] Since puritans had been vehement in their denunciation of 'popish' elements remaining in the Prayer Book, particularly where ceremonies were concerned, subscription to this article would mean compromising their deeply held beliefs.

James had hoped that the Hampton Court Conference would put

an end to divisions within the Church by responding to the desires of moderate puritans while making it plain to the radicals that they had no more to hope for, and no reason, therefore, to continue their resistance. He believed that the Conference had demonstrated the essential weaknesses in the puritans' arguments,

for we found mighty and vehement informations supported with so weak and slender proofs, as it appeared unto us and our Council, that there was no cause why any change should have been at all in that which was most impugned, the Book of Common Prayer . . . neither in the doctrine, which appeared to be sincere, nor in forms and rites, which were justified out of the practice of the primitive Church.[27]

However, the first Parliament of James's reign, which met in March 1604, showed that the many puritan sympathisers in the House of Commons were unprepared to accept the decisions of the Conference as final. On the contrary, they were all the more determined to rally to the support of those ministers who were threatened with deprivation because of their reluctance to conform. In June they approved the wording of a petition to be presented to James in which they complained of 'the pressing the use of certain rites and ceremonies in this Church; as the cross in baptism, the wearing of the surplice in ordinary parish churches, and the subscription required of the ministers, further than is commanded by the laws of the realm'. These things, they said, had been found by long experience

to be the occasions of such difference, trouble and contention in this Church, as thereby divers profitable and painful ministers, not in contempt of authority or desire of novelty (as they sincerely profess, and we are verily persuaded) . . . have been deprived; others of good expectation witheld from entering into the ministry; and way given to the ignorant and unable men, to the great prejudice of the free course and fruitful success of the gospel, to the dangerous advantage of the common adversaries of true religion, and to the great grief and discomfort of many of Your Majesty's most faithful and loyal subjects.[28]

James was not impressed by this petition. Taken in conjunction with the Commons' reluctance to press ahead with his plans for a statutory Union of England and Scotland, it seemed to confirm the presence in the House of members who were determined to prevent harmony rather than promote it. Hence, in his proclamation of July, he not only reaffirmed his belief 'that after so much impugning there appeareth no cause why the form of the service of God wherein they have been nourished so many years should be changed', but warned his subjects against 'the troublesome spirits of some persons who never receive contentment either in civil or ecclesiastical matters'.[29] Perhaps James had in mind Sir Francis Hastings, noted for his championship of the puritans both inside and outside Parliament. It was Hastings who, in April, had proposed the setting up of a Commons committee 'to consider of the confirmation and re-establishing of the religion now established within this kingdom; as also of the settling, increasing, maintaining and continuing of a learned ministry'.[30] The House acted on his suggestion, and Hastings subsequently played a major role in guiding the committee's deliberations. The King, who was anxious to implement the programme agreed on at Hampton Court, asked the Commons to confer with Convocation before drawing up any proposals of their own, but this suggestion was not well received. The Commons resented the implication that their actions should be subject to guidance from an institution which they regarded as inferior, but they did agree to confer with the bishops in their capacity as members of the Upper House.

When this conference took place, the Commons proposed that ministers should only be required to subscribe to those of the Thirty-Nine Articles which related to doctrine and the sacraments, and that none should be 'deprived, suspended, silenced or imprisoned for not using of the cross in baptism or the surplice'. There was no question, of course, of these proposals being adopted, since they had been ruled out at Hampton Court. Other proposals were, on the face of it, more acceptable, since they were concerned with providing a learned ministry and putting an end to pluralism.[31] But the bishops were convinced that the achievement of these desirable objectives would not be possible without re-endowing the Church, and there was no suggestion that the Commons were prepared to legislate in order to achieve this. The conference therefore came to nothing, and the Commons were left to their own devices. They passed Bills against pluralists and for the encouragement of a learned ministry, apparently on the assumption that all that was needed was legislation and the will to enforce it. When, in June, a draft Bill was introduced 'for a convenient portion to be assigned out of every impropriation, for the maintenance of a preaching minister' they promptly rejected it.[32] Nevertheless, the framers of the *Apology* insisted that the Commons were ready to have 'granted no small contributions, if in these (as we trust) just and religious desires we had found that correspondency from others which we expected'.[33]

It looks as though continuing criticism of the crown's ecclesiastical policy in the Commons, along with evidence of continuing puritan resistance to the imposition of conformity, made James more rather than less determined to enforce the Hampton Court settlement. In July he had given warning 'that what untractable men do not perform upon admonition, they must be compelled unto by authority',[34] and when, in the winter, he set out on a hunting expedition which took him into Cambridgeshire and Northamptonshire he became increasingly alarmed by the evidence of puritan support. One letter writer described how 'the puritans about Royston, to the number of about seven- or eight-and-twenty, presented to the King, as he was hunting there, a petition in favour of their ministers . . . The King took in ill part this disorderly proceeding [and] commanded them presently to depart'.[35] James reacted by announcing 'that from henceforth, without delay . . . the laws shall be put in execution'[36] and complained to Bancroft that hitherto the bishops seemed to have 'stood as men at a gaze, and have done nothing'.[37]

There was some truth in this complaint, for the hierarchy in general were not in favour of harsh measures. Archbishop Hutton of York, for instance, although disliking the 'fanatical zeal' of the puritans, believed that 'they agree with us in substance of religion, and I think all or the most part of them love His Majesty and the present estate'.[38] Even those clerics who accepted the need for action believed that this should be measured and not hasty. James Montagu advised Cecil that recalcitrant ministers should be ejected 'little by little, rather than . . . cut down at once; for I have ever found all controversies in religion to gather strength by opposition, and the party depressed to gain more by pity than ever they could by their piety'.[39] Many bishops held public as well as private conferences at which they tried to win their clergy over to conformity, and it was only under heavy pressure from the King that they instituted disciplinary proceedings against the recalcitrant. In the end, some ninety ministers were deprived of their livings, mostly in the early months of 1605 when James's anger against continued puritan agitation and fear of what it might portend was at its greatest. Many nonconformists were allowed to retain their livings, as were many ministers who refused to subscribe to the three articles laid down in the 1604 Canons. It was only those who refused either to conform or subscribe who were at risk, and not all of them by any means were ejected. The puritans claimed that three hundred of their brethren were eventually dismissed, but even if this figure had been correct it would only have represented some three per cent of the clergy; the actual figure was around one per cent.

James was alarmed by the fact that non-conforming ministers

found considerable support among the gentry, particularly in the diocese of Peterborough. In February 1605 he was presented with a petition signed by some forty Northamptonshire gentlemen complaining that deprivations would mean the loss of 'many faithful preachers [who have] by their conscionable and sincere teaching confuted papism, repressed Brownism and all other schismatical and heretical opinions carefully, beaten down sin and impiety power-fully, and have proved lights of great comfort and furtherance to us and all others Your Majesty's subjects'.[40] This petition had been drawn up by Sir Francis Hastings, which implied a link between it and the parliamentary campaign on behalf of the non-conformists, and was signed by Sir Edward Montagu (brother of James) who had been prominent among their defenders in the Commons. Sir Richard Knightley, another signatory, had been one of the lay organisers of the classical movement in the 1580s and had allowed his house to be used for printing the anti-episcopal *Marprelate Letters*. To the suspicious King this seemed evidence of a plot 'to deprave the state of the Church as it is established in our kingdom, and to bring in a form of presbytery, to the utter distraction of all monarchy'.[41]

James spent eight hours in Council discussing the petition, and made the revealing observation that the revolt in the Low Countries and the troubles in Scotland had started in just this manner. It was decided that the principal signatories should be dismissed from their offices as Deputy-Lieutenants and Justices of the Peace, and that the judges should be asked to rule upon the implications of the statement that if the King did not grant the petition many thousands of his subjects would be disappointed. The judges gave their opinion that this was an offence 'very near to treason, tending to the raising of sedition, rebellion and discontent among the people'. They also ruled that 'the King without Parliament might make orders and consti-tutions for the government of the clergy, and might deprive them if they obeyed not'.[42]

It seemed at this point as though the King, by mistakenly ident-ifying all puritans as Presbyterian subversives, would push them in that direction. However, in the course of investigating the Northamptonshire petitioners he came to realise that they were really 'good and loving subjects, rather blinded . . . with indiscreet zeal than otherwise carried by any disloyal intentions'.[43] He was also made aware how much his professed desire to reconcile the catholics to his rule by moderating the impact of the penal laws had alarmed the protestant majority of his subjects. He therefore went out of his way to emphasise his commitment to protestantism. The Lord

Chancellor reported him as declaring that 'in this religion he was born, bred, schooled, brought up; he hath maintained it with the danger of his life, and he will spend his life and best blood for the same and will die in it: and if he did doubt that his son would alter the same and set up popery, he would disinherit him'.[44]

James followed this up by announcing that he regarded the puritans as being 'in another rank than the papists, and he would go half way to meet them, and he loved and reverenced many of them, and if they would leave their opinions there were some of them he would prefer to the best bishopric that were void'.[45] In fact the deprivations did succeed in rooting out the hard core of Presbyterian militants within the ministry, and although they were frequently replaced by puritans, the new men were usually prepared to conform or, at any rate, to avoid proclaiming their non-conformity. The Church of England, in other words, remained under James largely as it had done at the death of Elizabeth, Calvinist in its theology, and with a majority of low-church ministers – a puritan Church, but one ruled over by a lay sovereign and an ecclesiastical hierarchy. It was a long way removed from the Genevan model, but it was unequivocally protestant, and in the last resort it was that which counted most.

THE REFORM OF THE MINISTRY

All shades of opinion within the Church were agreed upon two principal objectives, the creation of a learned ministry and the eradication of pluralism and non-residence. As far as the first of these was concerned, a gradual improvement had started in Elizabeth's reign and it continued throughout James's. Even in remoter dioceses the majority of ordinands by the second decade of the seventeenth century were graduates, and puritan ministers ceased to be an intellectual elite. Not all graduates were effective preachers, of course, but even in this respect the situation was improving, for combination lectures or 'exercises' did much to raise standards. A 'combination' was the name given to a panel of ministers within a given locality who took it in turns to preach on market days and other occasions in nearby towns. The preacher would usually be accompanied by his fellow members of the combination, and his sermon would be dissected in the discussion that followed, frequently over dinner. 'Exercises' were more like a seminar in which the most learned ministers guided the discussion while the rest took notes. Both devices were lineal descendants of the 'prophesyings' of Elizabeth's reign. The Queen had put an end to these in the southern province because she feared that they were the thin end of the Presbyterian wedge, but they were sanctioned (under episcopal licence) by the 1604 Canons and became one of the characteristic features of the Jacobean church – a form of self-help that improved not merely the intellectual quality of the parish clergy but also their self respect and social status.

Non-residence was a more intractable problem, for its roots were financial. As John Selden observed in his *History of Tithes* 'the souls of the parishioners suffered great famine for want of a fit pastor – that is, for want of fit maintenance for him; for without that, he is scarce to be hoped for'.[46] The same point was made by Richard Neile, at that time Bishop of Rochester, who told the Lords in 1610 that when he began his career as a curate, by the time he had 'paid all duties forth of my living, my means were so small as if it had not pleased God to send me a good master I could not have told what to have done; for of a living of a 100 marks *per annum* [not quite £67] a soldier that trails a pike shall eat more hot meat and have contenteder hours than he; and better were it to enjoy an annuity of £20 *per annum* and diet in a gentleman's house than a benefice of £80'. Archbishop Bancroft agreed that £80 was not a sufficient stipend for a preacher, but made the pertinent observation that he would be happy if he lived long enough to see every living in England worth as much.[47]

The bishops were much better off than the parish clergy, of course, but they received considerably less in real terms than their medieval predecessors, even though, unlike the unmarried clergy of the pre-Reformation period, they might well have families to support. The Bishop of Oxford described his income as being 'very small and so little that I cannot live without having some livings *in commendam* [i.e. in addition]'.[48] He may have been blinded by self-interest, but a lay observer, the lawyer James Whitelocke, took a similar view, that episcopal pluralism was caused by necessity rather than greed: when his friend, John Buckeridge, on his appointment to the see of Rochester in 1611, 'kept *in commendam* with it the parsonage of South Fleet in Kent, the vicarage of St Giles in London, and his place [as canon] at Windsor', Whitelocke noted this as evidence of 'how far from covetousness he had lived'.[49]

When Parliament was in session, the Commons kept up their pressure against pluralism and non-residency. In 1607 they passed a Bill to compel non-residents to provide a preaching minister at their own expense and delegated Sir Francis Hastings to carry it up to the Lords. The bishops were opposed to it, however, and it did not get beyond a first reading. This did not deter Sir Edward Montagu, who introduced his own Bill 'against non-residence and pluralities' shortly after the opening of the final session in 1610.[50] Another champion of the puritans, Nicholas Fuller, also submitted a Bill 'against non-residents' and both were given two readings before being sent to a committee over which Montagu presided.[51] This seems to have combined the two proposals into one, for a single Bill passed the Commons on 1 March 1610 and was sent up to the Lords with a special recommendation. It met with no better success than its predecessors, but this did not deter members of the next Parliament, in 1614, from giving two readings to a similar measure. It was welcomed by moderates like Sir Thomas Lake, who described it as 'a mean to further the growth of religion'. His suggestion of a conference with 'some of the Convocation house' was not taken up, but there was a certain amount of support for Sir Edwin Sandys' alternative suggestion that they should confer with the bishops as lords of Parliament. A less temperate contribution came from the aged Sir Anthony Cope, who had played a leading role in the Presbyterian campaign in Elizabeth's reign. Speaking from long experience, he said that parliaments had been passing Bills on this topic for thirty years, but that the abuses had continued to grow like Hydra's heads. Three-fifths of all clergy, he declared, were 'non-residents, drones, or scandalous ministers', and a 'soul-murdering non-resident is as dangerous to the soul as a murderer of the body to it'.[52] This Bill never proceeded beyond a second reading, and a similar one introduced into the 1621 Parliament was read once and then lost to sight.[53]

The Commons did not confine themselves to Bills. In July 1610 they included pluralism and non-residency in their petition of ecclesiastical grievances, arguing that 'although those that have pluralities of such livings and non-residence do frame excuse of the smallness of some livings, and pretend the maintenance of learning, yet we find by experience that they, coupling many of the greatest livings, do for the most part leave the least meanly furnished, and the best as ill served and supplied with preachers as the meanest'.[54] There was considerable truth in this accusation, and there is no doubt that the bishops could have done more to control the abuse of pluralism. But it did not escape their notice, any more than the King's, that it was the puritans and their sympathisers in the Commons who masterminded the campaign against these twin evils, and they distrusted their motives. Moreover, they resented the fact that their critics were the representatives of the landowners who had diverted Church revenues into their own hands and yet blamed the hierarchy for failing to cope with the consequences. Pluralism applied to tithes as well as livings, as Bancroft emphasised when he asked 'is the law good that giveth to a layman the tithes to two benefices and is it unlawful for a minister to hold two benefices?'.[55] Robert Cecil was one of the few laymen to acknowledge that fundamental reform of abuses in the Church demanded sacrifices on the part of the land-owners. 'Let us take from the laity out of the impropriations to give unto the Church', he proposed to the Lords in May 1610, and added that he would be willing to give the tenth part of all that he held.[56] His proposal was not taken up, but the Addled Parliament, in its brief meeting in 1614, had before it a draft Bill 'touching benefices impropriate, that the justice of assize and ordinary [shall] rate a reasonable living to a preaching minister'.[57]

One of the complaints made by critics of the Church and its episcopal administrators was that worthy ministers were dismissed for refusing to abandon their principles while unworthy ones were allowed to continue unchecked. In 1604, 1606 and 1610 the Commons passed Bills 'for reforming scandalous ministers',[58] the last of which would have given assize judges and Justices of the Peace power to punish delinquent clergy – a proposal which George Abbot, Bishop of London and a low-churchman, declared would 'leave the Church in worse estate than in the time of the persecuting emperors'.[59] In 1614 Nicholas Fuller introduced a Bill empowering judges and Justices to punish 'scandalous ministers, as drunkards or any other enormous vice', by fine and imprisonment for the first offence and deprivation for the second. This got no further than one reading, but in 1621 a similar Bill was read twice. Sir Dudley Digges maintained that it was unnecessary, 'because there are laws sufficient already to punish them, and . . . because it casts an aspersion upon the ministry'. Sir James Perrott said that Digges would be of another opinion if he lived in Perrott's part of the world, 'and whereas he thinks it a scandal to our ministry to punish scandalous ministers, I think it is not so, but it's a scandal rather to suffer them unpunished'. It was left to Dr Gooch to come to the defence of the ministry. Some of them, he admitted, were 'of small or no gifts', yet what better could be expected when livings were so poor? 'Many have but £4, £5 or £6 *per annum*, and what worthy man can you have for such a stipend?' But in general, he insisted, 'there were never better ministers since this kingdom stood'.[60] This was also the view of Lionel Cranfield, who included in his 'Notes for Parliament', drawn up in November 1621, the rhetorical question 'for true religion, whether it was ever more freely and more learnedly professed and taught? Whether the clergy were ever more honoured and more protected since the establishing of the true religion now established than since His Majesty's happy reign?'.[61]

JAMES I AND THE BISHOPS

Following the death of Whitgift in February 1604, James appointed Richard Bancroft as Archbishop of Canterbury. Bancroft was an exponent of *jure divino* episcopacy, and a disciplinarian very much in the mould of Whitgift, whose chaplain he had been. He took his stand on the Prayer Book and 1604 Canons, and told the Commons, in a conference in 1606, that 'there is no religion where [there] are no ceremonies. The hands and knees must be affected besides the heart'.[62] Like Whitgift, Bancroft believed that the puritans and their allies in Parliament aimed at the destruction of the established Church, as was shown by their support of non-conforming ministers, their attacks on High Commission and the *ex officio* oath, and their insistence that the King had no right to issue Canons without parliamentary approval. He therefore refused to accept reform measures coming from the Commons and effectively blocked their passage through the Upper House. He became, in fact, a staunch defender of the *status quo*, simply because any change was likely to be for the worse. At the same time he encouraged the parish clergy to hold their heads high and to press for a realistic valuation of tithes, even if this entailed taking legal action against their patrons and parishioners in the church courts.

Bancroft's policies led him into conflict with the judges over prohibitions (see p. 54), and with the common lawyers, whom he accused of unfair discrimination against the civil lawyers who practised in the ecclesiastical courts. Faced with such powerful adversaries, he needed all the support he could get from the King, and therefore exalted the royal authority. This led to accusations that he favoured arbitrary government, that 'by my means a course is entered into which tendeth to the overthrow of the common law, and to deprive His Majesty's subjects of their birthright; that I labour by all ways I can devise to make the King believe that he is one absolute monarch and may, *jure regio*, do what he list'.[63] Bancroft denied this charge, but the fact that it had been made is revealing. It shows that even before the advent to power of the Arminians there was an alliance of interests between the hierarchy and the crown, and that any Archbishop who set himself the task of holding back change would have to take his stand upon the prerogatives of the King, as supreme governor of the Church.

Although Bancroft took an exalted view of the episcopal office and valued ceremonies as an aid to worship, he did not belong to the high-church or Arminian minority among the episcopate which had been slowly gaining ground since its emergence in the 1590s. The most distinguished member of this group was Lancelot Andrewes, whom James made Bishop of Chichester in 1605 and subsequently elevated to the sees of Ely and Winchester. Andrewes was a distinguished scholar and an accomplished preacher in the somewhat convoluted style that was popular at Court. James relished his company, and when Bancroft died in November 1610 there was some expectation that James might select Andrewes in his place. James, however, chose the low-church George Abbot, whom he had only recently appointed to London. It seems likely that Bancroft had intended Abbot to succeed him, and there was the further consideration that Abbot would be more acceptable to the puritan element in the Church. This proved to be the case, for between Abbot's appointment and James's death in 1625 only two ministers are known to have been deprived for non-conformity, and the majority of puritans, both clergy and laity, seem to have found it possible to accept the minimum requirements laid down for Church membership. This did not mean that all puritans gave up their distinctive views and merged into the general mass. On the contrary, there was a tendency for the more committed ones to come together for private prayer and to covenant among themselves, and with God, to live a holy life. Some groups, such as that set up in Southwark by Henry Jacob in 1616, were semi-separatist, half in and half out of the Church. A few were separatist on principle, but generally speaking the Church of England under James and Abbot remained sufficiently flexible to be able to accommodate a wide range of attitudes.

This was reflected in the episcopate itself, for James was ecumenical in his approach to appointments and never allowed a single faction to gain control. He chose high-churchmen and low-churchmen, intellectuals and non-intellectuals, idealists and time-servers. Since the Church of England claimed to embrace the entire population, except for a handful of recusants, it was appropriate that its hierarchy should be similarly all-embracing. There was, however, an essential condition for the preservation of this state of affairs, and that was the avoidance of public controversy. One of James's main complaints against the puritans was that they insisted on discussing issues, such as predestination, which could only confuse and divide ordinary people. It may be that James's own views were changing. In 1604 he had announced his acceptance of predestination, on the grounds that 'election dependeth not upon any qualities, actions or works of man, which be mutable, but upon God His eternal and immutable decree and purpose'.[64] Some years later, however, he told Bishop Overall 'that it appeared to him a very bold attempt for men to dispute so nicely about such questions of God's predestination, and so peremptorily to decide matters as if they had been in heaven and assisted at the divine Council board'.[65]

THE ARMINIANS

James's objection to those who made dogmatic pronouncements on such questions was not confined to the puritans. When the distinguished Dutch theologian Conrad Vorstius echoed the views of Jacob Arminius (whom he had succeeded as professor of divinity at Leiden) by reacting against the rigid interpretation of the doctrine of predestination, emphasising instead man's freedom to shape his own life, James launched a successful campaign to have him censured and dismissed. His suspicion of the Arminians as both heterodox and stirrers-up of faction was nourished by Archbishop Abbot, and when, in 1618, the Dutch held a conference at Dort to decide how to deal with them, James instructed the English delegates to support the anti-Arminian majority. But here again he did so, in part at least, because the Arminians were challenging the consensus which had hitherto maintained peace within the United Provinces. It was wrong, said James, for ministers to 'deliver in the pulpit to the people these things for ordinary doctrines which are the highest points of schools [i.e. universities], and not fit for vulgar capacity'.[66]

Although the avoidance of public controversy remained James's policy, it became much more difficult to enforce after 1618. One reason for this was the emergence of Arminianism, not only in Holland but also, to an increasing extent, in England, as an open challenge to the existing Calvinist orientation of the established Church. Another was the intensification of anti-Spanish and anti-catholic feeling after the outbreak of the Thirty Years War. In 1622 James directed Archbishop Abbot to impose formal restraints upon sermons. In future no one below the degree of Bachelor of Divinity was to 'presume to preach in any popular auditory the deep points of predestination, election, reprobation, or the universality, efficacy, resistibility or irresistibility of God's grace; but leave these themes to be handled by learned men, and that moderately and modestly'.[67] This restriction upon controversial preaching was itself controversial, for many of James's subjects believed that at a time when protestantism was again under attack from the forces of international catholicism it was more essential than ever to proclaim the truth of the reformed faith, and to do so in a manner that admitted of no ambiguity.

There is little doubt that popular opinion, as reflected in the parliaments of 1621 and 1624, was deeply anti-catholic and therefore opposed to James's policy of seeking a marriage alliance with Spain, the leading catholic power. In 1623, when the Prince of Wales was actually in Spain, putting the last touches to the marriage treaty, a pamphlet appeared in the form of a letter from Archbishop Abbot to the King, condemning not simply James's pro-Spanish policy but also his toleration of catholicism, whereby it appeared that he was willing 'to set up that most damnable and heretical doctrine of the Church of Rome, the Whore of Babylon'.[68] Abbot denied any knowledge of, or share in, the authorship of this intemperate tract, but although he may have disapproved of its style he had a great deal of sympathy with its substance. So did many of his fellow bishops, but this was less true of the Arminians than of the low-churchmen. The Arminians were relatively unfanatical in their attitude towards the Church of Rome. They were prepared to recognise it as the mother church of Christendom, and although they acknowledged its corruptions – from which they claimed their own, Anglican, church was mercifully free – they declined to denounce the Pope as AntiChrist.

The Arminians' lack of fanaticism appealed to James, and this helped strengthen the bond that was already being forged by their support for the royal prerogative. In 1613, for instance, at the time of the Somerset divorce proceedings, the Arminians had wholeheartedly committed themselves to the King's view that his favourite's marriage should be annulled – unlike Abbot, who had incurred James's displeasure by opposing it. Richard Neile, a prominent Arminian, was said to have intrigued against Abbot, and in the following year he made a further bid for James's favour by defending his right to levy Impositions and attacking the Commons as 'a factious, mutinous, seditious assembly' that was striking 'at the very root of the King's prerogative, and did catch at his crown'.[69] A year later Neile's mentor, Lancelot Andrewes, told a meeting of the Privy Council which had been called to consider remedies for the crown's parlous financial condition 'that he thought it a very good preparation that the people might be instructed and taught that relief to their sovereign in necessity was *jure divino* and no less due than their allegiance and service'.[70]

In these and many other ways the Arminians had endeared themselves to James, and he valued their support even more in the closing years of his reign, when the consensus which he had enforced after Hampton Court was clearly breaking down. The puritan majority within the established Church had been prepared, however reluctantly, to conform with James's decisions on matters of ceremonial, but only because they believed him to be sound on doctrine. Now, however, they were less willing to trust his judgment, for on the issue of anti-catholicism, which for them was crucial, he seemed to be leaning dangerously towards the wrong side. From about 1620 onwards discontent with James's approach towards foreign affairs expressed itself more openly, and as puritanism came to be identified with aggressively anti-catholic and anti-Spanish attitudes it presented an increasing challenge to the King's right to determine his own course of policy. In other words the puritans once again appeared to be a dissentient and potentially dangerous faction.

The Church of England, however, was in many respects a puritan Church, and how could its members be dismissed as a faction? One answer to this was given by an Essex rector, Richard Montagu, in 1624. Montagu had been alarmed by the distribution among his parishioners of a catholic tract entitled *The Gag for the New Gospel* which asserted that the Church of England was essentially Calvinist. Montagu rejected this claim out of hand, and told his friend John Cosin how happy it would make him if the King could be persuaded 'to take strict order that these Allobrogical dormice [i.e. the Calvinists] should not so much as peep out in corners or by owl-light. This riff-raff rascals make us liable to the lash unto our other adversaries of the Church of Rome, who impute the frantic fits and froth of every puritan paroxysm to the received doctrine of our Church'.[71] Montagu set himself to write a defence of the Anglican church as he believed it was – or at least ought to be – and called it *A New Gag for an Old Goose*. In this he stressed the catholic elements in Anglicanism while playing down the Calvinist ones. His aim, as he informed Cosin, was 'to stand in the gap against puritanism and popery' and to show that the Church of England was a true Church and not a satellite either of Rome or Geneva.[72]

To many low churchmen this seemed like heresy, and a formal complaint against Montagu was presented to James's last Parliament in 1624. John Pym described the *New Gag* as being 'full fraught with dangerous opinions of Arminius, quite contrary to the [Thirty-Nine] Articles established', and the Commons resolved to call it to the attention of the Archbishop.[73] Abbot, after consulting with James, sent for Montagu and told him

you profess you hate popery and no way incline to Arminianism. You see what disturbance is grown in the Church and in the Parliament House by the book you lately put forth. Be occasion of no scandal or offence . . . Go home, review over your book. It may be divers things have slipped you, which, upon better advice, you will reform . . . Do not wed yourself to your own opinion, and remember we must give an account of our ministry unto Christ.[74]

This appeal might have succeeded with the older generation of high-churchmen typified by Andrewes, for they were not inclined to public controversy. But Montagu came at a time when religious passions were rising at both ends of the spectrum, and he felt impelled to speak out. Moreover, he believed he could count on the King's support, for when he explained his views to James, the King exclaimed 'By God, if this be popery, I am a papist!'.[75] This explains why it was that when Montagu, in response to Abbot's request, 'reviewed over' his book, he came to the conclusion that if anything he had understated his case. He remedied this by producing, in *Appello Caesarem*, a much more forceful exposition of his views. James referred the new book to Francis White, at that time Dean of Carlisle, who declared that it contained nothing contrary to the doctrines of the established Church, and authorised its publication. White was subsequently to be consecrated bishop by Richard Neile, which suggests that his sympathies were with the Arminians. Moreover, Neile himself, in association with William Laud, Bishop of St David's, wrote to the Duke of Buckingham on Montagu's behalf. He was, they said, 'a man every way able to do God, His Majesty, and the Church of England great service'. As for his opinions, they were, for the most part, 'such as are expressly the resolved doctrine of the Church of England, and those he is bound to maintain'.[76]

It was perhaps fortunate for James that he died in March 1625, before the Arminian challenge to the ecclesiastical *status quo* became a major issue and opened up an ever-widening gap between the crown and the political nation. He had managed to preserve the Elizabethan church for more than twenty years after the Queen's death, and this in itself was a considerable achievement. It seems unlikely that the Jacobean consensus could have been maintained in the turbulence created by the Thirty Years War, but its future was now in the hands of King Charles I.

NOTES AND REFERENCES

(*The place of publication is London, unless otherwise stated*)
1. **R. G. Usher** *The Reconstruction of the English Church* (1910). Vol. I, p. 56. (Hereafter Usher *Reconstruction*)
2. **The Political Works of James I**, ed. C. H. McIlwain (Cambridge, Mass. 1918), pp. 7–8.
3. **J. R. Tanner** (ed.) *Constitutional Documents of the Reign of James I* (Cambridge 1930), pp. 57–9. (Hereafter Tanner *Constitutional Documents*)
4. Tanner *Constitutional Documents*, p. 59.
5. Usher *Reconstruction*. Vol. I, p. 294.
6. Usher *Reconstruction*. Vol. I, pp. 295–96.
7. **James F. Larkin** & **Paul L. Hughes** (eds.) *Stuart Royal Proclamations*. Vol. I. *Royal Proclamations of King James I* (Oxford 1973), p. 62. (Hereafter Larkin & Hughes *Royal Proclamations*)
8. Larkin & Hughes *Royal Proclamations*, p. 63.
9. **F. Shriver** 'Hampton Court Revisited: James I and the Puritans', *Journal of Ecclesiastical History*. Vol. 33, 1982, p. 58.
10. **Sir Ralph Winwood** *Memorials of Affairs of State in the Reigns of Queen Elizabeth and King James I* (1725). Vol. II, pp. 13–14 (Hereafter Winwood *Memorials*); Tanner *Constitutional Documents*, p. 58.
11. **The Works of Francis Bacon** ed. James Spedding (1874). Vol. X, pp. 109–10. (Hereafter Bacon *Works*)
12. Winwood *Memorials*. Vol. II, p. 14.
13. Tanner *Constitutional Documents*, p. 62.
14. Larkin & Hughes *Royal Proclamations*, p. 14.
15. Tanner *Constitutional Documents*, p. 63.
16. Winwood *Memorials*. Vol. II, p. 14.
17. Tanner *Constitutional Documents*, p. 67.
18. Tanner *Constitutional Documents*, p. 67.
19. Winwood *Memorials*. Vol. II, p. 14.
20. Winwood *Memorials*. Vol. II, p. 14.
21. Winwood *Memorials*. Vol. II, p. 15.
22. Winwood *Memorials*. Vol. II, p. 15.
23. Winwood *Memorials*. Vol. II, p. 15.
24. Winwood *Memorials*. Vol. II, p. 15.
25. Larkin & Hughes *Royal Proclamations*, p. 90.
26. **J. P. Kenyon** (ed.) *The Stuart Constitution 1603–1688* 2nd edn. (Cambridge 1986), p. 123.

27. Larkin & Hughes *Royal Proclamations*, p. 75.
28. **Journals of the House of Commons 1547–1714** (1742). Vol. I, p. 238. (Hereafter *Commons Journals*)
29. Larkin & Hughes *Royal Proclamations*, p. 89.
30. *Commons Journals*. Vol. I, p. 172.
31. *Commons Journals*. Vol. I, p. 200.
32. *Commons Journals*. Vol. I, p. 244.
33. Tanner *Constitutional Documents*, p. 227.
34. Larkin & Hughes *Royal Proclamations*, p. 89.
35. Winwood *Memorials*. Vol. II, p. 36.
36. Tanner *Constitutional Documents*, p. 74.
37. Usher *Reconstruction*. Vol. I, p. 414.
38. Winwood *Memorials*. Vol. II, p. 40.
39. Usher *Reconstruction*. Vol. I, p. 414.
40. **W. J. Sheils** *The Puritans in the Diocese of Peterborough 1558–1610* Northamptonshire Record Society (1979), p. 110.
41. **Kenneth Fincham** & **Peter Lake** 'The Ecclesiastical Policy of King James I', *Journal of British Studies*. Vol. 24, 1985, pp. 176–77.
42. Usher *Reconstruction*. Vol. I, p. 420.
43. **B. W. Quintrell** 'The Royal Hunt and the Puritans 1604–05', *Journal of Ecclesiastical History*. Vol. 31, 1980, p. 54.
44. **W. P. Baildon** (ed.) *Les Reportes del Cases in Camera Stellata 1593–1609* (1894), p. 189. (Hereafter Baildon *Reportes*)
45. Baildon *Reportes*, p. 191.
46. **John Selden** *The Historie of Tithes* (1618), p. 486.
47. **E. R. Foster** (ed.) *Proceedings in Parliament 1610* (New Haven 1966). Vol. 1, pp. 111–12. (Hereafter Foster *Proceedings 1610*)
48. Foster *Proceedings 1610*. Vol. 1, p. 73.
49. **James Whitelocke** *Liber Famelicus* ed. J. Bruce. Camden Society (1858), p. 26.
50. *Commons Journals*. Vol. I, p. 393.
51. *Commons Journals*. Vol. I, p. 396.
52. *Commons Journals*. Vol. I, p. 482.
53. *Commons Journals*. Vol. I, p. 592.
54. Foster *Proceedings 1610*. Vol. 2, p. 256.
55. Foster *Proceedings 1610*. Vol. 1, p. 223.
56. Foster *Proceedings 1610*. Vol. 1, pp. 77, 234.
57. **Wallace Notestein, Frances Helen Relf & Hartley Simpson** (eds.) *Commons Debates 1621* (New Haven 1935); Vol. VII, p. 640. (Hereafter *Commons Debates 1621*)
58. Foster *Proceedings 1610*. Vol. 1, p. 123.
59. Foster *Proceeding 1610*. Vol. 1, p. 128.
60. *Commons Debates 1621*. Vol. II, p. 440.
61. *Commons Debates 1621*. Vol. VII. Appx. C, p. 618.
62. **S. B. Babbage** *Puritanism and Richard Bancroft* (1962), p. 7. (Hereafter Babbage *Puritanism and Bancroft*)
63. Babbage *Puritanism and Bancroft*, p. 8.
64. **Claire Cross** 'Churchmen and the Royal Supremacy' in Felicity Heal & Rosemary O'Day (eds.) *Church and Society in England: Henry VIII to James I* (1979), p. 30.

65. **John Platt** 'Eirenical Anglicans at the Synod of Dort' in Derek Baker (ed.) *Reform and Reformation: England and the Continent c. 1500–c. 1750* (1979), p. 224. (Hereafter Platt 'Eirenical Anglicans')
66. Platt 'Eirenical Anglicans', p. 223.
67. *Cabala sive Scrinia Sacra* (1691), p. 104. (Hereafter *Cabala*)
68. **P. A. Welsby** *George Abbot, the Unwanted Archbishop 1562–1633* (1962), p. 108.
69. *The Letters of John Chamberlain* ed. N. E. McClure (Philadelphia 1939), Vol. I, p. 533.
70. Bacon *Works*. Vol. XII, p. 202.
71. *The Correspondence of John Cosin, Lord Bishop of Durham* ed. G. Ornsby (1869). Vol. I, p. 32. (Hereafter Cosin *Correspondence*)
72. Cosin *Correspondence*. Vol. I, p. 21.
73. *Commons Journals*. Vol. I, p. 788.
74. **S. R. Gardiner** (ed.) *Debates in the House of Commons in 1625* Camden Society (1873), p. 35. (Hereafter Gardiner *1625 Debates*)
75. Gardiner *1625 Debates*, p. 46.
76. *Cabala*, p. 105.

CHAPTER SIX

The Nature and Functions of Parliament in Early Stuart England

MEMBERSHIP AND LENGTH OF SESSIONS

During the Tudor period, and particularly after the Break with Rome, Parliament had come to be accepted as an integral, though intermittent, element in the English system of government. Elizabeth summoned it as and when she thought fit, but in practice it met every three or four years. In James's reign Sir Edward Coke was to assert that annual parliaments were not only desirable but actually prescribed by statute, but the prevailing opinion seems to have been expressed by Bacon, who referred to the need to purge and restore 'the civil state' by 'good and wholesome laws made every third or fourth year in parliaments'.[1] James would presumably have agreed with this, for he had summoned the Scottish parliament at approximately three-year intervals, and he showed the importance he attached to these meetings by giving detailed supervision to their agenda and making sure that members were well informed about his wishes. The Scottish parliament was not a subservient institution, but James found it extremely useful, particularly since it brought him into direct contact with the magnates and elected representatives who formed the political nation in Scotland. James enjoyed and valued first-hand encounters, where he could explain his views and present his case in the most compelling manner, and partly because of this intimate relationship between the King and the members, the Scottish parliament was a highly effective body – in contrast to its English equivalent, which was much larger and far less amenable to direction.

James came to England not simply as a new King but also as the inaugurator of a new dynasty, and a meeting with Parliament was one of the most obvious ways in which to make himself known to his English subjects. This would have taken place soon after his arrival but for the outbreak of plague, which caused a postponement until January 1604, when writs were at last sent out. Because Elizabeth had been very mean when it came to creating peerages, only fifty-two lay lords were called to the Upper House, along with twenty-six spiritual ones – a situation that was to change dramatically with the inflation of honours that set in under James, for by 1615 there were eighty-one lay peers, and by 1628 this number had risen to 126. The House of Commons in 1604 consisted of 467 members, but this number also increased during the early Stuart period, both through enfranchisement by the crown and through the House's own policy of restoring the right of election to boroughs which had allowed it to lapse. The Long Parliament of 1640 continued this process by re-enfranchising seven boroughs, and thereby increased its membership to a nominal total of 507. In the Lower House the greatest prestige attached to the seventy-eight 'knights of the shire' who represented the thirty-nine English counties; there were also twelve representatives for the Welsh shires, which elected only one member each. The remainder of the House consisted of 'burgesses', so called because they sat for borough seats, though in fact the majority of them were gentry. The number of actual merchants in the House was usually only a little over forty – though these included the four representatives of London – and they were far less influential than the somewhat larger group of professional lawyers.

James's first Parliament assembled in March 1604 and remained in existence, though not in continual session, until the end of 1610. It sat for some 108 weeks in all, and after it was dissolved there was a lapse of three years until the brief nine-week session of the Addled Parliament in 1614. This was followed by a long intermission until 1621, when James's third Parliament met and sat for a total of twenty-two weeks. Just over two years later came his fourth and last Parliament, which met for fifteen weeks in 1624. James reigned in England for more than twenty-one years, during which time Parliament was in session for some 154 weeks. This gives an average of 7.3 weeks per year, which compares favourably with the comparable figure for Elizabeth of 2.7.

JAMES'S ATTITUDE TOWARDS PARLIAMENT

Although, on the face of it, James was a more 'parliamentary' ruler than Elizabeth, there was an undercurrent of fear among members of the Commons that the continued existence of Parliament could no longer be taken for granted. One reason for this was the all too obvious fact that representative institutions were fast disappearing from Europe as rulers concentrated authority in their own hands: as Sir Robert Phelips reminded the Lower House in 1625, 'we are the last monarchy in Christendom that retain our original rights and constitutions'.[2] Another was uncertainty about James's real attitude towards Parliament. He had a habit of referring to himself as an 'absolute' King, which was hardly reassuring, though, as he frequently stressed, he did not mean by this that he either wished or intended to ride roughshod over his subjects' liberties and rule in a despotic manner. After all, as he informed the two Houses in 1610, 'many things I may do without Parliament which I will do in Parliament; for good kings are helped by Parliament – not for power, but for convenience'.[3] James clearly intended his speech to be reassuring, but many of his listeners were more likely to have had their suspicions confirmed by the implications of his statement. James regarded Parliament as 'convenient', but what if it became inconvenient? And as for his reminder that he was not dependent upon Parliament for the exercise of his authority, this could be taken as a warning, even if none was intended, that in certain circumstances he might find it easier to rule without Parliament. Indeed, he did exactly this after the unhappy experience of the Addled Parliament, for six and a half years elapsed before writs were sent out for new elections. This compares with the longest period of intermission in Elizabeth's reign of just under five years.

James began with the assumption, which was well grounded in history, that parliaments came later in time than kings, 'and were not instituted before them (as many foolishly have imagined); but long after that monarchies were established were they first created'.[4] It followed logically from this premise that the function of Parliament was to serve the monarch, and that any privileges which it possessed had been granted by the monarch so that it could carry out this function. Parliament met at the King's command to do the King's business, and nothing irritated James more than the Commons' habit (as it seemed to him) of setting their own agenda and ignoring that which he and his ministers had outlined. Members of Parliament, and in particular of the Commons, frequently acted as though their time was their own, but James reminded the Speaker in December 1621 that it was 'not theirs, but ours' and that they should therefore use it well.[5] His resentment at the Commons' time-wasting was of long standing, for he had informed his first Parliament that 'when he looked into the gravity and judgment of this House, and of the long continuance of the Parliament' and saw 'so few matters of weight passed . . . he was moved with jealousy that there was not such proceeding as in love he expected'.[6] The same resentment surfaced in 1610, when James complained that 'the delay and lingering was so great' that despite a very long session 'only eight or ten days were spent in the business', and 'one half was consumed in nothing'.[7] James's growing conviction that the Commons' procedure was deliberately designed to frustrate his intentions materially affected his attitude towards Parliament. In October 1622 there was talk of summoning a new one, but Chamberlain reported that 'the King is so distasted with their tedious manner of proceeding that he will hardly be drawn unto it, unless matters be so prepared that there will be a more quick despatch'.[8]

James put much of the blame for what he regarded as unnecessary delays on dissident elements within the Lower House, many of them lawyers. In 1616 he delivered his opinion to the Privy Council that 'ever since his coming to the crown, the popular sort of lawyers have been the men that most affrontedly, in all parliaments, have trodden upon his prerogative',[9] and at the end of 1620, when he issued a proclamation concerning the forthcoming elections, he called on his 'well-affected subjects' not to give their vote to 'curious and wrangling lawyers who may seek reputation by stirring needless questions'.[10] James also warned them against 'young and inexperienced men that are not ripe and mature for so grave a council', no doubt thinking of the disastrous 1614 session in which, according to Bacon, 'three parts of the House were such as had never been of any former Parliament, and many of them young men, and not of any great estate or quality'.[11] Bacon had been a member of the Commons in 1614 so presumably knew what he was talking about. His view is confirmed by Chamberlain's comment, made shortly after the dissolution, that there had been too many 'bold and petulant speeches' and that the House was so disorderly 'that it was many times more like a cockpit than a grave council, and many sat there that were more fit to have been among roaring boys than in that assembly'.[12]

Even before he met his first English Parliament James had advised his subjects to take particular care when they went to the polls. In county elections they should vote for 'the principal knights or gentlemen of sufficient ability', while borough representatives should be chosen from among 'men of sufficiency and discretion, without any partial respects or factious combination'.[13] Unfortunately for the King he could do little more than exhort, and there is no evidence that the sort of advice offered in eve-of-poll proclamations had any effect. Nor was it necessarily the case that only young and inexperienced members of the Commons dared to criticise royal policies. Sir Edwin Sandys, for instance, came to be regarded as one of the leading opponents of the government in the first two parliaments of James I, but he was well over forty when he took his seat in 1604 and had a decade of parliamentary experience behind him. He suffered the major disadvantage, in James's eyes, of being a lawyer, but he could hardly have been described as of 'mean quality', since his father was Archbishop of York. Sandys was not motivated by personal animus against James. On the contrary, he went north to greet the new King as he journeyed south from Edinburgh and accompanied him into England, for which act of devotion he was rewarded with his knighthood. On the face of it he should have been, in Bacon's phrase, a 'peremptory royalist', but he chose to range himself among the crown's critics and James included him in the category of 'fiery spirits' who disturbed the harmonious relations that ought to have existed between the monarch and the representatives of his loving subjects assembled in Parliament.

James was notoriously short tempered and never bothered to conceal his feelings, but his outbursts of irritation against the House of Commons should not be taken as indicative of a desire to rule without Parliament. When James was feeling particularly bitter after the failure of the 1614 session he told the Spanish ambassador that the House of Commons consisted of 500 men without a head, who 'voted without order, nothing being heard but cries, shouts, and confusion' and that he was astonished 'that the kings his predecessors had consented to such a thing'. Yet he added the significant rider that he 'had found it thus when he came, so that he could not do without it'.[14] No doubt if James had started his rule in England with a clean sheet he would have constructed a form of government which either excluded Parliament, or, more likely, included a version much closer to the Scottish model, but given that he had no choice, James simply had to make the best of a bad job. Moreover, even from the King's point of view the parliamentary balance sheet was not entirely adverse. Parliament had its advantages as well as its drawbacks.

LEGISLATION

The principal function of Parliament was to legislate, and the statutes which it passed were binding upon all the King's subjects and enforceable in the courts of common law. Although the King acting alone had a limited power to legislate by issuing proclamations, this was narrowly circumscribed; only in Parliament could he exercise his supreme legislative function. In the second half of Henry VIII's reign the Break with Rome and subsequent religious changes had involved Parliament in a great deal of law making, but as Elizabeth's reign drew to a close the pressure was relaxing: indeed, the Lord Keeper informed members in 1593 that 'this Parliament is not for making of any more new laws and statutes, for there are already a sufficient number'.[15] Sir Edwin Sandys took a similar view in 1614, when he gave his opinion that 'this Parliament [was] not called for making of laws; rather for the execution'.[16] James, however, did not regard the two functions as mutually exclusive. Speaking in the same 1614 session he told a delegation from the Commons that 'hereafter he would call a Parliament either to make good laws or else to execute those which are already enacted'.[17] In some ways the emphasis on law-enforcement is puzzling, since Parliament had virtually no executive powers. But the representatives of the community were well placed to know what was amiss in the local-ities and what the government needed to do about it. In Parliament they had the opportunity to call the King's attention to their views and galvanise the Privy Council into action. Furthermore, since many of them were themselves Deputy-Lieutenants or Justices of the Peace, they were responsible for carrying out public policy at the local level, and a meeting of Parliament, at which matters of mutual concern could be discussed and appropriate responses formulated, helped them to establish their order of priorities.

The initiative in framing new laws come from members of Parliament rather than the crown. Of the seventy-two measures which were enacted in 1604, just over half were private, and the same proportion obtained in James's last Parliament in 1624. Private Bills were a very convenient means whereby corporations or private individuals could obtain a legal remedy for problems arising out of unclear or disputed property rights. Parliament could break trusts, override restrictive covenants or vested interests, and provide what was, in effect, swift justice – all the more valuable since it was incontestable. As for public Bills, many of these were drawn up by members who found that the particular problems of their constituents were widely shared, and that generally-applicable legislation was therefore more appropriate than a private measure. The crown would occasionally put forward legislative proposals. James's main concern in his first Parliament, for instance, was to secure the passage of measures to establish a full union of his two kingdoms of Scotland and England. Subsidy Bills were also a matter of prime concern for the royal government, while the 1610 session was dominated by Salisbury's attempt to push through the Great Contract. Yet even though the initiative in the Contract came from the crown, the scheme had been prompted by the fact that two of the major items with which it dealt, wardship and purveyance, had long been the subject of complaints in Parliament. In this instance, as in many others, the government was reacting to popular opinion.

REDRESS OF GRIEVANCES AND SUPPLY

While law-making was the principal function of Parliament, it was closely connected with another, the redress of grievances. Sir Edward Coke, speaking in the Commons in 1621, made the link explicit. As 'ill humours increase in the body and hurt the body if they be not purged', he explained, 'so likewise abuses and corruptions increase in the commonwealth. Therefore often parliaments are necessary, that good laws may be made to prevent and punish them'.[18] This view was widely shared, and members of the Lower House regarded it as their duty to make known the feelings of their constituents: in the words of Sir George Moore, 'our principal care [is] to speak for the commonwealth that continually speaketh to us'.[19] Raising grievances meant, in effect, complaining to the King about abuses in his government, and Parliament was a forum where this could be done without giving offence – in theory, at any rate. Moreover, the alternative to a constitutional redress of grievances might well be something much worse. As Bacon noted in 1610, 'take away parliaments, the wounds of the realm will bleed inward; sharp humours will not evaporate but exulcerate'.[20]

James recognised the value of this particular function of the Commons. When he addressed the two Houses in 1610 he singled out

two special causes of the people's presenting grievances to their King in time of Parliament. First, for that the King cannot at other times be so well informed of all the grievances of his people as in time of Parliament, which is the representative body of the whole realm. Secondly, the Parliament is the highest court of justice and the fittest place where divers natures of grievances may have their proper remedy, by establishing of good and wholesome laws.[21]

This explains his attitude towards the Commons' fierce attack upon monopolies in 1621. Far from resenting it, James gave the Commons his explicit approval, 'protesting that he held and found them a very wise Council and [one] which had discovered that unto him which he should never have known but too late: that his kingdom was like a garden overgrown with weeds, wherein he desired their help to pluck them up by the roots'.[22]

James drew a sharp distinction, however, between positive and negative criticism. 'You may meddle with the abuse of my commissions', he told the Houses in 1610, 'but not with my power of government', and to illustrate his meaning he warned them that while they had every right to complain about specific actions of the Court of High Commission they were not justified in calling for its abolition. James was also insistent that the grievances complained of must be genuine, and 'not, as it were, greedily sought out by you, or taken up in the streets . . . Ye should only meddle with such grievances as yourselves do know had need of reformation, or had informations thereof in your countries for which you serve: and not so to multiply them as might make it noised amongst the people that all things in the government were amiss and out of frame'.[23] In drawing this distinction James was in fact appealing to members' self-interest, for they all belonged to the political nation, that tiny minority of the population which, on account of its wealth and status, ruled over the majority. In the absence of a police force or standing army, the maintenance of social discipline depended upon ingrained habits of deference, which needed careful cultivation. By securing the redress of genuine grievances, the privileged minority could help allay social discontent; but if they went beyond this and called into question the whole structure of authority, they would be shaking the foundations of their own position.

James was not content simply to acknowledge the Commons' right to inform him of abuses in his government and to petition him for reformation; he added that by so doing they would enable him to 'show himself to be a just and faithful King unto you'.[24] The duty of a King was to act justly, because this promoted harmony and strengthened the bonds of love between him and his people. It also created an atmosphere of good will in which the subjects could freely express their affection in its most tangible form by supplying the

King's necessities. In James's own words, it was in Parliament that 'the King is to open himself in his wants, and the people to supply them. For this I minister – and will ever be ready, by God's help, to minister – justice and mercy unto my people. And where this is done on my part (which shall not fail) and on yours (which should not) the harmony will be sweet between Prince and people, and my throne and your place stand firm'.[25] The same point was made, more mellifluously, by Bacon when he described Parliament as the '*intercursus magnus*, the great intercourse and main current of graces and donatives from the King to the people, from the people to the King'.[26]

In other words, the granting of supply and the redress of grievances were two sides of the same coin. They were an integral and essential part of the 'frame of monarchy' which had given England such a long period of stability. The King could raise money by use of his prerogative, but as Bacon emphasised, this was 'slow coming in, and hath not conjoined with it the point of honour and reputation'.[27] Sir Thomas Lake, who was a Privy Councillor and shortly to become Secretary of State, indicated a similar attitude when he told a meeting of the Privy Council that was considering how to raise money, in September 1615, that he preferred 'the way by Parliament before any other, because it worketh to both the points of subsistence – that is, reputation as well as means – in settling of love and goodwill between the King and his people'.[28]

Redress of grievances, whether it came through Bills, proclamations, or the pardon for technical offences customarily granted by the King at the end of a parliamentary session, was not simply a thankoffering on his part for the supply voted by his subjects. It was also a clear demonstration that the Commons were fulfilling their responsibility towards their constituents. An 'addled' Parliament, in which no Acts were passed, did nothing for the reputation of its members. After the abrupt ending of the 1621 Parliament, for instance, when the Council ordered the collection of a Benevolence, John Chamberlain made the bitter comment that 'the wilfulness of the Lower House hath brought us to these terms'.[29] Members of the Commons were always involved in a difficult balancing act, for they had to put pressure on the King to secure the redress of what they (but not necessarily he) defined as grievances, yet to avoid pressing him so hard that he decided to cut his losses and bring proceedings to an end. If they voted supply too quickly they might be left with nothing to show for their pains: as Edward Alford put it, speaking in the troubled winter session of 1621, 'I did desire that in regard we had given away our two subsidies and done no good for our country, that we might have some care saving of our reputations, for I was ashamed that it should be bruited that we should do nothing but give away their monies and do nothing for them'.[30] Some members wanted to compel the King to grant them more time by stopping all business – going on strike, as it were – but Sir Thomas Wentworth declared that 'he had rather present his country [i.e. county] with good laws with a New Year's gift than feed them on Christmas Day with plums and hopes'. A few Bills were better than none, he argued; therefore 'let's all set to our hands, lest we return like children with empty vessels, ashamed'.[31]

One obvious solution to the problem with which the Commons were so frequently faced would have been to hold up their vote of supply until they had secured everything they wanted, but in James's reign they resorted to this device only once, in 1614, when it had disastrous consequences. The King regarded such tactics as blackmail, to which he would not yield. Furthermore, they ran counter to the belief that a Parliament should be a symbol of unity, a witness to the harmony between the King and his people. A voluntary offering by the House of Commons was the clearest possible demonstration of the subjects' love for their sovereign; its denial implied the contrary. Mr Brooke, speaking in the relatively harmonious first session of 1621, reminded fellow members of the Commons that 'it's reported among foreign nations that there is a distaste between the King and his people, and therefore they less fear us than heretofore. I would be glad that by our willingness to give, this ill conceit might now be taken out of their minds'.[32] The House duly voted two subsidies, and James responded by thanking them for 'this their free, noble, and no merchantlike dealing' which he felt confident would produce 'two notable effects. First, his honour and credit abroad; secondly, that it should breed such good blood in him as he would strive, nay hunt, to find out the grievances and oppressions of his loving subjects, and relieve them, and that therein he would meet with his subjects more than halfway'.[33]

James's reference to 'no merchantlike dealing' illustrates his deep aversion to any idea that concessions on his part should be traded for money; this was not the way in which a King should deal with his subjects or subjects with their King. It could be argued that his attitude, and that of the members of the Commons who expressed similar views, was hypocritical, for clearly there was a close link between the 'graces' granted by the crown and the 'donatives' proffered by the Commons. Members of the Lower House could be blunt in pointing this out. In 1610, when the Commons were trying to persuade James to give up Impositions and he merely offered to outlaw them for the future, they voted the niggardly sum of one subsidy and fifteenth, 'which a knavish burgess said – but in the hearing of few – would do the King much good and serve as a *subpoena ad melius responderum* ["a formal demand for a better response"]'.[34] No doubt the 'knavish burgess' was saying aloud what many members secretly believed, but it is significant that he confined his remark to a small circle and that even so it was noted. Mr Ashley, speaking in the 1614 Parliament, phrased the same sentiment in less offensive terms when he advised members 'to have Bills of grace passed, and to give proportionately according to the redresses'.[35] In 1621 he was more forceful in his expression: 'we must give presently [i.e. at once] because of present perils, but must have some retribution . . . Give with one hand and take with the other, in a parliamentary course'.[36]

These and many other comments in the same vein make it clear that both King and Commons acted on the assumption that supply and redress of grievances were intimately linked and that some sort of bargaining was inevitable if the demands of both parties were to be satisfied. But this was predicated upon an even more basic assumption, that it was the duty of subjects to relieve the King's necessities and the moral obligation of the King to remedy abuses in his government. Bargaining was a secondary stage, and if it became too pronounced it distorted the relationship between the King and the representatives of his people and led to the sort of merchantlike dealing that James abhorred. When the Commons gave, they should give freely; likewise with the King. To some extent it was simply a matter of style, but outward forms were held to embody inner truths, and the emphasis on honourable dealing within the context of a loving relationship helped to maintain a harmony that benefited all those who were involved.

AUCTIONING THE PREROGATIVE

The first major breach of this convention in James's reign came in 1610, when Salisbury proposed the Great Contract (see p. 174). The very term 'contract' implied merchantlike dealing, and this makes it even more surprising that James authorised Salisbury to take this particular step. No doubt Salisbury presented it to the King in as favourable a light as possible, playing down the element of bargaining. Indeed, it may be that his initial offer of ten specific concessions was all he originally had in mind, a ready-made package that the Commons could either accept or reject. If this was the case, then it was the Commons who, by brushing aside the ten points and insisting on the abolition of wardship, began the process of haggling.

James may have been persuaded by Salisbury that his financial position was so desperate that only unconventional measures could remedy it. If so, his anger at the collapse of the Contract would have been caused not simply by disappointment but by the awareness that he had broken with his deeply held principles to no effect. This would also explain the asperity which marked his comments on Salisbury after the Lord Treasurer's death. If the Great Contract had succeeded, then all doubts and reservations would have been submerged – at any rate for a time. But when it failed they were merely reinforced, as Bacon made plain when he submitted his opinion to the King in 1613 on the question of holding another Parliament. 'It was no marvel the last Parliament, men being possessed with a bargain, if it bred in them an indisposition to give' observed Bacon, and he advised James in any future Parliament to 'put off the person of a merchant and contractor, and rest upon the person of a King'.[37]

The Great Contract was a further breach with convention in that the King offered not merely to confine his prerogative within the bounds of law – which was what redress of grievances amounted to – but to abandon certain elements of it altogether. The distinction is not quite as clear-cut as it seems at first sight. Purveyance, for instance, had been so grievous in its execution, despite the existence of innumerable statutes designed to restrain it, that it was now widely viewed as being in itself an abuse. Perhaps for this reason Salisbury included it among the ten points which he offered to the Commons in February 1610. Wardship was a different matter, for although it was deeply resented it was not regarded either as illegal or as an abuse of the prerogative. There were abuses connected with it – as Salisbury acknowledged by proposing to make the application of wardship less onerous – but it clearly belonged in a different category from purveyance. Salisbury implied, by suggesting reform rather than abolition, that the King intended to retain wardship. Only subsequently did he, and James, put it up for sale.

Auctioning off aspects of the prerogative was a dangerous precedent, and one which James was careful not to repeat. By cancelling oppressive monopolies in 1621 he preserved the crown's right to grant patents in the first instance. This right was circumscribed by the Monopolies Act of 1624, the first statutory invasion of the prerogative, but that could be regarded as an act of grace on the part of the King and not the consequence of bargaining between him and the Commons. Much the same was true of James's proffer of appropriation of supply in 1624. Had he been left to his own devices James would probably not have made such a move, but by accepting Buckingham's proposal and taking the initiative himself he preserved the crown's theoretical rights while agreeing to limit them in this particular instance.

It was in 1628, under Charles I, that the next major auction of the prerogative took place, and on this occasion the element of bargaining was explicit, for the Commons deliberately held up their vote of supply until the King had accepted the Petition of Right which they had framed (see p. 338). Although their manoeuvre was successful, the Petition was less of a safeguard than it seemed, for it raised the question whether the crown could divest itself of its prerogatives. Salisbury, when he proposed the Great Contract, had explicitly excluded 'matters of sovereignty' inherent in the crown, and awareness of this important distinction may have prompted the Commons to insist, in 1628, that they were asking for nothing new, merely a clarification of the *status quo*. Charles was not convinced by their arguments and turned to the judges for advice. He asked them whether by granting the Petition 'he doth not thereby conclude himself from committing or restraining a subject for any time or cause whatsoever without showing cause?' The judges replied that 'every law, after it is made, hath its exposition . . . which is left to the court of justice to determine', but they assured him that 'although the Petition be granted, there is no fear of conclusion, as in the question is intimated'.[38] In other words, whatever the King might agree to do under parliamentary pressure, he could not, in the last resort, either deprive himself or be deprived of those prerogatives which formed an integral part of the English system of government. Not even Parliament could do this – except in circumstances where customary ways of doing things had been totally abandoned.

The final stage in parliamentary invasion of the prerogative began in November 1640, with the assembling of the Long Parliament. By this time, however, the balance of power between the King and the two Houses had shifted so markedly against him that although the element of bargaining was still present, insofar as the Commons agreed to finance the government only in return for the abolition of the prerogative courts and other concessions, Charles had virtually no choice. Either he accepted the Commons' terms or he ceased to be able to rule effectively, if at all. Whether his acceptance made any difference in the long run remains a moot point. Charles was accused, both at the time and subsequently, of being untrustworthy, but it could be argued that the Commons had forced him into this position by making him agree to part with inalienable prerogatives. In fact, by this time the conventions of the constitution were coming apart at the seams, and although traditional language was used it no longer corresponded to political realities.

PARLIAMENTARY JURISDICTION

In the early Stuart period Parliament had a judicial as well as a legislative role, and this became more marked than it had been since the late Middle Ages as the Commons turned their anger against those servants of the crown whom they accused of abusing the King's trust. If the culprit was a member of their own House they had the right to expel or imprison him. If not, they needed the co-operation of the Lords, who had inherited the residuary powers of the medieval High Court of Parliament. It was at the prompting of the Commons that the Lords began once again to exercise their powers of jurisdiction. The Commons moved hesitantly at first, and constantly turned to late-medieval precedents for guidance. When, in 1621, they stumbled upon evidence that no less a person than the Lord Chancellor had been taking bribes, they handed it over to the Lords, who then pursued their own investigations. Three years later, however, the Commons had refined their techniques, and when they attacked Lord Treasurer Middlesex they took over the whole business of prosecution. The process was well summarised by John Pym, speaking in April 1621:

That we have an interest in judgment, it is well known, for the High Court of Parliament is the great eye of the kingdom, to find out offences and punish them. At first it was but one House; after, it was divided for some causes, and as it is divided so is the power of it also divided. The power of inquisition is left to this House; the power of judgment to the Higher.[39]

Impeachment was a legal process, carried out in the King's name, but no early Stuart monarch ever attempted to inhibit such action by denying it his authority. The King had the right to issue a pardon under the great seal to anyone convicted and sentenced as a result of impeachment proceedings, and Charles I used this to rehabilitate Roger Mainwaring who, in 1628, had been disabled by the Lords' judgment from holding any ecclesiastical dignity. It was left to the Long Parliament to renew the action against Mainwaring, who by this time had become Bishop of St David's. The King could also bring pressure to bear upon the House of Lords to throw out an impeachment, but this could be counter-productive. In 1626, for instance, the Lords preferred co-operation with the Commons to compliance with the King's wishes, and Charles had to dissolve Parliament in order to prevent the impeachment proceedings against his chief minister, Buckingham, being carried through to a successful conclusion.

The major weakness of impeachment as a political weapon was that it depended upon proving that the accused person had been guilty of criminal behaviour. Buckingham was accused of 'misdemeanours, misprisions, offences and crimes',[40] Strafford of high treason, but these charges were difficult to sustain in view of the fact that both men had been acting in the King's name and with his full authority. In Strafford's case the evidence against him was so unconvincing that the Lords, despite the pressure of public opinion, were unwilling to convict. The Commons therefore had recourse to an Act of attainder, which recorded a judgment and pronounced sentence without the inconvenience of a formal trial. This was a much more nakedly 'political' procedure and therefore marginally more acceptable to those members of the Upper House who sympathised with the Commons' objective but did not wish to compromise their own integrity as judges.

THE COMMONS' PRIVILEGE OF FREE SPEECH

Historically speaking, Parliament was a council, an enlarged version of the *magnum concilium* to which the medieval rulers of England had turned for advice on great matters. But just as the Privy Council dealt only with topics submitted to it by the King, so Parliament – in theory at any rate – was not authorised to discuss 'matters of state' unless specifically invited to do so by the sovereign. Members were entitled to raise 'commonwealth' issues affecting themselves and their constituents, but other aspects of government, and in particular foreign affairs, were outside their terms of reference. Yet the writ of summons to parliaments formally instructed the newly-elected members that they were summoned to advise and deliberate with the King '*pro quibusdam arduis et urgentibus negotiis, nos, statum, et defensionem regni nostri Angliae et Ecclesiae Anglicanae concernentibus* ["about certain arduous and urgent affairs concerning the King, state, and defence of the realm, and of the Church of England"]'[41] In 1621, when war was threatening, James, in his opening speech to Parliament, called members' attention to the wording of the writ, thereby inviting, and authorising, them to take into their consideration the prerogative matter of foreign policy. However, this was a terrain with which the Commons were unfamiliar, and they trod with uncertain steps, looking for guidance all the way. In the end they misread the signals, and the 1621 Parliament, which had begun so harmoniously, ended with an open and bitter quarrel between the King and the Lower House over the question of the degree of free speech which it could lay claim to (see p. 140).

This was an issue which had caused tension in Elizabeth's reign, and the Queen had taken care to clarify her own attitude. The Lord Keeper informed members of the Commons in 1593 'that Her Majesty granteth you liberal, but not licentious, speech; liberty therefore, but with due limitation'. They had the right to give their opinion on proposed legislation, 'and therein to have a free voice'. This, he said, was 'the very true liberty of the House; not, as some suppose, to speak there of all causes as him listeth, and to frame a form of religion or a state of government as to their idle brains shall seem meetest. She saith no king fit for his state will suffer such absurdities'.[42] James took the same attitude as his illustrious predecessor, drawing a distinction between commonwealth matters, which members were free to raise and discuss, and the formulation of policy, which was solely his concern. He made his position plain in 1621 when he told the Lower House not 'to meddle with complaints against your King, nor with the Church, nor with state matters, nor with princes' prerogatives'.[43]

The distinction between commonwealth matters and matters of state was clear in theory but not, unfortunately, in practice, and demarcation disputes clouded relations between James and his parliaments. James assumed that any such disputes were for him to resolve. Parliament, as he saw it, met at his command to do his business. The privileges which were claimed by both Houses – and, in the case of the Commons, formally conceded by the King at the beginning of each Parliament, at the request of the Speaker – were to enable them to do the King's business more effectively, not to hold it up for reasons of their own. Hence James's insistence that such privileges were of grace and not of right: as he informed the Lower House in March 1604, 'he had no purpose to impeach their privilege, but since they derived all matters of privilege from him, and by his grant, he expected they should not be turned against him'.[44]

If, as James insisted, the Commons' privileges were of grace, it followed that he was under no compulsion to grant them, but this ran counter to most members' basic assumptions. How could they freely and fully debate the 'arduous and urgent' affairs which they were specifically summoned to consider if their ability to do so depended upon the whim of the ruler? The Commons' unofficial spokesmen therefore developed the counter-argument that the House's privileges were part of the fundamental frame of government, as inalienable as the royal prerogative – if not more so.

The first clear expression of this claim was given in the *Form of Apology and Satisfaction* drawn up by a Commons' committee in June 1604. It was never formally adopted by the House, which did not wish to provoke an open clash with the King, but James was aware of its contents, and it may be taken as representing the opinion of a majority of the members. The *Apology* declared unambiguously

first, that our privileges and liberties are our right and due inheritance, no less than our very lands and goods. Secondly, that they cannot be withheld from us, denied or impaired, but with apparent wrong to the whole state of the realm. Thirdly, that our making of request in the entrance of Parliament to enjoy our privilege is an act only of manners, and doth weaken our right no more than our suing to the King for our lands by petition.[45]

Even if James had accepted – which he never did – that the Commons held their privileges of right, he would not thereby have barred himself from defining their boundaries. Like Elizabeth before him, he insisted that the House should not debate prerogative matters without his explicit authorisation, and in 1610, during the last session of his first Parliament, he ordered it to stop discussing the prerogative levies on trade known as Impositions. However, the members were of the opinion that Impositions were taxes unsanctioned by parliamentary grant, and fell within the 'commonwealth' category since they were ultimately paid by their constituents as consumers. The Commons therefore informed James, in May 1610, that 'we hold it an ancient, general and undoubted right of Parliament to debate freely all matters which do properly concern the subject and his right or state; which freedom of debate being once foreclosed, the essence of the liberty of Parliament is withal dissolved'.[46]

It was issues such as Impositions, which were simultaneously matters of state and of commonwealth, which caused the most acerbic exchanges between James and the Lower House. There was no supreme court to act as arbiter, and even if James had been prepared to allow the judges to decide which category a particular topic belonged to, the Commons would never have accepted their decision. The judges were royal appointees, whose attitude might be affected by fear of losing their office. And in any case, the House of Commons – or so members believed – was an integral part of the High Court of Parliament, the highest court in the land, whose verdict in all disputed matters was final. It was therefore up to them to determine the limits upon their freedom of discussion, and they saw nothing wrong or unconstitutional in informing the King of their constituents' opinions, no matter how unwelcome to him these might prove.

When the King and the Commons reached deadlock over the question of freedom of speech, the King could always put an end to it by dissolution. However, this tended to diminish his reputation as well as his revenue, and James was always reluctant, unlike Charles, to take such a course. He did so in 1614, however, when he and the Commons were at loggerheads over Impositions, and again in December 1621 when he warned the Commons 'that none therein shall presume henceforth to meddle with anything concerning our government or deep matters of state'. This provoked the House into complaining that 'Your Majesty doth seem to abridge us of the ancient liberty of Parliament for freedom of speech . . . being our ancient and undoubted right and an inheritance received from our ancestors'. James, equally provoked, riposted with a reminder 'that your privileges were derived from the grace and permission of our ancestors and us' and that they should 'beware to trench upon the prerogative of the crown, which would enforce us, or any just king, to retrench them of their privileges'.[47]

The Commons were unwilling to allow such an assertion to pass unchallenged, since it struck at their very roots. They felt an imperative need to put on record in the most formal way a statement of their own position, so that the privileges which they had themselves inherited could be passed on, undiluted, to their successors. They therefore had recourse to a formal Protestation in which they declared

that the liberties, franchises, privileges and jurisdictions of Parliament are the ancient and undoubted birthright and inheritance of the subjects of England; and that the arduous and urgent affairs concerning the King, state and defence of the realm and of the Church of England, and the maintenance and making of laws and redress of mischiefs and grievances . . . are proper subjects and matters of counsel and debate in Parliament: and that in the handling and proceeding of those businesses every member of the House of Parliament hath, and of right ought to have, freedom of speech to propound, treat, reason and bring to conclusion the same: and that the Commons in Parliament have like liberty and freedom to treat of these matters in such order as in their judgments shall seem fittest.[48]

This was a forceful and succinct summary of the claims which the Commons had been formulating and refining since their first meeting in James's reign. Not simply were their privileges of right – as was indicated by the wording of the writ of summons which they carefully incorporated into the Protestation – but they were to be the umpires in all disputed cases, determining where the boundary was to be drawn between matters of state and of commonwealth. James could not allow such a claim to remain on record in the Journal of the House, since this might have been taken by subsequent generations as implying a tacit acceptance on his part of the principles laid down in it. James, no less than the Commons, acknowledged a duty to his descendants to hand on intact the prerogatives he had inherited. When, therefore, he sent for the Commons' Journal and tore out the Protestation, he was not indulging in a childish tantrum. He was demonstrating in the clearest and most symbolic manner that, whatever the Commons might assert, the ultimate arbiter in all disputed issues was the King.

THE COMMONS' PRIVILEGE OF FREEDOM FROM ARREST

Another privilege which the Speaker requested and the King granted at the opening of every Parliament was freedom from arrest. However, this applied only to *subpoenas* from courts of law, and not to the crown. On a number of occasions Elizabeth had ordered the arrest of members, though she usually took care to state that it was for offences committed outside the House and not for anything they had said or done within. James took the prudent course of calling members to account for their actions only after the session was at an end, despite his warning in 1621 'that we think ourself very free and able to punish any man's misdemeanours in Parliament, as well during their sitting as after'.[49] Following the brief but stormy meeting of the Addled Parliament in 1614, nine members were summoned to appear before the Privy Council, of whom four were subsequently imprisoned in the Tower. In 1621 Sir Edwin Sandys spent a month there, and after the dissolution of Parliament early in 1622 Sir Edward Coke and Sir Robert Phelips suffered the same fate, remaining confined until the late summer. Charles I broke with precedent in 1626 by ordering the arrest of Sir Dudley Digges and Sir John Eliot while Parliament was still in session, but the Commons reacted by refusing to do any business until the detained members were returned to them. Charles released Digges after five days, but held on to Eliot for a few more on the grounds that he had plotted outside the House to disrupt its proceedings.

Eliot took a prominent part in the events of 2 March 1629 which culminated in the Speaker being held down in his chair while resolutions critical of the King's policies were put to the House (see p. 350). He and eight other members were arrested on the following day, a week before the formal dissolution of Parliament. Charles initially intended to bring them to trial before Star Chamber, but this prerogative court expressed doubts about its competence to deal with issues involving parliamentary privilege, and in any case the action of the imprisoned members in suing out writs of *habeas corpus* meant that their cases would have to go before King's Bench. Charles observed the Petition of Right by revealing, in the reply to the writ, that the members were detained for sedition, and although a number of them made their submission and were thereupon released, Eliot, Denzil Holles and Benjamin Valentine were brought to trial in January 1630. The defence lawyers argued that offences committed in Parliament were only punishable there, but Charles had already asked for and received the judges' opinion 'that if a Parliament man, exceeding the privilege of Parliament, do criminally or contemptuously offend His Majesty in the Parliament House, and [is] not then punished, [he] may be punished out of Parliament'.[50]

The accused members were found guilty and sentenced to be imprisoned at the King's pleasure. Holles managed to make his escape, but Eliot was held in the Tower until his death two years later, while Valentine remained a prisoner until the eve of the Short Parliament. Charles did not abandon his claim to punish recalcitrant members even during the unfavourable circumstances of 1640. On the contrary, after the dissolution of the Short Parliament in May of that year he sent the chairman of the Commons' committee on religion to the Tower for refusing to hand over his papers, along with two other members, and ordered a search of the lodgings of John Pym, John Hampden and Sir Walter Erle. Eighteen months later he instructed his Lord Keeper to impeach five members of the Commons – including Hampden, Holles and Pym – before the House of Lords on a charge of high treason.

It is not easy to estimate the effect of imprisonment upon the self-selected and unofficial leaders of the Commons. Insofar as it indicated that they had stepped over the line that divided legitimate or constitutional expression of grievances from what the King regarded as unwarranted invasion of his prerogative, it may have served to restrain them. In the peaceful years of James I the King's assumption that those members of the Commons who provoked opposition to his policies were unprincipled hotheads found some acceptance, as is indicated by Chamberlain's reaction to the Addled Parliament. The 1621 Parliament seems to have been a watershed, for in its second session the question of foreign policy, involving as it did the highly emotional issue of religion, became paramount and remained so for the next decade. Criticism of royal policy now seemed to be based far more upon principle, and therefore attracted a wide measure of popular support. Imprisonment may have been an effective means of restraining dissidence under James, but in the heated atmosphere of the opening years of Charles's reign it was more likely to strengthen opposition, by creating 'martyrs', than to weaken it.

However outspoken the more vocal members of the Commons, the great majority, who said little or nothing, were anxious to avoid confrontation. While Parliament was in being, members could draw sustenance from their sense of corporate identity, but no sooner was the session ended than they became private individuals once again. Sir Henry Withrington's constituents warned him in 1621 not to place himself in the firing line. 'Take heed', they advised him. 'You see what is become of Sir Edwin Sandys. You are brave fellows whilst you are together, but what becomes of you when you are parted?'.[51] It was this awareness of the fundamental weakness of their position that prompted some members to propose that parliamentary privileges should be given a more secure foundation. In 1624, for instance, Edward Alford suggested enshrining them in statute. Sir Francis Seymour, however, looked at the problem from a different angle. Let the Commons assert the right to control their own privileges, for then the punishment of offending members would become the House's responsibility instead of the crown's.[52] James had already pointed out that if the Commons exercised an adequate control over the freedom with which members expressed themselves, he would have no occasion to intervene. Secretary Calvert, speaking on his behalf in the first session of 1621, told the Commons of James's confidence 'that there is no man will so far transgress the bounds of his duty as to give any cause to be questioned for speaking that which becomes him not in this place', and that if any member should 'happen to offend in that kind . . . this House will be more ready to censure him according to his desert than he to require it; whereby His Majesty shall have rather cause to thank the whole body of the House for their dutiful care and respect to his honour than to punish any particular member thereof'.[53]

If the Commons' view of what was 'unbecoming' had been the same as James's, then the King would not have needed to intervene. Difficulties arose from the fact that the two views were rarely identical. This had become apparent even in James's early parliaments. In February 1606, for example, when the House was considering the vexed question of the Union, Sir Christopher Piggot, in the words of the Journal, 'entered into by-matter of invective against the Scots and Scottish nation, using many words of scandal and obloquy ill beseeming such an audience'.[54] The Commons, if this account is to be believed, were deeply shocked, but so anxious were they to press on with the (King's) business in hand that 'his said speech was, for this day, with a general amazement, neglected, without tax or censure'.[55] James was furious when he heard what Piggot had said, and instructed the Council to punish him. The House, no doubt warned by its Councillor members, took pre-emptive action by expelling Piggot and sending him to the Tower. But had they not been prompted to do so, the Commons would probably have taken no action. They may have been shocked by Piggot's mode of expression, but he was only saying aloud what many of them really thought.

Another instance of the Commons' unwillingness to punish members for expressing themselves too freely came at the end of the 1614 session, when the House was in uproar after receiving a message from James warning of his intention to dissolve Parliament. John Hoskins, one of the lawyer members, made a speech full of invective against Scottish beneficiaries of James's liberality, and ended with a reference to the Sicilian Vespers. The clear implication was that if the King continued to show favour to the Scots he would provoke an insurrection. The House was obviously apprehensive about James's likely reaction to Hoskins's diatribe, for it was proposed 'that it should be put to the question whether any member . . . had spoken unbeseeming or scandalous speeches'. When the Speaker asked for names, Sir Henry Wotton called on 'Mr Hoskins to explain himself, what he meant by the Sicilian Vespers'. The diarist who records this incident could not make out Hoskins's reply, but the House was apparently satisfied by it, since it cleared him of all blame.[56] James, however, took a very different view of the matter, and Hoskins was one of the four members despatched to the Tower after the end of the session.

Similar differences of interpretation occurred during the early parliaments of Charles I. In 1626 he was deeply offended by the comment made by Clement Coke, one of Sir Edward's sons and a member of the Commons, that 'it was better to be eaten up by a foreign enemy than to be destroyed at home'.[57] However, the House was of the unanimous opinion 'that neither the words mentioned in Your Majesty's message, nor any other of seditious effect, were spoken by him'. It admitted that in the course of his speech Coke had let fall 'some few words which might admit an ill construction', but it pointed out that he had been instantly checked and asked to explain himself.[58] In the absence of any authoritative shorthand record there was scope for genuine disagreement about what had or had not been said in either House. When, for instance, Sir Dudley Digges presented the Commons' charges against Buckingham to the Lords, he seemed to imply that not only Buckingham but also Charles had been involved in hastening James's death. Charles was so affronted when he heard about this that he ordered Digges's immediate imprisonment, but the Lords subsequently resolved, by a substantial majority, that Digges had never spoken the words alleged against him.

THE PRIVY COUNCILLORS IN PARLIAMENT

Although Charles had been a regular attender in the Upper House when he was Prince, neither he nor James ever took part in debates after they became King. They therefore had no direct knowledge of what went on in Parliament, but had to rely upon reports from Privy Councillors and private members. James was often away in the country while Parliament was in session, but like Elizabeth before him he kept in close touch with events at Westminster. On Thursday 26 April 1621, to take one example, Sir John Jephson complained to the Commons of abuses in the Irish administration; on the following Monday Sir Lionel Cranfield, Master of the Wards and one of the principal Councillors in the Lower House, rose to his feet to report James's anger at Jephson's speech and his insistence that

Ireland had never been in so flourishing a state.[59] It was in this same first session of 1621, which saw the overthrow of the Lord Chancellor, Francis Bacon, that James warned members not to be carried away into a general attack upon his ministers. The very next day, however, Sir Francis Seymour accused the Lord Treasurer, Viscount Mandeville, of dereliction of duty. This was on Saturday 21 April. On the following Tuesday Cranfield informed the House 'that he found the King much discontent, thinking it had been an affront to his speech, saying it was strange his speech had not impression with the House'.[60]

Seymour defended himself by saying that he had spoken only as his conscience moved him, and that it was 'unhappiness to him to have the King misinformed of him'. In order to prevent similar 'misreports' in future, he proposed that 'no member of this House may acquaint the King with anything in question or debate here'.[61] Seymour, an outspoken critic of the government, was supported by a fellow dissident, William Mallory, who argued that any member found guilty of giving the King misleading information about events in the House should be severely punished. In a subsequent discussion of this same issue, Sir Nathaniel Rich referred to a statute of Henry IV's reign which provided 'that no member of either House should inform the King in any cause until it were at an end', and suggested that it should be reenacted.[62]

In the second session of the 1621 Parliament the issue of freedom of speech and the role of Councillors led to further passionate debate. Mallory made the valid point that 'His Majesty is wise, but we have not access to him. We may have things misreported, and be wronged to the King'.[63] Edward Alford was even more outspoken in his condemnation of the part played by Councillors. 'They that now sit with us are *pares* ['equals']; when shortly we shall be called into another room [i.e. the Council chamber] they then shall be our judges; and some must carry tales unto the King, and in carrying such tales misreport things oftentimes'.[64] Sir Dudley Digges, who had already suffered a brief spell of imprisonment for expressing himself too freely in the Addled Parliament, urged 'those that are near the King' not to aggravate matters by misreporting, and the House was sufficiently concerned to set up a committee to consider the matter.[65] The prevailing view was later incorporated into the Commons' Protestation, which concluded with the request 'that if any of the said members be complained of and questioned for anything done or said in Parliament, the same is to be showed to the King by the advice and assent of all the Commons assembled in Parliament, before the King give credence to any private information'.[66]

The accession of Charles I led to no apparent improvement in communications between the Lower House and the King. Members of the Commons clung to the belief that Charles was not accurately informed about either their actions or the intention behind them, and that this was the cause of the ill feeling which increasingly manifested itself. In June 1626 the Speaker expressed the Commons' distress at the thought 'that any misinformation or misrepresentation should at any time render their words or proceedings offensive to Your Majesty'. The King, he pointed out, heard not the words themselves but merely an echo of them, and 'words misreported, though by an echo, or but an echo of an echo, at a third or fourth hand, have oft a louder sound than the voice itself, and may sound disloyalty though the voice had nothing undutiful or illoyal in it'.[67] It was in order to put an end to such 'misreporting' – always assuming it actually took place – that in March 1628 Sir Peter Heyman put forward a Bill to secure the Commons' privileges of freedom of speech and freedom from arrest, which contained the provision 'that no information ought to be given to the King but by both Houses, to prevent all differences that may grow betwixt the King and his people'.[68] Nothing came of this, however, and Sir Thomas Wentworth subsequently gave voice to what had by now become virtually an article of belief in the Commons, that 'misinterpretation is the *malus genius* ['evil spirit'] of this place'.[69]

The Commons were doubtless sincere in believing that the lack of harmony between them and the King was due to 'misreporting' and not – as in fact was usually the case – to fundamental differences of approach and of opinion. They blamed Councillors for not giving the King an accurate account of what took place in the House, but all too frequently they ignored the guidance offered by Councillors and plunged into courses which led to confrontation and were not subject to any other interpretation than that which the King adopted. In April 1628, to give one example, Sir John Coke, who was the leading Councillor in the Commons, informed his fellow members 'with some grief . . . that notice is taken as if this House pressed not upon abuses of power only, but upon power itself'.[70] This was a simple statement of the truth, but the House was unable to accept it as such, and took refuge in the affirmation that 'no person or council can be greater lovers nor maintainers of the prerogative of the crown than we'.[71]

Coke was in a difficult position, for in his own words he was 'in a slippery way between His Majesty and his people'.[72] There was nothing unusual about this, for Privy Councillors had always been the main channel of communication between the King and the Commons. In Elizabeth's reign they had performed their task with outstanding success, but no sooner did James become King than things went wrong. One reason for this was the failure to keep a sufficient number of Councillors in the Lower House. When James's first Parliament assembled in 1604 there were only two Councillors in the Commons, neither of them in any way outstanding. By the beginning of the 1606 session the number had been reduced to one, Sir John Herbert. He was a Secretary of State, but his nickname of 'Mr Secondary Herbert' indicates the generally low opinion of his abilities. Indeed, an observer who had a decade of experience in Elizabethan parliaments behind him confided to a friend 'that I think the state scorneth to have any Privy Councillors of any understanding in that House'.[73]

During the first decade of his rule in England, James left the management of Parliament to his chief minister, Robert Cecil, whom he created Earl of Salisbury. Cecil had been a highly effective manager under Elizabeth, but after his elevation to the peerage he was confined to the House of Lords and had to try to guide the debates in the Commons by proxy. His critics complained that he kept too much power in his own hands, for fear of opening the way to rivals, and it may be that this accounts for the poor quality of the Councillors in the Lower House. If this is the case, it would explain why Cecil's death was almost immediately followed by a report that the King had been 'given to understand that he is ill served in Parliament by reason of the paucity of Councillors and officers of [the] household that were wont to bear great sway in that House'.[74] Shortly before the next Parliament met, in April 1614, James appointed Sir Ralph Winwood as Secretary of State. Winwood, a dour puritan who had served as ambassador to France and the United Provinces, was the sort of man who in normal circumstances would have exercised considerable influence over the Commons, but he was crippled by his lack of experience, for he had never been a member of the House. Furthermore, James, who was anxious to prevent a repetition of the bitterness and deadlock that had marked the previous parliamentary session in 1610, had listened to advice from Bacon and others that the government should prepare a programme for the forthcoming meeting and establish links with those elements in the Commons which were willing to carry it out. As far as the latter proposition was concerned, James did very little, but the rumours of a secret 'undertaking' led to an outcry that Parliament had been packed, and nothing that Winwood and his three fellow Councillors could do was of any avail.

After his experience with the Addled Parliament, James did not summon another until 1621. When this met, the House of Commons included all nine of the non-noble members of the Privy Council, but they had not been adequately briefed, nor did they act as a coherent block. It was one of them, Lionel Cranfield, who set off the attack upon referees which culminated in the overthrow of his fellow Councillor, Lord Chancellor Bacon. As for Sir Edward Coke, still at that time a member of the Council, he acted as though he was a free agent. In the turbulent second session he became even more wayward, and after it was over he was summoned before the Council to account for his actions. Chamberlain reported that 'it was told him he had incurred the King's displeasure for having forgotten the duty of a servant, the duty of a Councillor, and, as might be thought, the duty of a subject'. The King was angry not simply with Coke but with all 'his servants' in the House, and the Solicitor General, Sir Robert Heath, was said to be 'in danger for not interposing himself more earnestly'.[75] Even Secretary Calvert was blamed for not acting in accordance with James's instructions, but he pleaded in justification that he had been guided by 'advice and direction from the Prince'[76] – a clear indication that part of the reason for James's difficulties in this session was conflicting signals from the Court. In 1624, when James's last Parliament met, the Court was split right down the middle, but the predominance of the group led by the Prince and Buckingham, and the fact that the dissidents in the Lower House had been won over to it, ensured an unusually harmonious session.

Buckingham's success in 1624 may have led him to assume that the 1625 Parliament, the first of Charles's reign, would need little managing. He therefore failed to organise the conciliar element in the Commons, or to maintain his links with former dissidents. There was the further problem that the accession of Charles opened the way to active participation in the war that was already raging on the continent, and the planning of military and naval operations demanded a high degree of secrecy. Even if Buckingham had wished to take the Privy Council into his confidence it would not have been easy to do so, since a number of its members resented his monopoly of royal favour and would have preferred to maintain good relations with Spain rather than run the risks attendant upon war. Buckingham found it convenient to work with men like Sir John Coke

– not at that time a Councillor – on whom he knew he could rely, but one of the consequences of this was that he received scant support from the Councillors for some of his initiatives. The most striking example came towards the end of the first session, in July 1625, when Coke, acting on Buckingham's instructions, called for additional supply. In normal circumstances his plea would have been reinforced by speeches from the Privy Councillors, but on this occasion they remained silent, and Coke's proposal was brushed aside. Buckingham obviously learnt his lesson, for in the second session, at Oxford, the Councillors were marshalled behind his plea for further financial aid. Yet the House refused to follow their lead. Mistrust of Buckingham was by now so widespread that no amount of pressure would persuade members to commit themselves to support of his policies.

This distrust came to the fore in the 1626 Parliament, when Buckingham was impeached. His supporters in the House could do little to stem the tide of anger and suspicion which was flowing against him, and the Council was divided – as is shown by the fact that the impeachment was master-minded by the Earl of Pembroke, a Privy Councillor of long standing, and that at least two other Councillors, Lord Keeper Williams and George Abbot, Archbishop of Canterbury, were numbered among the Duke's enemies. The 1628 Parliament began more constructively, presumably because some sort of bargain had been struck between the King and Buckingham on one side, and the Duke's opponents on the other. Pembroke had been reconciled to Buckingham by a marriage alliance, while John Williams had been replaced as Lord Keeper by one of the Duke's clients, Sir Thomas Coventry. In the Lower House the principal government spokesman was once again Sir John Coke, but by this time he was Secretary of State and a member of the Council. He could count on the support of other conciliar members of the Commons, among them Sir Richard Weston, the Chancellor of the Exchequer, and Sir Humphrey May, the Chancellor of the Duchy of Lancaster. But their influence was limited by the fact that they were championing policies which were deeply unpopular.

Buckingham's removal from the scene made no difference, for in the second session of Parliament, in 1629, the Lower House was dominated by unofficial leaders who led it towards confrontation and dissolution. There was an eleven-year gap before the next meeting of Parliament, in April 1640, but Sir John Coke remained Secretary of State until shortly before the session opened, when Sir Henry Vane was appointed in his place. Vane never commanded the degree of respect that Coke had done, nor did he have a united Council behind him, for there were many members of it who had grave reservations about Charles's intentions and capabilities. In the Short Parliament, and even more in the Long Parliament, distrust of the King's ministers and – increasingly – of the King himself, ruled out the sort of compromises that had been possible in James's reign. The Privy Councillors' influence in the Commons had been eroded not so much by their lack of numbers or quality as by their identification with policies that the majority of members were no longer prepared to tolerate.

'TRIBUNES OF THE PEOPLE'

In the second half of Elizabeth's reign the pressure of legislative business had encouraged the development of committees to deal with specific aspects of the Houses' work. There were also 'general' committees, which were ultimately extended to include all the members, and thereby became, in effect, 'unofficial' meetings of the full House, in which the crown's presiding officer – the Speaker in the Commons, the Lord Chancellor or Keeper in the Lords – vacated his chair and no formal record was kept. The advantage of committees was that the standard rules of debate did not apply and members could therefore speak as often as they liked on the issue under discussion. Councillors, because of their prominence in the Elizabethan Commons, spoke more frequently there than other members, and it seems highly likely that the initiative in developing the system of committees came from them. However, with the decline in conciliar influence under James, a device that had previously worked in favour of the crown now began to work against it, for the vacuum left by official spokesmen was filled by unofficial ones. In the 1606 session Salisbury accused John Hare of acting as a 'Tribune of the People' and shortly afterwards Henry Yelverton, noted for his outspokenness, was referred to by a fellow member as 'the old Tribune of the House'.[77] Other terms used to describe critics of the royal government were 'the popular party' and 'the patriots'.[78]

Some of the 'Tribunes' were driven by distrust of the Court, which they regarded as a centre of intrigue, debauchery and corruption where only those addicted to popery and absolutism could flourish, and they therefore deliberately identified themselves with the opposite or 'Country' viewpoint which stressed the need to uphold both the protestant religion and the liberties of the subject. Nicholas Fuller and Edward Alford were typical 'Country' members, and in the unlikely event of their being offered office they would almost certainly have spurned it.[79] But there were other outspokenly critical members of the Commons who would have welcomed the chance to show how much better they could govern the country than those whom the King had entrusted with this task. Their complaints about abuses of power were genuine, but by voicing them as and when they did they were consciously or unconsciously bidding for office.

Those who sought power by challenging the government had to pick their way carefully through the minefield of early Stuart politics, and they often stumbled *en route*. By taking a critical or reforming stance they were likely to bring themselves to the King's attention, but they risked angering him so much that they destroyed their chances of advancement. In 1611, for example, there were rumours that Sir Henry Neville would shortly be made a Privy Councillor, but one of his close acquaintances thought this unlikely, on the grounds that Neville 'did not (like Sir Dudley Carleton) speak in Parliament for the King's demands, but ranged himself with those Patriots who were accounted of a contrary faction to the courtiers; which I think he would not have done if he had aspired to any Court employment'.[80] Neville was not the only aspirant to office who misjudged the effect of his actions in the Commons. James Whitelocke was another. He was hoping to be chosen Recorder of London in 1618, but, as he confided to his journal, he was 'barred from that, by high hand' because of 'a remembrance of my not pleasing the King in Parliament'.[81]

Whitelocke was ambitious and therefore adopted a lower profile and assiduously cultivated Bacon, whose star was at that time rising rapidly. His tactics paid off, for in due course he was appointed Chief Justice of the county palatine of Chester, at which time James bestowed the honour of knighthood upon him. Another dissident member of the Commons was William Hakewill, and when Queen Anne appointed him as her Solicitor in 1617 Bacon commented that it was 'no ill counsel to win or to remove such men'.[82] As an experienced Commons man himself, Bacon knew that only a handful of those who took a critical stand over certain issues were committed oppositionists. By a skilful combination of the carrot and the stick the rest could probably be won over, if only temporarily. In 1613, when James was considering summoning Parliament once again, Bacon reminded him of the need to take account of those members who had made up 'the popular party last Parliament; for the severing of them, intimidating of them, or holding them in hopes'. In order perhaps to encourage James to pursue this course, he added that 'the opposite party heretofore is now dissolved and broken. Yelverton is won; Sandys is fallen off; Crewe and Hyde stand to be Sergeants[-at-Law]; Neville hath his hopes; Martin hath money in his purse; Brock is dead'.[83]

In the event, Bacon's optimism about the collapse of opposition turned out to be unjustified, for the 1614 Parliament was even less tractable than its predecessor. Yet he saw no need to modify his belief that the royal government could always come to terms with its critics if it took appropriate measures. In 1620, when a new Parliament was in prospect, Bacon drew up lists of members whose support could be counted upon: these included not only 'the Privy Councillors and principal statesmen or courtiers' but also 'the gravest and wisest lawyers' and 'the most respected and best tempered knights and gentlemen of the country'. But at the same time he made a careful note of those 'who were the *boutefeus* ["firebrands"] of the last session [1614]: how many of them are dead; how many reduced [to conformity]; and how many remain'.[84]

Among the *boutefeus* of 1614 was Sir Robert Phelips, son of the Speaker of James's first Parliament. Phelips had come to prominence in the Addled Parliament as a doughty defender of the Commons' reputation against the insinuations of Bishop Neile (see p. 118), but it was his outspoken opposition to James's Spanish marriage project in the 1621 Parliament that led to his arrest and subsequent imprisonment. On the face of it, Phelips seems to be a 'Country' member of the same type as Edward Alford. But in fact he would have welcomed appointment to office – as he subsequently demonstrated by soliciting the post of ambassador to the United Provinces[85] – and his intervention in the heated debate that took place in December 1621 was designed to further royal policy rather than frustrate it. Writing from prison, Phelips protested his 'innocency from the crime of coming to the Parliament with a malicious and undutiful intention to oppose His Majesty's designs there . . . and how far I was from being possessed with such undutiful and unsafe affections as have been too uncharitably objected against me'. He had not spoken 'upon design or premeditation' but upon impulse, thinking that what he said 'might induce to His Majesty's ends'. Far from asserting the Commons' right to discuss matters of state, he stressed 'how unfit it is for private men to speak, and how impossible for them rightly to judge of the high designs and secret counsels of princes'.[86]

Phelips had come to grief because his own interpretation of royal objectives did not match the King's. A similar lack of congruity held back Sir Thomas Wentworth, who was also ambitious for office. In 1625, just before the opening of the second session of Parliament at Oxford, he was approached by one of Buckingham's agents and offered the Duke's 'good esteem and favour' if he agreed 'to comply with his ends'. Wentworth replied that he would be glad to serve him 'with quality of an honest man and a gentleman' and was of the opinion that in the ensuing session he 'performed what I had professed'. Yet he opposed the grant of additional supply, which was Buckingham's main objective, and affirmed that the Commons were under no obligation to meet the King's necessities, for 'the engagement of a former Parliament bindeth not this'.[87] Wentworth, like Phelips, seems to have assumed that the favour of the King and of powerful ministers could be secured solely by assurances of loyalty, and did not entail any commitment to defend their policies. This was an extraordinarily naive view and one which Wentworth rapidly abandoned after he became himself a minister, but it shows how a strong 'Country' element persisted in the thinking even of those members of the Commons who were ambitious for a career at Court.

The examples of Phelips and Wentworth may serve as a warning against the temptation to classify critics of royal policy in the Lower House as *de facto* members of a nascent opposition party. They regarded themselves as the King's well-wishers, not as his opponents. When they upheld the privileges of their House or the liberties of free-born Englishmen they did so in the not entirely unjustified belief that the King shared their basic assumptions. In their view the Commons constituted Bacon's ideal of 'a sufficient and well-composed House of the ablest men of the kingdom, fit to be advised with *circa ardui regni* (as the style of the writ goeth)'.[88] As the King's true counsellors they felt bound to give their opinions openly and honestly, but they intended no offence thereby and were upset and puzzled when offence was nevertheless taken. If their views did not always coincide with those of the government, this was only to be expected, but it did not affect their duty to give expression to them. It was up to the King and his ministers to make policy. The Lower House – except for those few members who held government office – was free from such a burden and could act with appropriate irresponsibility. The constitutional convention within which members operated was long established and had hitherto worked reasonably well. Under the combined pressures of population growth, inflation, financial stringency, economic recession, acute religious divisions, and above all, war or threats of war, it began to fall apart, but awareness of this only made members cling to it with increasing desperation. If was fear rather than arrogance, conservatism rather than ambition, loyalty rather than sedition, which conditioned their actions and reactions.

NOTES AND REFERENCES

(*The place of publication is London, unless otherwise stated*)
1. **Wallace Notestein, Frances Helen Relf** & **Hartley Simpson** (eds.) *Commons Debates 1621* (New Haven 1935). Vol. II, pp. 197–98. (Hereafter *Commons Debates 1621*) *The Works of Francis Bacon* ed. James Spedding (1874). Vol. X, p. 105. (Hereafter Bacon *Works*)
2. **S. R. Gardiner** (ed.) *Debates in the House of Commons in 1625* Camden Society (1873), p. 110.
3. **E. R. Foster** (ed.) *Proceedings in Parliament 1610* (New Haven 1966). Vol. 2, p. 105. (Hereafter Foster *Proceedings 1610*)
4. *Commons Debates 1621*. Vol. II, p. 3.
5. *Commons Debates 1621*. Vol. VI, p. 425.
6. **Journals of the House of Commons 1547–1714** (1742). Vol. I, p. 232. (Hereafter *Commons Journals*)
7. Foster *Proceedings 1610*. Vol. 2, p. 309.
8. **The Letters of John Chamberlain** ed. N. E. McClure (Philadelphia 1939). Vol. II, pp. 459–60. (Hereafter Chamberlain *Letters*)
9. Bacon *Works*. Vol. XII, p. 363.
10. **James F. Larkin** & **Paul L. Hughes**(eds.) *Stuart Royal Proclamations*. Vol. I. *Royal Proclamations of King James I* (Oxford 1973), p. 494. (Hereafter Larkin & Hughes *Royal Proclamations*)
11. Bacon *Works* Vol. XII, p. 181.
12. Chamberlain *Letters*. Vol. I, pp. 537–38.
13. Larkin & Hughes *Royal Proclamations*, pp. 67–8.
14. **Francisco de Jesus** *El Hecho de los Tratados del Matrimonio Pretendido por El Principe de Gales con La Serenissima Infanta de España Maria* ed. S. R. Gardiner. Camden Society (1869), p. 288.
15. **Conrad Russell** *Parliaments and English Politics 1621–1629* (Oxford 1979), p. 45.
16. *Commons Journals*. Vol. I, p. 457.
17. *Commons Debates 1621*. Vol. VII, pp. 632–33.
18. *Commons Debates 1621*. Vol. II, pp. 197–98.
19. *Commons Journals*. Vol. I, p. 462.
20. Foster *Proceedings 1610*. Vol. 2, p. 98.
21. **The Political Works of James I** ed. C. H. McIlwain (Cambridge, Mass. 1918), pp. 313–14.
22. Chamberlain *Letters*. Vol. II, pp. 357–58.
23. Foster *Proceedings 1610*. Vol. 2, p. 61.

24. *Commons Debates 1621*. Vol. II, p. 5.
25. *Commons Debates 1621*. Vol. VI, p. 366.
26. Bacon *Works*. Vol. XII, pp. 137–38.
27. Bacon *Works*. Vol. XII, p. 176.
28. Bacon *Works*. Vol. XII, p. 196.
29. Chamberlain *Letters*. Vol. II, p. 421.
30. *Commons Debates 1621*. Vol. III, p. 435, n. 16.
31. *Commons Debates 1621*. Vol. II, pp. 440–41.
32. *Commons Debates 1621*. Vol. II, p. 86.
33. *Commons Debates 1621*. Vol. V, p. 466.
34. **The Court and Times of James the First . . . transcribed by Thomas Birch** ed. R. F. Williams (1849). Vol. I, p. 122. (Hereafter *Court and Times James I*)
35. *Commons Debates 1621*. Vol. VII, p. 655.
36. *Commons Debates 1621*. Vol. V, p. 219.
37. Bacon *Works*. Vol. XI, pp. 370–71.
38. **W. J. Jones** *Politics and the Bench* (1971), p. 165. (Hereafter Jones *Politics and the Bench*)
39. *Commons Debates 1621*. Vol. II, p. 303.
40. **Roger Lockyer** *Buckingham: The Life and Political Career of George Villiers, First Duke of Buckingham 1592–1628* (1981), p. 321. (Hereafter Lockyer *Buckingham*)
41. *Commons Journals*. Vol. I, p. 140.
42. **G. R. Elton** (ed.) *The Tudor Constitution* 2nd edn (Cambridge 1982), p. 274.
43. *Commons Debates 1621*. Vol. VI, p. 372.
44. *Commons Journals*. Vol. I, p. 158.
45. **G. W. Prothero** (ed.) *Select Statutes and other Constitutional Documents illustrative of the Reigns of Elizabeth and James I* (Oxford 1913), p. 288. (Hereafter Prothero *Select Statutes*)
46. Prothero *Select Statutes*, p. 297.
47. Prothero *Select Statutes*, pp. 312–13.
48. Prothero *Select Statutes*, pp. 313–14.
49. Prothero *Select Statutes*, p. 310.
50. Jones *Politics and the Bench*, p. 166.
51. *Commons Debates 1621*. Vol. II, p. 485.
52. *Commons Journals*. Vol. I, p. 719.
53. *Commons Debates 1621*. Vol. V, p. 462.
54. *Commons Journals*. Vol. I, p. 333.
55. *Commons Journals*. Vol. I, p. 333.
56. *Commons Debates 1621*. Vol. VII, p. 652.
57. **John Rushworth** *Historical Collections* (1682). Vol. I, p. 225. (Hereafter Rushworth *Historical Collections*)
58. Rushworth *Historical Collections*. Vol. I, p. 244.
59. *Commons Journals*. Vol. I, pp. 593, 597.
60. *Commons Journals*. Vol. I, p. 589.
61. *Commons Journals*. Vol. I, p. 589.
62. *Commons Debates 1621*. Vol. II, p. 334.
63. *Commons Debates 1621*. Vol. III, p. 437.
64. *Commons Debates 1621*. Vol. II, p. 441.
65. *Commons Debates 1621*. Vol. III, p. 436.

66. Prothero *Select Statutes*, p. 314.
67. Rushworth *Historical Collections*. Vol. I, p. 397.
68. **Robert C. Johnson, Mary Frear Keeler, Maija Jansson Cole** & **William Bidwell** (eds.) *Commons Debates 1628* (New Haven 1977). Vol. II, p. 54. (Hereafter *Commons Debates 1628*)
69. *Commons Debates 1628*. Vol. III, p. 235.
70. *Commons Debates 1628*. Vol. II, p. 430.
71. *Commons Debates 1628*. Vol. II, pp. 436–37.
72. **Wallace Notestein** & **Frances Relf** (eds.) *The Commons' Debates for 1629* (Minneapolis 1921), p. 12.
73. *Court and Times James I* Vol. I, p. 60.
74. Chamberlain *Letters*. Vol. I, p. 359.
75. Chamberlain *Letters* Vol. II, p. 418.
76. *Commons Debates 1621*. Vol. VII. Appx. C, pp. 627–28.
77. *The Parliamentary Diary of Robert Bowyer 1606–1607* ed. D. H. Willson (Minneapolis 1931), pp. 42, 123 n. 1.
78. **D. H. Willson** 'The Earl of Salisbury and the "Court" Party in Parliament 1604–1610' *American Historical Review*. Vol. 36, 1931, p. 279.
79. **Robert Zaller** 'Edward Alford and the Making of Country Radicalism' *Journal of British Studies*. Vol. 22. 1983. **Roland G. Usher** 'Nicholas Fuller: A Forgotten Exponent of English Liberty' *American Historical Review*. Vol. 12. 1906–07.
80. **Historical Manuscripts Commission**. *Report on the Manuscripts of the Duke of Buccleuch & Queensberry* Vol. I. (1899), p. 102.
81. **James Whitelocke** *Liber Famelicus* ed. J. Bruce. Camden Society (1858), p. 679.
82. Bacon *Works*. Vol. XIII, p. 208.
83. Bacon *Works*. Vol. XI, pp. 367, 365.
84. Bacon *Works*. Vol. XIV, p. 116.
85. **Public Record Office** *SP 84*. 127, 144.
86. **Somerset Record Office** *Phelips MSS*. DD/PH/224, 82–90 fol. 145.
87. Lockyer *Buckingham*, p. 269.
88. Bacon *Works*. Vol. XIV, p. 116.

CHAPTER SEVEN

The Early Parliaments of James I 1604–1614

THE UNION

The opening session of James's first Parliament began with a dispute over which member had been returned for the county of Buckinghamshire. One of the candidates was Sir John Fortescue, a Privy Councillor whose presence in the Lower House would have been welcomed by the government. He had been defeated by Sir Francis Goodwin, but the Chancery office, which was responsible for the issue and return of writs, declared Goodwin's election invalid on the grounds that he had been outlawed for failure to pay his debts. This raised the issue, left unresolved since Elizabeth's reign, of who should decide whether or not an election was valid. It could also be held to affect the fundamental independence of the Lower House, for as Henry Yelverton warned its members, 'a Chancellor may call a Parliament of what persons he will by this course'.[1]

James, who, as a new ruler, was just as concerned to safeguard the rights of the crown as were the Commons to preserve those of Parliament, instructed the House to confer with the Lords before it took any further action. Members were so affronted by this 'extraordinary and unexpected' message[2] that they requested an audience with him in order to elaborate their claim that election returns were a matter for the House alone. James granted the audience, but when it took place he argued that 'by the law this House ought not to meddle with returns' on the grounds that these could be 'corrected or reformed by that court only [i.e. Chancery] into which they are returned'.[3] The Commons, not surprisingly, declined to accept this argument, and the dispute might have developed into an ugly confrontation had not James made another intervention a few days later. This time he informed the House, through the Speaker, 'that he was now distracted in judgment' and therefore 'desired and commanded, as an absolute King, that there might be a conference between the House and the judges'.[4]

The House was stunned into silence by this peremptory message, but there is no reason to assume that members were especially alarmed by James's use of the term 'absolute'. All he was asserting was his rightful authority as a monarch whose claim to the English throne was beyond challenge – a usage identical to that of the Speaker who, in his address of welcome to the new sovereign, had rejoiced in the realisation that 'we have but exchanged our exquisite Queen for an absolute King'.[5] What worried the Commons was the implication that the extent of their privileges might be determined by the judges, for it was part of their basic assumption that the House, as an integral constituent of the High Court of Parliament, should be immune from lesser jurisdictions, including those of the common-law judges. Perhaps it was for this reason that when they considered what their reply should be, one member urged them to petition the King 'that he will be pleased to be present, to hear, moderate and judge the case himself'.[6]

In the event, James was present, and the outcome of the conference was a compromise which left open the question of who should have the last word on disputed elections. The Commons accepted James's ruling that both Goodwin and Fortescue should be disbarred and that a new election should take place. In return, he acknowledged that the House was, as it claimed, a court of record and a judge (though not the sole one) of election returns.[7] The Commons were relieved at this outcome, which gave them more than had at one time seemed likely, and they sent a delegation to convey their thanks to the King. James took the occasion to pour balm upon any remaining wounds. The whole question, he insisted, had been 'unhappily cast upon him; for he carried as great a respect to our privileges as ever any prince did. He was no ground-searcher. He was of the mind that our privileges was his strength'.[8] This was, in effect, the end of the Buckinghamshire election dispute, for although it was referred to subsequently in the *Form of Apology*, the framers of that document were careful to state 'that the controversy was between the Court of Chancery and our court, an unusual controversy between courts about their pre-eminences and privileges'. There was no question, they insisted, of a clash between the Commons and the King, 'for God forbid that between so gracious a sovereign and so dutiful and loving subjects any difference should arise'.[9]

The *Apology* also made reference to another topic which had caused dissension between James and the Commons, namely the Union. 'True it is,' the framers admitted, 'we were long in treating and debating the matter of Union', but this was not because of any factious opposition to the King's desires. On the contrary, the causes of delay were to be found in the complexity of the issues involved: 'the propositions were new, the importance great, the consequences far-reaching and not discoverable but by long disputes' in which 'each [member] hath liberty to speak'.[10] James would have agreed about the importance of the Union, but for him the matter was a straightforward and relatively simple one. He was, by his descent from Henry VII, the heir of the Tudors as well as the Stuarts, and no sooner was he born than his mother, Mary, Queen of Scots, hailed him as 'the son whom I hope shall first unite the two kingdoms of Scotland and England'.[11] James had to wait nearly thirty-seven years for the fulfilment of his destiny, but soon after the news reached him, in late March 1603, that the throne of England was now his, he issued orders for new signets to be made in which the arms of England and Scotland should be united. He also informed the Scottish Council that from henceforth the former borderland between his two kingdoms would be 'the very heart of the country'.[12] It was in the same spirit that when he took possession of the English throne he promptly issued a proclamation in which he affirmed that he had 'found in the hearts of all the best disposed subjects of both the realms . . . a most earnest desire that the said happy union should be perfected, the memory of all preterite discontentments abolished, and the inhabitants of both the realms to be the subjects of one kingdom'.[13]

If James could have achieved a total fusion of England and Scotland by the exercise of his prerogative he would have taken the appropriate action immediately. Union, however, on whatever terms it was made, would involve alteration, or at least adjustment, of the laws of each state and this could not be done without Parliament; hence James's promise, in his proclamation, to consult 'the Estates and Parliaments of both the kingdoms' in order to 'make the same to be perfected'.[14] The first English Parliament of the new reign met on 19 March 1604, and when he addressed it a few days later James reminded the members that he had brought with him to the throne the priceless gift of internal peace. No longer should the Scots and English be enemies, nor was there any natural, as distinct from human, reason why they should ever have been so. 'Hath not God first united these two kingdoms both in language, religion, and similitude of manners?' James asked his audience. 'Hath He not made us all in one island . . . separated neither by sea nor great river, mountain, nor other strength of nature, but only by little small brooks or demolished little walls?'. All that was now required, as James saw it, was for the two Houses to bring the divine plan to fruition by removing the last obstacles that divided his twin kingdoms. 'I am assured,' he added, 'that no honest subject of whatsoever degree within my whole dominions is less glad of this joyful union than I am'. If there were any 'would-be hinderers of this work' they could only be 'blinded with ignorance or else transported with malice, being unable to live in a well-governed commonwealth, and only delighting to fish in troubled waters'.[15]

In his eagerness to bring about the Union, James either forgot or failed to realise that centuries of hostility and prejudice could not be eradicated overnight. As a Scotsman himself he knew that his native land was far from being a backwater of civilisation, given over to barbarism, but his newly-acquired English subjects, including those many members of the House of Commons who had never ventured north of the border, would take a lot of persuading that this was indeed the case. While James, as Bacon noted, 'hasteneth to a mixture of both kingdoms and nations faster perhaps than policy will conveniently bear',[16] the Commons preferred to put off the moment of decision. James gave them several weeks and then sent them a message to remind them that the groundwork of the statutory Union needed to be laid in the present session if it was to be put into effect during the ensuing one. His initiative was followed up by the Lords who proposed, at a conference with the Commons, that the names of *England* and *Scotland* should be subsumed in that of *Great Britain* and that both Houses should choose commissioners to meet with their Scottish counterparts and draw up detailed drafts of the appropriate legislation.

The Commons discussed this suggestion on 19 April and it became apparent that many members had doubts about the wisdom of the proposed course. In particular Sir Edwin Sandys argued against the change of name. This might seem a simple matter, he said, but 'the ground of every name is the nature of the thing' and the *thing* in question was an unknown quantity. It was not even certain that an English Parliament could 'make laws to bind *Britannia*'. Nor could it be assumed that the liberties won by earlier generations of Englishmen would be passed on to the newly-denominated Britons: 'as our predecessors have left us free,' he warned members, 'so [are] we to leave our successors without prejudice'.[17] The House found this argument convincing, despite Secretary Herbert's assurance that 'taking the name of *Britain* will not take away *England*', and resolved that it would not consider the change of name 'before the union in government be treated and resolved'.[18]

On the following day, 20 April, James addressed the joint committee for the Union set up by both Houses and proposed that Parliament should pass an Act giving statutory recognition to the Union which had already been brought about by his accession. Parliament should also authorise him to assume the title of *King of Great Britain*, and should appoint commissioners to confer with their Scottish counterparts about all the other details which needed to be settled before the union of states, as distinct from the union of crowns, could come into effect. Since opinion in the Commons was clearly divided over the major issues, particularly that of the new royal style, it was left to the joint committee for the Union to give a lead, but as Bacon (who was a member of the committee) informed the Commons on 25 April 'the more we wade, the more we doubt'.[19] In a debate on the following day Sir Edwin Sandys renewed his attack upon the proposed change of style: 'by this name [of *Britain*]', he declared 'the kingdom of England is dissolved'. It was all very well for James to protest that the change of name would not involve any change in the laws or liberties of his English subjects, but this was patently not the case: 'the King cannot preserve the fundamental laws by uniting' any more than a goldsmith, instructed to fuse two crowns into one, could do so and yet at the same time preserve the originals.[20]

Sandys was not simply being cantankerous. James, in an attempt to reassure public opinion, instructed the judges 'upon their consciences to God and their allegiances to me, to declare the truth if I may not at this time use the name of *Britain*, warranted by Act of Parliament, without the direct abrogation of the laws'.[21] No doubt he assumed that their reply would be favourable to him, but on 28 April Robert Cecil reported that 'all the judges of the realm have joined with the opinion of three parts of the House that the first hour wherein the Parliament gives the King the name of *Great Britany* there followeth necessarily . . . an utter extinction of all the laws now in force'.[22] The committee for the Union held its meeting on the same day, and the Lord Chancellor, as well as reporting the judges' decision, added that the King had never propounded the change of name 'definitively, but conditionally'.[23] Since the basic condition of preserving the fundamental laws could not, apparently, be met, the project was to be allowed to lapse. The committee decided that it was 'a thing left and no more to be spoken of'. Their attention was henceforth to be concentrated upon the naming of the commissioners.[24]

James's temper had clearly not been improved by the rebuff administered him by the judges, for in an attempt to speed up the Commons' proceedings he sent them a letter on 1 May in which he bluntly stated his view that the project of the Union had not been 'so willingly embraced by you as the worthiness of the matter doth well deserve . . . Nothing can stay you from hearkening unto it but jealousy and distrust either of me, the propounder, or of the matter by me propounded. If of me, then do ye both me and yourselves an infinite wrong . . . but if your distrust be of the matter itself, then distrust ye nothing but your own wisdoms or honesties'. He urged them not to allow themselves to 'be transported with the curiosity of a few giddy heads' but, 'by the away-taking of that partition wall which already, by God's providence, in my blood is rent asunder, to establish my throne and your body politic in a perpetual and flourishing peace'.[25] The Commons resented this admonition and were only just dissuaded from pressing for an audience at which they could justify their action – or, rather, inaction. James assured them, in a subsequent message, that had they come to him he 'would have explained himself and endeavoured to have given them satisfaction'. Now that they had decided not to do so, however, 'he alloweth . . . their course, because he taketh it to proceed from their love'.[26]

The Commons remained sensitive to the accusation that they had engaged in unnecessary delaying tactics, as was shown by their angry reaction to the publication by John Thornborough, Bishop of Bristol, of *A Discourse plainly proving the evident Utility and urgent Necessity of the desired happy Union of England and Scotland*, which, according to one member, tended 'to the derogation and scandal of the proceedings of the House'.[27] On 1 June the Commons appointed a committee 'to peruse and survey the book published by the Bishop of Bristol' in readiness for a conference on the matter with the Lords, but on the same day they also gave a second reading to the Bill for naming commissioners, which was described, not without cause, as being 'like winter fruit, that ripens slowly'.[28] The third reading followed the next day and the Bill was sent up to the Lords, who received it 'with great applause'.[29] The last apparent obstacle to harmony was removed when the Bishop of Bristol made a public apology in the Upper House for unintentionally defaming the Lower, but the self-justificatory references to the Commons' behaviour made in the *Form of Apology* drawn up shortly afterwards showed that a residue of bitterness remained.

James ordered the commissioners to hold their first meeting on 20 October 1604, but on that very day he issued a proclamation in which he announced that

seeing there is undoubtedly but one head to both peoples, which is ourself, and that unfeignedly we have but one heart and mind to communicate equally to both states, as lines issuing from one centre, our justice, our favours, and whatsoever else dependeth upon the unity of our supreme power over both . . . we have thought good to discontinue the divided names of *England* and *Scotland* out of our regal style, and do intend and resolve to take and assume unto us . . . the name and style of *King of Great Britain*.[30]

It seems likely that James was following the advice of Bacon, who had not only drawn up a draft proclamation himself – though it differed considerably from the one that was actually issued – but had argued in favour of this particular course, on the grounds that a proclamation, unlike a statute, left the law intact: 'for then the usual names must needs remain in writs and records, the forms whereof cannot be altered but by Act of Parliament, and so the point of honour satisfied. And again, your proclamation altereth no law, and so the scruple of a tacit or implied alteration of laws [is] likewise satisfied'.[31]

Bacon was technically correct, and indeed the judges, when they gave their opinion about the adverse effects of a change of style, had only been considering a statutory alteration. Yet the decision to effect by proclamation what Parliament had declined to effect by statute was a calculated affront. Moreover it brought to the fore the thorny question of the relationship between the royal prerogative on the one hand and statute and common law on the other that was already causing apprehension among many of James's subjects. James had hoped that the Union would be swiftly and painlessly achieved and would symbolise not merely the friendship between his two kingdoms but also the harmony that would characterise relations between him and his newly-acquired English subjects. In the event the effort to achieve the statutory Union had quite the opposite effect. It left James dissatisfied with the Commons – or certain elements of it – and the Commons increasingly apprehensive about the constitutional assumptions of their new ruler. As the framers of the *Form of Apology* put it, 'what cause we, your poor Commons, have to watch over our privileges is manifest in itself to all men. The prerogatives of princes may easily, and do daily, grow; the privileges of the subject are for the most part at an everlasting stand'.[32]

The English and Scottish commissioners appointed by their respective parliaments took a mere six weeks to conclude their discussions, and by early December had agreed draft proposals. The English Parliament was due to reassemble in February 1605, but an outbreak of plague forced a postponement until the late autumn. When at last it did meet it was under the shadow of the Gunpowder Plot, and after a relatively short session, taken up mainly with supply, it went into recess until the winter of 1606. When he opened the third session James immediately returned to the subject of the Union, which he described as 'the greatest and weightiest matter of all'.[33] He called upon the Houses to take three major items into their consideration. The first was 'that all laws and ordinances of hostility might be extinguished', since 'there was now no cause of hostility or war' between England and Scotland. The second was 'freedom of commerce and traffic', and the third 'that those that were born his subjects before he was King of England may have this benefit, to be esteemed his subjects now he is King'. He concluded with an exhortation which shows that he had lost none of his enthusiasm for or commitment to this great project: 'therefore now let that which hath been sought so much and so long and so often by blood and by fire and by the sword, now it is brought and wrought by the hand of God, be embraced and received with an Hallelujah . . . and let all at last be compounded and united into one kingdom'.[34]

On 20 November 'the Instrument of the Union, signed and sealed by thirty-nine English and twenty-eight Scottish commissioners', was sent down from the House of Lords for the Commons' consideration.[35] This made specific proposals for the abolition of the hostile laws and the freeing of trade between the two kingdoms. As for the question of nationality, the commissioners were of opinion that the *post-nati* – i.e. 'all those subjects of both the realms born since the decease of Elizabeth, the late Queen of England' – were automatically citizens of the newly-united state; the *pre-nati*, born before James's accession to the English throne, would need to be naturalised by statute. However, in order to quieten fears in both kingdoms about a possible take-over of positions of power and responsibility by natives of the other, the commissioners proposed that the *pre-nati*, though in all other respects to be fully naturalised, should be barred from public office outside the kingdom in which they had been born.[36]

There was no enthusiasm in the Commons for any of these proposals, particularly that of naturalisation insofar as it affected the Scots, and despite repeated admonitions from the Lords they took their time over considering them. Nicholas Fuller, a lawyer and outspoken critic of some of the crown's policies, attacked the whole idea of a general naturalisation. If a man had two meadows, he said, one of which was bare (i.e. Scotland) and the other fertile, would he willingly take down the hedge which divided them? If he did so 'the cattle will rush in in multitudes, and much against their will return'.[37] Bacon did not accept this comparison. 'There is great difference between men and beasts', he argued. Cattle ranged swiftly from one field to another in search of food, but men and their families 'must have stock, means, acquaintance, time of settling'. If Scots had been poised to move south they would have acted 'in this springtime of the King's coming', but few in fact had done so. He urged members to take a broader view, to 'put off private consider-ations and raise our thoughts to the public state', and warned them that 'if there be not a further union by naturalisation, the nature of things doth bear that these kingdoms must break'.[38] Bacon was a respected member of the Lower House but on this issue he was almost certainly in a minority: the majority were of the opinion expressed by a committee that *pre-nati* and *post-nati* should be treated alike because neither had automatic rights of naturalisation. In other words, as Sir Edwin Sandys put it, the Scots were 'better than aliens, but not equal with natural subjects'.[39]

It looked as though the Commons might formalise their opinion by passing a resolution to this effect, and Salisbury encouraged the Speaker to absent himself from the House on the excuse of illness rather than allow this to happen. He was not simply concerned to save the King from further embarrassment; he also wanted to avoid a clash between the Commons and the judges, for at a conference with a Lords' committee in February 1607 the judges, with only one dissenting voice, had given their opinion that the *post-nati* were natural-born subjects of both kingdoms. This was in line with the advice given to James shortly after his accession by the law officers of the crown and with his statement in the proclamation announcing his change of style 'that immediately upon our succession divers of the ancient laws of this realm are *ipso facto* expired, as namely that of . . . the naturalisation of the subjects'.[40] James referred to these judicial opinions when he addressed Parliament on the last day of March 1607. 'I do not deny', he added, 'but judges may err as men, and therefore I do not press you here to swear to all their reasons . . . But remember also it is as possible, and likely, your own lawyers may err, as the judges. Therefore, as I wish you to proceed herein so far as may tend to the weal of both nations, so would I have you, on the other part, to beware to disgrace either my proclamation or the judges'.[41]

Earlier in his speech James had expressed his astonishment at the way in which the simple issue of Union, as he regarded it, had taken up so much time: 'I protest unto you all, when I first propounded the Union I then thought there could have been no more question of it than of your declaration and acknowledgment of my right unto this crown, and that, as two twins, they would have grown up together'. He admitted that he had been over-confident and so sure of the benefits to be gained that he had not anticipated any hostility towards the project: 'I knew mine own end but not others' fears'. He did not conceal his distaste at the way in which the Commons had added 'delay unto delay, searching out, as it were, the very bowels of curiosity', but he acknowledged that 'great matters do ever require great deliberation before they be well concluded' and he assured the members that 'if you will go on, it matters not though you go with leaden feet, so you make still some progress'.[42]

When Parliament reassembled after the break for Easter the Commons again took up the subject of the Union, and Sir Edwin Sandys made the somewhat surprising suggestion that instead of discussing the specific issues put before them by the commissioners they should consider how to bring about a total and complete fusion of the two states. This had originally been James's hope and intention, but the determination of both parliaments to preserve the fundamental laws of their respective kingdoms had compelled him to opt for a partial union. Sandys's suggestion, coming as it did at this late stage, was almost certainly a delaying tactic: given the time spent on relatively straightforward issues, the task of combining English and Scottish law would have dragged out into eternity. On 2 May 1607 James intervened once more to express his opposition to a so-called 'perfect' union, warning the Commons that 'these men that thus interpret, mark them well and you shall find that they propound and pray for that they would most shun'. In any case, he argued, the Union as now projected was 'no more unperfect . . . than a child, that is born without a beard . . . Upon the late Queen's death the child was first brought to light, but to make it a perfect man, to bring it to an accomplished union, it must have time and means. And if it be not [perfect] at the first, blame not me. Blame time. Blame the order of nature'.[43]

James may still have been hoping for a resolution of the question of naturalisation, but there could be none by parliamentary means, for the Commons remained obdurate. They now turned their attention to the hostile laws and on 4 May 1607 gave the first reading to a Bill to abolish them. But even on this topic progress was slow, for as Sir Thomas Wilson observed, members 'fell . . . to mincing every word, both in the title and the preamble'.[44] It was 28 May before Bacon reported from committee that the Bill was almost ready – 'in sight of land; even now anchored'[45] – and it did not receive its third reading until 6 June. This was not the end of the story, however, for the Lords found the Bill defective and proposed a number of amendments. These were accepted by the Commons at the end of June, and the Hostile Laws Bill became law shortly afterwards. None of the other measures proposed by the commissioners was enacted: the mountain had laboured and brought forth a mouse. The legal status of the *post-nati* was eventually clarified by the judges, who gave their verdict, in Calvin's Case, that they were 'in reason and by the common law of England, natural-born subjects within the allegiance of the King of England, and enabled to purchase and have freehold and inheritance of lands in England'.[46] What the Commons had denied the King, the common law – or at any rate its judges – had given him, but this merely confirmed many members in their belief that they knew the law better than its official guardians. Insofar as there was ever any possibility that the judges might be able to act as umpires in disputed constitutional matters, it disappeared in the wake of Bate's Case in 1606 and Calvin's Case in 1608.

PURVEYANCE

James had no doubt that the Union was the principal issue for consideration by his first Parliament, but his order of priorities was not shared by the members. On the first working day of the session, 'after prayers ended and the House [of Commons] settled, with expectation of what should be propounded for the weal of the common subject', Sir Robert Wroth put forward a number of 'matters of most importance', which made no reference to the Union but included wardship, monopolies, and 'the general abuse and grievance of purveyors and cart-takers'.[47] Purveyance was the crown's right to buy provisions and services for the royal household at below market prices, and it had long been a cause of complaint. Prior to the accession of Elizabeth I some forty statutes had been passed defining the limits of purveyance and attempting to eradicate abuses, but the Queen refused to allow any further legislation on this topic for fear that it would erode her rights completely and thereby weaken her financial position. Nevertheless, there was continuing opposition to purveyance and an increasing volume of complaints against the arbitrary actions of the Board of Green Cloth, the household department responsible for provisioning, which claimed exclusive jurisdiction in this sphere.

Public anger, as reflected in the House of Commons, had become so intense by 1589 that John Hare introduced a Bill to limit the powers of the Board of Green Cloth by involving Justices of the Peace, more in tune with local interests, in its jurisdiction. The Queen headed off this challenge by offering to reform abuses, and four members of the Commons, including Hare and Wroth, were appointed to confer with the Privy Council on this matter. Meanwhile the Treasurer, Lord Burghley, pressed ahead with his programme of making composition agreements with the counties and the importing merchants. These had the advantage of substituting defined burdens for uncertain obligations, and thereby reduced the area of dispute. But the Green Cloth, subject to inefficiency and corruption, was never easy to control, and it slipped its shackles almost entirely after the death of Burghley in August 1598.

In 1602 Elizabeth announced her intention to take action. 'I will not suffer this dishonourable spoil and increase that no prince ever before me did', she declared. It was an offence to God and a great grievance to her loving subjects, 'who I understand daily complain, and not without cause, that there is increase daily of carriage and provisions taken from them at low prices and wastefully spent within my Court'.[48] The Green Cloth was once again threatened with reform, but it was saved by the death of Elizabeth in the following year. The problem of purveyance, along with many others, was handed over to James, but he was even more dependent on the system than his predecessor, since he had three households to maintain – his own, Queen Anne's, and Prince Henry's. Moreover his progress through southern England in the summer and autumn of 1603 involved the requisitioning of hundreds of carts, whose aggrieved owners doubtless made their views known to the members elected to James's first Parliament.

Robert Cecil, unlike his father, had little interest in the details of household administration and was also considering the possibility of abandoning some of the crown's more disputed prerogatives, such as wardship and purveyance, in return for statutory provision for an increase in the King's permanent revenue. Wroth was probably acting on Cecil's behalf when he put forward his proposal in March 1604, but while the Commons were prepared to negotiate over the abolition of wardship, their anger against the purveyors was so great that they determined to take direct action. They initially considered a Bill, but on second thoughts they decided to proceed by the less contentious way of a petition, which Hare helped to draft. This began by recalling the 'many good and wholesome statute laws' made to restrain abuses in purveyance, but declared that in spite of them the King's subjects were

mightily oppressed, charged, and disquieted by sundry grievances daily put in use as well by Your Highness's purveyors, [cart-]takers and their ministers, in doing contrary to the laws in most points, as also by Your Highness's officers of the Green Cloth in sending forth commissions directly contrary to the appointment of the foresaid laws and in maintaining the unlawful and unreasonable doings of the said purveyors.[49]

James made a conciliatory reply, expressing his regret 'that the general expectation of relief and solace should be frustrated by these men' and assuring members that while he 'would not neglect the punishment of that which is past' he would also make 'provision for that which is to come'.[50] He ended by inviting the Commons to confer with the Lords and the Privy Council about appropriate reform measures. At this conference the Lords proposed that purveyance should be bought out at a cost of £50,000 a year, thereby putting an end not merely to abuses but to the entire system. When the Commons discussed this proposal, Hare suggested accepting it in principle but lowering the compensation to £20,000 per annum. He was supported by other members, but there was no general agreement on how to proceed, and meanwhile feelings were further inflamed by the Green Cloth's reply to the charges made against it, in which the officers denied the existence of abuses and insisted on the overriding need to uphold the King's prerogative. The House eventually decided to postpone further consideration of the question until the next session.

When the debate on purveyance resumed, in January 1606, Hare put forward a Bill which was far more radical than it seemed. Its principal objective was 'the better execution of sundry statutes touching purveyors and cart-takers', but the effect of this would have been to remove the crown's right to buy goods at lower than market rates and to make the common-law courts, and not the Board of Green Cloth, the arbiter in all disputes. In subsequent conferences with the Lords, Salisbury showed his dislike of these proposals, and insisted that the strained royal finances could not sustain the loss of purveyance unless equivalent recompense was provided. However, many members refused to accept that they should buy out prerogatives which were contrary to statute. Henry Yelverton said he would 'rather compound for common thieves in the highway', and another member asserted that composition would be neither possible nor just, since they had no obligation to pay for that which 'is already ours'.[51] In the event the House insisted on going ahead with Hare's Bill, which was given its third reading on 18 March 1606 and despatched to the Lords. At the same time the Commons provided a sweetener by adding a third subsidy to the two they had already voted.

The Bill made no progress in the Lords, who took their stand on the judges' decision that the existing system of purveyance was in accordance with the law. Meanwhile James had issued a proclamation 'for prevention of future abuses in purveyance' which called attention to the fact that those agents who had been accused of taking up 'far greater quantities of provisions for our house and stable than ever came or were needful for our use' had been prosecuted by the Attorney General in Star Chamber, where many of them had received 'condign punishment by fine, imprisonment, pillory and losing of their ears'. The King expressed the hope that this action would be taken as evidence of his 'good intention to reform abuses' and that his subjects would therefore 'willingly continue their obedience and conformity to those courses for furnishing such provisions as are necessary for us' in view of the fact that purveyance was 'one of the most ancient flowers of the crown'.[52] This proclamation was given a formal reading in the Commons on 25 April, but the House was not impressed. Less than a week later it gave a first reading to a new Bill 'to restrain purveyors, that they exceed not the limits of their commissions',[53] which was subsequently modified in such a way that it became a repeat of Hare's former measure. Although this Bill passed the Commons, the Lords refused to accept it, on the grounds that they had already rejected its predecessor and namesake.

There, for the time being, the matter rested. It was taken up again when Parliament met for its final session in 1610 as part of the negotiations for the Great Contract. This ambitious scheme was a development of Wroth's proposal of 1604, and had it ever come into effect it would have signalled the end of purveyance. The collapse of the Great Contract, and the subsequent dissolution of Parliament, left purveyance unchallenged until 1621, when a Bill 'for carts and carriages' was introduced. This laid down that all purveyance of horses, carts and carriages must be by commission under the great seal, but that the Justices of the Peace were to fix the rates to be paid. They were also made responsible for punishing any purveyor or his agent found guilty of breaking the law, and the officers of the Green Cloth were deprived of their power of imprisonment. The crown's representatives in the Lower House warned members against proceeding in this fashion. The Solicitor General, Sir Robert Heath, argued that the Bill would entirely take away 'the King's prerogative of purveyance for carriages', and he was supported by the Treasurer of the Household, Sir Thomas Edmondes, who added that removing this prerogative 'would be to rob the crown of a flower'.[54] The Chancellor of the Duchy, Sir Humphrey May, adopted a more philosophical line: 'there be some diseases incurable', he said, 'and in some things we can never take the abuse of things from the use. My motion is that we may debate this with the King's officers and let the Bill sleep till we have tried whether we can ease the subjects by that course'.[55] However, members knew from their own experience that consultations led to nothing but fine words and empty promises. They therefore pressed on with the Bill and gave it three readings before the end of the session brought about its premature demise. A similar Bill passed through all its stages in the Lower House in the 1624 Parliament, but once again came to nothing.

Even if the Commons' attempts to deal with purveyance by legislation had been successful it is doubtful whether any great change would have occurred in practice. The Speaker of James's first Parliament had reminded members in May 1604 that a Bill could not bind the King, for he could always 'grant a *non obstante* and dispense with it'.[56] This was the opinion of Sir Edward Coke, who stated in his *Reports* that 'no Act can bind the King from any prerogative which is sole and inseparable to his person, but that he may dispense with it by a *non obstante* . . . Purveyance for the King and his household is incident solely and inseparably to the person of the King; and for this cause the Act of Parliament held in the time of Henry III *De Tallagio Non Concedendo* . . . which bars the King wholly of purveyance, is void'.[57] Not all lawyers agreed with Coke: Bacon, for instance, argued that purveyance, unlike the doing of justice, was not part of the 'essential and inseparable' prerogative, and could therefore be relinquished by the King if he saw fit.[58] Nevertheless, the lack of clarity about the relationship between purveyance and the prerogative – and, for that matter, the relationship between prerogative and the law – left open the question of how effective any attempt to control purveyance by legislation would be. The Commons themselves complained of the disregard by the King's agents of some forty statutes dealing with purveyance, yet they pursued the apparently illogical course of trying to add a forty-first. In effect they were doing little more than registering their strong feelings on this subject.

In retrospect it seems clear that the Commons would have achieved positive results if only they had acknowledged the truth of the King's claim that he could not afford to give up purveyance without compensation, and had agreed to a settlement of the issue on the lines sketched out by Salisbury. Their reluctance to do this arose from two causes. The first was the fear – which, as Coke's pronouncement showed, was well grounded – that the King might wriggle out of any bargain and take the benefits without giving anything of substance in return. The second was their passionate concern to uphold the letter of the law, particularly where it affected the subjects' property. Why should they buy out illegal practices? Why should they pay to have back what was really theirs? If they compensated the King for breaking the law, they would merely encourage him to break it yet again. Their attitude was defensive rather than aggressive, but by standing firm on what they insisted were their legal rights they ruled out the possibility of a compromise solution, offended the King, and drove him into the very courses from which they had been trying to divert him.

THE GREAT CONTRACT

Although Wroth had bracketed purveyance and wardship in his speech at the beginning of the 1604 Parliament, there was an essential difference between the two, as far as the Commons were concerned, for while they regarded purveyance as, at best, quasi-legal, they accepted that the King had a prerogative right to wardship. For this reason they were prepared to consider composition, and they proposed to offer James 'a perpetual and certain revenue out of our lands, not only proportionable to the utmost benefit that any of his progenitors ever reaped hereby, but also with such an overplus and large addition as in great part to supply His Majesty's other necessities'.[59] It was not the Commons' fault that this promising initiative came to nothing, for it was Salisbury who changed his mind and decided not to pursue the matter.[60] Nevertheless, they could not act of their own accord, and therefore had to wait until 1610, when

Salisbury once again proposed a bargain over wardship in the shape of the Great Contract. At a conference on 24 February he emphasised that 'his demand was double: supply, to discharge the King's debts, and support to maintain his state'.

Salisbury went on to explain that repayment of the debts would require £300,000, while a further £150,000 would be needed for the navy, and a similar amount for the establishment of a contingency fund. In other words, the King was asking for £600,000 by way of supply. He would, in addition, require £200,000 annually for support, though in practice this figure would be diminished by 'retribution' to the subjects of those prerogative revenues which he was prepared to part with. These, as Salisbury made clear, did not include 'matters of sovereignty inherent in him, as to call Parliament, his coin, proclamations, war', but James was content to abandon those rights which were proving onerous to his people. Salisbury made specific mention of ten of these – all of them relatively minor, except for purveyance, which, as Salisbury said, 'were a great ease and contentment to the subject if it were extinguished'. There was no hint of abolishing wardship. Indeed one of the provisions, that the relatives or friends of wards should be granted custody of them at fixed and reasonable rates, implied that the King intended it to continue.[61]

It may be that Salisbury, as an old hand at the political game, was reserving wardship as a trump card; but it is equally possible that he genuinely believed that reform of the system rather than outright abolition would be the best course. He may have been influenced by the fact that as well as being Lord Treasurer and Secretary of State he was also Master of the Court of Wards and stood to lose a substantial part of his income if this particular feudal incident was abolished. However, the Commons ignored his ten points and instead asked to know whether James was prepared, in principle, to part with wardship. Salisbury told them the King would not make an immediate reply to this question, and he urged them meanwhile to give careful consideration to the propositions he had put forward. They should not, he said, 'disvalue [these] because they were offered unto us, but rather highly to value them because they were never offered before by any King of this realm unto his subjects'.[62] Nevertheless, he left all options open by adding that if they did compound for wardship they must make a realistic estimate, taking into account the King's present income from this source. Once again, the House declined to consider the ten points but insisted on knowing the King's mind about wardship. They had to wait a further ten days until they were at last informed by the Lord Privy Seal, the Earl of Northampton, that James had given them leave 'to treat concerning the discharge of tenures and all dependances thereupon'.[63]

The Commons now had, in Northampton's phrase, 'the fair Helen which we all did woo',[64] and on 26 March they informed the Lords of their willingness 'to offer for this of tenures alone, and the dependances thereupon, the sum of £100,000 *per annum*'.[65] They had to wait over a month for the King's response, and when it came it amounted to a rejection. Salisbury reminded them that when he had originally put forward the figure of £200,000 for support, this had been for the ten points, which did not include the abolition of wardship; 'and if we thought then, without tenures, that demand to be just, shall we now, casting in the wards, think it enough?'.[66] Yet he did not wish them to abandon negotiations. If they were prepared to offer '£200,000 a year above whatsoever we defalked [i.e. took away] from him [the King] by our contract', they could have not only the wards but also purveyance and the other items in his original propositions, as well as 'what else the Parliament shall think fit . . . not meddling with any matter that bears the mark of sovereignty'.[67]

The Commons did not take up Salisbury's suggestion, and negotiations therefore came to a halt. However, on 2 June they decided to reopen the whole question and to estimate the value not of wardship only but also the remaining seven items from Salisbury's original list – the other three were concerned with feudal tenures and would automatically disappear if wardship was abolished. Not all the members approved of this move, which clearly implied a reconsideration of the Commons' bargaining position. Sir John Savile thought that the £100,000 already offered was as much as the country could afford, and expressed the wish 'that the name of "support" . . . had never been known'. He also argued that 'if we bargain for those seven things offered – which are all either the straining of the prerogative royal upon the liberties of the subjects, or abuses of inferior officers – we shall find that every Parliament there will be something or other found wherein the subject will be grieved, and will be enforced to give a further support for the discharge thereof to the King, so that it will be as usual to give a support as a subsidy'.[68]

The House appointed a committee to consider the matter, and there it was left while members took part in the ceremonies connected with the creation of Prince Henry as Prince of Wales. When Salisbury addressed a joint conference a few days later, on 11

June, he reminded his hearers of the cost of the Prince's installation and of the urgent need to restore the crown's finances in view of the tensions created in Europe by the assassination of Henri IV. He stressed that he appreciated the Commons' hesitation about committing their constituents to permanent and regular taxation for the support of the crown, and therefore suggested that at this stage they should concentrate on supply, by voting subsidies. Then, during the summer recess, they could consult with their constituents and come back prepared to make a bargain over support. He added that consideration of grievances should likewise be postponed, thereby implying that redress would depend upon compliance with the King's wishes over support.

In the course of his speech, Salisbury had confessed that 'the King's demand of £240,000 *per annum* . . . was a great demand'.[69] This was a higher figure than anything yet put forward, and presumably included £40,000 to compensate for the loss of revenue if wardship was abolished. It did not induce the Commons to take a more conciliatory attitude. On the contrary, they rejected Salisbury's implication of a link between support and redress of grievances, and insisted that until they had received a reply to their petition of grievances they would not even consider voting supply. As one member put it, 'if we should now return into our country with nothing for the good of the commonwealth, they would say that we have been all this while like children in catching butterflies'.[70] They were only mollified when Sir Julius Caesar, the Chancellor of the Exchequer, revealed that he had been 'commanded by His Majesty to signify unto them that he was willing to receive their grievances presently'.[71]

Caesar suggested, no doubt with Salisbury's approval, that the House should vote two subsidies, 'whereby His Majesty might be the better encouraged to extend his grace and favour towards us'.[72] Even so the Commons remained obdurate until Caesar announced a further concession. The King, he said, now promised not merely to receive the petition of grievances but also to give his answer to it before the summer recess. At the same time he would state his minimum terms for the Great Contract. Members responded to this olive branch by turning their attention at last to supply, but even though they agreed in principle to offer a niggardly single subsidy, they were unwilling to do so until they were satisfied about their grievances. These were formally presented to James on 7 July; he gave a partial answer on the 10th; and on the following day, the 11th, the Commons resolved to grant him one subsidy and one fifteenth.

Meanwhile, on 26 June, the King had announced his readiness to accept £140,000 for the Contract. This was a net figure, and if the wards and purveyance were both valued at £40,000 it would amount to £220,000 gross. In other words, the King had dropped £20,000 since 11 June. The Commons were not prepared to go as high as £220,000. On 16 July they decided to offer £180,000. Only on the following day, after Salisbury had made known the King's willingness to accept £200,000, but not a penny less, did the Commons raise their offer. The Great Contract was therefore concluded at the cost of £200,000 *per annum* for the abolition of wardship and purveyance and the other seven prerogative revenues left over from Salisbury's original ten. No mention was made of supply, though the grant of one subsidy came nowhere near the £600,000 first asked for. A memorial of the Contract was drawn up and deposited with the Lords, who ordered it to be entered in their Journal. Nothing was said about how the £200,000 *per annum* was to be raised, but it was agreed that it should be 'stable and certain to His Majesty' and that it should not be levied on essentials such as bread and beer or upon the labouring poor.[73] The Lords formally accepted the memorial on the morning of 23 July, and in the afternoon the King prorogued Parliament until 16 October.

During the recess, members were supposed to sound out opinion among their constituents. Having accepted the Contract in principle they should no doubt have recommended it, but the House had been split over the question, and although no division had been called it was estimated that the majority in favour was only about sixty.[74] This meant that a large number of members were still opposed to the Contract, and they may have sought support for their views from their constituents instead of encouraging them to approve of it. Whatever the case, the atmosphere when Parliament reassembled was distinctly unpropitious. Many members delayed their return, and those who did appear at Westminster showed a marked lack of enthusiasm for carrying the Contract to completion. Salisbury tried to stir them up by reminding them that the present situation could not drag on indefinitely: 'you are wise,' he told them, 'and able to consider what it is to leave a King in want, an exhausted treasure, a decayed revenue, the flowers of the crown cropped'. He acknowledged that the Contract was 'a child born after much difficulty, a King full of apprehension, a Lower House full of doubt', but he urged members not to ask for more than was reasonable for fear that they would lose what they already had. 'I speak not by way of menace', he assured them. 'I do not say the King shall send you an

Empson and a Dudley. But this I say: the King must not want'. If there was no Contract, James would have to 'abate his expenses and look carefully to his estate', and this would not be a painless operation. 'Some of you will have a wipe by the way', he warned them; but on no account must the King 'lack [in order] to please you'.[75]

In the debate that followed the report of Salisbury's speech, Sir Maurice Berkeley tried to pinpoint the reason for the Commons' reluctance to carry the Contract through to conclusion. 'Either it must be the want of company that hath made us so backward in this business', he said, 'or it must proceed of somewhat else which makes us more cold in the business than we were in the end of the last session'.[76] He did not specify what this 'somewhat' was, but his opinion became obvious when he proposed that they should call for the King's answer to their petition of grievances to be read over, and consider whether or not it was satisfactory. The Commons approved of this course of action, for they still had reservations about a number of grievances, including prohibitions, proclamations, and, above all, Impositions (see below). Their attitude was probably a reflection of that of the country as a whole, as was indicated by Sir Thomas Beaumont's report that when he went home to Leicestershire during the recess he had been pressed by his constituents 'to tell them whether the Impositions, which were resolved in Parliament to be unlawful, were determined by the King to be laid down'. They also asked that the annual sum granted to the King should not be levied on land alone.[77] These two issues were closely linked, for many members of the House were determined that part of the £200,000 granted to the King should consist in confirmation of the existing Impositions. In other words they would 'give' the King some £70,000 or so which he was already receiving and which he and the judges regarded as rightfully belonging to him.

Before the Commons had time to reconsider the King's reply to their grievances they were summoned to his presence. James chided them for their dilatoriness, and complained that 'as his estate lay a-bleeding, so his honour lay a-bleeding; for to require help of his people and be denied were a disgrace both to him and his people'. He had cause enough 'to have a loathing and satiety of this Contract', but he was prepared to honour his commitments if only the Commons did the same. What he could not tolerate was further delay. He therefore called upon them to give him 'an answer affirmative or negative to your memorial'.[78] When the Commons considered this speech, some members expressed their resentment at the charge of dilatoriness and proposed drawing up a remonstrance justifying their conduct, but on 6 November the King made a last, and decisive, intervention, this time via the Speaker. James began by recalling that it had never been 'his intention, much less his agreement, to proceed in the Contract finally, except he should receive as well supply as support'. What he required by way of supply was £500,000. This was 'far inferior to his necessities', but it was witness of his readiness 'to give relief to the desires of his subjects'. As for support, he would not accept 'of any course of levy which shall not be firm and stable and free from grieving the poorer sort of subjects, or which shall diminish any part of the profit which he doth now receive'.[79] In short, he wanted '£200,000 *de claro*'.[80]

The King insisted, quite correctly, that he had been consistent in his position on the Contract. When Salisbury first proposed it he emphasised the need for supply as well as support, and asked for £600,000. Presumably the £500,000 now demanded by the King took account of the extra subsidy and fifteenth granted by the Commons, which were worth about £100,000. As for support, the King's insistence on '£200,000 *de claro*' seems at first sight to go well beyond the £140,000 net which had formed the basis of the draft agreement enshrined in the memorial. However, the context of James's speech makes it clear that he was not breaking his promise by demanding additional compensation for lost revenues. What he required was no more, and no less, than he had accepted on 17 July. If the Commons wanted additional concessions, they would have to pay for them. If they wished to compensate the officers of the Court of Wards for the loss of their jobs, they must make appropriate provision. Above all, if they intended to bring Impositions within the scope of the Contract, they would have to provide the King with an equivalent revenue by way of compensation.

The members of the Lower House knew exactly what James meant, for when they debated his message one of their number said that the worst thing was that the King 'would have no part of this money [to] be levied out of Impositions, which he conceived to be understood by these words "that there must be no diminishing of the revenue which the King now receiveth"'.[81] The debate showed that by this stage lack of enthusiasm for the Contract had given place to outright hostility, and on 9 November the Commons informed James of their decision not to proceed in it. Some days later Salisbury floated the idea of a mini-Contract on the lines of his original ten points, but the Commons were not interested. In the words of one member, 'since we cannot get the fair Helen, we will not woo her foul apron'.[82]

James had good reason to feel let down. No ruler enjoys having his financial dirty linen washed in public, and James, with his exalted view of the monarch's role and authority, found it particularly distressing. He had relied on Salisbury's advice, but, not for the first time, Salisbury had misread the mood of the Commons. He should surely have realised that a collection of highly conservative country gentlemen could not quickly or easily be persuaded to accept what was in fact a major innovation. Yet as Lord Treasurer, Salisbury had a detailed knowledge of the royal finances which was denied to all but a handful of members of Parliament. He also, of course, knew just how desperate the situation was. The crown could survive for some time still on a hand-to-mouth basis, but in his view its long-term security demanded a radical reconstruction of its financial base. This was what Salisbury proposed – and what was only eventually accomplished after the collapse of the monarchy and its subsequent restoration in 1660. In many ways it is a tribute to Salisbury that the Great Contract came as close as it did to success. Had it been put into effect it would have redounded to his credit. As it was, he had to take the blame for failure. James criticised him for clinging to the Contract long after it should have been abandoned: 'your greatest error hath been that ye ever expected to draw honey out of gall, being a little blinded with the self-love of your own counsel in holding together of this Parliament, whereof all men were despaired (as I have oft told you) but yourself alone'.[83]

The King, who longed to be free of the canker of want, felt bitter at the collapse of his hopes, for which he held the Commons in large part responsible. He reminded Salisbury that he had kept this his first Parliament in being for seven years, 'and from them received more disgraces, censures and ignominies than ever Prince did endure'.[84] Yet even if the Great Contract had been carried through to a conclusion it is doubtful whether the King's needs would have been effectively relieved. Sir Julius Caesar, the Chancellor of the Exchequer, gave his opinion that wards were worth £44,000, purveyance £50,000, and the other prerogative revenues with which the King had agreed to part £21,000, making a total of £115,000. When this was subtracted from the additional revenue of £200,000 to be voted to the King, he would have stood to gain only £85,000. Moreover, the additional revenue was a fixed sum, and its real value would inevitably have been eroded by continuing inflation. It was highly likely that in due course the crown would find itself once again in debt, but extremely unlikely that Parliament would once again come to its relief. In Caesar's words:

after this Contract [is] passed, the King may undoubtedly resolve to receive no more subsidies or fifteenths from his subjects in time of peace. For that is parcel of their groundwork, whereupon they are proposed to win their countries' consent to this Contract. For neither shall the King need it, as they pretend, having that yearly portion from them; neither will their countries be able to furnish any more than that £200,000 a year.[85]

Caesar was of the opinion that the King would be better advised to abandon the Contract and exploit his prerogative revenues. Wardship, he thought, could easily yield an additional £40,000, purveyance £20,000, and other miscellaneous sources £25,000, thereby providing James with the £85,000 net which was all that he stood to gain by the Contract. As for the debt, he proposed a whole series of measures which he believed would effectively eliminate it. Caesar was almost certainly over-optimistic where debt reduction was concerned, but his insistence that the prerogative revenues were expansible was well grounded. After 1610 the crown survived for another thirty years with only occasional grants of parliamentary supply. During the Personal Rule, Charles I received the equivalent of a subsidy every year by levying Ship Money, and by 1640 Impositions were yielding nearly a quarter of a million pounds annually. It is most unlikely that Parliament would have provided revenue on this scale.

The negotiations over the Great Contract provide little support for the view that in James's reign the Commons rarely took the initiative, and that apparent disputes between them and the crown were really reflections of divisions within the royal Council. It seems probable that the Council was divided over the Contract. Indeed, the memorandum from Caesar – who was Salisbury's right-hand man in the Treasury – proves that there were divergent views even among the Councillors who specialised in financial matters. It is possible that some of those who opposed Salisbury, either for personal reasons or out of principle, stirred up opposition in the Lower House, but there is no evidence of this. The Councillor who stood to gain most from discrediting the Treasurer was the Lord Privy Seal, the Earl of Northampton, but he appears to have given Salisbury his full support in public, whatever private reservations he may have had. The Commons acted as they did, and drove a very hard bargain, because they believed it to be in their best interests to do so. By rejecting Salisbury's original proposal they persuaded James, much against his will, to agree to divest himself of part of his prerogative. But this was the limit of their achievement, for in the subsequent negotiations they showed – nor for the first time, nor for the last – a lack of realism where sums of money were involved and a stubborn refusal to pay a worthwhile price for the concessions they demanded. It was this, rather than any Court intrigue, which aborted the Contract.

IMPOSITIONS

The rights of the subject were founded upon property – in Maitland's phrase, 'constitutional law seems at times to be but an appendix to the law of real property'[86] – but the increasing poverty of the crown from the late sixteenth century onwards drove it to courses of action which appeared to infringe the principle that subjects could not be deprived of their property without their consent. Purveyance, for instance, amounted in the eyes of many members of the Commons to nothing less than robbery carried out by the King's agents in open defiance of statutory restrictions. Impositions were regarded as another example of prerogative erosion of the subjects' property rights, and were therefore fiercely resisted. In 1606 the Commons included the Imposition upon currants in their petition of grievances, and also gave three readings to a Bill 'concerning taxes and Impositions upon merchants and other subjects of the realm'.[87] In his reply to the petition, James referred to the 'suggestion that this Imposition [upon currants] would not be found warrantable by law' and announced that 'for satisfaction of all parties interested therein' he had decided to remit 'the determination thereof to such proceedings in law as is usual in like cases'.[88]

By the time this reply was given, in November 1606, the Exchequer Court had already considered the question of the Imposition on currants in Bate's Case (see p. 77), and had given judgment in favour of the crown. There the matter rested for a time, for in the third session of James's first Parliament the attention of the Commons was focussed upon the Union. In 1610, however, the House returned to the attack and appointed a committee to search the records and see whether the precedents avouched by the crown's lawyers in Bate's Case were valid. Before members could get down to discussion of the issue, however, James intervened by ordering them not to question his prerogative 'in the case of Impositions, for that was determined by judgment in the proper court and could not be undone but by [writ of] error'.[89] This order was immediately challenged by Thomas Wentworth, who argued that the decision in

Bate's Case had no general application. 'No other man in England is bound by that judgment', he declared, 'but he may try the law in a new action . . . And though three or four judges have given their opinions, should this bind the whole commonwealth perpetually?'. All courts, said Wentworth, were involved in discussing prerogative matters from time to time, so why should the Commons, which was an integral part of Parliament, the highest court of all, be barred from so doing: 'if we shall once say that we may not dispute the prerogative, let us be sold for slaves'.[90]

James, who was anxious to press ahead with the Great Contract, tried to lower the temperature by explaining that he had not intended to bar the Commons from discussing particular Impositions but only his right to levy them. 'You ought not to question what the King may do', he instructed them; 'but if there be inconvenience in . . . one or two of the Impositions which you desire to have taken away, then you must consider what you will offer me for them or what recompense in lieu of them'.[91] The House resented James's insistence that it should not discuss the general question of his right to impose, nor was it impressed by his claim that 'all kings Christian . . . have power to lay Impositions'.[92] In the ensuing debate Nicholas Fuller called on members to be 'true to the King and true to ourselves' by letting him know 'what by the laws of England he may do'.[93] Fuller also repeated parts of a speech made earlier by James Whitelocke, who had affirmed

that the English nation was accounted in times past by all others in three special respects: 1. that that which is the subjects' cannot be taken from them without their consent, but by due course of law; 2. that laws cannot be made without the consent of the three estates; 3. that the Parliament consisting of these three estates was the armamentary or storehouse wherein these things were safely reposed and preserved, as well the laws of the land as the rights and proprieties of the subjects to their lands and goods; and that the special privilege of Parliament is to debate freely of all things that shall concern any of the subjects in particular, or the commonwealth in general, without any restraint or inhibition.[94]

Whitelocke's view commanded general support, and the House resolved to proceed by a petition of right asserting its claim 'to debate freely all matters which do properly concern the subject'. As far as Impositions were concerned, the House denied that it was attempting to reverse the Exchequer judgment of 1606 – even though it insisted that this, 'being only in one case and against one man [Bate] . . . can bind in law no other but that person'. All it wished to do was to find out the grounds for the Exchequer barons' decision, in view of 'a general conceit . . . that the reasons of that judgment may be extended much farther, even to the utter ruin of the ancient liberty of this kingdom and of your subjects' right of propriety of their lands and goods'.[95] In his reply to this petition, James insisted that he was not asking for any more than 'that which other virtuous and good Kings of England had. Neither would he meddle with our *meum et tuum* [literally 'mine and thine', i.e. property], neither would he impose upon lands and goods, but only upon merchandise imported and exported, and that only in Parliament'.[96]

James's principal concern was to allay the Commons' fears about Impositions so that they could concentrate on the Great Contract. There was no formal link between the two issues but they were closely related. Indeed, James himself had acknowledged as much when he said 'that as this cause of Impositions was fit to be handled for the ease of the subject, so this other business of support was necessary to be handled for the good of the kingdom'.[97] The Commons responded to his overture by giving further consideration to the question of support, and then turned once again to Impositions. On 16 June 1610 they heard the report of the committee which had inspected the legal records in the Tower and the Exchequer, and then launched into a mammoth debate which was not concluded until 2 July. This was dominated by the lawyers, who conducted what was in effect an exercise in constitutional analysis by means of detailed examination of precedents drawn from statute and common law. The upshot was recorded by a non-lawyer member, Dudley Carleton. 'All this debate', he wrote, 'was at grand committees, the Speaker being in the House but not in his chair; and when the powder was all spent on both sides, we grew in the end to this peaceable conclusion – not to put the question of the right to condemn hereby the judgment of the Exchequer in the matter of currants, whereof all this is the consequence, but to frame a petition by way of grievance, implying the right, though not in express terms'.[98]

James was fully prepared for this manoeuvre. Indeed it was one of Salisbury's closest associates, Sir Walter Cope, who had suggested to the Commons that they should be 'petitioners to His Majesty to refer the Impositions present to a committee of Parliament, to reform the same where need is; and that His Highness would be pleased that an Act may pass that no Impositions may be hereafter set but by Parliament'.[99] James made it plain in his reply to the petition that he could not afford to give up existing Impositions unless the Commons provided recompense, but that there would be no new ones except with Parliament's consent. A Bill to this effect passed rapidly through all its stages in the Commons and was sent up to the Lords, who gave it a first reading on 20 July. Three days later Parliament was prorogued and the Bill disappeared from sight. When the Houses reassembled after the summer recess the Commons were preoccupied with the question of whether or not to complete the Contract. Had they done so, it is likely that the Bill on Impositions would have been revived and formally enacted. In the event, it foundered along with the Contract.

The grievance of Impositions did not go away, however, and it was taken up again by Parliament in 1614. On 14 April the Commons gave a first reading to a Bill 'concerning taxes and Impositions upon merchants and other subjects of the realm, and upon their wares, goods and chattels', which declared Impositions to be illegal, despite the Exchequer judgment in their favour.[100] After a debate on the second reading, the King sent for the Commons and reminded them that at his accession he had made no change in the Councillors and judges bequeathed him by his predecessor. It was these Elizabethan Councillors who had assured him that Impositions were among the flowers of his crown, and these Elizabethan judges who had confirmed that they were lawful. He was willing to let the verdict in Bate's Case be challenged by a writ of error, and would abide by the final decision of the judges, but he would die a hundred deaths rather than allow his prerogative to be taken from him by other means.[101]

The Commons were aware that if they were to have any chance of legislating Impositions out of existence they would need the co-operation of the Lords. They therefore drew up a lengthy statement of their case, which they hoped would convince the peers, and called for a conference at which they could present it. However, the Lords were unwilling to agree to a conference at this stage. They may have been shocked by the tone of the debate in the Lower House, for Sir Edwin Sandys had put forward the dangerous view that the authority of kings rested upon popular consent and that tyrants could be dethroned, while the impulsive Thomas Wentworth recalled that Henri IV of France, who had burdened his country with taxes, 'had died by a knife like a calf'.[102] When the Lords considered the Commons' request for a conference. Richard Neile, Bishop of Lincoln,

opposed himself very bitterly against it, alleging that he thought it no way fit to admit of any parley in a matter of that nature, which did not strike any more at the branches but at the root, yea, at the very crown and sceptre itself; adding further . . . that the Lower House was known to be composed of such turbulent and factious spirits as, if they should give way to a communication or treaty with them, they were like to hear such mutinous speeches as were not fit for those honourable personages to lend their hearing to.[103]

Reports of Neile's speech provoked uproar in the Commons, and they were not content until the Bishop had formally apologised and protested that he had never meant to impugn their loyalty. The conference, however, did not take place, for James was losing patience and had informed the Commons on 3 June of his intention to dissolve Parliament unless they voted supply. The House discussed this message but could not bring itself to make a positive reponse. It decided to inform the King 'that the Impositions lately laid on goods and merchandise in so huge a number, which none of his most royal progenitors have done before him, have been the occasion that they could not so freely give as they intended'. Since James had publicly affirmed his right to impose and to hand on these revenues to his heirs, a vote of supply might be held to imply recognition of his claim. The House had therefore decided that until 'it shall please God to ease us of these Impositions, whereby the whole kingdom doth groan, we cannot, without wrong to our country, give Your Majesty that relief which we desire'.[104] On this unharmonious note the Addled Parliament came to an end.

Seven years passed before James once again summoned Parliament, and when the Commons got down to business in 1621 they focussed their attention upon monopolies, which relegated Impositions to the background. The second session of 1621 was taken up primarily with foreign affairs, and the same issues dominated the 1624 Parliament. In April 1624, however, the Commons spent some time discussing the causes of the continuing depression in English commerce, and decided that one of these was the over-burdening of trade by Impositions of various sorts. This could have provoked another stormy debate, but with war on the horizon the House was not seeking confrontation, and it therefore resolved 'that the dispute of the royal right of imposing now . . . be declined'.[105] A month later the issue was raised again, and a committee was appointed 'to take into consideration the claim of the subject against Impositions'.[106] Nothing came of this initiative, but the House did resolve that an additional duty on exported cloth, levied from 1618 onwards and known as the pretermitted customs, 'is against law and shall be presented to His Majesty as a grievance'.[107] These stirrings of discontent showed that the anger provoked by Impositions was still present among members. They could do nothing while James was alive, but in the following year, when the accession of a new monarch reopened the question of duties on trade, they broke with precedent by refusing to make the customary lifetime grant of Tonnage and Poundage. In this indirect way the issue of Impositions contributed to the souring of relations at the very outset of Charles I's reign.

NOTES AND REFERENCES

(*The place of publication is London, unless otherwise stated*)
1. *Journals of the House of Commons 1547–1714* (1742). Vol. I, p. 939. (Hereafter *Commons Journals*)
2. *Commons Journals.* Vol. I, p. 156.
3. *Commons Journals.* Vol. I, p. 158.
4. *Commons Journals.* Vol. I, p. 166.
5. *Commons Journals.* Vol. I, p. 148.
6. *Commons Journals.* Vol. I, p. 166.
7. *Commons Journals.* Vol. I, p. 168.
8. *Commons Journals.* Vol. I, p. 171.
9. **J. R. Tanner (ed.)** *Constitutional Documents of the Reign of James I* (Cambridge 1930), pp. 224–25. (Hereafter Tanner *Constitutional Documents*)
10. Tanner *Constitutional Documents*, p. 226.
11. **D. H. Willson** 'King James I and Anglo-Scots Unity' in W. A. Aiken & B. D. Henning (eds.), *Conflict in Stuart England* (1960), p. 43.
12. **James F. Larkin & Paul L. Hughes** (eds.) *Stuart Royal Proclamations.* Vol. I. *Royal Proclamations of King James I* (Oxford 1973), p. 19.n. (Hereafter Larkin & Hughes *Royal Proclamations*)
13. Larkin & Hughes *Royal Proclamations*, p. 19.
14. Larkin & Hughes *Royal Proclamations*, p. 19.
15. *Commons Journals.* Vol. I, p. 43.
16. *The Works of Francis Bacon* ed. James Spedding (1874). Vol. X, p. 77. (Hereafter Bacon *Works*)
17. *Commons Journals.* Vol. I, pp. 950–51.
18. *Commons Journals.* Vol. I, p. 179.
19. *Commons Journals.* Vol. I, p. 957.
20. *Commons Journals.* Vol. I, pp. 186–87.
21. *Letters of King James VI & I* ed. G. P. V. Akrigg (1984), p. 225. (Hereafter James I *Letters*)
22. Bacon *Works.* Vol. X, p. 200.
23. *Commons Journals.* Vol. I, p. 962.
24. *Commons Journals.* Vol. I, p. 962.
25. *Commons Journals.* Vol. I, pp. 193–94.
26. *Commons Journals.* Vol. I, p. 199.
27. *Commons Journals.* Vol. I, p. 226.
28. *Commons Journals.* Vol. I, p. 983.

The Early Stuarts

29. *Commons Journals*. Vol. I, p. 984.
30. Larkin & Hughes *Royal Proclamations*, p. 96.
31. Bacon *Works*. Vol. X, p. 226.
32. Tanner *Constitutional Documents*, p. 222.
33. *Commons Journals*. Vol. I, p. 314.
34. *Commons Journals*. Vol. I, p. 315.
35. *Commons Journals*. Vol. I, p. 318.
36. *Commons Journals*. Vol. I, p. 323.
37. *Commons Journals*. Vol. I, p. 334.
38. *Commons Journals*. Vol. I, pp. 336–37; 1015.
39. *Commons Journals*. Vol. I, p. 345.
40. **S. R. Gardiner** *History of England from the Accession of James I to the Outbreak of the Civil War 1603–1642* (1884). Vol. I, p. 325 n. 2.; Larkin & Hughes *Royal Proclamations*. 95.
41. *Commons Journals*. Vol. I, p. 360.
42. *Commons Journals*. Vol. I, p. 358.
43. *Commons Journals*. Vol. I, p. 367.
44. Bacon *Works*. Vol. X, p. 343.
45. *Commons Journals*. Vol. I, p. 376.
46. **G. W. Prothero** (ed.) *Select Statutes and other Constitutional Documents illustrative of the Reigns of Elizabeth and James I* (Oxford 1913), p. 446.
47. *Commons Journals*. Vol. I, pp. 150–51.
48. **Allegra Woodworth** 'Purveyance for the Royal Household in the Reign of Queen Elizabeth' *Transactions of the American Philosophical Society*. Vol. 35. Part 1. 1945 pp. 16–17.
49. *Commons Journals*. Vol. I, p. 190.
50. *Commons Journals*. Vol. I, p. 193.
51. *Commons Journals*. Vol. I, p. 274.
52. Larkin & Hughes *Royal Proclamations*, pp. 137–38.
53. *Commons Journals*. Vol. I, p. 303.
54. **Wallace Notestein, Frances Helen Relf** & **Hartley Simpson** (eds.) *Commons Debates 1621* (New Haven 1935). Vol. III, pp. 305–06. (Hereafter *Commons Debates 1621*)
55. *Commons Debates 1621*. Vol. III, p. 307.
56. *Commons Journals*. Vol. I, p. 978.
57. ***The Reports of Sir Edward Coke, Kt***. (1738). Part XII, pp. 18–19.
58. ***The Parliamentary Diary of Robert Bowyer 1606–1607*** ed. D. H. Willson (Minneapolis 1931), p. 65.
59. *Commons Journals*. Vol. I, p. 227.
60. **Pauline Croft** 'Wardship in the Parliament of 1604' *Parliamentary History*. Vol. 2. 1983.
61. **S. R. Gardiner** (ed.) *Parliamentary Debates in 1610*. Camden Society (1862), pp. 13–16. (Hereafter Gardiner *1610 Debates*)
62. Gardiner *1610 Debates*, p. 21.
63. Gardiner *1610 Debates*, p. 27.
64. Gardiner *1610 Debates*, p. 28.
65. **E. R. Foster** (ed.) *Proceedings in Parliament 1610* (New Haven 1966). Vol. 2, pp. 66–7. (Hereafter Foster *Proceedings 1610*)
66. Gardiner *1610 Debates*, p. 151.
67. Gardiner *1610 Debates*, p. 151.

68. Gardiner *1610 Debates*, p. 46.
69. Gardiner *1610 Debates*, p. 53.
70. Gardiner *1610 Debates*, p. 55.
71. Gardiner *1610 Debates*, p. 56.
72. Gardiner *1610 Debates*, p. 56.
73. Gardiner *1610 Debates*, p. 124.
74. Foster *Proceedings 1610*. Vol. 2, p. 284.
75. Foster *Proceedings 1610*. Vol. 2, p. 301.
76. Foster *Proceedings 1610*. Vol. 2, p. 305.
77. Foster *Proceedings 1610*. Vol. 2, p. 318.
78. Foster *Proceedings 1610*. Vol. 2, pp. 309–11.
79. Foster *Proceedings 1610*. Vol. 2, pp. 314–16.
80. Gardiner *1610 Debates*, p. 128.
81. Foster *Proceedings 1610*. Vol. 2, p. 317.
82. Gardiner *1610 Debates*, p. 136.
83. James I *Letters*, p. 317.
84. Bacon *Works*. Vol. XI, pp. 236–37.
85. Gardiner *1610 Debates*, p. 178.
86. **F. W. Maitland** *The Constitutional History of England* (Cambridge 1908), p. 538.
87. *Commons Journals*. Vol. I, p. 312.
88. *Commons Journals*. Vol. I, p. 317.
89. Foster *Proceedings 1610*. Vol. 2, p. 82.
90. Foster *Proceedings 1610*. Vol. 2, pp. 82–3.
91. Foster *Proceedings 1610*. Vol. 2, p. 104.
92. Foster *Proceedings 1610*. Vol. 2, p. 102.
93. Foster *Proceedings 1610*. Vol. 2, p. 109.
94. Gardiner *1610 Debates*, p. 37.
95. *Commons Journals*. Vol. I, p. 431.
96. Foster *Proceedings 1610*. Vol. 2, p. 115.
97. Foster *Proceedings 1610*. Vol. 2, p. 116.
98. *The Court and Times of James the First . . . transcribed by Thomas Birch* ed. R. F. Williams (1849). Vol. I, p. 122. (Hereafter *Court and Times James I*)
99. Gardiner *1610 Debates*, p. 109.
100. *Commons Journals*. Vol. I, pp. 464, 466.
101. *Commons Debates 1621*. Vol. VII, pp. 632–33.
102. *Commons Debates 1621*. Vol. VII, p. 644.
103. *Court and Times James I*. Vol. I, p. 316.
104. *Commons Debates 1621*. Vol. VII, p. 651.
105. *Commons Journals*. Vol. I, p. 760.
106. *Commons Journals*. Vol. I, p. 787.
107. *Commons Journals*. Vol. I, p. 782.

CHAPTER EIGHT

The Later Parliaments of James I 1621–1624

MONOPOLIES

The financial pressures which drove the crown into levying Impositions had also encouraged it to grant patents of monopoly for revenue purposes rather than the protection of new inventions. This was of doubtful legality, for in the Case of Monopolies (Darcy *v* Allen) in 1602 the judges had resolved that monopolies were inherently prejudicial to the subjects' welfare. 'The end of all these monopolies', they declared 'is for the private gain of the patentees, and although provisions and cautions are added to moderate them, yet . . . it is mere folly to think that there is any measure in mischief or wickedness'. They condemned monopolies on three principal grounds. The first was 'that the price of the same commodity will be raised; for he who has the sole selling of any commodity may and will make the price as he pleases'. The second was 'that after the monopoly [is] granted the commodity is not so good and merchantable as it was before, for the patentee, having the sole trade, regards only his private benefit and not the commonwealth'. The third and last was that a monopoly 'tends to the impoverishment of divers artificers and others who before, by the labour of their hands in their art or trade, had maintained themselves and their families, who now will of necessity be constrained to live in idleness and beggary'.[1]

The issue of monopolies had already caused trouble between the crown and the Commons in the closing years of Elizabeth's reign, and in 1601 Laurence Hyde, a lawyer member of the House, had put forward a Bill to declare monopoly patents illegal. The Queen preempted parliamentary intervention in this prerogative matter –

which was also, of course, a commonwealth one – by promising to take action herself, but little had been done by the time she died. James began where Elizabeth had left off, and in a proclamation of May 1603 he forbade any person 'to use or execute any manner of charter or grant made by our late sister, the Queen deceased, of any kind of monopolies . . . except such grants only as have been made to any corporation or company of any art or mystery, or for the maintenance or enlargement of any trade of merchandise' until these had been subjected to scrutiny by the Privy Council.[2] However, James soon found that the financial pressures which had induced Elizabeth to grant monopolies were driving him in the same direction, as was the need to devise new (and inexpensive) ways in which to reward crown servants and courtiers. The problem with such grants was that they benefited the King at the expense of his subjects, and to this extent weakened the bonds of affection that were the fundamental strength of the monarchy. Salisbury was anxious to restrain James's extravagance and to demonstrate that the King's largesse would not be a burden on his people. He therefore persuaded James to accept the 'Book of Bounty', drawn up in late 1608 and printed in 1610, by which the King bound himself not to grant monopolies and other 'things contrary to our laws'.[3]

Although James continued to make monopoly grants, he observed his self-imposed limitation by instructing the crown's law officers to examine all proposals and report on their legality and their 'convenience' (i.e. the extent to which they seemed likely to produce genuine benefits). This system was not foolproof, however. In 1608 Sir Francis Bacon, as Solicitor General, considered Sir Stephen Proctor's scheme for taking over the collection of fines arising from breaches of penal statutes, which were concerned with the detailed regulation of certain manufactures, particularly that of woollen cloth. In his report, Bacon informed James that these statutes were an unhappy legacy of Henry VII's reign and that his subjects were so ensnared in them 'that the execution of them cannot be borne'. Bacon was of the opinion that the replacement of common informers by a single officer specially appointed for the purpose would lead to more efficient and more humane enforcement of these laws. His clear impression was that 'the purpose and scope' of Proctor's project was 'not to press a greater rigour or severity in the execution of penal laws, but to repress the abuses in common informers and some clerks and under-ministers that for common gain partake with them'. On these grounds, therefore, he approved it, but added that 'if it had tended to the other point, I for my part should be very far from advising Your Majesty to give ear unto it'.[4] Proctor was duly issued with a patent appointing him sole Collector and Receiver of Fines on Penal Statutes, but his activities were reported to Parliament in 1610, and the Commons laid charges against him before the Lords. There seems little doubt that Proctor had abused his position by bullying, blackmailing, and shady dealing, since his principal objective, as the judges had foreseen in 1602, was private enrichment. Bacon was correct in stating that the appointment of one officer instead of many was a *prima facie* improvement on the existing situation. What he and the referees in all monopoly cases failed (or were unable) to take into account, was the motivation of the projector. Many a scheme looked good on paper but turned out in practice to be something very different.

As James's reign went on and his financial position worsened, the number of monopoly grants increased. In July 1620 Chamberlain reported that 'the world doth even groan under the burden of these perpetual patents, which are become so frequent that whereas at the King's coming in there were complaints of some eight or nine monopolies then in being, they are now said to be multiplied to so many scores'.[5] Bacon could see a storm coming. In November 1620 he warned Buckingham 'that in the number of patents which we have represented to His Majesty as like to be stirred in by the Lower House of Parliament, we have set down three which may concern some of your lordship's special friends'. He advised him therefore to 'put off the envy of these things, which I think in themselves bear no great fruit, and rather take the thanks for ceasing them than the note for maintaining them'.[6] Buckingham would have done well to follow Bacon's advice, for the patents in question included one for the licensing of inns, held by Sir Giles Mompesson, which came under attack soon after Parliament met.

Mompesson's patent had been granted in 1617, after the judges had pronounced it to be in accordance with the law and the Privy Councillors had accepted that it would be 'convenient'. 'The pretences of this patent', as a Commons' committee subsequently reported, were firstly 'forasmuch as there was a great disorder by the abuse of inns, many [persons] of their own authority having taken upon them to keep inns, contrary to the law and themselves being unfit'; secondly, 'because Justices of Peace had no authority to restrain innkeepers and punish them'; and finally 'because the justices of assize were not at leisure to meddle with it'.[7] Mompesson was authorised to maintain a general supervision of inns, ensuring that they were well managed, 'as also to contract with persons of substance and good report for the erecting of new inns in places convenient, taking such fines and reserving such rents to His Majesty as the patentees should agree for'.[8] He was now accused of having 'much abused the King's trust by licensing of disorderly alehouse-keepers and innkeepers, albeit formerly put down for their ill course of living by Justices of Peace; and that he had not reformed any abuse, nor refused to license any that would give money, whereby the subject was not only much oppressed, but proceedings of justice much scandalised'.[9]

Mompesson was a member of the Commons, which therefore had authority to proceed against him for unworthy conduct, but not to sit in judgment on his activities as a patentee. For this they needed the co-operation of the Lords, to whom they sent up a detailed list of charges. At this point Mompesson fled abroad, but the Lords duly sentenced him, in his absence, to be degraded from the order of knighthood, to be perpetually banished, and to pay a fine of £10,000. Meanwhile, the Commons had initiated action against another of their members, Sir Francis Michell, who had been associated with Mompesson in the ruthless enforcement of a monopoly patent for gold and silver thread. He likewise was presented to the Lords, who sentenced him to be degraded, fined and imprisoned. Among the beneficiaries of the gold and silver thread monopoly was Buckingham's half-brother, Sir Edward Villiers. His full brother, Christopher Villiers, shared in the profits of a patent for alehouses, which the Commons also condemned. This patent had been justified on the grounds that the Justices of the Peace who were responsible for licensing alehouses allowed them to increase in number and to become centres of drunkenness and disorderly conduct. There was considerable truth in this criticism, but a House of Commons which numbered many magistrates among its members resented the appointment of patentees to supplement and, to some exent, control the Justices' activities, and was only too happy to include this particular patent among the grievances it investigated.

Although James was at fault insofar as he had granted the monopoly patents which were now the subject of complaint, he diverted criticism by asserting his ignorance of the abuses that had been committed. In his opening speech to Parliament, in January 1621, he confessed that he had been 'much deceived in doing many things hurtful to myself and prejudicious to my people in point of grant' and promised to revoke harmful patents as long as they were called to his attention 'in right manner and by orderly information'.[10] The Commons were only too happy to accept these assurances, which left them free to investigate abuses without fear of provoking a clash with the King, and they were content to follow the lead given by Privy Councillors such as Sir Edward Coke and Sir Lionel Cranfield. When the names of the referees for Mompesson's patent for inns were revealed, Sir Edward Coke declared that 'if these did certify it, no king in Christendom but would have granted it. Therefore His Majesty is free from all blame in it'.[11] Cranfield was equally concerned to place the blame on the referees. 'The King was ever jealous and would not refer [a patent] to those whose names were in it', he said. 'If the referees be in fault, can he do himself more honour than to call them to account? If the fault be not in them but in the executioners, do you not think that the King will punish them that shall abuse his grace?'.[12] Non-Councillors such as Sir Dudley Digges took up the same theme. The King, said Digges, had made plain his dislike of monopolies ever since coming to the throne, and 'howsoever they have been procured of him, yet is not His Majesty's honour to be impeached in it, because he hath ever been most careful never to grant them before he hath referred them to learned and honourable persons, both for the lawfulness and conveniency'. The real villains, Digges insisted, were the patentees themselves, for although they 'had a virgin's face . . . their hands and feet were like griping talons. They pretended the profit of the King and good of the kingdom. What more fair? But they intended only their own gain, though procured by unjust vexation and oppression. What more cruel?'.[13]

Although the Commons could complain of specific monopolies and present offending patentees to the Lords, they had no power to overthrow a grant made by the King. This was why Sir Edward Coke was of the opinion that 'it's necessary that some law be made for the time to come that no monopoly be granted, and they that procure any such may incur some great punishment'. This, he felt sure, would 'kill the serpent in the egg'.[14] Since monopolies were a prerogative matter, the King's permission had first to be sought before legislation could be embarked upon. There was no difficulty about this, for James welcomed the idea of a Bill as a means of freeing him from the endless importunities of suitors. No sooner was his approval announced than the Commons gave a first reading to a Bill which Coke had ready and which was aimed, as one member recorded, 'against all monopolies; hereafter to be inhibited and to be tried in the King's courts; and that those that take forth such patents, commissions or grants shall enter into recognisances; and he that findeth himself aggrieved shall have treble damages'.[15] During its passage through the House the Bill was considerably amended, so that new inventions, as well as the rights of towns, cities and companies, were excluded from its provisions. It finally passed the Commons on 12 May and was sent up with a special recommendation to the Lords. They eventually rejected it, perhaps because the courtier element, which profited from monopoly grants, was more strongly represented in the Upper House than in the Lower.

When he addressed the assembled members of Parliament on 26 March, shortly before its adjournment for a long summer recess, James announced his intention to 'strike dead' the patents for inns, alehouses, and gold and silver thread. He also confessed that he felt 'ashamed (and it makes my hair stand upright) to consider how . . . my people have been vexed and polled by the vile execution of projects, patents . . . and such like'.[16] James put his promise into effect a few days later, when the three patents were repealed by proclamation. July saw the issue of another proclamation 'declaring His Majesty's grace to his subjects touching matters complained of as public grievances'. This reiterated James's 'hatred and detestation' of all suits which claimed as their objective 'the common good and profit of his subjects' but were in reality aimed at private gain. It then announced that eight specific monopoly grants, including those for playing-cards and tobacco pipes, had been voluntarily surrendered by their patentees and would be permanently suppressed. A further ten patents – which were principally delegations of the crown's prerogative powers in matters such as 'pardoning or dispensing with the conversion of arable land into pasture' – were 'fully and absolutely' revoked. The proclamation concluded with a list of seventeen monopolies which could henceforth be challenged at common law by 'all and every persons that at any time hereafter shall find themselves grieved, injured or wronged' by them.[17]

The Commons' campaign against monopolies in the 1621 Parliament was remarkably successful, in large part because they had the King as well as public opinion on their side. But James's acknowledgment of the fact that he had been deceived by those he trusted was a reminder, if one was needed, that he could not be relied on to stand firm against the importunities of suitors, and that the situation might well deteriorate once again. The only way in which to prevent this was by legislation, and in 1624, therefore, the Bill against monopolies was reintroduced and this time completed its passage through both Houses. It sanctioned monopoly grants for new inventions but limited them to fourteen years. It also left untouched the privileges of chartered companies and corporations.

This provided a loophole for Charles I's Lord Treasurer in the period of personal rule, for although the King could no longer increase his revenues through monopoly grants to individuals he had a clearly defined legal right to make them to corporations. In early 1632, therefore, he authorised the setting up of a company of soap-makers who were to pay into the Exchequer £4 for every ton which they sold. The company did not have a monopoly of soap manufacture, but it was authorised to inspect and control rival products, which amounted to much the same thing. The 'Westminster Soapers', as the projectors were called, became deeply unpopular, particularly since many of them were catholic, but the government supported them because it needed their money, This was true of other companies also, and in the Grand Remonstrance the Long Parliament complained of the 'monopolies of soap, salt, wine, leather, sea-coal, and, in a manner, of all things of most common and necessary use'.[18]

FOREIGN POLICY IN THE 1621 PARLIAMENT

James I's main reason for summoning Parliament at the beginning of 1621 was not to unleash an assault upon projectors and patentees but to obtain a vote of supply which would enable him to take effective action in support of his son-in-law, the Elector Frederick (see p. 19). When he addressed the assembled members on 30 January he declared that in this cause he would not spare 'my crown, my blood, and the blood of my son here'. But he could do nothing, he added, without the aid of his people, and he trusted they would 'not be wanting, this cause being the cause of religion and the inheritance of my grandchildren'.[19] The King's demand came at an inopportune moment, for the economy was deep in recession, and Chamberlain reported 'that England was never generally so poor since I was born as it is at this present'.[20] James needed £200,000 merely to set out an army, but the Commons felt unable to vote more than two subsidies, worth some £160,000. They deliberately refrained from adding the customary tenths and fifteenths since these bore heavily on the poorer sections of society, which were already hard pressed. Recognising that two subsidies were, in Sir Edwin Sandys' phrase, 'no proportion for the regaining of the Palatinate', they accepted his suggestion that they should offer them 'as a present of love to the King, without any other consideration'.[21]

James expressed his pleasure at this 'free, noble, and no-merchantlike dealing' on the part of the House,[22] and looked forward to the speedy passage of the subsidy Bill. When, in mid-March, there was a threat of delay from an impending conference with the Lords about monopolies, he sent a message to the Commons, asking them to postpone it. The House, at Sir Edward Coke's suggestion, stood bare-headed to receive the royal messenger, and replied that while it would attend the conference it would make sure that the King's business did not suffer thereby. James, who – perhaps rightly – valued gestures of goodwill almost as highly as money, was delighted with this response, and informed the House that 'never any of his royal progenitors found more obedience, love and duty from their subjects than hath been expressed unto him this Parliament, and by this assembly of his Commons'.[23]

The unusually harmonious relations between the King and the Lower House were not even imperilled by the overthrow of Francis Bacon, the Lord Chancellor and head of the royal administration. When the Commons, during the course of their investigations into abuses, came across evidence that Bacon had accepted bribes, they resolved to pursue the matter and bring charges against him before the Lords. Bacon was not unduly worried, for he was on good terms with the favourite, Buckingham, and he took it for granted that the King would not allow the royal authority to be questioned, albeit obliquely, by an attack upon his principal minister. However, Bacon's confidence turned out to be ill founded. As one of the referees for many of the patents complained of by the Commons, he would make a suitable scapegoat; moreover, by throwing him to the wolves, Buckingham might be able to divert attention from the involvement of members of his own family in unpopular monopolies. James could have insisted on saving his Chancellor, but he neither wished, nor could afford, to appear to be sanctioning corruption in high places: as he told the Lords, 'so precious unto me is the public good that no private person whatsoever, were he never so dear unto me, shall be so respected by me . . . as the public good'.[24] Bacon took the hint and pleaded guilty, thereby averting a formal trial before the Lords which would have brought the King's government into even further discredit.

James dismissed Bacon from office, but he gave a clear signal that this was not to be regarded as permission for an all-out assault upon the administration. Addressing the two Houses on 20 April he warned members not to 'hearken to every particular man's complaint which concerns himself alone, but [only] when it concerns a multitude. Look not upon judges as they are judges, but as they are corrupt judges . . . Let not this Parliament be a Domesday wherein all books may be opened, but a jubilee wherein we may rejoice'.[25] When, on the very next day, Sir Francis Seymour criticised Sir Henry Montagu, Coke's successor as Chief Justice of King's Bench, who had recently been created Viscount Mandeville and given the white staff of Lord Treasurer, James swiftly intervened and instructed the House to go no further along this path.

The Commons did as they were told, and found an outlet for their zeal, and an opportunity, as they thought, to demonstrate their loyalty both to God and their King, in devising punishments for Edward Floyd, a Roman Catholic barrister who had dared to criticise the Elector Palatine and his wife. But on this occasion, as on others, they allowed their emotions to carry them away, for in fact they had no jurisdiction over Floyd, who was not a member of the House and had not brought himself within its purview by infringing its privileges. James decided on an adjournment, to let passions cool, but the Commons were apprehensive that this might be a prelude to dissolution. Their over-reaction was attributable perhaps to a guilty conscience, for the House had ordered its own business so badly, by appointing too many committees, frequently with overlapping memberships, that draft Bills had become bogged down in them. Rather than blame themselves, however, the Commons preferred to follow Sir Edwin Sandys' suggestion that they should ask the King to allow them more time. 'The eyes of all the kingdom, and hearts, are upon us', he declared. 'They stand expecting and gazing after the good that we will bring them'. These sentiments were echoed by Sir Richard Grosvenor, who asked 'when we come into the country, what will they think of us? We have given subsidies, and have brought home nothing for them. I pray God we be not subjects of their fury'.[26] Sir Lionel Cranfield, Master of the Wards and one of the principal government spokesmen in the Commons, tried to calm the House by giving an assurance that dissolution was not intended and that, although the King was determined upon a recess, Parliament would be recalled in November. He was supported by Secretary Calvert, who called on members to 'prepare as many Bills as we may',[27] but they remained suspicious and apprehensive and more inclined to do nothing than to co-operate in what they regarded as a premature and unjustified end to their meeting.

The sudden change of tone was commented on by Sir Edward Cecil, who gave his opinion that 'some ill members have shortened this session' and that 'someone hath cast a bone twixt us and the King'.[28] Cranfield thought the same. 'If any man have a mind to discontent the King and the country and to hinder all good, he may further us to this discontented departure . . . We went on fairly a long time, even till Easter, contending on both sides who should do more, the King or us; and I think many wise men in the House know how, and by whom, we are now interrupted and diverted'.[29] This somewhat cryptic observation is clarified by a memorandum from Cranfield to the King, presented after the close of the session, in which he affirmed that the Earl of Southampton 'consorted himself during the time of Parliament with those young lords in the Upper, and those knights and burgesses in the Lower, House which were most stirring and active to cross the general proceedings and to asperse and infame the present government'. Indeed, according to Cranfield, 'scarce one speech concerning any public grievance . . . was uttered in Parliament by any other man than some bosom friend, or ordinary guest at the least, of the said Earl', who had been 'active in ripping up supposed enormities in the state . . . and yet so cold (or rather so stone dead) in advising of means to support the King'.[30]

Southampton was arrested after the end of the session, along with Sir Edwin Sandys, who was supposed to be the chief link between him and the Commons. Southampton was no friend of Buckingham, and favoured a far more aggressive foreign policy than James had in mind. No doubt he used his influence to try to bring this about, but it is difficult to believe that he and possibly Sandys were responsible for creating a mood of apprehension in the Commons. The sudden news of an adjournment before their work had been completed was enough to alarm members, and the abrupt end of the previous Parliament gave grounds sufficient for their fears. The King went some way to calm them by allowing the Commons to decide for themselves 'whether they would sit till midsummer and have then a prorogation of the Parliament, or rise presently and so have it but adjourned'. The House preferred an adjournment, since this did not put an end to the session, but it professed its inability to get any Bills ready for the royal approval, on the grounds of lack of time. James was not inclined to accept this excuse. 'He said that they had longer time of sitting than parliaments formerly had, and that he had sent them sundry admonishments to husband their time well; which, if they had done and fallen in with the commonwealth's business in any reasonable time, they had ended with somewhat, having now done nothing'.[31]

James emphasised that he had no complaint about the majority of members, 'but some he found in the House rather affected to their own fancies than to his just commandments, and who, to cross him, brought into the Parliament strange matters, notwithstanding his many messages sent unto them to take heed of such diversions'.[32] This sort of comment often stung the House into protesting its innocence, but on this occasion it decided to demonstrate its good-will and loyalty by concluding its meeting 'with what His Majesty began, concerning the Palatinate'.[33] With a 'general acclamation and waving of hats'[34] the Commons, at Sir James Perrot's suggestion, passed a resolution 'that if His Majesty's pious endeavours by treaty . . . shall not take that good effect which is desired . . . they shall be ready to the utmost of their powers, both with their lives and fortunes, to assist him so as by the divine help of Almighty God . . . he may be able to do that with his sword which by a peaceable course shall not be effected'.[35] With this resounding declaration the members brought the first stage of the 1621 Parliament to a close.

When it reassembled in November, foreign affairs were at the top of the agenda, for James's special envoy, John Digby, had just returned from Vienna, and informed the Houses that he had found the Emperor intransigent and unwilling to make any concession over the restoration of the Palatinate. Digby's opinion, as recorded by one of his listeners, was 'that the King must either abandon his children and the Palatinate, or declare himself for war'.[36] The Upper Palatinate was occupied by imperial troops, and the Lower Palatinate, on the Rhine, was threatened with the same fate. Only a few towns were holding out, through the presence of an English volunteer force under Sir Horace Vere, but the mercenary leader, Count Mansfeld, who had previously commanded Frederick's army in Bohemia, was prepared to join up with Vere if only money were provided at once.

The debate on Digby's speech opened on 26 November, and it quickly became apparent that opinion in the House was divided. Sir Benjamin Rudyerd believed that the maintenance of Mansfeld's forces in the Palatinate would be a cheaper option than raising and despatching a new English army. Sir James Perrot, on the other hand, thought that England was 'poorer than it was [and] money more scarce' and that a war of diversion against Spain would be not only more effectual but also more profitable.[37] Sir Robert Phelips also favoured a war of diversion. He thought that in the present depressed state of the economy little could be done for the Palatinate: 'our inabilities are too patent. We have lost trade. Money is wanting. Many other defects which neither the Parliament nor Lords of Council have yet redressed. To exhaust our treasure in our doubtful state, for religion, were dangerous'. A small sum, which the King could easily find from his own resources, would be sufficient to keep Mansfeld in the field until the spring, when Parliament could give serious consideration to the question of supply. Meanwhile, they should demonstrate their overriding commitment to the cause of religion by suppressing the English papists: 'let's so fight for the Palatinate that we secure ourselves at home'.[38]

Phelips was challenged by Secretary Calvert, who insisted that only by intervening in the Palatinate could James rally protestant Europe to Frederick's cause. 'If the King have had his sword sheathed too long', he said, 'let's not keep it in longer. Let's remember our own protestation and not fall off our own offer'.[39] There was some support for Calvert, but Thomas Crew brought out into the open the doubts felt by many members about the King's attitude. James had professed his determination to recover the Palatinate from the House of Austria without provoking war with Spain. Indeed, he was actively engaged in trying to achieve a Spanish marriage for his son, Charles, and for this reason he wanted to play down the religious element in the conflict over the Palatinate. Yet the prevailing view in the Commons was that Spain was the real enemy; it was, in Phelips's words, 'the great wheel of Spain' which kept 'the little wheel of Germany' in motion.[40] Given this fact, said Crew, they should fight the King of Spain abroad and the papists at home. He would 'consent to give willingly and freely' if only 'we might know who were our enemies'. He also expressed the hope that 'our Prince might be matched to one of our religion'.[41]

James did not welcome the expression of such sentiments, for he was still hopeful of regaining the Palatinate by diplomacy, with the aid of Spain. It might be, as Sir Thomas Edmondes, the Treasurer of the Household, observed, that in due course a firmer line would have to be taken against Spain, 'but His Majesty, in his wisdom and justice, doth not think it fit to apply this cauter to the wound till he shall see how the King of Spain, who professeth such inward friendship to him, will avow these last proceedings of the Emperor'.[42] James was working on the assumption that the Spaniards were acting in good faith, but was such an assumption justified? Sir Edward Coke thought not. 'The great Armado of Spain', he recalled, 'came while we were treating of peace with Spain. Therefore take heed of treaties'.[43] Phelips agreed with Coke. He was convinced that the overriding aim of the Spaniards in all their negotiations was 'for advancing the Romish religion. Rome our unplacable adversary. Spain the Pope's dearest child. Involved together'.[44] Yet he also agreed with Coke that now was not the time for a declaration of war against Spain. They should consider how best to keep Mansfeld's army in existence during the winter, when no campaigning was possible, and leave all major decisions to their next meeting in the spring.

Calvert had called on members to honour the commitment they had made in their protestation of 4 June, but Sir Nathaniel Rich argued that this had bound them principally to the defence of religion, 'whereof the Palatinate [was] but a branch'.[45] Heneage Finch thought otherwise. 'One particular branch of our declaration is for defence of the Palatinate', he said. 'Tis not a binding act, but an obligation to our hearts, and an army there will keep a hook in the jaws of the lion'.[46] Nevertheless, Finch took the view that there was no need for immediate supply. They should press ahead with their own business, including enforcement of the penal laws, while they waited for further guidance from the King. Sir William Cope reinforced this argument by pointing out that the subsidies which had already been voted would not be fully collected until May 1622, and that any new grants could not begin until June or August of that year. In the end, the House decided to go into committee to discuss three specific issues. The first was 'the state of religion, and for a petition to His Majesty for execution of laws against Jesuits, papists, etc'. The second was how much should be given for the Palatinate, and 'when, and of the manner'. The third and last was the framing of a petition to James 'for passing Bills and making an end of this session before Christmas'.[47]

The committee on the whole decided that one subsidy should be voted 'for the present relief of the Palatinate, to be paid in February next',[48] and the House, now in formal session, confirmed this without a dissenting voice. Members then returned to the more congenial business of 'commonwealth' matters, including consideration of the case of two patentees, Lepton and Goldsmith, who were said to be involved in a plot to discredit Sir Edward Coke and were rumoured to have the support and encouragement of Buckingham. However, the House was abruptly brought back to foreign affairs by Sir George Goring, one of Buckingham's close associates. Goring referred to a letter which James had written to Philip IV of Spain, calling on him either to procure a cease-fire in Germany or to break with the Emperor. He then proposed that the Commons should ask James, 'in case the King of Spain shall not condescend to either of these so just and reasonable demands . . . to declare unto them that he will not spare to denounce war as well against the King of Spain . . . as against the Emperor or any other that shall go about to

dispossess them [Frederick and Elizabeth] of their ancient inheritance'.[49] Goring must have been speaking with James's knowledge
and approval, and the purpose of his motion was presumably to
draw a declaration from the House which the King could use as a
diplomatic weapon in his campaign to persuade Spain that unless she
intervened to secure the restoration of the Palatinate she would find
herself involved in war with England.

Manoeuvres of this sort were always risky, since the House had
only limited knowledge and even more limited understanding of the
King's motives, and could not be relied upon to give the sort of
precise and controlled response that he expected and needed. Things
went wrong almost immediately, for Sir Robert Phelips, who
frequently allowed his heart to lead his head, not merely endorsed
Goring's motion but added to it. As a consequence, the House's
petition, in its final form, included the request that 'our most noble
Prince may be timely and happily married to one of our own religion'.[50] This was despite a warning from Sir Edward Sackville,
another of the crown's spokesmen in the Commons, that 'it is the
privilege of princes to marry where they list; and since we are so
careful of our own privileges he would not have us seek to limit our
Prince'.[51] James regarded the proposed marriage between Charles
and the Infanta Maria as his trump card, and therefore he was
unlikely to react favourably to such a request, particularly since at
the very moment when he received it he had been shown evidence
suggesting that the Spaniards were indeed acting in good faith and
that he stood to gain far more from co-operation with them than
from confrontation. He sharply rebuked the Commons for
debating 'matters far above their reach and capacity'[52] and thereby
sparked off a series of increasingly acerbic exchanges that culminated
in the Commons' Protestation and the abrupt end of the session (see
p. 140).

The sudden transformation of harmony into bitterness in
December 1621 was due essentially to misunderstanding. James, who
alone was responsible for the framing of foreign policy, wished to
use the Commons for his own purposes by prompting an initiative
from them which he could claim to be a spontaneous expression of
public opinion. An open direction to the Lower House would have
been self-defeating; it might also have goaded the Commons into
an assertion of their right to decide their own order of business.
James had therefore to proceed by winks and nods, indicating the
path he wished them to take but not defining it at all precisely. The
Commons misread his directions and felt genuinely aggrieved when

he accused them of trespassing into areas which were out of bounds.

Communications were always a problem where Crown–Commons' relations were concerned, as James had recognised in 1610 when he summoned thirty selected members to a private conference with him and asked them to tell him frankly what they thought about his financial necessities. According to one account 'they departed exceedingly well and graciously used by the King to every particular man's contentment'.[53] However, when the Commons discussed this informal and innovative procedure, grave doubts were expressed about its propriety. William Hakewill argued that it was potentially dangerous, for the King 'might, by thirty, twenty, or as he please, send for and so know the opinion of the whole House – which is a great infringing of our privileges and contrary to the orders of the House'.[54] Hakewill's arguments clearly struck a chord among his hearers, for a draft order was drawn up

that such private conferences by any of the members of this House, not directed by the counsel and wisdom of this House nor warranted by the authority of the same, do very much tend to the weakening and infringing of the ancient liberty and freedom of this council, and may in future times become very prejudicial as well to the King as to the subject, and that also the same is contrary to the practice and rules of former parliaments.[55]

James never repeated this experiment, but he continued to prefer informal discussions, of the sort that he had employed so effectively with the Scottish parliament, to formal exchanges in which his personality could not be brought into play. The House of Commons, on the other hand, chose to keep its distance simply because members valued their independence. They would have acknowledged the truth behind James's observation that 'in your country villages you are like ships in a river, which look like great things' whereas 'at London you are like ships in a sea, which show like nothing'.[56] Power lay with the King and his Council, and members of Parliament, as individuals, were liable to be reduced or overawed by it. The House's insistence upon its corporate personality and privileges was prompted more by fear than assertiveness, more by weakness than strength. The same factors made it reluctant to follow the lead of Privy Councillors in the Commons, and as a consequence, from the closing years of Elizabeth's reign onwards, the royal government made increasing use of 'unofficial' links. The first session of the 1621 Parliament was an exception, in that Councillors such as Cranfield and Coke commanded the respect of the House, mainly because they shared the attitudes and objectives of its members towards monopolies. In the second session, however,

Cranfield's guidance was lacking, since he had been elevated to the Lords, and Coke was behaving in an increasingly maverick manner. As a consequence, links between the government and the Commons became blurred, and the use of non-conciliar intermediaries such as Goring made matters worse. A lot of the problems of the second session could have been avoided through better communications, and this lesson was not lost on Buckingham when he returned to England from Madrid in late 1623.

FOREIGN AFFAIRS IN THE 1624 PARLIAMENT

Buckingham and Prince Charles had come back from their Spanish venture with a much clearer and more realistic appreciation of the international situation. They were determined to push James into a new course in foreign policy, from peace to war, and since they could not rely on the Council they determined to appeal to Parliament. Buckingham began his preparations by reconciling himself with notable dissidents in the Upper House, such as the Earls of Oxford and Southampton and Lord Saye, for whom he secured a viscountcy. He also won over key figures in the Lower House, among them Sir Robert Phelips, who apparently undertook to speak in favour of supply for a war against Spain if the favourite managed to bring this about. The difficulty inherent in such manoeuvres was that the House was so jealous of its independence that it quickly became suspicious of any member whom it suspected of selling out. Chamberlain reported that the Commons would no longer 'be led along by their old *duces gregis* ['leaders of the flock'] Sir Edwin Sandys, Sir Dudley Digges, and Sir Robert Phelips, for they have so little credit among them that though they speak well, and to the purpose sometimes, yet it is not so well taken at their hands, for still they suspect them to prevaricate, and hold them for undertakers'.[57] Like a modern trade union, the House of Commons was more concerned to defend the rights of those whom it represented than to assume governmental functions along with the corresponding obligations.

James opened what was to be the last Parliament of his reign on 19 February 1624, and by asking the members 'for their advice whether he should proceed any further in his treaties with Spain about the match of the Prince or concerning the restitution of the Palatinate'[58] he was inviting them to discuss foreign policy, which normally lay within the sphere of the prerogative. This initiative was followed up by Buckingham a few days later, when he gave a joint meeting of both Houses a detailed survey of the whole course of the Spanish negotiations. It amounted to a demonstration of Spanish perfidy, and the favourite can have been in no doubt what answer would be given to the question he posed, whether the King should continue the negotiations or 'trust in his own strength and . . . stand upon his own feet'.[59]

The Commons did not immediately seize the opportunity that James and Buckingham had presented to them. Having burnt their fingers once, in December 1621, they did not wish to risk a repeat performance. This time, however, they were given a lead by the Lords, who had said little or nothing about foreign policy in the preceding Parliament but were now rallying behind Buckingham and Prince Charles, who was a regular attender. Significantly, it was not one of Buckingham's clients but Sir Benjamin Rudyerd, whose links were with Buckingham's rival, the Earl of Pembroke, who opened the debate in the Commons by proposing that they should humbly 'advise His Majesty to break off both the treaties of match and Palatinate'.[60] He was supported by all the other speakers, and on 3 March Sir Edward Coke informed the Lords that the Commons had 'unanimously resolved to break both the treaties'.[61] The end of negotiations was highly likely to be followed by war, but although many members expressed bellicose sentiments there is no evidence that they wanted an immediate opening of hostilities. Sir Edwin Sandys gave voice to their attitude when he advised the House 'to restrain our answer to His Majesty's proposition . . . whether it were fit for him to hold any further treaty with Spain or not. To proceed only to answer this, and not, as yet, to meddle with the consequences'.[62] It may be that the Commons felt that one step at a time was sufficient: they were moving into what was for them unknown territory and they could not be sure of James's reaction. It may also be the case that Buckingham's supporters in the House deliberately played down the issue of war at this stage for fear that the members of the Commons – who were aware of the sufferings of their constituents and unwilling to impose further burdens upon them – might take fright and draw back.

The Lords and Commons were now working closely together on drawing up a statement, for presentation to James, of their reasons for wanting an end to the 'Spanish treaties'. At this point the Earl of Southampton observed that when they gave their formal advice to the King, he 'might . . . object there might be, upon this, a breach with Spain, and war, and . . . might demand what assistance we would afford'.[63] The Lords thereupon resolved 'that in the pursuit of this advice we will assist His Majesty with our persons and fortunes, according to our abilities, as becometh good and obedient subjects'.[64] This resolution deliberately echoed Perrot's motion of 4 June 1621, which the Commons had passed with acclamation, and no doubt the Lords were hoping that they would do the same on this occasion. But when Southampton's associate, Sir Edwin Sandys, reported this resolution to the House, its only effect was to rouse a heated debate about the privileges of the Commons where money grants were concerned, and in the end the Lords' proposal was laid aside.

During the course of the debate John Glanvill had argued that 'to provide for war before it be propounded to us is to christen a child before it was born', and suggested that if the King did raise the matter they should simply reply 'that they did not presume to advise upon the means of maintaining a war till he propounded it'.[65] The Commons knew that James remained a pacifist at heart and they had no intention of providing him with money which might be spent merely on reduction of his debts. James, on the other hand, was experienced in the ways of parliaments and was reluctant to commit himself to war unless and until he was assured of adequate funding. It was Buckingham who found the way out of this dilemma by persuading James that when he replied to the address of the two Houses he should invite them to 'choose a committee to see the issuing out of the money they give for the recovery of the Palatinate'.[66] James also assured them that

if, upon your offer, I shall find the means to make the war honourable and safe, and that I resolve to embrace your advice, then I promise you, on the word of a King, that although war and peace be the peculiar prerogatives of kings, yet as I have advised with you in the treaties on which war may ensue, so I will not treat nor accept of a peace without first acquainting you with it and hearing your advice, and therein go the proper way of Parliament in conferring and consulting with you.[67]

When the Lords considered James's reply, Lord Treasurer Middlesex stressed the debts the King had contracted through his foreign policy. Diplomatic missions, the Prince's journey to Spain, and support of the Elector Frederick had cost more than £660,000. The subsidies voted in 1621 and other contributions had brought in £370,000, which left a deficit of £290,000. Middlesex proposed that when the question of supply was discussed, provision should be made for elimination of this deficit as well as for war expenditures, but the Prince brushed this aside as a dangerous diversion, insisting that 'supply for the main [business] is to have priority'.[68] In the Commons the debate was opened by Sir Benjamin Rudyerd who urged members 'to make some proportion presently for His Majesty's own supply, to sweeten parliaments' and proposed the setting up of a Council of War 'for the securing Ireland, strengthening our forts, furnishing the navy, and assisting the Low Countries'.[69] There was one significant omission from this list of strategic priorities, namely the Palatinate: presumably Rudyerd and his patron Pembroke believed that inclusion of this would reopen the debate about a diversionary war and delay the voting of supply. Secretary Conway took much the same line when he pressed the House not to concern itself with details at this stage. 'Give the King such an answer as that he may declare himself', he told them. 'The rest will follow in their time'.[70] In the end the Commons accepted the lead given earlier by the Lords and resolved 'that in pursuit of our advice we will be ready, upon His Majesty's declaration to break off both the treaties, to assist, both with our persons and abilities, in a parliamentary manner'. This was done 'with a general acclamation, without any one voice to the contrary'.[71]

The Lords joined with the Commons in presenting this resolution to James on 14 March. The King thanked the Houses for their general offer of assistance, which, he assured them, he valued 'more than millions of subsidies', but he added the pertinent comment that 'except particular means be set down it will neither be a bridle to the adversary of that cause, nor a comfort to my friends who shall join with me'. He then descended to specifics and asked for five subsidies and ten fifteenths for the 'great business' as well as an annual payment of one subsidy and two fifteenths to eliminate his debts.[72] This double demand was most unwelcome to the Commons, and Buckingham and the Prince immediately set to work to persuade James to accept less. Three days later Buckingham was able to report that James had dropped his insistence upon eliminating the crown's debts and would be content with six subsidies and twelve fifteenths – equivalent to some £780,000 – for the war. This was still a huge amount of money, but if the Commons voted it they would have control over its expenditure. Buckingham also assured them that once they had made this commitment the King would forthwith break off negotiations with Spain.

The Commons spent two days debating the question of supply. It soon became apparent that members were shocked by the size of the sum demanded, but the Councillors in the House dampened down disquiet by insisting that there was no need to vote the whole amount at once. Sir Thomas Edmondes, the Treasurer of the Household, suggested that all the King expected at this stage was 'some competent sum, to enable him to support the charge of a fleet, Ireland and the Low Countries'. He thereupon proposed three subsidies.[73] Edmondes was supported by Sir Richard Weston, the Chancellor of the Exchequer, who admitted that 'the sound of six subsidies and twelve fifteeenths [was] very fearful' but added that they could limit themselves by way of immediate provision to 'so much as the present necessity requires'.[74] John Glanvill was of the same opinion, but pointed out that they would have to commit themselves to a specific sum because the King had warned them 'that general terms will not carry it'. As for the amount, it would have to be 'an extraordinary overture that must draw the King from peace. If this give the King occasion not to declare, where are we then? . . . [It is] better to fall into the arms of England than Spain. We bestow what we do upon ourselves'.[75] Sir Henry Vane made the further point that if the Commons' response to the King's overture was inadequate, 'parliaments will not be so frequent'. In addition they risked incurring the 'distaste also of him that is to succeed'.[76]

The Commons eventually resolved, without one dissenting voice,

that after His Majesty shall have been pleased to declare himself for the utter dissolution and discharge of the two treaties for the marriage and the [restoration of the] Palatinate, the House, in pursuit of their advice given to His Majesty, and towards support of the war which is likely to ensue – and more particularly for those four points proposed by His Majesty: namely, the defence of this realm, the securing of Ireland, the assistance of our neighbours the States of the United Provinces, and the setting-out of His Majesty's royal navy – will grant, for the present, three subsidies and three fifteenths, to be . . . paid unto the hands, and expended by the direction, of such . . . commissioners as shall hereafter be agreed on in this present session of Parliament.[77]

The Lords approved of this, and the two Houses drew up a joint draft of the declaration to be made to the King when their resolution was formally presented. Buckingham took the precaution of showing this to James beforehand, and reported that the King had only two objections. The first was to the statement that the war would be for the defence of the 'true religion'. This, said James, would be unacceptable 'in respect of the help he hopeth to have from divers catholic princes'.[78] The second was to the absence of any mention of eliminating the crown debts. The Houses dealt with the first point by removing all mention of religion. As for the second, Buckingham assured the King that 'though we had omitted it now, yet in due time we would take it into consideration'.[79]

In a ceremony at Whitehall on 23 March James formally accepted Parliament's offer, but he warned members that the sum voted was only 'sufficient for the present entrance into the business'. He now publicly committed himself to break off the two treaties, but on the understanding 'that you will make good what you have spoken, and that in what you advise me unto, you will assist me with your wisdom, monies and forces, if need require'.[80] In other words, James saw the future conduct of the war as depending upon the fulfilment of the general promises given by both Houses. Where war aims were concerned, he insisted that the recovery of the Palatinate must come high on the list. He was also insistent that he alone should decide on strategy. He would appoint a Council of War to advise him, but its deliberations must of necessity be kept secret. 'Whether, therefore, I shall send two thousand or ten thousand, whether by sea or by land, north or south, by diversion or otherwise . . . that must be in the council of mine own heart, and that you must leave to the King'. The parliamentary commissioners were to oversee the expenditure of the monies that had been voted, 'yet how much shall go out, or how little, must be in the power of the King, whose war it is, whose stewards they are'.[81]

Although James and the two Houses were slowly edging towards each other, there was still a substantial gap dividing them. James had committed himself to ending current negotiations with Spain about the marriage of his son and the restoration of the Palatinate but had not promised to break off relations altogether. Indeed he was still hoping that the clear evidence of parliamentary pressure for war would encourage the Spaniards to make meaningful concessions. Moreover, although he had envisaged the possibility of war he had not declared it or even named the enemy. As for Parliament, the members had agreed to vote three subsidies but had not yet done so. They expected to be given evidence that naval and military operations were under way, yet even the preliminary stages of these were dependent upon the supply of money, for the crown had none of its own to spare.

Another major difference was over the nature and purpose of the war. James was concerned above all to secure the restoration of the Palatinate and was thinking in terms of an expedition to achieve this. He did not see such an operation as leading inevitably to war with Spain, for the Spanish occupation force in the Palatinate was there in the Emperor's name and service. James therefore hoped that the recovery by the Elector Frederick of what was rightfully his could be accomplished without involving England in hostilities with the greatest military power in Europe. Many members of the Lords and Commons, however, believed that Spain was the enemy they should be fighting and that religion was the true cause at stake. War against catholic Spain had the further advantage of offering rich rewards through capture of enemy prizes. A self-financing war was the mirage which hovered before the eyes of members of Parliament, for this would enable them to fulfil their commitment to God's cause without imposing financial burdens upon God's people.

When the two Houses reassembled at the beginning of April, after a brief Easter recess, Buckingham tried to persuade the Commons to authorise the raising of loans for war purposes on the security of the forthcoming subsidies. Sir John Eliot, who was at this time Buckingham's client, called this a 'matter of great importance' since 'the season of the year requires haste',[82] but the House was not prepared to break with precedent over this sensitive issue. Instead, it spent several days discussing the reasons for the decay of trade, which served as a reminder, if any was needed, of the financial constraints upon its freedom of action. The House also took up the question of recusants, for as Sir Robert Phelips said, 'Spain can do us no harm unless he have a party here in England'.[83] Sir Robert Heath, the Solicitor General, suggested that the Commons should 'make it a piece of our petition to His Majesty never to entertain treaty that may entangle us with the like inconvenience again', and this was adopted.[84] The petition, calling for much stricter enforcement of the laws against popish priests and recusants, was, in effect, a rebuttal of James's insistence that the impending war had nothing to do with religion. James realised this and responded by holding up the departure of the despatch to Spain announcing the breaking-off of negotiations. A major clash of wills was only averted by the action of the Prince, who persuaded his father to let the despatch go in return for an assurance that the petition would be modified in such a way as to make it acceptable to him. The Lords, and eventually the Commons, followed the Prince's lead, but only because he gave a formal promise in the Upper House 'that whensoever it should please God to bestow upon him any lady that were popish, she should have no further liberty but for her own family [i.e. household], and no advantage to the recusants at home'.[85]

The Prince now put pressure upon the Commons to expedite the subsidy Bill, and Buckingham, with James's permission, gave details of the despatch ordering the breaking-off of the treaties with Spain. This was followed up by the Duke's close associate, Secretary

Conway, who called on the Commons to deal with the major remaining question of supply. 'The necessity of going on with this', he said, was 'very necessary. Delay will be very dangerous'.[86] The subsidy Bill was given its first reading on 22 April. The second followed on the 24th, after James had accepted the petition on religion. The Commons were encouraged by indications that the commitment to war was genuine – on the part of Buckingham and the Prince, at any rate, if not on the King's. Commissioners had been appointed to negotiate terms of an alliance with the Dutch; there was talk of a combined expedition against Spain; and the mercenary commander, Count Mansfeld, was already in London, discussing his terms for leading an Anglo-French force to recover the Palatinate (see p. 24).

The Spanish ambassadors in London had hitherto been counting on James to nullify the bellicose instincts of the Prince, the favourite and Parliament, but they were increasingly alarmed at the way in which James was being pushed towards war. They struck a counter-blow by revealing to James the details of a 'plot', which they claimed to be masterminded by Buckingham, to shut him away in one of his country houses so that he no longer had control of government. The ever-suspicious King took these accusations seriously, as did Buckingham, though for different reasons. Buckingham knew that there were elements at Court which opposed the whole idea of war with Spain, and would have welcomed the opportunity to topple him from power. Chief among these was Lord Treasurer Middlesex. Indeed, in 1623, when Buckingham was away in Spain, his agents at Court had warned him that Middlesex was intriguing against him. While Middlesex remained in office and in James's confidence he was a threat to the entire anti-Spanish policy which Buckingham had embraced. As the controller of the royal finances he was also the embodiment of those fiscal measures such as Impositions which the Commons most resented. The overthrow of Middlesex would therefore be not only a warning to Buckingham's opponents among the pro-Spanish group at Court but also a signal to the Commons that financial reform was on the agenda. On 5 April Sir Miles Fleetwood, who may have been acting on Buckingham's behalf, laid charges against the Treasurer before the Commons, who duly impeached him before the Lords. On 13 May Middlesex was sentenced to be deprived of his offices, fined £50,000, imprisoned in the Tower, and barred from Court. He had been a dedicated and effective crown servant, as James openly acknowledged. It was not corruption but politics which led to his destruction.

Although the subsidy Bill had received two readings and gone into its committee stage, it was only making slow progress. The main reason for this was the need to define the responsibilities of the commissioners who were to oversee the expenditure of the subsidies, but it was also the case that the longer the session lasted the more chance the Commons had of enacting commonwealth Bills. The 1621 Parliament had been abortive in this respect, but 1624 saw the passing of well over thirty public Acts, principal among them that which restricted the crown's right to grant monopolies. Work on the subsidy Bill was more or less completed by 14 May when it was reported from committee to the House. It declared, 'by the authority of this present Parliament, that the said two treaties are by Your Majesty utterly dissolved' and provided three subsidies and three fifteenths 'for the maintenance of that war which may hereupon ensue, and more particularly for the defence of this your realm of England, the securing of your kingdom of Ireland, the assistance of your neighbours the States of the United Provinces and other Your Majesty's friends and allies, and for the setting forth of your navy royal'. The monies raised by this grant – which the Bill described as 'the greatest aid which ever was granted in Parliament to be levied in so short a time' – were to be paid to parliamentary treasurers, who were listed by name. They in turn were to disburse them only on the instructions of the Council of War, whose members were also recorded by name. It was further provided 'that as well the said treasurers as the said persons appointed for the Council of War . . . shall be answerable and accountable for their doings or proceedings herein to the Commons in Parliament when they shall be thereunto required by warrant under the hand of the Speaker of the House of Commons'.[87]

The Solicitor General, Sir Robert Heath, was aware that from the King's point of view the Bill had several deficiencies. The most important of these was the failure to include the recovery of the Palatinate among the four specified objectives. Heath therefore suggested that this should be added, and that assistance to the Low Countries should be confined to what was necessary 'as a means to recover the Palatinate'.[88] The Commons were in no mood to compromise, however. They insisted on engrossing the Bill as it had been reported, and on 21 May they gave it a third and final reading. The session was now drawing to a close, and the Lords had time only for a cursory consideration of what was a long and complex Bill before they also passed it. The last stage came on 29 May when James accepted the subsidy Bill, but with an ill grace. Edward Nicholas, who was present on the occasion, recorded the King as saying 'that the preamble of the subsidy Bill being made without his advice and contrary to his interests, he must alter it by marginal notes'. This was received, according to Nicholas, 'with such murmurs and signs that both His Majesty and the lords saw how much it was disliked, as being beyond all precedent or order'.[89]

The 1624 Parliament was in many ways an exceptional one. For the first time in James's reign a reversionary interest had emerged and the Court was divided between James and his supporters, who were either opposed to war altogether or at best lukewarm in their attitude, and the adherents of Prince Charles and Buckingham, who were fully committed to it. The 'Prince's party' was well organised in both Houses, and the positive achievements of the session were largely due to this. But James was by no means a cipher, and the Commons' reluctance to commit themselves wholeheartedly to support of the war was due in part to their fear, which was well grounded, that he would take their money but still seek a negotiated settlement with Spain. They gave as little as they could, with vague assurances about the future. Buckingham and the Prince were prepared to accept these because they had little choice. They were counting on speedy victories to swing public opinion behind them and force the Commons to open their purse strings more widely. In retrospect it seems that they were mistaken and would have been better advised to work for agreement with the Commons on both the nature of the war and the level at which it should be funded. But they were at the mercy of events over which they had no control. Great armies were in movement on the continent of Europe and if England was to intervene effectively she needed to do so speedily, before the tide had turned irrevocably in favour of the Habsburgs. The Lord Keeper's words to Parliament in 1628 were of equal applicability to the 1624 session: 'we may dandle and play as we will with the hourglass that is in our power, but the hours will not stay for us, and an opportunity once lost cannot be regained'.[90]

NOTES AND REFERENCES

(*The place of publication is London, unless otherwise stated*)
1. *The Reports of Sir Edward Coke, Kt.* (1738). Part XI, p. 86v.
2. **James F. Larkin** & **Paul L. Hughes** (eds.) *Stuart Royal Proclamations.* Vol. I. *Royal Proclamations of King James I* (Oxford 1973), p. 12. (Hereafter Larkin & Hughes *Royal Proclamations*)
3. **Wallace Notestein, Frances Helen Relf** & **Hartley Simpson** (eds.) *Commons Debates 1621* (New Haven 1935). Vol. VII. Appx. B. Part 2, p. 491. (Hereafter *Commons Debates 1621*)

4. ***The Works of Francis Bacon*** ed. James Spedding (1874). Vol. XI, p. 98. (Hereafter Bacon *Works*)
5. ***The Letters of John Chamberlain*** ed. N. E. McClure (Philadelphia 1939). Vol. I, p. 311. (Hereafter Chamberlain *Letters*)
6. Bacon *Works*. Vol. XIV, pp. 148–49.
7. *Commons Debates 1621*. Vol. II, p. 108.
8. *Commons Debates 1621*. Vol. V, p. 478.
9. *Commons Debates 1621*. Vol. V, p. 479.
10. *Commons Debates 1621*. Vol. VI, p. 372.
11. *Commons Debates 1621*. Vol. II, p. 108.
12. *Commons Debates 1621*. Vol. II, p. 90.
13. *Commons Debates 1621*. Vol. II, p. 180.
14. *Commons Debates 1621*. Vol. II, p. 194.
15. *Commons Debates 1621*. Vol. II, p. 210.
16. **John Rushworth** *Historical Collections* (1682). Vol. I, p. 26. (Hereafter Rushworth *Historical Collections*)
17. Larkin & Hughes *Royal Proclamations*, p. 513–16.
18. **S. R. Gardiner** (ed.) *The Constitutional Documents of the Puritan Revolution 1625–1660* (Oxford 1906), p. 212.
19. *Commons Debates 1621*. Vol. VI, p. 371.
20. Chamberlain *Letters*. Vol. II, p. 342
21. *Commons Debates 1621*. Vol. II, p. 91.
22. *Commons Debates 1621*. Vol. V, p. 466.
23. *Commons Debates 1621*. Vol. VII. Appx. C, p. 578
24. **Roger Lockyer** *Buckingham: The Life and Political Career of George Villiers, First Duke of Buckingham 1592–1628* (1981), p. 99. (Hereafter Lockyer *Buckingham*)
25. *Commons Debates 1621*. Vol. II, p. 306.
26. *Commons Debates 1621*. Vol. II, p. 407.
27. *Commons Debates 1621*. Vol. II, p. 408.
28. *Commons Debates 1621*. Vol. III, p. 357.
29. *Commons Debates 1621*. Vol. III, p. 363.
30. *Commons Debates 1621*. Vol. VII, Appx, p. 616.
31. *Commons Debates 1621*. Vol. VI, pp. 406–08.
32. *Commons Debates 1621*. Vol. VI, p. 408.
33. ***Journals of the House of Commons 1547–1714*** (1742). Vol. I, p. 639. (Hereafter *Commons Journals*)
34. *Commons Journals*. Vol. I, p. 639.
35. Rushworth *Historical Collections*. Vol. I, p. 36.
36. *Commons Debates 1621*. Vol. II, p. 437.
37. *Commons Journals*. Vol. I, p. 645.
38. *Commons Debates 1621*. Vol. III, p. 451.
39. *Commons Debates 1621*. Vol. III, p. 454.
40. *Commons Journals*. Vol. I, p. 645.
41. *Commons Journals*. Vol. I, p. 647.
42. *Commons Debates 1621*. Vol. VII, Appx. C, p. 619.
43. *Commons Debates 1621*. Vol. III, pp. 466–67.
44. *Commons Journals*. Vol. I, p. 649.
45. *Commons Journals*. Vol. I, p. 649.
46. *Commons Debates 1621*. Vol. III, p. 471.

47. *Commons Journals.* Vol. I, p. 649.
48. *Commons Journals.* Vol. I, p. 650.
49. Lockyer *Buckingham*, p. 108.
50. Lockyer *Buckingham*, p. 109.
51. Lockyer *Buckingham*, p. 110.
52. **J. R. Tanner** (ed.) *Constitutional Documents of the Reign of James I* (Cambridge 1930), p. 279. (Hereafter Tanner *Constitutional Documents*)
53. **E. R. Foster** (ed.) *Proceedings in Parliament 1610* (New Haven 1966). Vol. 2, p. 338. (Hereafter Foster *Proceedings 1610*)
54. Foster *Proceedings 1610.* Vol. 2, p. 342, n.7.
55. Foster *Proceedings 1610.* Vol. 2, p. 391.
56. Bacon *Works.* Vol. VII, p. 175.
57. Chamberlain *Letters.* Vol. II, p. 549.
58. *Commons Journals.* Vol. I, p. 670.
59. Rushworth *Historical Collections.* Vol. I, p. 125.
60. *Commons Journals.* Vol. I, p. 675.
61. *Commons Journals.* Vol. I, p. 676.
62. *Commons Journals.* Vol. I, p. 676.
63. *Commons Journals.* Vol. I, p. 729.
64. *Commons Journals.* Vol. I, p. 729.
65. **R. E. Ruigh** *The Parliament of 1624* (Cambridge, Mass. 1971), p. 194. (Hereafter Ruigh *1624 Parliament*)
66. Ruigh *1624 Parliament*, p. 199.
67. Ruigh *1624 Parliament*, p. 200.
68. Ruigh *1624 Parliament*, p. 202–03.
69. *Commons Journals.* Vol. I, p. 732.
70. *Commons Journals.* Vol. I, p. 733.
71. *Commons Journals.* Vol. I, p. 733.
72. Ruigh *1624 Parliament*, p. 211.
73. *Commons Journals.* Vol. I, p. 740.
74. *Commons Journals.* Vol. I, p. 741.
75. *Commons Journals*, Vol. I, p. 742.
76. *Commons Journals*, Vol. I, p. 742.
77. *Commons Journals.* Vol. I, p. 744.
78. Ruigh *1624 Parliament*, p. 229.
79. *Commons Journals.* Vol. I, p. 746.
80. Ruigh *1624 Parliament*, p. 230.
81. Ruigh *1624 Parliament*, p. 231.
82. *Commons Journals.* Vol. I, p. 752.
83. *Commons Journals.* Vol. I, p. 752.
84. *Commons Journals.* Vol. I, p. 752.
85. *Commons Journals.* Vol. I, p. 756.
86. *Commons Journals.* Vol. I, p. 772.
87. Tanner *Constitutional Documents*, pp. 375–77.
88. Ruigh *1624 Parliament*, p. 254.
89. *Calendar of State Papers, Domestic Series, of the Reign of James I. 1623–1625* (1859), p. 261.
90. **Robert C. Johnson, Mary Frear Keeler, Maija Jansson Cole & William Bidwell** (eds.) *Commons Debates 1628* (New Haven 1977). Vol. II, p. 8.

CHAPTER NINE
Charles I and the Constitution

THE NEW KING

James I died on 27 March 1625 at the great mansion of Theobalds
which he had rebuilt and embellished and made an appropriately
regal setting for the hunting excursions which he enjoyed so much.
He had never established himself in the affections of his people as
his predecessor, Queen Elizabeth, had done, nor did he have her
natural dignity or her instinctive sense of when to use the common
touch. But he was by no means unpopular. In March 1619 John
Chamberlain had told his correspondent, Dudley Carleton, of the
concern that had been created by reports that the King was unwell.
'I am glad to see the world so tenderly affected towards him', he
added, 'for I assure you all men apprehend what a loss we should
have if God should take him from us, and do earnestly enquire, and
in general heartily wish and pray for his welfare'.[1] James's faults
were only too apparent, but they should not be allowed to conceal
his considerable achievements. He kept his country at peace for more
than twenty years, he prevented religious divisions from tearing
Church and state apart, and despite rhetorical flourishes about the
unlimited authority of divinely-appointed kings he held the
monarchy to the course prescribed by common law.

It is often assumed that the long speeches with which James
regaled his parliaments were so much verbal flatulence, and treated
as such; but repeated references to them in the opening parliaments
of his son's reign show that they had made their mark. Sir Nathaniel
Rich, speaking in March 1628, recalled James's declaration that
'whosoever should bid the King go against law was a viper',[2] and
in the same debate Sir Robert Phelips reminded the House that 'our

late King said, were he to choose a law, he would choose our common law'.[3] In short, James's repeated professions of his commitment to customary ways and legal methods had had their effect in preserving the image of the King as a constitutional ruler despite his recourse to unpopular measures such as Impositions. James may have been too much in love with the sound of his own voice, but he was addressing members of a political nation that fed on long sermons. The tongue-tied Charles was briefer and pithier, but for that very reason he often lost his case by default.

The switch from garrulity to reticence was not the only contrast between the new reign and the old. James's Court had not been renowned for its high morality. The daughter of Sir Allen Apsley – Victualler of the Navy and governor of the Tower of London – who married the puritan Colonel Hutchinson, condemned 'the bawdry and profane abusive wit, which was [its] only exercise', along with its 'fools and bawds, mimics and catamites'.[4] Like many of her contemporaries she welcomed the accession of Charles, who was 'temperate, chaste, and serious', an opinion echoed by Chamberlain, who reported in April 1625 that 'the Court is kept more strait and private than in the former time'. The new King, he noted, 'is very attentive and devout at prayers and sermons, gracing the preachers and assembly with amiable and cheerful countenance, which gives much satisfaction'.[5]

Charles had every reason to assume that his reign would open with a honeymoon period. He was a young man, not yet twenty-five, who had won golden opinions by his conduct in the parliaments of 1621 and 1624 and for the way in which he had resisted the blandishments of the Spaniards during his stay at Philip IV's court in 1623. Yet in one crucial respect he carried over into his reign the most unacceptable feature of his father's, namely the primacy of the Duke of Buckingham in the royal counsels. Buckingham had come to be regarded as the embodiment of all that was wrong with the Jacobean state, and there were many people who hoped and prayed that the accession of a new ruler would see the casting-off of the old favourite. However, they were quickly disillusioned, for as the two men stood by the bedside of the dead King, Charles assured the grieving Duke that 'you have found another that will no less cherish you'. When Charles left for London he took Buckingham along with him, confirmed him in all his offices, and presented him with a golden key which gave him the right of entry to all the royal palaces.[6]

Charles was a reserved man who found it difficult to make

friends, but Buckingham, both before and during the time they had spent together in Spain, had broken through this carapace of shyness and established a durable relationship. Sir Robert Cotton showed himself to be a perceptive observer when he commented, during the attack on Buckingham in the Parliament of 1626, that Charles would 'never yield to the Duke's fall, being a young man, resolute, magnanimous, and tenderly and firmly affectionate where he takes'.[7] It was not only a question of personal feelings, however. Charles was convinced that Buckingham, who had risen by service to the crown, was a devoted and capable adviser, pursuing policies that were in the best interests of the country. Attacks on him were prompted, or so Charles believed, by ignorance, jealousy, and – more sinisterly – the desire to undermine the monarchy. In these circumstances it was clearly incumbent on the new King to stand firm and not give way to ill-informed popular clamour.

CHARLES'S ATTITUDE TOWARDS PARLIAMENT

Charles had begun his parliamentary apprenticeship in 1621, and James explained that he had instructed his son to attend the Lords so that 'when it shall please God to set him in my place [he] will then remember that he was once a member of your House and so be bound to maintain all your lawful privileges and like the better of you all the days of his life'.[8] Charles was a regular attender at debates, and Chamberlain reported that 'his affability and courtesy in the Parliament hath won him great reputation and love'.[9] No doubt the Prince welcomed this release from his rather restricted upbringing and the opportunity it gave him to meet the leaders of the political nation and share in their discussions. He even relished his encounters with Sir Edward Coke, for after that worthy had enlivened a conference with the story of a friar who went to Rome and was so overwhelmed with the splendour of the papacy that he declared St Peter had been a fool to embrace prayer and poverty, Charles told Coke 'I am never weary of hearing you, you do so well mix pleasant things with these sad and serious matters'.[10]

His experiences in the 1624 Parliament, coming on top of those in 1621, can only have confirmed Charles in his favourable impression of Parliament as an institution. Indeed, his original intention when he became King was to reconvene the assembly elected in 1624. Only after it had been pointed out to him that his father's death had automatically ended its life did he order writs to be sent out for a new one. This may account for the notable lack of government guidance in the first session of 1625, but it also seems likely that Charles was counting on the goodwill which he had earned as Prince to sustain him now that he was King. The Lord Keeper, when he opened proceedings, referred to the key role played by Charles in what he called the 'happy' Parliament of 1624, which, he said, 'may assure us that he will hereafter be to parliaments as a soul in the body, and cannot never pretend himself a stranger to the customs, or forgetful of the wishes and desires, of Parliament'.[11] The same sentiment was voiced by Sir Benjamin Rudyerd, who stressed that the Prince had broken the cycle of 'distastes' between James and his parliaments which had been 'the chief cause of all the miseries of the kingdom'.[12] This, he added, was hardly surprising, given the fact that Charles 'hath been bred in parliaments, which hath made him not only to know but to favour the ways of his own subjects'.[13]

Charles opened his first Parliament with a reminder that its members were bound by the commitment given a year earlier to support the King if the actions which he took in response to their advice to break off negotiations with Spain led to war. Lord Keeper Coventry made the same point. 'His Majesty', he told the two Houses, 'puts his fame, his reputation . . . upon us . . . As soon as he shall be known for a valiant prince, you shall be esteemed a faithful people'.[14] This was more than a rhetorical flourish, for from the very outset of his reign Charles took commitment to the war which he had embarked on as the touchstone of loyalty to him. He never doubted for one moment that the 1624 Parliament had made such a commitment. Indeed, the Subsidy Act passed by that Parliament was declared by its own words to be 'an ample testimony of our dutiful affections and sincere intentions to assist you . . . for the maintenance of that war'.[15] Yet in 1625 the Commons, for reasons which will be considered elsewhere (see p. 326), refused to honour their predecessors' promise. Far from voting ample supply, they even called the crown's ordinary revenue into question by declining to make the traditional lifetime grant of the Customs duties, Tonnage and Poundage.

Charles was profoundly disturbed by the Commons' unwillingness or inability to respond to his appeal. As Rudyerd later observed, 'the King certainly is very tender of his present honour and of his fame hereafter',[16] and Charles did not conceal his puzzlement and bitterness at the way in which his commitment to a justified and apparently popular war, and in particular to his foreign allies, had been undercut by what he regarded as an inexplicable and wilful abdication of responsibility on the part of Parliament. In a moment of despair he was said to have asked Buckingham 'What can I do more? I have engaged mine honour to mine uncle of Denmark and other princes. I have, in a manner, lost the love of my subjects. What wouldst thou have me do?'.[17] He showed his anger by dissolving his first Parliament when it refused to increase its grant of two subsidies, but its successor was even less tractable, for although the Commons declared their willingness to vote four subsidies and three fifteenths they carefully refrained from embodying this grant in a Bill and made it plain that they would do so only after their grievances had been redressed. Since the main grievance in their eyes was the continued supremacy of Buckingham in the King's counsels, they were really demanding his dismissal as the price of supply. Charles regarded this as blackmail, an affront to his dignity, and a breach with established conventions. Rather than give way, he dissolved Parliament.

Charles had now been King for just over a year, and during that time his attitude towards Parliament had undergone a fundamental change. As an active member of the Upper House in both 1621 and 1624 he had gained an inside knowledge of the working of Parliament that was denied his father and he therefore had less reason to be suspicious of it as an institution. James had found Parliament to be in many respects an unknown quantity, and while he genuinely wanted to establish harmonious relations with it, he sometimes doubted whether this was possible. Nor was he alone in his doubts. His first Lord Chancellor, Ellesmere, was so shocked by the Commons' attitude in 1610 that he committed to paper his view that 'the popular state ever since the beginning of His Majesty's gracious and sweet government hath grown big and audacious, and in every session of Parliament swelled more and more. And if way be still given unto it (as of late hath been) it is to be doubted what the end will be'.[18] There are indications that by the middle of 1626 Charles was veering towards this view. The Venetian ambassador reported hearing complaints 'from the King and the dependants of the Duke of Buckingham . . . that the parliamentarians are too audacious, and that His Majesty ought not to suffer his dignity and reputation to be taken away from him by his subjects'.[19] At about the same time an anonymous author informed the King 'that this great opposition against the Duke of Buckingham is stirred up and maintained by such who, either maliciously or ignorantly . . . seek the debasing of this free monarchy; which because they find not yet ripe to attempt against the King himself, they endeavour it through the Duke's side'. Charles should therefore hold fast, he advised, because Buckingham's overthrow would be 'the cornerstone on which the demolishing of his monarchy will be builded'.[20] It was surely more than a coincidence that Charles's proclamation denouncing the remonstrance against Buckingham echoed this advice by declaring that 'through the sides of a peer of this realm, they [the Commons] wound the honour of the sovereign'.[21]

In a declaration which he issued to defend his action in dissolving the 1626 Parliament Charles laid the blame firmly on 'the violent and ill-advised passions of a few members of the House [of Commons]' who, 'for private and personal ends ill beseeming public persons trusted by their country . . . wilfully refused to hearken to all the gentle admonitions which His Majesty could give them, and . . . wholly forgot their engagements to His Majesty for the public defence of the realm'.[22] Even before the session was brought to a close, fears had been expressed that the days of parliaments in England were numbered. Sir Dudley Carleton reminded the Commons that representative assemblies had existed in many countries until the monarchs 'seeing the turbulent spirits of their parliaments . . . began to stand upon their prerogatives, and at last overthrew the parliaments throughout Christendom, except here only with us'. The implication of Carleton's speech was clear: if there was a continuing lack of harmony between the King and the two Houses, Parliament would no longer be of any value to the royal government, and Charles would be 'enforced to use new counsels'.[23]

CHARLES AND THE LAW: THE FORCED LOAN

Evidence of just such a change of course was swiftly forthcoming, for the dissolution of Parliament had put an end to any hope of supply from that quarter, but urgent defensive measures needed to be taken in view of reports that the Spaniards were preparing to invade. Furthermore, in September news reached England of the defeat of Charles's principal ally, Christian IV of Denmark, in the battle of Lutter. The King took this very much to heart, and assured the Danish ambassador, with tears in his eyes, 'that he would render his uncle every assistance, even at the risk of his own crown and hazarding his life'.[24] He then presided over a Council meeting lasting four hours in which the members considered how to fulfil the King's promise. Attempts to raise money by a Benevolence had been a complete failure, so the Council now decided to levy a forced loan. Some of the Councillors proposed that the King should pledge himself to repay the loan out of future parliamentary subsidies, but Charles would not hear of it. 'They might pledge his word and crown', he said, 'but there was to be no question of Parliament'.[25] Indeed, such was the strength of his feelings that he was reported to have forbidden his Council even to mention Parliament, since 'he did abominate that name'.[26] Charles's anger sprang from his belief that Parliament had been guilty of disloyal conduct at this crucial moment when not only his honour but the fate of Europe were at stake. The response to the Forced Loan would be an indication of whether the Commons were an accurate reflector of public opinion.

Forced loans, levied from individuals by privy seal letters, had long been a feature of Tudor and early Stuart public finance, but the 1626 levy was significantly different, since all subsidy payers were assessed for it, at the rate of five subsidies. It was, in other words, parliamentary taxation without parliamentary sanction, and as such it ran counter to many Englishmen's most deeply-held beliefs. Charles's view seems to have been that where Parliament had failed in its duty it was incumbent upon the sovereign to act. Insofar as Parliament's failure indicated a lack of respect for the royal authority, this must be countered by inculcating in all subjects the primary duty of obedience. The sermons given by Sibthorpe and Mainwaring of which the Commons subsequently complained (see p. 309) were an integral part of this process, and Charles showed his approval by insisting on their publication.

Charles had no wish to act illegally, nor did he believe he was doing so. He called on the judges to validate the Loan, but when they declined to do so, he dismissed Sir Ranulph Crewe – who had been Speaker in the Addled Parliament – from his post as Chief Justice of King's Bench. He replaced him with Sir Nicholas Hyde, who had won favour by helping to draft Buckingham's reply to the charges laid against him by the Commons in 1626. Charles intended his action as a sign that he was determined to be obeyed, but the news of the judges' resistance had the opposite effect and prompted mounting opposition. Altogether some seventy gentlemen were imprisoned for refusing to subscribe to the Loan. Five of them carried their challenge one stage further by suing out writs of *habeas corpus*, demanding to know the cause of their detention. They assumed that the crown would reply that it was for failing to subscribe to the Forced Loan, and that the ensuing trial would centre round the question of the Loan's legality. However, the Council, when it drew up the reply, simply stated that the knights had been imprisoned *per speciale mandatum domini regis* ['by special command of our lord the King'].

There had never been any question that in matters affecting state security the crown had the right to imprison without showing specific cause, and Sir Edward Coke had informed the Commons in 1621 that 'one committed by the body of the Council [is] not bailable by law'.[27] What the judges usually did in such cases was wait to be informed privately by the Council of the true causes for imprisonment, and then decide whether or not to award bail. This was the course they took in November 1627. They were in a difficult position, for except in the most general sense there was no threat to state security involved in the action of Loan refusers. The crown was using a legal technicality to avoid discussion of the major issue at stake, yet the conventions of the law made it difficult, if not impossible, for the judges to set aside the Council's reply and to decide on the legality of forced loans. They were, after all, the King's servants, committed to the maintenance of the·existing structure of state and society. It was an underlying assumption of the English legal tradition that the sovereign had to be trusted. If in practice he proved untrustworthy, there was little that the law could do about it.

The judges in the Five Knights Case declined to pass judgment. They merely remanded the prisoners in custody pending a further hearing, no doubt hoping that the Council would, as was customary, inform them of the true nature of the prisoners' offence. Failing that, the knights themselves could sue out another writ of *habeas corpus* and start the ball rolling again. In other words, while the judges had not taken a stand on the defence of English liberties, neither had they endorsed the action of the crown. Loan refusers and their many supporters might regard this as a betrayal, but the Solicitor General, Sir Robert Heath, took a different view. He had hoped for a clear judgment in favour of the crown, and although none had been given, he tried to have one inserted in the official record of the King's Bench proceedings so that it could be used as a precedent on future occasions. Had it not been for the summoning of the 1628 Parliament he might well have succeeded, and the effect of his action would have been, as Sir Robert Phelips commented, to 'determine the question against us for ever and ever'.[28]

Charles, who was not a lawyer, is unlikely to have understood – or even, perhaps, to have been aware of – the details of Heath's devious manoeuvres, but he would undoubtedly have approved of Heath's overall aim of strengthening royal authority. Charles was more authoritarian than his father and lacked the philosophical bent that had given James at least some appreciation of views with which he was not himself in sympathy. Admittedly James had dismissed Sir Edward Coke from the Chief Justiceship of King's Bench, but only after that stubborn and cantankerous genius had tried his patience beyond the limits of endurance. Charles's dismissal of Crewe was of a totally different character, for Crewe had never challenged the royal authority. He was deprived of his office simply because he and his fellow judges were unable to accept Charles's interpretation of the law. It may be that Charles's action made the judges more amenable to conciliar control, but to the extent that it did so it called in question their role as umpires in disputes affecting the prerogatives of the crown and the liberties of the subject. Yet Charles was doing no more than the Commons had done when they refused to accept the judges' verdict in such matters as Impositions and the Union. Both King and Commons were so convinced not merely of the justice but of the legality of their case in certain highly controversial questions that they were not prepared to accept arbitration. In the last resort the Commons regarded themselves as the guardians and interpreters of the law. Charles did likewise.

Opposition to the Loan had been prompted by the fear that it would open the way to permanent prerogative taxation and thereby eliminate the need for parliaments. Charles blamed such fears on deliberate misrepresentation by 'malevolous persons' and declared that 'it is far from our heart . . . to make this any annual or usual course of raising monies'. On the contrary, 'we are fully purposed to call a Parliament so soon as conveniently we may, and as often as the commonwealth and state occasions shall require it'. The success of the Loan, far from threatening the existence of parliaments would actually strengthen it, for 'our people's affections now showed unto us in this way of necessity . . . shall the sooner invite us to the frequent use of parliaments'.[29]

CHARLES AND THE LAW: THE PETITION OF RIGHT

The success of the Loan in financial terms (see p. 246) could be taken as an indication of the subjects' loyalty, and the moderates on the Council used this argument to try to persuade the King to revert to a parliamentary course. Charles was reluctant to do so, particularly in view of the fact that the failure of the Ré expedition (see p. 29) had struck a further blow at the reputation of his chief adviser, Buckingham. With the war still continuing, Charles was more than ever aware of the danger of being held to ransom by the Commons, forced to sacrifice both his minister and his policy in return for parliamentary supply. In January 1628, therefore, he instructed his Councillors to 'enter into consideration of all the best and speediest ways and means you can for raising of monies . . . the same to be done by impositions or otherwise as . . . you shall find to be most convenient in a case of this inevitable necessity, wherein form and circumstances must be dispensed with rather than the substance be lost or hazarded'.[30] Despite the crippling shortage of money, Charles also made funds available for the levying in Germany and the Low Countries of a thousand mercenary cavalrymen, 'to be brought over into this kingdom for our service'.[31]

Charles subsequently explained that this force – which was never in fact raised – was intended to be sent to his uncle, the King of Denmark. This may have been the case, but the 'Excise Commission' and the 'German Horse' could have provided a means by which to establish Charles's rule upon a firmer, more 'absolute' basis, following the pattern already established in European states. Charles's reference to 'inevitable necessity', and his use of this to justify the abandonment of conventional 'form and circumstances', are evidence of his readiness to adopt new patterns of government, at least in the short term. Yet although he made his views known to the Privy Council, he never attempted to browbeat members or to force them to line up behind him. There were elements in the Council who would have supported a hard-line approach, with greater insistence upon the prerogative powers of the crown, but they were outnumbered by the moderates, and in the end Charles went along with the majority. This may indicate that he was at heart a conservative, anxious to rule in a conventional manner if only he could do so and at the same time pursue the policies which he believed to be in the nation's best interests. Or alternatively, it could imply that although he had absolutist inclinations he saw no way of carrying them into effect. The Loan had been a success in large part because the Council was united in levying it. There would be no such unity, however, if Charles chose to pursue 'new counsels', and given the fact that he had no police force or standing army he would be unable to enforce his will in the face of widespread resistance.

Charles's motivation remains obscure, because he never expounded his attitudes in the open and detailed way that had characterised James I. Unlike his father, Charles was not a systematic thinker, and he had no fully worked out theory of absolutism which he intended to carry into effect. Had there been an English Richelieu to translate his emotional responses into political reality, Charles might have been a very different, and more successful, ruler, but the Duke of Buckingham, despite the fears expressed in Parliament, was neither willing to embrace such a role nor capable of playing it. All the indications suggest that Charles's main concerns were short term. He needed to raise money, and to raise it quickly, in order to honour the commitments he had made to his friends and allies in the Thirty Years War, and eventually he allowed himself to be persuaded that the best means towards this end was Parliament.

When the third Parliament of Charles's reign assembled in March 1628 it quickly became apparent that the King was determined to achieve a reconciliation with his subjects. His chief spokesman in the Commons, Sir John Coke, acknowledged that there had been abuses of power. 'Has there been any defence made of that which has formerly been done?', he demanded. 'His Majesty being a young King and newly come to his crown, which he found engaged in a war, what could we expect in such necessities? His Majesty called this Parliament to make up the breach. His Majesty assures us we shall never have the like cause to complain. He assures us the laws shall be established. What can we desire more?'.[32] The moulders of opinion in the Commons, particularly Sir Thomas Wentworth, recognised the need to make a generous gesture in response to this acknowledgment, and the House agreed, in principle, to vote five subsidies. The King was delighted: 'although five subsidies be inferior to my wants, yet it is the greatest that ever was; and now I see with this I shall have the affections of my people, and this will be greater to me than the value of many subsidies'. Charles was not given to expressing his innermost feelings in public, but this seems to be one of the rare occasions on which he did so. The genuineness of his response is indicated by his further observation that 'at the first I liked parliaments, but since – I know not how – I was grown to a distaste of them. But I am now where I was. I love parliaments. I shall rejoice to meet with my people often'.[33]

Charles accepted that the Commons had a right to call for the end of abuses in his government, including the most recent one of the imprisonment of Loan refusers without cause shown. 'For their grievances', he told Sir John Coke, 'let them go on, in God's name. Why should any man hinder them? If they should not do it, they should not deal freely with me'.[34] The Commons did indeed go on, and eventually produced the Petition of Right, but this was not what Charles had in mind. He had told Coke 'let me but see that they rely on me, and they shall find what they little expect';[35] in other words, he wanted the Commons to demonstrate their trust in him by relying on his royal word and his sense of honour to preserve their liberties. He informed the Commons that 'he holds the statute of Magna Carta, and the other six statutes insisted upon for the subject's liberty, to be all in force, and assures you that he will maintain all his subjects in the just freedom of their persons and safety of their estates, and that he will govern according to the laws and statutes of this realm, and that you shall find as much security in His Majesty's royal word and promise as in the strength of any law you can make'.[36] However, in return for acting as 'the best of our kings' Charles expected the Commons 'to match ourselves with the best subjects by not encroaching upon that sovereignty and prerogative which God has put into his hands for our good, and by containing ourselves within the bounds and laws of our forefathers'.[37]

What Charles had offered the Commons, as Sir John Coke reminded them, was an assurance that the laws 'shall be so executed that we shall enjoy as much freedom as ever. This . . . binds the King further than the law can. First, it binds his affections, which is the greatest bond between King and subjects, and it binds his judgment also . . . Nay, it binds his conscience. This confirmation before both Houses is in the nature of a vow'.[38] The point was put even more forcefully by another Councillor, Sir Humphrey May, when he argued 'that sweetness, trust and confidence are the only weapons for us to deal with our King; and that coldness, enforcement and constraint will never work our ends. Let us take the King's heart if we will compass all we desire. If we have not his heart, what will law or anything else do us good?'.[39] Charles, as has already been noted, was a young man who gave his affection sparingly, but once given it formed a firm bond. When he came to the throne he took it for granted that he had his subjects' love and goodwill, but the experience of his first two parliaments persuaded him otherwise. The third Parliament was intended to bring about a reconciliation, but while members of the Commons were profuse in their expressions of trust and confidence in their sovereign, their actions seemed to Charles to imply 'coldness, enforcement and constraint'. By failing to capture the King's heart, by failing indeed to make any attempt to do so, they demonstrated their lack of understanding of Charles's nature. As a consequence they endangered the very liberties which they were so anxious to preserve.

During their preparatory work on the Petition of Right the Commons constantly asserted that they wanted no new liberties but only confirmation of those which Englishmen had long claimed as their birthright. Charles took their words at face value, and in his first answer to the Petition he therefore committed himself to preserve not only the 'just rights and liberties' of the subject but also the 'just prerogative' of the crown.[40] This failed to satisfy the Commons, so Charles authorised the formal second answer which gave the Petition the force of law (see p. 344). It also emphasised the resemblance between the Petition and statutes, which were likewise ratified by a formula in old French pronounced at the King's command. The big difference, of course, was that statutes actually made law, whereas the Petition – or so the Commons had repeatedly insisted – merely clarified it. This, presumably, was why Charles followed his second answer by a reminder that he had granted no more than in his first, 'for the meaning of that was to confirm all your liberties, knowing (according to your own protestations) that you neither mean nor can hurt my prerogative'.[41] It would also explain why he subsequently ordered that the printed version of the Petition should include only his first answer and his comments on the second, not the ratifying formula. This seemed to many members of the Commons like double dealing, but there was a logic in Charles's attitude, and in practice he adhered to the letter of the Petition. After the collapse of the Personal Rule, the King was accused of having infringed it by collecting Tonnage and Poundage and also Ship Money without parliamentary grant, but Charles asserted that these had long formed part of the royal prerogative and were therefore beyond the scope of the Petition.

Charles put an end to the first session of the 1628 Parliament after the Commons presented a remonstrance against Buckingham, for in his view they had 'fallen upon points of state which belong to me to understand better than you'.[42] During the recess Buckingham was murdered, and his assassin confessed that it was through 'reading the remonstrance of the House of Parliament [that] it came into his mind

[that] by . . . killing the Duke he should do his country great service'.[43] Given the close relationship between Charles and Buckingham, and the King's awareness that the leaders of the Commons were in a sense, accessories to his murder, there was considerable uncertainty whether Parliament would be reconvened. Charles had already been voted five subsidies and was unlikely to receive more, but he had still not been given the customary grant of Tonnage and Poundage. Since, as he frequently professed, he was only collecting this out of necessity, until such time as Parliament should put it upon a statutory basis, it made sense to give the Commons another opportunity to pass the appropriate legislation. Now that Buckingham, whom they had hated and feared, was no longer on the political scene, there seemed a real possibility that the outstanding issues which stood in the way of harmony between the King and the Lower House could be resolved: in the words of one observer 'all things by His Majesty's personal order . . . are provisionally so disposed that he may the better hope for a fair and loving meeting with his people'.[44]

This optimism turned out to be unjustified, for the 1629 session ended not merely in deadlock but with an open act of violence (see p. 350). In the declaration which he issued to explain and defend his action in dissolving Parliament, Charles emphasised that he had not been 'unmindful of the preservation of the just and ancient liberties of our subjects, which we secured to them by our gracious answer to the Petition [of Right] . . . having not since that time done any act whereby to infringe them'. Nevertheless, the House of Commons, carried away by 'ill affected men', had extended its privileges in an uprecedented manner, intending, by this means, 'to break . . . through all respects and ligaments of government, and to erect an universal over-swaying power to themselves, which belongs only to us, and not to them'.[45]

While Buckingham was alive, said Charles, he was regarded as 'the only wall of separation' between the King and the people. But his death had made no difference, for the 'envenomed spirits which troubled then that blessed harmony between us and our subjects' were still at work, suggesting 'new and causeless fears which in their own hearts they know to be false'. This led Charles to the same conclusion as the anonymous adviser who had written to him in 1626, that 'the Duke was not alone the mark these men shot at, but was only as a near minister of ours taken up, on the by, and in their passage to their more secret designs, which were . . . to abate the powers of our crown and to bring our government into obloquy, that in the end all things may be overwhelmed with anarchy and confusion'. This, said Charles, he would never permit, and although he pledged himself 'to maintain our subjects in their just liberties', he expected them in return to 'yield as much submission and duty to our royal prerogatives, and as ready obedience to our authority and commandments, as hath been promised to the greatest of our predecessors'.[46]

This declaration may be taken as a definition of Charles's constitutional position, as he saw it. Because he believed that the House of Commons, misled by some of its members who were aiming at sedition, had gone beyond its prescribed bounds, he had put an end to the Parliament. Whether he would ever have summoned another had not the Personal Rule collapsed remains a moot point, but there is no indication that Charles intended to effect radical changes in the way in which he administered his kingdom. Admittedly Parliament was an integral part of the 'framework of government' which he was committed to uphold, but it had never been more than an intermittent element. The King might choose to summon it frequently, if not regularly, but he was under no obligation to do so. The main function of Parliament from the crown's point of view had always been the granting of supply, and non-parliamentary rule was virtually impossible in time of war. After the dissolution of Parliament, therefore, Charles swiftly made peace with France and Spain. This relieved the pressure on his finances and enabled him to live off his ordinary revenue, supplemented by prerogative levies such as fines for failing to take up knighthood or encroaching on the royal forests (see p. 267).

CHARLES AND THE LAW: SHIP MONEY

The most lucrative of these devices, and the most far-reaching in its constitutional implications, was Ship Money, for it called into question even more dramatically than the Forced Loan of 1626–27 the relationship between the prerogatives of the crown and the liberties of the subject. Richard Chambers – a London merchant who had already acquired a certain notoriety by refusing to pay Tonnage and Poundage, and whose use of force to try to recover his goods from the Customs officers was taken up by Parliament in 1629 – stood out against the 1635 levy of Ship Money and sued the Lord Mayor of London for wrongfully imprisoning him. When the case came before King's Bench in 1636, Sir Robert Berkeley, one of the judges, was reported as saying 'that there was a rule of law and a rule of government, and that many things which might not be done by the rule of law might be done by the rule of government'.[47] In a sense he was merely confirming what Chief Baron Fleming had asserted in Bate's Case (see p. 47), but Charles would not have accepted the implication that the actions of his government in this instance were unlawful. In February 1637 Charles called on the judges to advise him whether he had the right to command his subjects to provide ships for the defence of the kingdom if he believed it to be in danger. In their reply the judges confirmed that 'when the good and safety of the kingdom in general is concerned, and the whole kingdom in danger, Your Majesty may, by writ under the great seal of England, command all your subjects of this your kingdom, at their charge, to provide and furnish such number of ships . . . for such time as Your Majesty shall think fit . . . and that by law Your Majesty may compel the doing thereof in case of refusal'.[48]

Although all twelve judges signed this opinion, two or three of them – including Sir George Croke – apparently did so unwillingly. They were given an opportunity to reconsider the matter at the end of 1637 when the case of John Hampden – a wealthy Buckinghamshire landowner who had refused to pay Ship Money on the grounds that it was unlawful – was brought before the whole judicial bench sitting in the Exchequer Chamber. Hampden's counsel accepted that the King had the right to levy Ship Money in times of emergency but argued that no such emergency existed. Oliver St John pointed out that the writ itself allowed seven months for the ships to be provided, 'and thereby it appears that the necessity in respect of time was not such but that a parliamentary consent might in that time have been endeavoured for the effecting of the supply'.[49] This view was refuted by Sir Robert Berkeley when he delivered his judgment. He declared that it was 'a dangerous tenet, a kind of judaizing opinion, to hold that the weal public must be exposed to peril of utter ruin and subversion, rather than a charge such as this, which may secure the commonwealth, may be imposed by the King upon the subject without common consent in Parliament'.[50] Sir John Finch, who concurred with Berkeley, insisted that the King was acting according to law. As King, he was 'given the interest and sovereignty of defending and governing the kingdom', and it was a well-established rule that 'the law commands nothing to be done, but it permits the ways and means how it may be done'. To give the King the responsibility for defending his people and yet at the same time to deny him the means to do so would be to render the law 'imperfect, lame and unjust'.[51]

The apparent failure of the judges to defend the rights of individual Englishmen in Bate's Case and the Five Knights' Case had undoubtedly lowered them in popular esteem. Indeed, Sir John Eliot had accused them of conspiring with the officers of the crown 'to trample on the spoils of the liberty of the subject',[52] and Charles had complained of the way in which 'young lawyers' sitting in the Commons, had taken upon them 'to decry the opinions of the judges'. Some, indeed, had gone so far as to maintain 'that the resolutions of that House must bind the judges', which was, in Charles's opinion, 'a thing never heard of in ages past'.[53] Yet the judges were far from being supine upholders of royal authority. In Hampden's Case five of the twelve gave judgment for the defendant, and Sir George Croke stated quite baldly that Ship Money was 'against divers statutes' and that

no pretence of prerogative, royal power, necessity, or danger, doth or can make it good . . . The common law of England sets a freedom in the subjects in respect of their persons, and gives them a true property in their goods and estates, so that without their consent – that is to say their private, actual consent, or (implicitly) in Parliament – it cannot be taken from them.[54]

THE PERSONAL RULE

Croke's judgment, as news of it spread, carried far more weight in the country than did that of Berkeley. Yet Berkeley's view that the law was not meant for 'King-yoking', but was, on the contrary, 'an old and trusty servant of the King's . . . his instrument or means which he useth to govern his people by',[55] was not in the least eccentric or unfounded. Lawyers had been prominent, as members of Parliament, in upholding the rights of the subject, but they were equally aware of the need for effective government. The anarchic behaviour of the Commons in 1629, under the leadership of the impulsive Eliot, caused many of them to re-order their priorities. William Noy, who defended the Forced Loan resisters and condemned the King's action in levying Tonnage and Poundage without parliamentary consent, accepted office as Attorney General in October 1631 and became one of the principal instruments of prerogative rule. Sir Dudley Digges, who had been a thorn in the side of James I, bought himself a Mastership of the Rolls; while Edward Littleton – who had played a major part in the parliamentary campaign for the Petition of Right and in 1629 supported the action of a fellow member of the Commons, John Rolle, in refusing to pay Tonnage and Poundage – became Recorder of London at the King's instance in December 1631, Solicitor General in 1635, Chief Justice of the Common Pleas in January 1640, and Lord Keeper a year later.

Noy and Littleton, like the non-lawyer Wentworth, may have decided that after Charles's acceptance of the Petition of Right they could hold office with a clear conscience. But they were also the heirs of Bacon, who had looked to the King rather than Parliament for effective government. Charles gave the impression at the outset of his reign that he would come closer than his father to the Baconian ideal. To take one example, James had appointed a number of commissions to enquire into the fees taken by office-holders, but these had achieved nothing. In 1627 Charles appointed a new commission and gave it his active support. It seemed for a time as though there might be a genuine attempt to reduce, if not eliminate, corruption and the abuse of patronage, and in the first years of its existence the commission was meeting twice a week. In spite of this high level of activity, however, it achieved little of significance, and by 1640 it was moribund. As so often in the early Stuart period, it had been frustrated by the crown's financial needs. Pecuniary motives took precedence over reform, and corrupt practices were tolerated because they produced money. It was also the case that the deficiencies of the administration were built into it, and reconstruction was impossible unless preceded by demolition. Charles clearly had the wish, and to some extent the will, to be an effective reformer, but the abuses which the commission uncovered were all too often the perquisites of courtiers and other members of the political nation whom Charles could not afford to alienate. The existing system might be unsatisfactory from a theoretical point of view, but it had the sanction conferred by long continuance and even if it functioned inefficiently it functioned nevertheless.

The Personal Rule, which could have been a watershed in English history, turned out to be nothing of the sort. The royal government confined its activities within the bounds of the common law, as defined by the judges, and was concerned above all to preserve the *status quo*. In secular, as distinct from religious, matters, Charles was not an innovator, nor did he create the instruments, such as a standing army, which alone might have enabled him to carry through innovative policies in the face of widespread opposition.

Charles's conservatism and his legalism provided his regime with the requisite degree of acceptance, and although many aspects of his government were resented there was no effective challenge to it. Even the hated Ship Money was paid, and it looks as though the Personal Rule could have endured indefinitely had not Charles brought about its demise by provoking a revolt in Scotland (see p. 319). It was foreign intervention, in the shape of the Scots, and not an internal English uprising, that led to the summoning of Parliament in April 1640.

A QUESTION OF TRUST

The Short Parliament was in many respects a re-run of the early parliaments of Charles's reign, which had also met under the shadow of war. In 1640, as in 1625 and 1626, Charles was still thinking in terms of victory and assumed – or at any rate hoped – that Parliament was of the same frame of mind. He had summoned it in order to obtain supply which would enable him to crush the Scottish revolt, and he believed that this must take precedence over redress of grievances. This was why the Solicitor General, speaking on Charles's behalf, called on the Commons to demonstrate their trust in him. 'They had the word of a King and a gentleman for redress of their grievances' he assured them, adding that Charles's 'honour was as dear unto him as his life'. They would have to trust the King at some stage, and 'seeing . . . that we must trust him in the future, then as well in civility as [in] good manners that trust ought to be in him in the first place; which if we should do, then he would lend a gracious and princely ear to our grievances, and grant as much as we could in justice ask'.[56] A similar appeal was directed to the Lords, who made a positive response to it. In the words of the Lord Keeper, 'they all resolved to trust him, and said they would take the word of a King (and that some also added "of a gentleman")'.[57]

The Commons declined to follow the lead given by the Lords. After their experience of what many of them regarded as arbitrary rule they were unwilling to trust the King – not, at any rate, until he had bound himself by statute to end such abuses as unparliamentary taxation. In the opinion of Edward Hyde, who was a member of the Short Parliament, 'the House generally [was] exceedingly disposed to please the King and to do him service'.[58] but the Commons did not accept Charles's order of priorities. The eleven years of personal rule had merely confirmed them in their belief that they could not supply the King until they knew what was theirs to give. During the course of the next few weeks the outline of a possible bargain took shape, centring round the abolition of Ship Money, but it came to nothing. One reason for this was disagreement over how much Ship Money was worth, but more important was Charles's sense of betrayal. Once again, as in the early part of his reign, he had called on the representatives of his people to help him in his (and their) hour of need, and they had failed to respond. Far from making the sort of gesture that would capture the King's heart they had demonstrated their profound distrust of him by insisting upon a statutory fettering of his prerogative. Charles reacted as he had done fifteen years earlier, by bringing proceedings to an abrupt close.

There was nothing inevitable about Charles's subsequent decision to summon another Parliament. His main concern was to suppress the Scottish revolt without making concessions over religion, and if his armies had been victorious in the field he would probably have reverted to personal rule. It was the rout of his troops at Newburn, in August 1640, that made another Parliament necessary. The general assumption was that its principal task would be to make peace with the Scots, but Charles did not share this. The Scots, as he saw it, were still rebels, and their victory at Newburn made no difference to this fact. On the contrary it demonstrated the need for a greater commitment on the part of his subjects. Parliament, as he informed the members in his opening speech, had been summoned for two purposes: 'first, the chasing out of the rebels; and the other is the satisfying your just grievances'.[59] It is conceivable that if Parliament and the nation had united behind Charles in a patriotic crusade against the Scottish invaders, the revolt might have been put down. But there was no enthusiasm for such a course. For one thing, dislike of Charles's religious policies was widespread, and those of puritan inclination regarded the Scots as fellow sufferers under the Arminian scourge, who had not so much rebelled as stood firm in defence of their liberties and set an example which the English should follow. But even those who were not puritan seem to have felt that the war was not worth fighting, simply because there was no possibility of winning it. The situation was a repeat of that in 1625 and 1626, when Charles had reacted to defeat in a way that was quite contrary to that of his subjects. He had continued to believe in the possibility of victory long after they had abandoned hope. The same was true in 1640.

The big difference between the earlier Parliaments and that of 1640–41 was that the latter included members who were in close touch with the 'enemy' and using them to secure concessions from the King that he would not have contemplated in other circumstances. These men were the 'malicious and ambitious spirits' whom the Lord Keeper had warned the Short Parliament to beware of.[60] They were the same dissident elements whom Lord Chancellor Ellesmere had identified in 1610, and who had subsequently disrupted the harmony of Charles's opening parliaments – or so he was convinced. Charles, like his father, had been unable to isolate and destroy these elements, but as long as they existed there would be no possibility of reconciling the King with his subjects. In January 1642 Charles made a belated attempt to free the Houses from their malign influence by impeaching five members of the Commons and one of the Lords, and when this failed in its immediate effect he resorted to force in an attempt to bring them to justice. It may be that even at this eleventh hour the King was hoping to rally what he believed to be the moderate and loyal majority behind him, but he was no more successful on this occasion than he had been before. Two months after his attempted *coup* the two Houses passed the Militia Ordinance which deprived him of control of the armed forces of the kingdom. To Charles, this was clear proof that the 'malignant persons' were still in control, still pursuing what he described as their 'mischievous designs and intentions' and aiming to 'seduce our good subjects from their due obedience to us'.[61] It may have been with a sense of relief that having failed to undermine their influence in Parliament he now turned to open confrontation with them on the battlefield.

NOTES AND REFERENCES

(*The place of publication is London, unless otherwise stated*)
1. ***The Letters of John Chamberlain*** ed. N. E. McClure (Philadelphia 1939). Vol. II, pp. 225–26. (Hereafter Chamberlain *Letters*)
2. **Robert C. Johnson, Mary Frear Keeler, Maija Jansson Cole & William Bidwell** (eds.) *Commons Debates 1628* (New Haven 1977). Vol. II, p. 130. (Hereafter *Commons Debates 1628*)
3. *Commons Debates 1628*. Vol. II, p. 130.
4. **Lucy Hutchinson** *Memoirs of the Life of Colonel Hutchinson* (1902), p. 84.
5. Chamberlain *Letters*. Vol. II, p. 609.

6. **Roger Lockyer** *Buckingham: The Life and Political Career of George Villiers, First Duke of Buckingham 1592–1628* (1981), p. 234. (Hereafter Lockyer *Buckingham*)
7. *The Court and Times of Charles the First . . . transcribed by Thomas Birch* ed. R. F. Williams (1849). Vol. I, p. 101. (Hereafter *Court and Times Charles I*)
8. **John Rushworth** *Historical Collections* (1682). Vol. I, p. 25. (Hereafter Rushworth *Historical Collections*)
9. Chamberlain *Letters*. Vol. II, p. 359.
10. **Wallace Notestein, Frances Helen Relf** & **Hartley Simpson** (eds) *Commons Debates 1621* (New Haven 1935). Vol. V, p. 43.
11. **S. R. Gardiner** (ed.) *Debates in the House of Commons in 1625* Camden Society (1873), p. 10. (Hereafter Gardiner *1625 Debates*)
12. *Journals of the House of Commons 1547–1714* (1742). Vol. I, p. 800. (Hereafter *Commons Journals*)
13. Gardiner *1625 Debates*, p. 10.
14. Gardiner *1625 Debates*, p. 2.
15. **J. P. Kenyon (ed.)** *The Stuart Constitution 1603–1688* 2nd edn. (Cambridge 1986), p. 64. (Hereafter Kenyon *Stuart Constitution*)
16. *Commons Debates 1628*. Vol. III, p. 128.
17. *Court and Times Charles I*. Vol. I, pp. 103–04.
18. **E. R. Foster** (ed.) *Proceedings in Parliament 1610* (New Haven 1966). Vol. I, p. 276.
19. *Calendar of State Papers and Manuscripts relating to English Affairs existing in the Archives and Collections of Venice*. Vol. XIX 1625–1626 (1913), p. 462.
20. *Cabala sive Scrinia Sacra* (1691), pp. 255–57.
21. **Richard Cust** *The Forced Loan and English Politics 1626–1628* (Oxford 1987), p. 18. (Hereafter Cust *Forced Loan*)
22. Rushworth *Historical Collections*. Vol. I, p. 410.
23. Rushworth *Historical Collections*. Vol. I, p. 359.
24. Cust *Forced Loan*, p. 39.
25. **Richard Cust** 'Charles I, the Privy Council, and the Forced Loan' *Journal of British Studies*. Vol. 24. 1985, p. 210. (Hereafter Cust 'Charles I and the Forced Loan')
26. Cust 'Charles I and the Forced Loan', p. 213.
27. *Commons Journals*. Vol. I, p. 610.
28. **J. A. Guy** 'The Origins of the Petition of Right Reconsidered' *Historical Journal*. Vol. 25, 1982.
29. **James F. Larkin** (ed.) *Stuart Royal Proclamations*. Vol. II, *Royal Proclamations of King Charles I 1625–1646* (Oxford 1983), p. 111.
30. *Commons Debates 1628*. Vol. IV, p. 242.
31. *Commons Debates 1628*. Vol. IV, p. 180.
32. *Commons Debates 1628*. Vol. III, p. 189.
33. *Commons Debates 1628*. Vol. II, p. 325.
34. *Commons Debates 1628*. Vol. II, p. 282.
35. *Commons Debates 1628*. Vol. II, p. 282.
36. *Commons Debates 1628*. Vol. III, p. 125.
37. *Commons Debates 1628*. Vol. III, p. 213.
38. *Commons Debates 1628*. Vol. III, p. 268.

39. *Commons Debates 1628.* Vol. II, p. 481.
40. *Commons Debates 1628.* Vol. IV, p. 52.
41. *Commons Debates 1628.* Vol. IV, p. 182.
42. *Commons Debates 1628.* Vol. IV, p. 352.
43. Lockyer *Buckingham*, p. 458.
44. *Court and Times Charles I.* Vol. II, p. 2.
45. **S. R. Gardiner** (ed.) *The Constitutional Documents of the Puritan Revolution 1625–1660* (Oxford 1906), pp. 90, 91, 95. (Hereafter Gardiner *Constitutional Documents*)
46. Gardiner *Constitutional Documents*, pp. 97–8.
47. W. J. Jones *Politics and the Bench* (1971), p. 123. (Hereafter Jones *Politics and the Bench*)
48. Jones *Politics and the Bench*, p. 202.
49. Kenyon *Stuart Constitution*, p. 99.
50. Kenyon *Stuart Constitution*, p. 100.
51. Kenyon *Stuart Constitution*, p. 102.
52. Jones *Politics and the Bench*, p. 76.
53. Gardiner *Constitutional Documents*, p. 93.
54. Jones *Politics and the Bench*, pp. 187–88.
55. Gardiner *Constitutional Documents*, pp. 121–22.
56. **Esther S. Cope** & **Willson H. Coates** (eds.) *Proceedings of the Short Parliament of 1640.* Royal Historical Society (1977), p. 231. (Hereafter *Proceedings of Short Parliament*)
57. *Proceedings of Short Parliament*, p. 177.
58. **Edward, Earl of Clarendon** *The History of the Rebellion and Civil Wars in England* ed. W. Dunn Macray (Oxford 1888). Vol. II, p. 70.
59. **Conrad Russell** 'Why did Charles I call the Long Parliament?' *History.* Vol. 69. 1984, p. 380.
60. *Proceedings of Short Parliament*, p. 133.
61. Gardiner *Constitutional Documents*, pp. 248–49.

CHAPTER TEN

The Royal Finances under Charles I

THE CUSTOMS FARM

Charles I ordered the collection of Tonnage and Poundage from the outset of his reign, without waiting for the parliamentary sanction which he assumed would be quickly forthcoming. The great farm of the Customs had been leased at an annual rent of £140,000 until 1621, when a new syndicate took over after agreeing to pay £160,000. Its principal members were Sir John Wolstenholme, who was virtually born into the business since his father had been a Customs officer under the Tudors, Henry Garway (see pp. 9–10), Abraham Jacob, and the enormously wealthy Sir Maurice Abbot, brother of the Archbishop of Canterbury. This syndicate surrendered its lease in 1625 because it found that in the continuing trade depression it could not afford such a high rent. It tried to secure a new one at a lower figure but was outbid by a group which included Sir William Cockayne – apparently undamaged by his earlier involvement in the disastrous scheme to reorient the English cloth trade (see p. 5) – and Sir Paul Pindar, who had made a fortune out of commercial and financial operations in Italy and the Levant. Wolstenholme and Jacob transferred their allegiance to the Pindar syndicate, which was said to have secured Buckingham's support – no doubt at a price – but Garway and Abbot were left out in the cold. They blamed Buckingham for their exclusion, and they may have influenced the Commons' decision, taken shortly afterwards, to decline making a lifetime grant of Tonnage and Poundage to the King. Abbot had obvious connections with Buckingham's critics through his brother, while Garway was a leading figure in the East India Company which had accused the favourite of extorting money from it.

The new lease was set to run for five years at a rent of £150,000, and in view of the disruption in trade likely to be caused by England's involvement in war, and also the uncertainty about the legal status of the Customs duties in the absence of a parliamentary grant, the King gave his royal word to reimburse the farmers if the rent proved to be excessive. There were some people, most notably the financier John Harrison, who argued that Customs farms were a wasteful means of raising revenue and that the crown would be better advised to call them in and resume direct administration of the duties. The climate of opinion in the early years of Charles's reign was favourable to reform (see p. 234), and it may be that what was intended as a first step on this road was taken in 1628, when annual leases were issued. But if this was indeed the intention it came to nothing. One reason for this was that the crown's need for money was too great for it to risk embarking on an experiment with a principal source of its ordinary revenue. But a much more important factor in the survival of the Customs farmers was the big loans they provided for the King. In 1625 and 1627 they made advance rent payments of about £25,000, and in 1633 and 1635 of £30,000. These were on the security of the current year's revenue, but in 1626, and regularly from 1629, they were advancing large sums to be repaid from the income of the subsequent year. In 1631 and 1632 these sums were in the order of £60,000; thereafter, until the end of the Personal Rule, they averaged £20–30,000. In 1633, however, the crown began granting three-year leases, and this encouraged the farmers to make additional advances of some £30,000 in each of the years 1634–36, which were secured on revenues to be collected two years ahead. Their willingness to extend their commitment did not help them, however, when it came to renewing their lease in 1638, for by that time William Juxon was Treasurer and he favoured a syndicate which included a fellow courtier, Sir George Goring. This made an initial offer of £165,000 a year, but it only secured the contract after it had agreed to raise its bid to £172,500.

Although trade flourished in the peaceful years of the 1630s, the new rent cut into the profits of the syndicate and reduced its ability to loan money to the crown at just the moment when the Scottish crisis (see p. 320) caused a marked deterioration in the King's financial position. Goring was therefore squeezed out, and the King pleaded with Pindar to take his place. The treachery of the Scots, said Charles, 'had brought him into so sad condition as that his crown lay at the stake, and [he] therefore desired him to help him'.[1]

Pindar, who was moved to tears by Charles's unaccustomed eloquence, did join the syndicate, and during the next few months it advanced well over £100,000 to the King – though probably not so much as the £250,000 which it later claimed. Pindar and his fellow farmers suffered for their loyalty, for Parliament treated them as accomplices in the imposition of prerogative rule. In 1641 a Bill was prepared for the confiscation of their estates, but they were eventually allowed to commute this into a fine of £150,000 – a heavy penalty in view of the fact that they stood no chance of recovering the large sums they had advanced to the crown. Their fate may serve as a reminder that major interests in the City committed themselves to the King rather than Parliament as the political crisis developed in and after 1639.

THE CROWN'S CREDITORS

The Customs farmers were not the only individuals who lent money to the royal government. The naval and military expeditions of the 1620s could not have been mounted without the assistance of the international financier Philip Burlamachi, who acted as the crown's principal contractor. In the period 1625–29 he made loans amounting to several hundred thousand pounds, many of which were never repaid, so that he went bankrupt in 1633. Sir William Russell, the Treasurer of the Navy, was another major creditor of the crown, and so was the Victualler, Sir Allen Apsley. In 1626, when Buckingham was trying to set out a fleet for joint operations with the Dutch, Apsley engaged himself to the tune of £25,000 but informed the Duke that 'for want of payment his credit would extend no further'.[2] Buckingham thanked him for his 'extraordinary forwardness to supply (even beyond your own abilities) the great wants of the ships' and begged him not to slacken his efforts. 'I would not press you to help any further', he explained, 'but that His Majesty's present occasions urge it . . . Your care and help at this pinch will add much to the merit of your care of His Majesty's service'.[3] Apsley was a rich man, as is indicated by the fact that the crown owed him £100,000 at the time of his death in 1630. This was not the case with the captains and junior officers of the navy, yet they were all expected to pledge their personal credit in order to keep their ships in commission. Even the sailors were constrained to subsidise the crown, for their meagre wages were often months in arrears. At all levels of the early Stuart state public and private finance were inter-mingled, and this created a climate of opinion which tolerated a degree of corruption that would today be unacceptable. Men who had advanced private money to the state, or had not been paid for their public services, saw nothing wrong in recouping their losses if the opportunity came their way.

Buckingham owed his wealth to royal favour, but this made him particularly aware of his duty to spend what was now his own on the King's service. In 1627 he laid out £10,000 on preparations for the Ré expedition (see p. 29), and a year later he told the mutinous sailors – driven into desperate courses by the fact that their wages were nine or ten months overdue – that 'I have parted with mine own money to pay you, and engaged all mine own estate for your satisfaction'.[4] Buckingham was an exception only in the amounts he lent. Other courtiers also advanced money to the crown, some no doubt in hope of future favour, but many because they acknowledged a moral obligation to assist the King in his time of need. In 1628 the Privy Councillors contributed not far short of £10,000 towards the cost of the expedition designed to relieve La Rochelle, but this was as nothing compared with the enormous loan which they raised in response to Charles's appeal in December 1639 (see below).

When he ascended the throne in March 1625 Charles was short of money to cover his initial expenses, and he therefore turned to the City of London. The response of the corporation was con-ditioned by the fact that the greater part of the loan of £100,000 made to James I in 1617 was still outstanding, but it agreed to advance a further £60,000 on the security of crown lands with a capital value considerably in excess of £200,000. A year later, more money was needed for immediate defence measures against a threatened Spanish invasion. The Council demanded £100,000, but the City professed its inability to raise such a large sum at short notice, and in the end a mere £20,000 was provided. A major reason for the poor response was the reluctance of City businessmen to throw good money after bad, for the crown had a poor record as a debtor. Fear of a further rebuff may have contributed to Charles's decision to raise money instead by a forced loan (see p. 223), but although that was successful in purely financial terms this was partly because he had committed himself not to make it a precedent.

Without forced loans, and with only a faint prospect of parlia-mentary supply, Charles needed the City more than ever. In the early part of 1628, therefore, he agreed to a complicated transaction whereby the City undertook to wipe the slate clean and advance an additional £120,000 in return for the handing over to it of crown lands with a nominal yearly value of £14,000. These were to be sold off, and the proceeds used to repay all those individuals and companies who had contributed to the various loans and were still waiting for their money back.

PARLIAMENTARY SUPPLY

One of the first casualties of the shift from a peace to a war policy in the period following the return of Charles and Buckingham from Spain in 1623 was Lord Treasurer Middlesex (see p. 212). He was replaced by a former Chief Justice, Sir James Ley, subsequently created Earl of Marlborough, who was charged with the thankless task of finding enough money to pay for the crown's policies. The 1624 Parliament voted three subsidies and three fifteenths, which eventually brought in a quarter of a million pounds, but by the time the 1625 Parliament met £100,000 had been spent on the English forces serving with the Dutch, £60,000 on Mansfeld's expedition, £40,000 on the navy, and £80,000 on defence preparations in England and Ireland. This meant that Charles had already paid out £40,000 more than the subsidies would bring in, and he needed another £150,000 at once if the work already in hand was not to come to an abrupt halt. As for the future, he had promised to pay £20,000 a month to Mansfeld, to keep him in the field, and £30,000 a month to his uncle, Christian IV of Denmark, who was the only protestant prince of any importance actually engaged in hostilities. Moreover Buckingham was preparing a combined expedition against Spain which eventually cost about £500,000. In other words, Charles's requirements were not far short of a million pounds, and the Commons' vote of two subsidies, worth under £130,000, was clearly inadequate. Sir John Coke was speaking no more than the truth when he told Parliament in July 1625, shortly before the end of its first session, that additional supply was urgently needed (see p. 327).

Despite being summoned to Oxford for a second session the Commons declined to make any further grant (see p. 332). The government was left to scrape up money as and where it could, and Charles was only able to fulfil his immediate obligations to Mansfeld and Christian IV by borrowing £70,000 from Burlamachi. Preparations for the Cadiz expedition went ahead, financed in part by the

Queen's dowry of £120,000, but the deficiencies that made themselves apparent after the fleet sailed were the consequence of inadequate and irregular funding. Mansfeld's comments about his own predicament go far towards explaining the failure of the Cadiz expedition also. 'Unless I have the full amount', he said, 'I shall be unable to do anything worthwhile. Past experience has shown that the furnishing of money in driblets and at long intervals is the surest way to lose and waste it to no purpose'.[5]

Following the dissolution of his first Parliament, Charles turned to the long-established practice of levying loans from selected individuals. The privy seal writs which were despatched to them called 'for supply of some portions of treasure for divers public services which, without manifold inconveniences to us and our kingdom, cannot be deferred'.[6] However, the response to this appeal was so unenthusiastic that Charles abandoned the scheme for the time being. The continuing economic depression created genuine difficulties for potential contributors, and the two subsidies voted by the 1625 Parliament were now being collected, so the loans were unfortunate in their timing. They also provoked a negative response from those who believed that Parliament was not simply the appropriate but the only means whereby to offer financial aid to the sovereign.

By the opening of 1626 the shortage of money was so acute that the defence of the kingdom could no longer be assured. In February Captain Pennington wrote to Buckingham from Portsmouth asking him 'to take some speedy course for our supply; otherwise we must be constrained to discharge our men and let the ships ride destitute, for without victuals we cannot keep them'.[7] Buckingham used whatever sources were available. Attacks on enemy commerce resulted in the capture of ships or their cargoes which could be sold as prizes, and this source alone yielded £50,000 in 1626 – not far short of a parliamentary subsidy. Buckingham was also putting heavy pressure upon the East India Company to pay £10,000 prize money for its operations against Portuguese ships. The Company eventually paid up, and the money was all spent on the navy, but this did not endear the Lord Admiral to its governor, Maurice Abbot, who made sure that the case was brought to the attention of the Commons when they initiated impeachment proceedings against Buckingham. It was the Commons' attack upon his chief minister which led Charles to dissolve his second Parliament before the subsidy Bill had completed its passage. He was now, if such a thing was possible, even worse off than he had been before Parliament began its deliberations.

The strengthening of the navy was a paramount consideration, in view of the threat of Spanish invasion, and in June 1626 the Privy Council ordered the port towns 'to furnish ships at their own charges for the defence of the kingdom, as they did in the year 1588'. But many of the ports were in decline, as a consequence of the economic depression, or, in some cases, of attacks from the Barbary corsairs or the dreaded Dunkirk privateers. The Council therefore instructed the adjoining counties to come to the aid of the ports, but this provoked an outraged response. The Dorset magistrates declared that they could not 'find any precedent for being charged in a service of this nature', to which the exasperated Council could only reply 'that state occasions and the defence of a kingdom in times of extraordinary danger do not guide themselves by ordinary precedents'.[8]

This argument from necessity, with its undertones of an absolute prerogative, was used to justify the levying of a new-style forced loan in the autumn and winter of 1626–27 (see p. 223) – after the failure of an appeal to subjects to show their loyalty by contributing to a Benevolence. The gross yield of the Loan was only a little short of £270,000, which meant that it was worth five subsidies. Without it the Ré expedition (see p. 29) could never have been mounted, but the failure of that expedition, taken in conjunction with the King's promise that the Forced Loan would not be repeated, made recourse to Parliament inevitable. One of the Treasury officials had already warned Buckingham in September 1627 that 'His Majesty's revenue of all kinds is now exhausted. We are upon the third year's anticipation beforehand; land, much sold of the principal; credit lost; and at the utmost shift with the commonwealth'.[9] Charles secured short-term relief by a further loan from the City, as described above, and in January 1628 one official observed with delight that 'the stream begins to run again which hath been too long frozen up'.[10] But as fast as the money came in it went out, much of it to pay the billeting costs of the soldiers returned from Ré, and although the Council, on Charles's instructions, considered a whole range of possibilities, including the imposition of an excise, the general feeling was that only Parliament could provide the sums that were required to relieve the King's necessities.

THE TREASURERSHIP OF RICHARD WESTON, EARL OF PORTLAND

The five subsidies voted by Charles's third Parliament brought in £275,000, but the refusal of the Commons, in the 1629 session, to make a grant of Tonnage and Poundage, and the events of 2 March (see p. 350), persuaded Charles that he had no more to hope for from that direction. In July 1628 he had replaced the seventy-eight-year-old Marlborough as Lord Treasurer by Richard Weston, who had acquired a detailed knowledge of public finances during his long spell as Chancellor of the Exchequer. Weston had first been elected to Parliament in 1614, but it was not until after his appointment to the Privy Council in 1621 that he became one of the crown's principal spokesmen in the Lower House. As a client of Buckingham, he suffered from the distrust which was focussed on the favourite, while as Chancellor he had to defend the collection of the Customs duties even though these had not been voted by Parliament. His elevation to the peerage in April 1628 meant that he ceased to be a member of the Commons, but this did not save him from a savage attack by Sir John Eliot, who accused him of 'building on the foundation of the great master of his preferment, the Duke of Buckingham'. Eliot went on to denounce Weston as 'the head of the papists and Jesuits' and also an underminer of liberties through his insistence upon 'exacting from merchants what is not due, by altering of the customs of this kingdom'.[11]

Eliot's attack and the events of 2 March confirmed Weston in his belief that a period of rule without Parliament would be desirable as well as beneficial. He was also in favour of peace, as the only way in which to ease the strain upon the royal finances, and this was much more feasible now that Buckingham had been removed from the scene. Weston had learnt his trade under Cranfield, but in many ways he was closer in temperament to Queen Elizabeth's conservative Treasurer, Lord Burghley, as he showed in his attitude towards Customs farming. Direct administration of these duties by the crown might have yielded more in the long run, but Weston saw no point in radical overhaul of a system that, for all its deficiencies, actually produced money. It benefited him as well as his royal master, for Weston was no more scrupulous than his predecessors when it came to making lucrative deals. One critic summed up the position in his comment that there was no possibility of getting rid 'of the old way of farming' since this would have gone against 'the interests of that great man [Weston] and of the farmers, his creatures'.[12]

Weston reinstituted the regular weekly reports of Exchequer transactions which had been a feature of Burghley's regime, and kept a very close watch on the spending departments to try to ensure that they did not exceed their assignments. He also persuaded the King to limit his generosity where grants of pensions and annuities were concerned, with the result that they declined by thirty-five per cent during his period in office. Despite Weston's rumoured inclinations towards Roman Catholicism he substantially increased recusancy fines; in 1630 these had contributed a mere £5,000 to the Exchequer, but by the time of his death this figure had risen to £26,000. Weston also gave strong support to the proposal to fine all those who, though technically eligible for knighthood, had not taken it up (see p. 267), and thereby added some £175,000 to the King's coffers.

Over the whole course of his Treasurership, Weston – who was created Earl of Portland in 1633 – increased the crown's ordinary revenue by some twenty-five per cent, bringing it up to well over £600,000 a year. He also managed to reduce the accumulated debt from £1.5 million when he took office to £1.16 million when he died. Undoubtedly the major reason for his success was the withdrawal of England from the Thirty Years War, for this made possible a sharp decline in defence expenditure. During the opening years of Charles's reign some half a million pounds a year had been consumed by naval and military preparations, but by 1631 this amount had been more than halved and in 1625 it stood at a mere £66,000.

LORD TREASURER JUXON

After Portland's death, in March 1635, the King put the Treasury into commission, but it was widely assumed that he would eventually appoint Sir Francis Cottington to the post. Cottington had been Chancellor of the Exchequer and Portland's right-hand man, but this close relationship with the former Treasurer proved his undoing, for it earned him the hostility of Archbishop Laud, who was a prominent member of the anti-Portland faction. Laud would probably have preferred his friend and ally, Sir Thomas Wentworth, to be given the Treasurership, but Wentworth was now the King's Lord Deputy in Ireland where he was fully occupied. Laud therefore promoted the claims of his colleague and protege William Juxon, Bishop of London. Clerical Treasurers had been common before the

Reformation, but they were not a feature of protestant England. Nevertheless, at Laud's insistence the King broke with tradition and in March 1636 appointed Juxon as Lord Treasurer.

Juxon was an honest and hard-working administrator who continued what were now the standard policies of trying to restrain expenditure at the same time as he expanded revenue. During his first two years in office his task was considerably eased by the fact that trade was flourishing and the income from duties on it was therefore steadily growing. The new lease of the Customs which Juxon negotiated in 1638 increased the rent payable by £22,500. Meanwhile the income from the Impositions originally devised by Salisbury in 1608 rose from £55,000 in 1636 to £130,000 in 1638; in the following year it fell back sharply, but 1640 saw it recover to more than £140,000. Impositions added since Salisbury's day brought in £70,000, and the pretermitted customs £36,500, giving a total revenue from prerogative levies on trade of close on a quarter of a million pounds a year – the equivalent by 1640 of five subsidies. Juxon also benefited from the sharp increase in receipts from the Court of Wards, after the appointment of Cottington as Master in 1635. At the end of James's reign, it will be recalled, wardship had been worth some £40,000 a year to the crown, but in 1637 Charles was receiving £62,000 from this source, and by 1640 that figure had risen to £76,000.

THE CRISIS OF 1640–41

The peaceful and prosperous years of the Personal Rule came to an end in 1639 when Charles decided to use force to crush the revolt in Scotland (see p. 320). His decision was made easier by the fact that his finances seemed able to bear the strain. Income was roughly in balance with expenditure, and assuming that the crisis did not drag on, its costs could probably be covered by loans. But the crisis was not quickly resolved. Although Charles spent £185,000 on military operations in 1639 the Scots were undefeated and it was estimated that his charges in 1640 would amount to £600,000. There was no obvious way in which to raise such sums. When Charles called on the City to lend him £100,000 the corporation protested its inability to do so and offered a free gift of £10,000 instead. It soon became apparent that in the 1640s as in the 1620s the crown could not engage in war, with any hope of success, unless it had the financial backing of Parliament. In December 1639, therefore, Charles announced his intention to summon Parliament in the following spring, and appealed to his Privy Councillors to raise the funds necessary to keep operations going until it met. They responded by pledging their own credit and advancing more than £200,000.

When Parliament eventually assembled, Charles pressed for a grant of twelve subsidies and let it be known that he would be prepared, in return, to abandon Ship Money. This was rejected by the Commons, and rather than engage in protracted haggling Charles put an end to the session, thereby forfeiting whatever hope there had been of parliamentary supply (see p. 356). He was still determined to crush the Scots revolt, even though the army which he had raised was costing him £40,000 a month, and in July 1640 he ordered the confiscation of silver bullion worth £100,000 which English and Spanish merchants had placed in the Tower for safe keeping. This was to be adulterated with copper and used for the issue of a new and debased coinage, but when Charles realised that the debased coins would be employed for payments to the crown as well as by it, he agreed to abandon the scheme. However, he held on to a third of the bullion, treating it as a loan on which the government would pay interest. Another £50,000 was raised by Cottington, who bought pepper from the East India Company in return for tallies secured on future revenues, and immediately sold it on the open market. It was also at this time that Charles made a bid to improve his creditworthiness by persuading Sir Paul Pindar to rejoin the Customs farm.

In August 1640 Charles set out for York, to join his army. In the same month, however, the Scots moved south into England, routed the King's forces who were defending the Tyne crossing at Newburn, and occupied Newcastle. Defeat in the field left Charles with no option but negotiation, and peace talks opened at Ripon in September. The Scots were now in possession of the counties of Durham and Northumberland, and demanded £850 a day to cover their occupation costs. This was designed to force the King's hand, and although Charles summoned a great council of peers to advise him what to do, he had already bowed to the inevitable by deciding to call another Parliament. The peers, when they heard of his decision, expressed their willingness to act as guarantors for a loan of £200,000 which the City now agreed to make.

Charles was still determined to renew the struggle against the Scots, and hoped to find assistance from Parliament when it met. In particular, he wanted the Commons to give him, at long last, the lifetime grant of Tonnage and Poundage which he had been waiting for since his accession. But the members did not share his objectives. Their main concern was to put an end to the abuses of government that had marred the previous eleven years, and to limit the King's freedom of action in the sphere of government. Although they regarded the prerogative taxes on trade as illegal, they were willing to confirm them by statute on a short-term basis while they worked out a long-term solution. In June 1641, therefore, they passed the first in a series of Acts which granted Tonnage and Poundage to the King for two months at a time. Charles, when he accepted this, announced his intention henceforth to 'put himself wholly upon the love and affection of his people for his subsistence' – an intention that he reaffirmed at the beginning of 1641, when he informed the Lords of his willingness to abandon 'what parts of my revenue . . . shall be found illegal or grievous to the public' and to rely 'entirely upon the affections of my people'.[13]

On the face of it, Charles had little choice. When he summoned the Long Parliament his total income was about £900,000, but this included the levies on trade which were of doubtful legality. If these were removed, the figure would be cut by two-thirds, for the other sources were of limited value. By the end of 1641 the crown lands, depleted by the sales of the previous half century, were yielding not much more than £100,000 a year. Wardship brought in some £75,000, recusancy fines £18,500, and first-fruits and tenths from the clergy £18,000. All in all, Charles could expect to receive something over £300,000 from non-commercial sources, but this would not cover his ordinary expenditure. Annuities and pensions by themselves consumed nearly £90,000 a year; another £70,000 went to maintain the Queen and the royal family, while Elizabeth of Bohemia and her children were subsidised to the tune of £20,000. There were, in addition, the costs of the royal household, which in 1641 were in the region of a quarter of a million pounds.

Yet if Charles could not survive without Tonnage and Poundage, could he afford to pay the price that was being asked for it? Even at this late stage in his reign, Charles was hoping for a renewal of that fruitful interchange of 'graces' and 'donatives' which his predecessors had enjoyed. The granting of Tonnage and Poundage in its accustomed form would be a clear indication that the conventions were being observed and that his reliance upon the affections of his people was not misplaced. On the other hand, a continuing refusal to make the customary grant would imply continuing disloyalty, an intention to break with the conventions by depriving the King of his traditional rights and keeping him in perpetual leading strings. As Charles became gradually convinced that this was indeed the aim of the leaders of the Commons he decided that the price was too high. Anything was preferable to being a shadow King; even, in the last resort civil war.

NOTES AND REFERENCES

(The place of publication is London, unless otherwise stated)
1. **Robert Ashton** *The Crown and the Money Market 1603–1640* (Oxford 1960), p. 105. (Hereafter Ashton *Crown and Money Market*)
2. Ashton *Crown and Money Market*, p. 166.
3. **Roger Lockyer** *Buckingham: The Life and Political Career of George Villiers, First Duke of Buckingham 1592–1628* (1981), p. 341. (Hereafter Lockyer *Buckingham*)
4. Lockyer *Buckingham*, pp. 413, 447.
5. Lockyer *Buckingham*, p. 249.
6. Lockyer *Buckingham*, p. 273.
7. Lockyer *Buckingham*, p. 303.
8. Lockyer *Buckingham*, p. 339.
9. **F. C. Dietz** *English Public Finance 1485–1641. Vol. II. English Public Finance 1558–1641* (New York 1932), pp. 241–42.
10. Lockyer *Buckingham*, p. 424.
11. **Wallace Notestein** & **Frances Relf** (eds.) *The Commons' Debates for 1629* (Minneapolis 1921), p. 170.
12. Ashton *Crown and Money Market*, p. 98.
13. **S. R. Gardiner** *History of England from the Accession of James I to the Outbreak of the Civil War 1603–1642* (1884). Vol. IX, p. 400; **Conrad Russell** 'Charles I's Financial Estimates for 1642' *Bulletin of the Institute of Historical Research*. Vol. 58. 1985.

CHAPTER ELEVEN

Government and Society in Early Stuart England

THE COURT

In early Stuart England the government was the King. Appointed by God and not accountable to any human institution, the King alone was responsible for the formulation and execution of policy. Where formulation was concerned he could turn for advice either to a body like the Privy Council or to private individuals, but the choice of whether and whom to consult remained his alone, and he was free to accept recommendations or reject them, entirely as he pleased. Similarly with execution, he had ministers who were responsible for the administration, but they were appointed *durante beneplacito* ('at his good pleasure') and held office only as long as he approved of their conduct. The King of England was not, of course, a Sultan, an absolute ruler wielding powers of life and death over his subjects in an entirely arbitrary manner. As a Christian he was bound by the moral law, and as the governor of a long-established state his freedom of action was in practice curtailed by custom, tradition and routine. Furthermore, the King had no standing army and no police to enforce his will. He was therefore dependent for the exercise of his authority upon the co-operation of the political nation which governed the local communities. Its members were accustomed to obey the King's orders even when they disapproved of them, but no sovereign could afford to take their obedience for granted and assume that he had an absolute right to it.

The noblemen and gentry who constituted the political nation had a vested interest in upholding the royal authority since it was the linchpin of the social order from which they benefited. They also gained both profit and prestige from their share of royal patronage, for the King had an enormous range of offices, places, pensions, titles, and outright gifts available for distribution. As the Earl of Northampton reminded his fellow peers in 1614, '[we] prefer our sons, our nephews, our allies and friends to the King's service in hope of bountiful reward upon allowance of their desert', and he described the 'gift offices' which the King disposed of as 'the seeds of satisfaction'.[1] However, these seeds were in short supply, for galloping inflation in the second half of the sixteenth century forced the crown to husband its resources, and as inflation continued throughout the entire early Stuart period so also did the pressure to economise. The problem was made more acute by another contemporary phenomenon, population expansion, which had affected the political nation like all other sections of society.

There were, in short, more and more people seeking a diminishing supply of royal patronage, and this gave a key role to the courtiers and other intermediaries who facilitated its distribution. Until his death in 1612 Robert Cecil, Earl of Salisbury, was the principal distributor, but with the collapse of 'Cecil's Commonwealth' the situation became more fluid. Robert Carr, the royal favourite, picked up part of Salisbury's inheritance, but other parts went to the Howards, while the King retained certain 'gift offices' in his own hands. The marriage between Carr and Frances Howard reunited the separate parts, but not for long, since the Howards were overthrown by the palace *coup* which brought George Villiers, future Duke of Buckingham, into the limelight.

By 1616 Buckingham was firmly established as the King's favourite and thenceforth was a major influence upon the distribution of royal patronage. But he was not the only one. Early in his career he clashed with the Earl of Pembroke, now Lord Chamberlain, over the appointment of a new Chancellor of the Duchy of Lancaster. Buckingham had promised this office to Cranfield, but Pembroke wanted it for Sir Humphrey May and eventually he prevailed. Three years later, in 1621, Buckingham again pressed Cranfield's claim, this time to the Lord Keepership, which had been left vacant by the fall of Bacon. On this occasion it was not Pembroke but James himself who was the stumbling block, for the King was determined to give the post to a churchman, and it therefore went to John Williams, at that time Dean of Westminster. Buckingham had a clearer run – though even here not an entirely clear one – with lesser appointments. He helped mould the career of Sir Dudley Carleton by bringing him back from the Hague, where he was a long-serving ambassador, and securing his elevation to a viscountcy and his appointment as Secretary of State. Carleton's fellow ambassador at Brussels, William Trumbull, was also brought home, to serve as secretary to the Council of War, but only after he had made clear his willingness to accept Buckingham as his sole patron. No doubt he was prompted to do so by one of his correspondents who warned him that 'you absurdly stray in your means if your *Ora Pro Nobis* be not directed to the right saint. I have no conceit of those petty ones who for their own selves can obtain no grace except they bow and beseech at the shrine of the great one. Direct your suit to His Majesty by *his* hand if you will think to prosper, and be speedy'.[2]

James I never became politically dependent upon Buckingham. He relished the involvement in public affairs that was thrust upon him by his high office, and was too certain of his own judgment to wish to abdicate his authority, except in minor matters. The accession of Charles I in 1625 brought about a significant change, for although he was very conscious of his kingly dignity and determined to be obeyed, he worked so closely with Buckingham in state business that it was virtually impossible to say where Charles's authority ended and the Duke's began. The Earl of Pembroke, a long-time rival and enemy of Buckingham, came to terms with the new circumstances by abandoning open opposition to the favourite after the failure of the impeachment attempt in 1626, and agreeing to a marriage alliance between the Herbert and Villiers families. Sir Thomas Wentworth, an ambitious and outspoken member of the Commons, also acknowledged that Buckingham's supremacy was a fact of political life, and in 1628 agreed to become his 'creature'. His reward was swift in coming, for he was immediately elevated to the peerage and appointed Lord President of the Council of the North.

After Buckingham's removal from the scene, in August 1628, the Court was once again the scene of faction fighting, as ambitious politicians and their adherents struggled for influence over the King. There was nothing unusual about this. In the words of an Elizabethan sea-dog, Sir William Monson, 'he that will live at Court must make his dependency upon some great person, in whose ship he must embark his life and fortune . . . He that settles his service upon one of them shall fall into the disfavour of another, for a Court is like an army ever in war, striving by stratagems to circumvent and kick up another's heels'.[3] The existence of competing factions at the seat of power acted in some ways as a safety valve, providing a means for the expression of differing points of view. But faction feuding needed to be held within strict limits, for otherwise it might become so bitter that it threatened the stability, indeed the very existence, of the regime – as had been shown at the end of Elizabeth's reign, in the struggle between Cecil and Essex. One way of avoiding this was by creating a monopoly of patronage by a single group or individual. Salisbury's dominance of the first decade of James's reign enabled the new ruler to establish himself and his dynasty, and the same might well have been true of Buckingham and Charles I if the favourite's tenure of power had lasted as long as Salisbury's. Given that all early modern states had a built-in tendency towards instability, there was much to be said in favour of concentrating power at the centre: Richelieu, who made himself the conduit through which Louis XIII's favour flowed, and infiltrated his 'creatures' into key positions in the administration, demonstrated the effectiveness of just such a system.

Although factions were made up of individuals hungry for power, they were not necessarily without principles. Buckingham's rise to favour, which led to the overthrow of the Howards, had been engineered by the 'protestant faction' led by Pembroke and Archbishop Abbot. This group blamed the Howards for what they regarded as the pro-Spanish tilt of James's foreign policy. They wanted the King to assume the leadership of protestant Europe, and make Parliament and the people his partners in this crusade. Having failed to win over James to this course by means of persuasion, they took the dangerous gamble of trying to replace his favourite, Robert Carr, Earl of Somerset, who was the kinsman and patron of the Howards. Their manoeuvre was successful, but the rapid rise of Villiers made no difference to James's foreign policy, since he formulated it himself and used his favourites merely as executants. Another 'political' faction emerged during the 1630s, in opposition to Lord Treasurer Portland, who was committed to a policy of peace and retrenchment with no recourse to Parliament. The Earls of Holland and Northumberland led this faction, which favoured war with Spain and alliance with France. Like the members of the earlier 'protestant faction' they had puritan connexions and wanted the King to rule in collaboration with Parliament, but they included among their associates a number of anti-Spanish catholics and, for a time, enjoyed the support of the French-born Queen, Henrietta Maria.[4] Yet they were no more successful than their predecessors in persuading the King to change course, and although Charles eventually summoned Parliament in the spring of 1640 he did so not in response to pressures from Court factions but because of the collapse of his authority in Scotland.

THE PRIVY COUNCIL

Under the first two Stuarts, as under their Tudor and medieval fore-runners, the royal Court was the centre of government. Routine administration was carried out by the Privy Council, which at the end of Elizabeth's reign had only thirteen members. James immediately doubled its size, partly in order to incorporate his leading Scottish advisers but also to make it representative of a wider range of political opinion. The accession of Charles I was followed by a further expansion of the Council, and by 1630 it had forty-two members. However, under Charles as under James, the active membership was very much smaller than the nominal total. In 1613–14, at which time there were twenty-three Councillors, the average attendance at meetings was just under ten. When Parliament was in session, and more Privy Councillors were in town, as many as sixteen might attend, but the usual number was between eight and twelve, and on two occasions there were only five members present. Similarly in 1629–30 business was usually transacted by twelve or thirteen members, with numbers sinking as low as five, and on one occasion three. In the earlier period the regular attenders were headed by Archbishop Abbot, Lord Chancellor Ellesmere, and the Lord Privy Seal, the Earl of Northampton. In the 1630s the Lord Privy Seal, at this time the Earl of Manchester, attended eighty-three out of the ninety-nine meetings, which put him well ahead of Lord Keeper Coventry and the two Secretaries of State (Dudley Carleton, Viscount Dorchester, and Sir John Coke), whose attendance record was in the mid-seventies. Charles himself was recorded as being present on only nine occasions.

Most of the business with which the Privy Council dealt was routine, and matters of high policy were intermingled with relatively trivial issues. The Council more often than not responded to outside pressures rather than initiating policy, and systematic discussion of any topic was always liable to be interrupted by an unforeseen intervention. On one occasion, for example, the Earl of Northampton complained that 'this day the French ambassador comes . . . and hinders our proceeding to the consideration of other causes recommended by the King. For we never receive any direction by rule that is not crossed by some springing occasion, before unlooked-for, that must likewise be considered'.[5] In the 1630s the Council improved its procedures by setting up standing committees to deal with matters of perennial concern such as Ireland, the militia, and trade, as well as *ad hoc* ones for short-term issues. At the same time the

257

clerk of the Council began making indexes to its registers and drawing up monthly lists of unfinished business. When the Council focussed its attention upon a particular topic it could be remarkably effective, as it showed in its supervision of the Forced Loan in 1626–27 and the subsequent collection of Ship Money. Over a longer period it also carried through an extensive retraining and re-equipment programme for the county militias. But it suffered from inadequate staffing, for the four ordinary and five or six extraordinary clerks were insufficient to deal with the enormous range of business for which the Council was responsible. Moreover the officers of state and household officials who constituted the Council had departments of their own to run, and simply could not devote the necessary time and attention to developing collective policies. Indeed, they were fully occupied merely in ensuring that the decisions which the Council did take were put into practice.

Because the Privy Council was a formal body it had a more or less formal membership, but this made it unsuitable for the discussion of sensitive matters. When Prince Charles was in Madrid in 1623 – in order, as he hoped, to conclude the long-drawn-out negotiations for a marriage between himself and a Spanish princess – he asked his father to 'advise as little with your Council in these businesses as you can'. James assured him, in reply, that 'you need not doubt but I will be wary enough in not acquainting my Council with any secret in your letters'.[6] By the time Charles became King, war with Spain was certain, and since the Privy Council was split over this question, Charles took most of the major decisions on strategy in association with Buckingham alone. Details of naval and military operations were the concern of the Council of War which James had appointed in 1624. This included soldiers and sailors whose experience of operations made them invaluable but who would never have been eligible for membership of the Privy Council.

It was at about this time, in the mid-1620s, that the first references appeared to 'Cabinet Councils', a term of opprobrium, suggesting secret conclaves at which sinister decisions were taken. One such 'Cabinet' was the Privy Council committee for Scottish affairs, whose eight members were nominated by the King in 1638. It acted as the main advisory body to Charles during the next few years, and although its membership covered a broad spectrum of opinions, it was widely assumed to be responsible not only for the Bishops' Wars but also for plans to bring over an army from Ireland. The belief on the part of Charles's opponents that lack of good counsel had led to the breakdown of confidence in his government explains the demand in the Nineteen Propositions of 1642

that no public act concerning the affairs of the kingdom, which are proper for your Privy Council, may be esteemed as of any validity, as proceeding from the royal authority, unless it be done by the advice and consent of the major part of your Council, attested under their hands: and that your Council may be limited to a certain number, not exceeding five and twenty, nor under fifteen.[7]

THE COURT OF STAR CHAMBER

In the second half of Elizabeth's reign and under James I the Archbishop of Canterbury was virtually the sole representative of the clergy on the Privy Council, though from 1621 onwards there was a second clerical member in the shape of the newly-appointed Lord Keeper, John Williams, at that time Dean of Westminster but shortly to become Bishop of Lincoln. In 1628, however, Charles appointed William Laud, Bishop of Bath and Wells, and Richard Neile, Bishop of Winchester, to the Council. There, in 1636, they were joined by William Juxon, chosen by Laud to succeed him as Bishop of London, and subsequently, through Laud's influence with the King, given high secular office as Lord Treasurer. The presence of three or four bishops on the Council did not turn it into a clerical body, for they were outnumbered by the thirty or so lay peers and half a dozen commoners, but Privy Councillors were *ipso facto* judges of the prerogative court of Star Chamber, and Laud and Neile were regular attenders at the court's sessions. Star Chamber had hitherto been well respected; indeed, Sir Edward Coke described it as 'the most honourable court (our Parliament excepted) that is in the Christian world, both in respect of the judges of the court and of their honourable proceeding according to their just jurisdiction and the ancient and just orders of the court'.[8] The membership of the court included, in addition to the Privy Councillors, the two Chief Justices, who ensured that its proceedings, though lacking in the formality of the common law, were in accord with its principles.

Most of the cases that came before Star Chamber were brought by private individuals. Government actions, initiated by the Attorney General, amounted usually to some ten or twelve per cent of the total, but this figure rose to eighteen per cent during the Personal Rule. The Attorney General brought more than 175 of these actions in the period 1631–40, charging the accused with such offences as infringing monopoly patents, carrying out depopulating enclosures, demanding extortionate fees (if they were office-holders), and remaining in London despite royal proclamations ordering all those without legitimate business in the capital to return to their estates. Star Chamber had always been concerned with the enforcement of royal proclamations, but the impetus behind the spate of prosecutions in the 1630s was financial. The King needed money, and fines were a useful source of income: as Pym complained in April 1640, 'the Star Chamber now is become a court of revenue'.[9]

Association with the unpopular policies of the Personal Rule did much to undermine the reputation of Star Chamber. So too did its close link with Laud, who used it to punish critics of the episcopal hierarchy and infringers of the ecclesiastical discipline which he was so concerned to enforce. The savage sentences against Prynne, Burton and Bastwick (see p. 314) were delivered in Star Chamber, and the court became notorious for imposing heavy fines on gentlemen and ordering their ears to be cropped and noses slit. This unsavoury reputation was hardly justified. Corporal punishments had formed part of the armoury of the Elizabethan and Jacobean Star Chamber and had provoked little comment even when gentlemen were involved. Under Charles I such punishments were invoked on relatively few occasions, and although heavy fines were a more common penalty they were rarely collected in full. It was guilt by association rather than the actual abuse of its own powers which led the Long Parliament to dissolve Star Chamber in 1641.

THE ASSIZE JUDGES AND THE BOOK OF ORDERS

The very existence of prerogative courts in early modern England is an indication that no hard and fast line was drawn between the government and the judicature. The King was the chief executive, he was also the fount of justice, and these two roles were so closely linked that they often overlapped. One consequence of this was that the common-law judges were also administrative agents of the crown. Twice a year – except for the northern counties, which received only annual visitations – the judges went on circuit, holding assizes in the principal towns throughout the kingdom. Their primary function at the assizes was to try criminal cases that the Justices of the Peace regarded as too serious or too difficult for their own resolution, but they were also required to investigate the effectiveness of local government and of the magistrates who were responsible for carrying it out. James I made this plain when he addressed the judges in Star Chamber before the spring assizes in 1616: 'remember that when you go your circuits you go not only to punish and prevent offences, but you are to take care for the good government in general of the parts where you travel . . . You have charges to give to Justices of Peace, that they do their duties when you are absent as well as present. Take an account of them and report their service to me at your return'.[10]

The King, or the Lord Keeper acting on his behalf, would call the attention of the judges to specific topics of concern, which varied from year to year. In June 1618, for instance, Bacon instructed them to take particular account of 'recusants, the ill affected disease of this kingdom', of 'poverty, beggars and vagabonds', and of 'alehouses [and] nuisances of manners'.[11] Bacon was speaking at a time when the English economy was slowly recovering from the collapse set off by the Cockayne scheme (see p. 5), but it took a sharp downturn in 1620 and the government was concerned about the effect on the poor, who might be driven by desperation into violent courses. A Parliament was in prospect, and Bacon proposed that before it met the crown should show its concern for the general welfare by setting up standing commissions to handle specific problems. The most pressing of these was poor relief, and in January 1620 James authorised the establishment of a commission to deal with this and the associated problem of vagrancy. The commission was the brainchild of a Northamptonshire country gentleman, Sir Henry Montagu, who had succeeded Sir Edward Coke as Chief Justice of the King's Bench and was to become Lord Treasurer in December 1620. This particular initiative was short-lived, for it did not survive the fall of Bacon. In late 1630, however, when the economy was once again in severe recession, and the political crisis signalled by the violent end of the parliamentary session in 1629 had created fears of instability, Montagu – by now Earl of Manchester – put forward a revised version of his scheme. This provided the basis for the Book of Orders issued in 1631.

In its final form the Book consisted of eight orders and twelve directions. The orders instructed the Justices of the Peace to hold regular monthly meetings to supervise the work of their subordinate officials in the hundreds and parishes. They were also to make quarterly reports to the sheriff, who would pass them on to the assize judges for eventual presentation to the Privy Council. The directions required Justices to pay special attention to the provision of poor relief, the prevention of vagrancy, and the enforcement of the apprenticeship laws. There was nothing particularly novel about this initiative on the part of the Council. It had been the custom ever since Henry VIII's reign for the government to notify magistrates about its principal concerns, and the first printed Book of Orders dates from the middle of Elizabeth's reign. Other Books were issued from time to time to deal with the specific problems of dearth and plague, and the latest editions of these had been despatched to magistrates only in 1630. The 1631 Book of Orders did break with precedent in one respect, by calling for regular reports, but this provision was more honoured in the breach than in the observance. Reports were sent in sporadically, if at all, and they became increasingly stereotyped. One reason for this was the Justices' resentment at central government interference in what they regarded as their own domain. In the words of a Northamptonshire magistrate, 'it is observed to be a rule of discreet policy in general businesses to make a general answer, lest by descending too far into particulars something should be fastened upon which may produce an unexpected prejudice'.[12]

The Book of Orders won acceptance insofar as it coincided with the aims and objectives of the local governors. Its directions focussed the attention of Justices upon issues that were already of major concern to them, and its orders amounted to little more than the codification of what was already current practice in many areas. Intense and prolonged conciliar supervision might have produced superficially better results, but this was never a possibility. In fact a conciliar commission was set up in 1630, charged with overseeing local administration, and at a later stage groups of Privy Councillors were appointed to check on the work of the assize judges in their respective circuits. But the Councillors were too busy to give their full attention to such matters, and their interest declined as more pressing issues came to the fore. The Book of Orders, then, was not part of a long-term plan for the reinvigoration of conciliar government and the imposition of central control over the localities. On the contrary, it was a short-term response to the crisis brought about by the failure of the 1630 harvest – the worst of the entire early Stuart period – and it was entirely traditional in its approach.

THE JUSTICES OF THE PEACE

Although Justices of the Peace were nominated by the Lord Chancellor or Keeper, his choice was limited. In theory the crown was unfettered and could, if it thought fit, raise men from the dust to serve it. But the Justices, like their royal master, had no armed force at their disposal. In a deferential society they commanded respect because of their birth, their wealth, and their status. There were frequent complaints about their inefficiency, their corruption and their factiousness. James, in his Star Chamber address of 1616, criticised various sorts of Justices. There were the 'slowbellies that abide always at home, given to a life of ease and delight', but they were no more obnoxious than the 'busybodies' who would 'have all men dance after their pipe and follow their greatness'. There were also those who 'go seldom to the King's service but when it is to help some of their kindred', and the rather more sinister sort who 'in every cause that concerns prerogative give a snatch against a monarchy through their puritanical itching after popularity'.[13]

Dissatisfaction with the quality of many Justices led James to institute a major review of the Commission of the Peace in 1616–17, as a consequence of which more than 140 magistrates were left out while well over 200 new ones were brought in. This served merely to increase numbers, which had been steadily growing since the mid-sixteenth century: in Sussex, to take but one example, there were twenty-three resident Justices in 1570, thirty-nine at James's accession, and fifty by 1621. This trend was not reversed until the appointment of Sir Thomas Coventry as Lord Keeper in 1625. He promptly removed twenty-one magistrates from the Sussex bench and ensured that thereafter it never rose above thirty-five. There were similar cuts in other counties, with the consequence that in some places Justices of the Peace were thin on the ground and hard pressed to cope with the volume of work required of them. As early as 1626 one Somerset Justice complained of being 'weary of the burden and charge' of his office, 'especially now there is none in the division but myself. It is sessions every day all the day long here, [so] that I have no time for my own occasions, hardly to put meat into my mouth'.[14]

In theory all the Justices were supposed to assemble four times a year for Quarter Sessions – usually held in the county town, but sometimes rotated through a number of urban centres – but in practice absenteeism was common and attendance fluctuated. From Elizabeth's reign onwards there was also an increasing tendency to hold

263

informal petty sessions, where only two or three Justices might be present, and the Book of Orders tried to standardise this practice by requiring regular monthly meetings. Standardisation was difficult, however, for different counties had different requirements, and they cherished their quasi-independence. At Quarter Sessions the Justices dealt with cases brought before them by the grand jury of the shire – a body of some fifteen or so lesser landholders, empanelled by the sheriff, which was supposed to be representative of the county community and sufficiently knowledgeable to be able to distinguish between those charges which deserved formal trial and those which were malicious, factious or flimsy. The Justices would normally deal with judicial matters first, though the more serious cases would be stood over to the assizes, and then attend to such perennial problems as the maintenance of highways and bridges, the licensing or suppression of alehouses, the building and management of houses of correction, the apportionment of responsibility in bastardy cases, and the levying of local rates, including the poor rate.

The effectiveness of the Justices of the Peace in governing the local communities derived in large part from the fact that they were themselves resident there. Indeed, all the gentry, whether or not they were appointed to the Commission of the Peace, acted as guardians of the established order, for their continuing presence in the countryside served to maintain the traditional bonds between them and their inferiors. This function was important at all times, but particularly so at a period when population growth and inflation were putting severe strains upon the structure of society. For this reason Tudor and early Stuart governments tried to curb the tendency for some members of the gentry to spend part of the winter in London. In a proclamation issued soon after his arrival, James referred to reports

from all parts of our kingdom that by the remove of great numbers of the principal gentlemen out of the several counties – as well of such as have charge there, as Deputy-Lieutenants or Commissioners for Musters or for the Peace, as others – with their whole families, both the execution of things incident to their charge is omitted, and hospitality exceedingly decayed, whereby the relief of the poorer sort of people is taken away, who had from such houses much comfort and ease towards their living.[15]

In order to remedy this situation James commanded all nobles and gentlemen who had no valid reason to be in the capital to leave forthwith. However, the fact that further proclamations to the same effect were issued both in James's reign and in Charles's suggests that such exhortations were of limited effect.

SHIP MONEY

After the 1626 Parliament, which had seen a concerted attempt to overthrow Buckingham, the Commission of the Peace and the Lieutenancy were purged of the Duke's enemies. If this pressure had been maintained, it is conceivable that the royal government might have created a corps of local rulers much more in sympathy with its aims. However, initiatives of this sort were invariably short-lived, for although it was relatively easy to dismiss dissident Justices it was not so easy to replace them with men of equal standing. In practice, therefore, the Justices retained a considerable degree of autonomy, and it was probably for this reason that when the government decided to levy Ship Money in 1634 it by-passed them and instead used the sheriff as its agent in every county. Technically Ship Money was not a tax but a rate, and the writs implied that each levy was self-contained, an immediate response to an emergency situation created by the depredations of 'certain thieves, pirates, and robbers of the sea, as well Turks, enemies of the Christian name, as others'.[16] Indeed, the formal demand was not for money but ships, and London initially insisted on supplying these. In all other cases, however, the ships were 'commuted' into a lump sum estimated by the Council, and the 'emergency' proved to be of long duration since the writs were issued annually from 1634 until the end of the Personal Rule. Moreover, from 1635 Ship Money was levied on inland towns and counties as well as the maritime regions, on the grounds that 'that charge of defence which concerneth all men ought to be supported by all'.[17] There was no precedent for this, although in the closing stages of Elizabeth's reign her Council had been planning a similar extension, and in 1628 Charles had announced his intention of charging all the counties with the cost of the fleet he was setting out.[18]

The funds raised through the annual levies of Ship Money were all spent on the navy, but even if this had been generally known (and believed) it would probably have had little effect on public opinion, which was hostile to the whole idea of prerogative taxation. A further cause of resentment came from the size of the sums demanded: Sussex, for example, which had contributed £16,000 to the twelve subsidies voted by Parliament in the 1620s, was required to pay out £28,000 over six years for Ship Money. Taking the country as a whole, Ship Money brought in about £190,000 a year during the first three years of its collection, which was equivalent to three and a half subsidies. This is in part a reflection of the

265

declining value of the subsidy, caused largely by the fact that the country gentlemen who were responsible for collecting it consistently under-assessed themselves. The Privy Council had issued repeated exhortations stressing the need for them to be more realistic in their estimates, but these had been of no more effect than water off a duck's back. What Ship Money demonstrated was that a determined Council could impose a higher level of taxation than was customary, but only in the absence of Parliament. It risked alienating the local communities by its actions, but in fact it was remarkably successful in collecting the sums it prescribed until the government's authority was undermined by the outbreak of rebellion in Scotland. It achieved its success by putting heavy pressure on the sheriffs, who were held personally responsible for raising the sum decided upon for their county, even after the end of their year's tenure of office. It also brought pressure to bear upon other holders of local office by instructing the sheriffs, as in 1637, to inform it of all such who had 'expressed their averseness to this so great and necessary service', in order that it could take appropriate action against them.[19]

The payment of Ship Money was not confined to rich landowners. Sheriffs were instructed, when they made arrangements for detailed assessments, to take into account money as well as land, which meant that many tradesmen were brought into the net. So were many small freeholders who had hitherto been exempt from national (though not from local) taxation. As a consequence, a much larger section of the population was affected by Ship Money than by subsidies: in Essex, for instance, there were 3,200 names on the subsidy roll by 1640, but 14,500 people were assessed for Ship Money. This involvement of elements below the level of the political nation also applied to the business of collecting Ship Money, for the sheriff, after receipt of the writ, would issue warrants to the high constables of the hundreds, instructing them to proceed with assessment. They in turn would summon the petty constables and leading figures in the local parishes to assist them in this task. In Cheshire, which had seven hundreds, each divided into two administrative units, the sheriff had to deal directly with fourteen high constables and more than 400 petty ones. High constables were usually drawn from the ranks of the lesser gentry or yeomen, petty constables from the 'middling sort' of substantial farmers and well-established craftsmen or tradesmen. In other words, the levy of Ship Money had an impact upon sections of society which would not normally have been directly affected by the actions of the royal government. One

consequence of this was to promote the growth of political awareness among them.

The majority of those who paid Ship Money may have done so
unwillingly, but they were in no position to challenge the authority
of the sheriff. Open defiance came from those higher up the social
scale, beginning with Lord Saye and Sele, who not only refused to
pay but sued the constable and sheriff who distrained his property.
The government carefully avoided picking up this gauntlet, but after
the judges' confirmation of the legality of Ship Money the Council
decided to take up the challenge from a wealthy Buckinghamshire
landowner, John Hampden, and allowed his case to come to court
(see p. 232). Of the twelve judges, seven gave their judgment for
the crown, but if Charles hoped that the majority decision in his
favour would reconcile his subjects to payment of Ship Money, he
was mistaken. Clarendon's opinion was that

when they heard this demanded in a court of law as a right, and found it
by sworn judges of the law adjudged so, upon such grounds and reasons
as every stander-by was able to swear was not law, and . . . instead of
giving were required to pay, and by a logic that left no man anything which
he might call his own . . . they thought themselves bound in conscience to
the public justice not to submit.[20]

Clarendon's comment is a reminder that while the law buttressed
the King's authority through binding his subjects to obedience, it
did so only as long as they accepted that the law – or, rather, the
judiciary which interpreted it – was impartial. To the extent that
their trust in law was eroded, so was the authority of the crown.

DISTRAINT OF KNIGHTHOOD AND THE FOREST LAWS

Ship Money was the fiscal device which imposed the most severe
strain upon relations between the central government and the local
communities, but it was not the only one. Under an old law which
had long been in abeyance, owners of land worth £40 a year were
required to take up knighthood, and in 1627 it was decided to levy
fines on all those who had failed to do so. At first this was left to
the sheriffs, but in 1630 the Council appointed special commissioners
for each county, operating under the supervision of the Exchequer.
Fines were based upon subsidy assessments, and ranged from a £25
minimum for Justices of the Peace to £10 for lesser landowners.

Many of those affected were well below the level of the county elite, for after a century of inflation £40-worth of land was no longer an indication of great wealth or high social standing. This was one reason why those persons who were technically eligible for knighthood had never taken it up; had they done so they would have been required to assume responsibilities in local administration for which they felt themselves to be socially unsuited. Well over 9,000 landowners were compelled to compound for their 'oversight', and Distraint of Knighthood enriched the Exchequer by close on £175,000. There was little overt resistance to this device, but its unpopularity was indicated by the Long Parliament's action in abolishing it, in 1641. Like Ship Money, Distraint of Knighthood highlighted the gap between law and justice and weakened those bonds of respect and affection which bound subjects to their King.

Another fiscal device which had the same effect was the arbitrary extension of the forest boundaries from 1634 onwards. Forests were areas originally set aside as game reserves for the crown, and were subject to a special law. Over the course of many centuries the forests had shrunk in size, and the initial aim of the enquiries undertaken by the Attorney General, William Noy, in 1634 was to determine their present limits. It was only after Noy's death in that same year that another lawyer, Sir John Finch – who, as Speaker, had suffered from the violence that attended the end of the 1629 session of Parliament – persuaded the King to extend the forest boundaries to the maximum they had ever attained in the Middle Ages. They now covered entire counties, such as Essex and Northamptonshire, and many hundreds of people were accused of offences against forest law having never been aware that they were subject to it. More often than not they were also offered the option of buying their way out of the forest, which made the fiscal motive behind the entire operation even more transparent. The total of fines imposed came to over £80,000, but a significant amount of this was still unpaid by 1641, when the Long Parliament restored the forest boundaries to their Jacobean limits. Charles's manipulation of the forest laws contributed to his alienation of the political nation, for as Clarendon observed, the 'burden lighted most upon persons of quality and honour, who thought themselves above ordinary oppressions, and [were] therefore like to remember it with more sharpness'. Clarendon also condemned the 'over-activity' of lawyers such as Noy and Finch 'who should more carefully have preserved their profession and the professors from being profaned to those services which have rendered both so obnoxious'.[21]

MILITARY CHARGES

Prerogative taxation, particularly in the form of Ship Money, was resented not only on its own account but because it added to an already heavy financial burden on the local communities. In the Short Parliament Sir William Savile, one of the members for Yorkshire, declared that 'the freeholders about him told him at his coming, they did not care how many subsidies were given so that grievance of the Ship Money were taken away'. He was challenged, however, by two other Yorkshire MPs, who alleged 'that there were other grievances besides the Ship Money, as coat-and-conduct money and other military charges, which far exceeded that of Ship Money . . . Indeed, Sir John Hotham said the military charge upon that county was £40,000, whereas the Ship Money was but £12,000'.[22] Military charges were of two sorts. First of all there were those connected with the county militias or trained bands. In theory every able-bodied man between sixteen and sixty was liable for part-time service in his county militia, but in the sixteenth century warfare was becoming an increasingly professional business as pikes and firearms, which required skilled operation, replaced bows and billhooks. In 1573, therefore, the government decided that 'a convenient number' of militia men should be selected from the general mass in order that they could be 'tried, armed and weaponed, and so consequently taught and trained'.[23]

The cost of supplying weapons for the trained bands was substantial, as was that of exercising them, for the men had to be paid for their days off work. The Justices of the Peace levied a militia rate to meet these expenses, using the subsidy assessments as a guide. This created a great deal of resentment, for the subsidy assessments were increasingly outdated and no longer reflected the actual distribution of wealth within the local communities. A further grievance arose in the latter part of Elizabeth's reign as military responsibilities within the shires were handed over to the Lord Lieutenants and their Deputies. Whereas a county might have fifty or more JPs, only three or four of these were likely to be appointed as Deputy-Lieutenants, and relations between this small elite, in close touch with the central government, and the general body of the magistracy were often strained. Little could be done while Elizabeth was alive, but among the petitions presented to James at his accession was one asking for the abolition of the Lieutenancy as an 'unnecessary and inconvenient' office, particularly now that war was about to give way to peace. The King's service, according to the petitioners, 'may be done with

269

more ease and expedition by the Justices of Peace in their precincts, who may see the musters, levies, etc. as well performed and keep the soldiers in use of arms at their set times'.[24]

There was a widespread feeling that the administration of the militia was unsatisfactory, depending as it did upon a mixture of common and statute law and prerogative action. In 1604 Parliament took the first step towards reform by repealing the Marian Act 'for having of horse armour and weapon'[25] upon which the Elizabethan militia system had been based. However, it put nothing in its place, presumably because any new Act would have had to deal with the central problem of financing the trained bands, which in turn would have involved reassessment of the subsidy with all that that implied. This meant that the militia became increasingly a prerogative responsibility, at a time when the prerogative itself was under increasingly hostile scrutiny. This did not matter a great deal during the opening years of James's reign, after the conclusion of peace with Spain in 1604, for the militia, in the words of one Lord Lieutenant, underwent a period of 'long vacation and rest'.[26] In 1614 the Earl of Essex, who mustered the Staffordshire trained bands, reported that they were so out of practice that they could hardly stand up straight, let alone use their weapons properly,[27] and there is no reason to assume that his experience was exceptional.

The 'long vacation' of the militia came to an end after 1612, as the operations of Spinola in Cleve and Julich raised fears of a Spanish invasion of England. The Council ordered the resumption of regular training and the replacement of old-fashioned calivers by muskets, and it kept up a steady pressure which markedly increased after the outbreak of the Thirty Years War in 1618. In 1623 the Council sent out a new training manual, based upon the practice of the Dutch, but this had only a limited effect because the mustermasters, the paid officials who were responsible in every shire for instructing the militiamen, were unfamiliar with the latest techniques. Little more was done while James was alive, but no sooner had Charles ascended the throne than he announced his determination to create a 'perfect' or 'exact' militia, and in 1626 he recalled a number of English serjeants from service with the Dutch forces and seconded them to the counties for training purposes. He intended this as a short-term measure, but in many counties they stayed on for two or three years.

These professionals helped to bring about a considerable overall improvement in the quality of the trained bands, but performance varied from one area to another, depending in part upon the degree of commitment of the Lord Lieutenant and his Deputies, and also upon the attitude of the local population. In the West Country, for instance, where the threat of raids by marauding pirates was taken seriously, there was only slight opposition to military rates and measures, but this was not the case in East Anglia, which was suffering from the prolonged depression in the cloth trade and industry. The Deputy-Lieutenants of Norfolk, aware that since the repeal of the 1558 Act there was no statutory basis for their authority, and afraid that they might be called to account by a House of Commons that was suspicious of the Deputy-Lieutenancy as a potential instrument of absolutism, appealed to the Council for support against 'wilful refusers or negligent defaulters'. The Council ignored their request, however, and in effect the militia system in Norfolk ceased to function. There was no improvement until 1629–30, when the Lord Lieutenant of Norfolk, the Earl of Arundel, sent his son down to the region to restore order and impose discipline.[28] He succeeded where the Council and its agents had failed – a reminder that in early Stuart England magnates were still men of influence, exercising a natural as well as a delegated authority.

The second category of 'military charges' covered the costs of raising levies for service outside the kingdom. When these were required, the Privy Council would instruct the Lord Lieutenant of every county to press a specified number of men, who were to be able-bodied but not members of the trained bands. During the war years of the second half of Elizabeth's reign such demands had been frequent, but James brought peace with him, and only at the very end of his reign did pressing start again. In late 1624 the Council ordered the raising of 12,000 men for service under Count Mansfeld. A further 10,000 were demanded for the Cadiz expedition in 1625, and 6,000 more for the initial stages of the Ré expedition in 1627. The county authorities would usually take advantage of this situation to empty their jails and rid themselves of undesirable elements of the population, but the heavy demands of the war years in the mid-1620s meant that such resources were not, of themselves, sufficient. The counties now had to part with husbandmen and labourers who were useful members of society, and in the summer of 1627 the Deputy-Lieutenants of Dorset told the Council that they had been able to raise their quota only with great difficulty and to the accompaniment of 'lamentable cries of mothers, wives and children'.[29] As a rule, however, the unwilling conscripts were drawn from the dregs of the populace and represented a major threat to law and order. The Mansfeld levies who made their way to Dover in late 1624 were a foretaste of things to come: in the words of one report 'they straggle up and down, and not only spoil and take what they list, but do also terrify the poorer sort of inhabitants and molest and offend all that pass upon the highway'.[30]

The pressed men were usually so poor that they had to be provided with a coat and sometimes other items of clothing before they could be despatched to the nominated rendezvous under the care of specially appointed 'conductors'. The cost of the clothing and of the conductor's fee was met by levying a separate rate for 'coat-and-conduct money'. In theory this expenditure was merely a short-term expedient, for the Exchequer acknowledged an obligation to reimburse the counties for all the sums they spent on military purposes. In practice, however, the Exchequer was so short of money that it could not do so, and the burden therefore fell on the local communities. One of the reasons for the relative success of the Forced Loan in 1627 was the assurance that the first call on it would be repayment of sums owing to the counties. The collection of coat-and-conduct money was an unpopular, time-consuming and often fruitless occupation, and many officials had to dig into their own pockets to raise the required sums. In Sussex, for example, the high constables of the hundreds parted with £20 or £30 apiece in 1625, and the Deputy-Lieutenants pressed the Council 'that some present course may be taken that these monies may be speedily paid; otherwise we shall not be able hereafter, upon like occasions, to command the constables the furtherance of His Majesty's service'.[31] In fact it was not until 1627 that the Forced Loan made possible the repayment of these sums, by which time further expenditure was necessary in order to raise levies for the Ré expedition. Additional military charges were incurred, particularly in coastal counties, through the billeting of troops either before their embarkation or after their return. In 1626–27 Sussex had to provide lodgings for about 800 men for nearly a year, at a cost of some £3,500, and at least as much was spent on clothing and equipping the troops. The Forced Loan in Sussex brought in just under £6,000, but this proved insufficient to meet outstanding debts, let alone finance new outlays.

The long delay in repaying military charges, and the fact that some of them were never repaid, account for their unpopularity and for the lack of enthusiasm for the war in general. While Charles and his advisers were pressing for immediate and substantial supply in 1628, to enable the King to meet his obligations to foreign allies and play a full part in the major war that was raging on the continent, the Commons were demanding an end to billeting. 'Great companies of soldiers', they complained, 'have been dispersed into divers counties of the realm, and the inhabitants, against their wills, have been compelled to receive them into their houses and there to suffer them to sojourn'. Such a practice was a cause of 'great grievance and vexation of the people', particularly since it was held to be 'against the laws and customs of this realm'.[32] In the Petition of Right the Commons secured the King's promise 'to remove the said soldiers and mariners' and an assurance that his people would not be 'so burdened in time to come'.[33] There could be no clearer illustration of the difference of viewpoint between Whitehall and the local communities. What the King perceived as being in the national interest would all too often appear to his subjects as a specious excuse for intolerable and ultimately unacceptable fiscal pressures.

POVERTY AND VAGRANCY

A royal proclamation published in December 1615, declared that non-residency on the part of the local governors had led to 'the increase and multiplying of rogues, vagabonds and beggars'.[34] It was indeed the case that the problems of poverty and vagrancy were becoming increasingly apparent, and increasingly intractable. There simply was not enough work available, particularly in rural areas, for all those who needed it. Land also was in short supply, and although holdings could be and were fragmented, this was no long-term solution, for a smallholding of four or five acres was insufficient to provide a living. More and more small farmers either sold up to larger ones or took on part-time labouring work. In good times they could probably make ends meet, but when harvests were poor or the economy was depressed they were left without resources. Many people, especially young men, tried to break out of this vicious circle by moving to another part of the country, and from the mid-sixteenth century onwards there was a pronounced drift from the poorer uplands of the north and west to the more urban areas of southern England.

London attracted some 7,000 migrants annually, who settled in the suburbs outside the city walls where the writ of the municipal authorities did not run. Speculative landlords took advantage of population pressure to jerry-build new houses and fill existing ones to bursting point. The government tried to check this, and a proclamation of 1608 denounced 'the continual new buildings and increase of buildings in and near about the City of London', which, it declared, 'doth draw together such an overflow of people, specially of the meaner sort, as can hardly be either fed and sustained, or preserved in health, or governed; which doth not only threaten, but hath already bred and brought forth at divers times dearth of victuals, infection of plague, and manifold disorders'.[35] Further proclamations designed to check the growth of London and inhibit overcrowding were issued throughout the early Stuart period, especially after plague attacks, such as the severe visitation of 1625. They were of little or no effect, however, and although Charles I restrained new building in the capital he thereby merely increased pressure on existing accommodation. A survey carried out in 1637 found that one house contained eleven married couples and fifteen single persons, that another had eighteen lodgers, and that the Company of Freemasons, far from setting an example, had joined the profiteers by dividing up its hall into tenements.

London had been a pioneer in developing schemes for the relief of poverty, and had first imposed a compulsory poor rate in 1547. It also took over the old royal palace of Bridewell and turned it into a house of correction, where 'sturdy beggars' were punished and set to work. Other towns followed London's example, and Parliament ultimately gave statutory sanction to these local initiatives with an Act of 1572 authorising the imposition of a poor rate, and another of 1610 making the provision of houses of correction compulsory. The basic tenet of the poor law, as it had been defined by Parliament at the very end of Elizabeth's reign, was that parishes were responsible for the relief of their 'impotent' poor – i.e those who were unable to work, on account of age or disability – and for the punishment of 'sturdy rogues' who were sound in body but unwilling to undertake gainful employment. The assumption behind this distinction was that work was available for all those who really wanted it, but this was palpably untrue. In the open-field areas of the midlands a flexible approach to the problems of overpopulation was inhibited by strong manorial ties and reluctance to abandon customary practices. People who could not find work had little alternative but to seek it elsewhere, and they frequently migrated to forest and pastoral regions which were less densely settled and where manorial organisation was weak. A variety of crafts could be practised in these regions, including spinning and weaving the raw material 'put out' by the itinerant wool merchants, and these occupations provided employment·and a living for many thousands of newcomers. But this quasi-industrial economy was susceptible to fluctuations in international as well as domestic trade, and the depression which set in from the 1620s caused severe hardship. The forest dwellers were already notorious for their lack of discipline, and the depression sparked off riots in many areas, particularly in the west of England. It also prompted emigration from the forest-pastoral regions, mainly into the towns, thereby exacerbating the problem of urban poverty.

While necessity compelled many people to pluck up their roots and move from one part of England to another – or, in the 1630s, to the New World – it turned others into permanent vagrants. With food prices rising and real wages falling, begging might well offer a better prospect than poorly paid casual work. If a beggar could make 6d a day, which was by no means unfeasible, he would be just as well off as a farm labourer who counted himself lucky if he was paid £9 a year. Local authorities were prepared to license begging for those, such as maimed sailors and soldiers, who would otherwise have been a burden on the community, but licences were easy to forge, and a great deal of unauthorised begging went on. Vagrants were not necessarily full-time beggars; like modern gypsies they would, in addition, make and sell artefacts, do odd jobs, and even undertake short-term employment where this was available.

Despite reports of vagrants moving round the country in large bands, terrorising the population, they generally travelled in groups of two or three, and consisted mainly of young single men who either had no wife and children or had abandoned them. There were, of course, female vagrants, many of them pregnant unmarried women who had been turned out of their homes or jobs or had fled out of a sense of shame. Some vagrants confined their travels to the region around their 'home' – however this was defined – and were more or less tolerated. Others went further afield, moving in fits and starts, and settling for a time in places where the prospects of lawful or unlawful gain looked promising. It was this which particularly alarmed the parochial and urban authorities, for the law laid down that after twelve months in the same place a person acquired rights of residence and was therefore eligible for relief. Local communities were hard put to it to relieve their own poor and regarded indigent newcomers as a prospective additional burden. Vagrants were therefore usually whipped or put in the stocks, to discourage them from either staying or returning, and then sent on their way. Magistrates were supposed to arrange for them to go back to their native parish or last place of settlement, but this was easier said than done, and many vagrants clung to their particular lifestyle for lack of anything better and regarded the occasional punishments as an occupational hazard.

In July 1616 James I issued a proclamation 'for punishing of vagabonds, rogues and idle persons' which required the local authorities in London and the adjoining counties to appoint Provost Marshals. These were to carry out 'diligent search . . . as well in the fields as in the highways and streets' for all 'idle vagrant men and masterless men', whom they were to despatch to houses of correction for appropriate punishment.[36] In fact the use of Provost Marshals only became widespread in the 1620s and 1630s, and even then was far from universal. The Sussex magistrates nominated a Provost Marshal for each division of the county in 1624 and were so pleased with the results that they maintained the system for fifteen years. A similar scheme was adopted in Worcestershire in the next decade, with two Marshals, each attended by a footman, appointed 'to ride from place to place for apprehending and punishing of rogues'.[37] Full-time Provost Marshals were far more effective than the part-time constables in rounding up vagrants, but their salary, usually in the region of £20 a year, was a drain on local resources, and this was one reason why they were not employed in all counties. Another was the dislike of innovation, particularly in matters affecting the liberty of the subject, for Provost Marshals were linked in the public consciousness with the unpopular military levies of the 1620s and with the imposition of martial law, which had been condemned in the Petition of Right.

Although vagrants and unlicensed beggars were liable to harassment and were often held responsible for the petty pilfering and general disorderliness that seemed to be afflicting late Elizabethan and early Stuart England, there was genuine concern about the incidence and effect of poverty, and genuine attempts were made to soften its impact. Private charity played a major part in this, particularly the trusts set up by rich parishioners either during their lifetimes or after their deaths. Indiscriminate doles were no longer favoured, but monies were often provided for the distribution of food and clothing to those who were most in need, or, more specifically, for the provision of tools for men seeking work. Public charity was usually set in motion as a response to bad harvests or a trade recession. Magistrates would commandeer grain and either give it to the poor or sell it at a subsidised price. They would also impose restrictions on brewing, since this consumed supplies of barley, a normally cheap grain which was therefore favoured by the poor. They provided work for the able-bodied in houses of correction, maintained at the public expense and looked after by full-time Overseers of the Poor. They apprenticed pauper children, in the hope that these would subsequently be able to look after themselves. As for the 'impotent' poor, they gave them outdoor relief in the shape of food, money and sometimes accommodation. By twentieth-century western standards the poor relief system was harsh, but by the standards of the time it was remarkably humanitarian. Self-interest as well as charitable impulses played a part, of course, for the more affluent members of society were all too aware that starving and hungry men were fuel for rebellion, and that unrest, once it broke out, was difficult to contain. Yet except for a few isolated instances the poor did not starve, and the local communities acknowledged their responsibilities by accepting what was for them an unprecedentedly high level of local taxation in the poor rate. This may account for the fact that until the collapse of the monarchy after 1641 there was no major uprising in England. However primitive the mechanisms for relieving poverty, they served to blunt its cutting edge.

THE IMPOSITION OF A MORAL ORDER

Vagrants and masterless men were symbols of disorderliness, and as such threatened the stability of the existing social system. In the open-field areas of the lowlands, where manorial control was usually strong, disorderly elements could either be contained or expelled, but this was not the case in the forest-pasture regions. Until the flood of new arrivals from the mid-sixteenth century onwards, these had been sparsely populated and often outside the effective range of manorial or magisterial supervision. One observer described 'the people bred amongst woods' as 'naturally more stubborn and uncivil than in the champion [i.e. arable] countries' and this verdict was confirmed by the seventeenth-century antiquary John Aubrey, who referred to them as living in a lawless fashion and caring 'for nobody, having no dependence on anybody'.[38] The rapid expansion of these wood-pasture communities made them if anything more lawless, and the same was true of the towns in southern England, particularly the suburbs where the poor found refuge.

The threat to order prompted the emergence in many places of self-selected elites drawn from the 'middling sort' of lesser gentry, yeomen farmers and prosperous tradesmen. They might hold official positions as constables, Overseers of the Poor, or even magistrates, but their effectiveness derived from the determination with which they enforced what they regarded as a moral order. Alehouses were closed down, since they encouraged idleness and drunkenness and offered shelter to vagrants and other undesirables. Church ales, dancing round the maypole, and other traditional festivities were suppressed because they stimulated licentiousness and were an affront to decency. The mothers of bastard children were severely punished, not simply because they had done wrong but also because they had imposed an additional burden upon the community. The poor were duly relieved, as long as they were respectable, but poverty itself came to be regarded as the consequence of sin and something not far removed from a crime.

The imposition of a moral order had much in common with puritan demands for a tighter spiritual discipline, and indeed the two attitudes were mutually reinforcing. Sabbatarianism, for instance, implied both the suppression of Sunday games and also, at compulsory church services, the indoctrination of the entire population in the twin virtues of godliness and good living. Where the parish priest was of puritan inclination he would often be the nucleus around which the local elite revolved, and religious attitudes and social policies would be fused into one. This accounts for the shock felt by such communities at the triumph of the Arminians in the 1630s and the imposition of Laudianism. In the Essex village of Terling, for example, the authority of the elite was called into question when their leader, the vicar, was first suspended and then, in 1631, deprived for refusing to conform to the Prayer-Book service. For a time his place was taken by his curate, who continued the rejection of such 'popish' practices as wearing a surplice, kneeling to receive communion, and signing with the cross, but eventually he too was forced out. Private patronage ensured the appointment of another puritan as vicar, but his influence in the community was diminished by the fact that, as he later recalled, he was in 'weakness and in fear and in much trembling . . . all the prelates' times'.[39] It was the undermining of their authority which most offended the local elites, for the converse of puritan discipline, as they saw it, was popish or pagan anarchy. The royal government, through its *Declaration of Sports* (see p. 316), appeared to be encouraging the ungodly multitude, the profaners of the sabbath, at the expense of the godly minority who upheld both the sabbath and the social order.

It would be quite wrong to suggest that puritanism was the religion only of the successful middling sort, or that local government in all areas had fallen into the hands of puritan elites. But it does seem to be the case that traditional attitudes had greater strength and vitality in the arable areas than in wood-pasture regions and big towns. During the Personal Rule, the royal government came out in favour of the older, all-embracing culture against the newer and narrower puritan discipline. It also upheld established authority – including, of course, that of the bishops – and cut down both the pews and the pretensions of the puritan elites. This might imply that the civil war, when it came, was a struggle between the old England and the new, between the arable and the wood-pasture areas, between the countryside and the towns. But such simplifications are misleading because they leave out a whole host of other factors, not least the complexity of human motivation. When men and women were forced to choose sides – which most of them were intensely reluctant to do – they did so for a variety of reasons; indeed, their reason sometimes pulled them in one direction while their emotions tugged in another. Geographical location, social position, and cultural inclination were important (and, until recently, relatively unnoticed) factors, but they were not the only, nor necessarily the decisive, ones.

NOTES AND REFERENCES

(*The place of publication is London, unless otherwise stated*)
1. **E. R. Foster** (ed.) *Proceedings in Parliament 1610* (New Haven 1966). Vol. 1, p. 265.
2. **Berkshire Record Office** *Trumbull MSS.* XVIII, 76.
3. **'Sir William Monson's Account of the Navy'**. British Library *Additional MSS.* 9298.
4. **R. M. Smuts** 'The Puritan Followers of Henrietta Maria in the 1630s' *English Historical Review*. Vol. 93. 1978.
5. **Linda Levy Peck** *Northampton: Patronage and Policy at the Court of James I* (1982), p. 88.
6. **D. H. Willson** *The Privy Councillors in the House of Commons 1604–1629* (Minneapolis 1940), pp. 19–20.
7. **S. R. Gardiner** (ed.) *The Constitutional Documents of the Puritan Revolution 1625–1660* (Oxford 1906), p. 251. (Hereafter Gardiner *Constitutional Documents*)
8. **G. R. Elton** (ed.) *The Tudor Constitution* 2nd edn. (Cambridge 1982), p. 175.
9. **J. P. Kenyon** (ed.) *The Stuart Constitution 1603–1688* 2nd edn. (Cambridge 1986), p. 187.
10. *The Political Works of James I* ed. C. H. McIlwain (Cambridge, Mass. 1918), p. 338. (Hereafter James I *Political Works*)

11. ***The Works of Francis Bacon*** ed. James Spedding (1874). Vol. XIII, p. 315.

12. **Anthony Fletcher** *Reform in the Provinces: The Government of Stuart England* (1986), p. 58. (Hereafter Fletcher *Reform in the Provinces*)

13. James I *Political Works*, p. 340.

14. Fletcher *Reform in the Provinces*, pp. 10–11.

15. **James F. Larkin** & **Paul L. Hughes** (eds.) *Stuart Royal Proclamations*. Vol. I. *Royal Proclamations of King James I* (Oxford 1973), pp. 21–22. (Hereafter Larkin & Hughes *Royal Proclamations*)

16. Gardiner *Constitutional Documents*, p. 105.

17. Gardiner *Constitutional Documents*, p. 106.

18. **R. J. W. Swales** 'The Ship Money Levy of 1628' *Bulletin of the Institute of Historical Research*. Vol. 50, 1977.

19. **J. H. Gleason** *The Justices of the Peace in England 1558 to 1640* (Oxford 1969), p. 81.

20. **Edward, Earl of Clarendon** *The History of the Rebellion and Civil Wars in England* ed. W. Dunn Macray (Oxford 1888). Vol. I, p. 150. (Hereafter Clarendon *History of the Rebellion*)

21. Clarendon *History of the Rebellion*. Vol. I, pp. 148, 156.

22. **J. T. Cliffe** *The Yorkshire Gentry from the Reformation to the Civil War* (1969), pp. 317–18.

23. **L. O. J. Boynton** *The Elizabethan Militia* (1967), pp. 16, 91. (Hereafter Boynton *Elizabethan Militia*)

24. **A. Hassell Smith** 'Militia Rates and Militia Statutes 1558–1663' in Peter Clark, Alan G. R. Smith & Nicholas Tyacke (eds.) *The English Commonwealth 1547–1640* (Leicester 1979), p. 100. (Hereafter Hassell Smith 'Militia Rates')

25. Hassell Smith 'Militia Rates', p. 94.

26. Boynton *Elizabethan Militia*, p. 212.

27. Boynton *Elizabethan Militia*, p. 216.

28. Fletcher *Reform in the Provinces*, pp. 302–03.

29. **S. J. Stearns** 'Conscription and English Society in the 1620s' *Journal of British Studies*. Vol. XI. 1972, pp. 5–6.

30. **Roger Lockyer** *Buckingham: The Life and Political Career of George Villiers, First Duke of Buckingham 1592–1628* (1981), p. 210.

31. **Anthony Fletcher** *A County Community in Peace and War: Sussex 1600–1660* (1975), p. 194.

32. Gardiner *Constitutional Documents*, p. 68.

33. Gardiner *Constitutional Documents*, p. 69.

34. Larkin & Hughes *Royal Proclamations*, p. 357.

35. Larkin & Hughes *Royal Proclamations*, p. 193.

36. Larkin & Hughes *Royal Proclamations*, p. 361.

37. Fletcher *Reform in the Provinces*, p. 210.

38. **Joan Thirsk** (ed.) *The Agrarian History of England and Wales*. Vol. IV *1500–1640*. (Cambridge 1967), p. 111.

39. **Keith Wrightson** & **David Levine** *Poverty and Piety in an English Village: Terling 1525–1700* (1979), p. 161.

CHAPTER TWELVE

The Roman Catholics in England 1603–42

JAMES I AND THE CATHOLICS 1603–1605

When James I became King of England in 1603 his new subjects included some 40,000 men and women who had clung to the Roman Catholic faith despite the dangers and difficulties to which they were exposed under the penal legislation passed in Elizabeth's reign. To a large extent they were the unwilling and unhappy victims of an international power struggle in which the temporal ambitions of the King of Spain had become inextricably bound up with the missionary zeal of Counter-Reformation Roman Catholicism. They wished to be simultaneously good catholics and loyal subjects, but given that Elizabethan England was at war with Spain, the most threatening of catholic powers, and that Spanish policies received, to a greater or lesser extent, the support of the papacy, it is hardly surprising that the government regarded them as potential traitors and treated them accordingly. They despaired of any change of attitude while the war continued, but they hoped that the accession of a new sovereign, who had not been involved in hostilities with Spain and was known to be a peacelover, would bring about an improvement in their condition.

They had reason to hope, for James had already assured the Earl of Northampton, the unofficial spokesman for the English catholics, that he would not 'persecute any that will be quiet and give but an outward obedience to the law'. On the contrary, he would be more than willing 'to advance any of them that will by good service worthily deserve it'.[1] He explained his position at greater length to Robert Cecil. 'I will never allow in my conscience that the blood of any man shall be shed for diversity of opinions in religion', he told him, but added that he did not mean thereby to encourage a proliferation of the catholic faith: 'I would be sorry by the sword to diminish their number, but I would also be loth that, by too great connivance and oversight given unto them, their numbers should so increase . . . as, by continual multiplication, they might at last become masters'. He drew a sharp distinction between, on the one hand, lay catholics and, on the other, the seminary priests and Jesuits who administered to their spiritual needs. He was prepared to accept the lay catholics at their own valuation, as loyal (though in his view misguided) subjects, but he regarded the Jesuits as 'venomed wasps and firebrands of sedition'. The secular priests (see p. 284) were marginally better, since they professed their loyalty to the crown, but even they were liable to have their consciences 'commanded and overruled by their Romish god'.[2] In other words, James had no objection to catholics as such but only to their links with a papacy which claimed the right to act as the ultimate arbiter in temporal as well as spiritual affairs, not merely excommunicating but even deposing rulers who refused to acknowledge its supremacy.

James, then, was not anti-catholic, except insofar as catholicism implied disloyalty. He told his first English Parliament that 'I acknowledge the Roman church to be our mother church, although defiled with some infirmities and corruptions . . . And as I am none enemy to the life of a sick man because I would have his body purged of ill humours, no more am I enemy to their church because I would have them reform their errors'.[3] By the same token, James was not anti-papal, only opposed to the temporal pretensions of the papacy. He informed a foreign ambassador 'that he recognised . . . the Pope as the Universal Vicar of the whole Church, with spiritual authority over all',[4] and prior to 1603 he had been in direct contact with Clement VIII, as part of a diplomatic campaign to ensure his peaceful succession to the English throne. Clement had promised support, encouraged by the fact that James's wife, Anne of Denmark, was a catholic convert. He pressed James to educate his eldest son, Prince Henry, in the old faith, and for some years he had high hopes that James himself might be persuaded to abandon protestantism and return to the papal fold. There was never any realistic chance of this, though James was reported to have said that he 'would be gladly reunited with the Roman church and would take three steps in that direction if only the church would take one'.[5] It is difficult to imagine James agreeing to accept orders from anybody in religious matters, on which he prided himself for his learning and judgment. If he ever did conceive of a reunion it would have been on the basis of equality between the churches and their respective heads. And an essential condition would have been the renunciation by the papacy of all claims to exercise a temporal jurisdiction over the secular rulers of Christendom. James made this clear in a proclamation of February 1604 when he proposed that a general council should be called to settle religious differences between the Christian churches and also 'to make it manifest that no state or potentate either hath or can challenge power to dispose of earthly kingdoms or monarchies, or to dispense with subjects' obedience to their natural sovereign'.[6]

The principal purpose of the February 1604 proclamation was to command all Jesuits and seminary priests to quit the kingdom. This was in accordance with James's belief that lay catholics, left to their own devices, would be prepared to accept a minimum level of conformity and put their loyalty as subjects before their scruples of conscience. He dealt with the catholics as he dealt with the puritans, by trying to release what he felt sure was the moderate majority from the grip of a radical and uncompromising minority. Indeed, by ordering the banishment of the Jesuits and seminary priests he hoped to create a climate in which ordinary catholics could remain unmolested, largely freed from the impact of the penal laws. Even recusancy fines were reduced, with the result that the income from them, which had been close to £8,000 a year prior to his accession, dropped to below £1,500 in 1604, and a year later was only a little above £2,200.

It seemed to many catholics that their hopes were on the way to being fulfilled, and they noted the contrast between James's relative tolerance and the harsher attitude of the 1604 Parliament, which passed an Act calling for the 'due execution of the statutes' not simply against the missionary priests but also against 'any manner of recusants'.[7] If contemporary reports are to be believed, catholics and crypto-catholics took advantage of the more relaxed atmosphere to come out into the open. Their protestant adversaries, apprehensive at what they regarded as the King's over-permissiveness, kept a diligent watch, and it may be that they allowed their imagination to run away with them. What mattered, however, was not so much the facts of the case as the general impression, and this was summed up by one letter-writer who reported that 'it is hardly credible in what jollity they [the catholics] now live. They make no question to obtain at least a toleration if not an alteration of religion; in hope whereof many who before did dutifully frequent the [parish] church are of late become recusants'.[8] Archbishop Hutton of York was of the same opinion, for he told Cecil in December 1604 that the 'papists and recusants . . . of late, partly by this round dealing against puritans and partly by reason of some extraordinary favour, have grown mightily in number, courage and influence . . . I assure your lordship 'tis high time to look unto them. Very many are gone from all places to London, and some are come down to this country in great jollity, almost triumphantly'.[9]

James's investigations into the puritan petitioning campaign (see p. 100) made him aware of the extent to which his soft-line approach towards the catholics was alienating him from the prot- estant majority of his subjects. He therefore signalled a change of course – in appearances at any rate – by making plain his detestation of the catholic religion and informing the Council in February 1605 that 'if I thought my son would alter the religion now established, especially to the Romish religion, so contrary to truth and so full of error, I would give my crown and kingdom from him, and I would rather die childless, and bury them before me, than they should do it'.[10] In the same month Dudley Carleton described how 'the sword now begins to cut on the other edge and to fall heavily on the papists' side, whereof there were twenty-eight indicted at the last sessions at Newgate',[11] and in June Sir Henry Neville reported that James had sent for the judges and instructed them to see that the laws against recusants were put into operation. Neville regretted, however, that none of the missionary priests in prison were likely to be executed, 'for they are the root and fountain of all mischief'; and he summed up the prevailing attitude towards the English cath- olics in his comment that 'howsoever they pretend now to seek only impunity, yet that obtained, assuredly they will not rest there till they have obtained a further liberty. Therefore, if we mean not to grant all, we were as good deny all, and put them to an issue betimes, either to obey or not'.[12]

THE GUNPOWDER PLOT AND THE OATH OF ALLEGIANCE

Although the initial period of *de facto* toleration had passed, catholics were still shielded from the full impact of the penal laws, and might have remained so, despite parliamentary pressure, but for the Gunpowder Plot of November 1605. This audacious plan to blow up the entire government and legislature was the work of a small and unrepresentative band of young catholic malcontents, reacting against the conclusion of peace between England and Spain in August 1604. For several decades English catholics had looked to Spain for support – though the majority in Elizabeth's reign probably deplored armed intervention and plots against the Queen's life – and had clung to the belief that the Spanish government would never agree to a peace treaty unless it included specific provisions for the repeal of the penal laws. Now their eyes had been opened, for the Treaty of London included no such provisions. Philip III and his ministers still professed concern for the condition of their coreligionists in England, but had implicitly abandoned their commitment to change it. In effect the English catholics had been told that they must work out their own salvation. This created a mood of desperation in some quarters that led to the embracing of desperate measures. The Gunpowder Plot was the outcome.

It was a tragedy for catholics that the Plot apparently confirmed everything that their most bitter opponents had long been asserting' – namely that all catholics were potential traitors and must be treated as such. Parliament reacted by intensifying the penal laws. The 1606 session saw the passing of an Act 'to prevent and avoid dangers which may grow by popish recusants', which forbade them to live in or near London, or to practise the law, or to hold any public office. Another Act, 'for the better discovering and repressing of popish recusants', gave the King authority to seize two-thirds of their lands rather than impose the £20 a month fine set by Elizabethan legislation, which was deemed to be too light a penalty for the richer catholics. However, the most important provision in this Act required all suspected recusants to take an oath which bound them not merely to 'bear faith and true allegiance to His Majesty, his heirs and successors' but also to acknowledge that 'the Pope, neither of himself nor by any authority of the church or see of Rome . . . hath any power or authority to depose the King, or to dispose [of] any of His Majesty's kingdoms or dominions, or to authorise any foreign prince to invade or annoy him or his countries, or to discharge any of his subjects of their allegiance and obedience to His Majesty'.[13] This oath had been carefully devised by James,

to the end that I might hereby make a separation . . . between so many of my subjects who, although they were otherwise popishly affected, yet retained in their hearts the print of their natural duty to their sovereign; and those who, being carried away with the like fanatical zeal that the Powder-Traitors were, could not contain themselves within the bounds of their natural allegiance, but thought diversity of religion a safe pretext for all kind of treasons.[14]

The Oath of Allegiance demonstrates the consistency of James's policy of splitting the radicals from the moderate majority, and is evidence that he preserved a balanced and unfanatical approach to the catholic problem even in the turbulent wake of the Gunpowder Plot. Indeed, he hoped that the acceptance of the Oath by the catholics would demonstrate to his subjects in general that catholicism was not synonymous with treachery, thereby lowering the temperature of religious debate and allowing the catholics once again to enjoy an inferior but relatively unmolested existence. His tactics were initially successful, for many catholics, priests as well as laymen, took the Oath. However, its final provision proved a stumbling block, for this required the taker to swear

that I do from my heart abhor, detest and abjure, as impious and heretical, this damnable doctrine and position, that princes which be excommunicated or deprived by the Pope may be deposed or murdered by their subjects or any other whosoever. And I do believe, and in my conscience am resolved, that neither the Pope nor any person whatsoever hath power to absolve me of this oath or any part thereof.[15]

It was one thing for catholics to accept that the Pope had no right to depose earthly rulers; it was quite another for them to affirm that such claims were 'impious and heretical' and that the Pope had no power to absolve them from an oath. The papacy was swift to condemn the Oath and ordered catholics not to take it. This order was widely ignored, but it prevented the general acceptance of the Oath upon which the King had been relying.

James showed his anger by producing *An Apology for the Oath of Allegiance* in which he asserted that he had given catholics 'a good proof that I intended no persecution of them for conscience' cause, but only desired to be secured of them for civil obedience'.[16] The publication of this tract was part of a pamphlet war, in which the leading papal champion was the distinguished philosopher and controversialist, Cardinal Bellarmine. James's emergence on the European stage as the hammer of the papacy won him acclaim and respect at home and thereby contributed to the stability of the Jacobean Church, but it did nothing to reconcile those of his catholic subjects who had reservations about the Oath. James never succeeded in incorporating the catholics within the state Church. They remained, in his own words, 'disconformable in religion from us' and therefore 'but half my subjects, . . . able to do but half service, and I to want [i.e. lack] the best half of them, which is their souls'.[17]

Bellarmine's riposte to the *Apology* stung James into reissuing this work with a long preface or *Premonition* which more than doubled its length. It was now addressed 'to all most mighty monarchs, kings, free princes, and states of Christendom' and called on them to reject papal pretensions. James was no longer concerned merely to attack the papal claim to temporal power; he now argued that the Pope had no overriding authority even in spiritual matters. 'As I well allow of the hierarchy of the Church for distinction of orders', he wrote, 'so I utterly deny that there is an earthly monarch thereof, whose word must be a law and who cannot err in his sentence by an infallibility of spirit. Because earthly kingdoms must have earthly monarchs, it doth not follow that the Church must have a visible monarch too; for the world hath not one earthly temporal monarch'.[18] This challenge to the papacy was consistent with James's belief that the Roman church was simply one, and not the purest, among a number of Christian churches. While he was prepared to give the Pope pride of place as *Princeps Episcoporum*,[19] the 'Prince of Bishops', on historical grounds, he did not accept that Rome had a monopoly, or even primacy, when it came to religious truths. He regarded the Church of England as in many respects superior to Rome, and rejected suggestions that it was heterodox in its doctrines. He demonstrated his own orthodoxy and dislike of innovation by attacking Vorstius and the Dutch Arminians (see p. 116), and by ordering the burning at the stake of two Englishmen convicted of heresy.

THE ENFORCEMENT OF THE PENAL LAWS

Although James was temperamentally averse to the shedding of blood over differences of religion, he was too much of a politician not to realise that a hard-line approach could, in certain circumstances, place him in an advantageous position. This is why meetings of Parliament were usually preceded and accompanied by greater stringency in the enforcement of the penal laws. Similar considerations account for the fact that nineteen missionary priests were executed during James's reign. This was considerably fewer than the 124 who suffered under Elizabeth, and no doubt the number would have been even smaller if James had had a free hand. However, he always had to take into account public reaction and the possibility of a backlash which would weaken his authority. By letting the law take its course from time to time he defused a potentially explosive.

situation, but his private views may be glimpsed in a proclamation of June 1606 ordering all Jesuits and missionary priests to quit his kingdoms. This was issued, according to James, 'with no other purpose but to avoid the effusion of blood, and by banishing them presently out of our dominions, to remove all cause of such severity as we shall otherwise be constrained to use'.[20] Another example of his natural clemency came in the following year, when he instructed the judges to deal mercifully with captured priests who were willing to take the Oath of Allegiance, and even with those who were only prepared to engage in discussion, as long as they 'showed not arrogance and violence'. 'The King's word', as Bacon recorded, 'was "No torrent of blood"'.[21]

When the 1610 Parliament assembled, James attempted to deflect criticism of his lax enforcement of the penal laws by shifting the responsibility to his servants. 'I must blame both the judges and you, my lords of the clergy', he insisted, and showed his concern by instructing them to 'take care this Parliament that the papists be from time to time strictly presented and, according to the statutes already made, duly punished'. Yet he reminded them to draw a distinction between 'ancient papists' and 'apostates'. The latter, he declared, 'shall never have my favour or good looks', but as for the ancient papists, 'there is divers of them so honest and so fair-conditioned men as if I were a subject I could be contented to live and spend my time with them'.[22] The main work of this Parliament in the religious sphere was the passing of an Act which obliged all office-holders to take the Oath of Allegiance and imposed a financial penalty upon the husbands of recusant wives.

The short-lived Addled Parliament of 1614 saw further complaints about the ease with which catholics evaded the penal laws. The King was implicitly criticised for allowing English catholics to attend services at the chapels of foreign ambassadors, and also for permitting these ambassadors, at their departure from England, to take with them a number of imprisoned priests, most of whom, it was asserted, soon made their way back again. There were the usual reports 'that young gentlemen and others are taken and carried over to St Omer, to the English seminary there, to be instructed', and that popish books were sent across from St Omer for distribution in England. Undervaluation of recusants' lands, it was claimed, diminished the threat of having two-thirds confiscated for non-attendance at their parish church, and there was general agreement 'that for want of execution of the laws, and noblemen's favours, the number of recusants did increase'.[23]

CATHOLIC ARISTOCRATS AND OFFICE-HOLDERS

The Commons had some grounds for their suspicion that certain members of the nobility were favourably inclined towards catholicism. It was virtually impossible to enforce the penal laws against noblemen and their wives, and they played a major role in keeping the old faith alive. In the mid-1620s, when the catholic episcopate was restored, the first two bishops found succour and safety in the houses of Viscount Montagu at Cowdray, Lord Arundell at Wardour, and the Earl of Shrewsbury at Grafton. These were representatives of 'old' families, but the new creations of the early Stuart period added to the number of catholic aristocrats: indeed, by the eve of the civil war some twenty per cent of the peerage was catholic, compared with about one per cent of the population as a whole. Many catholic peers steered clear of public life, but not all were able or willing to take this approach. Local office-holding was one of the customary responsibilities of landowners, and the crown did not pay a great deal of attention to their religious beliefs when it made appointments. In 1626 the Commons drew up a list of catholics who held official positions in the localities. It was headed by Buckingham's father-in-law, the Earl of Rutland, who was Lord Lieutenant of Lincolnshire, Northamptonshire, Nottinghamshire and Rutland, despite being a catholic convert. It also included Emanuel, Lord Scrope, created Earl of Sunderland in 1627, who served as Lord President of the Council of the North from 1619 to 1628 although the Commons had already presented him as a recusant and accused him of 'continuing still to give suspicion of his ill-affection in religion'.[24]

Open or covert adherents of the old faith were to be found even at the royal Court and in the administration, despite James's public avowal 'that if he thought any of his Council were popish, or did favour the papists, or countenance them, or hinder the proceedings of the law against them, he would remove them from his Council'.[25] The Earl of Northampton, Lord Privy Seal, was the most notorious of these Court catholics, and later in the reign there was a cluster of catholic converts among the kindred of the favourite, Buckingham. Sir George Calvert, appointed Secretary of State in 1619, declared himself a catholic six years later; Francis Cottington, secretary to Prince Charles and subsequently Chancellor of the Exchequer, conformed outwardly but was widely assumed to be sympathetic towards catholicism, which he openly embraced shortly before his death in 1652; Richard Weston, who preceded Cottington as Chancellor of the Exchequer and rose to be Earl of Portland and Lord Treasurer under Charles I, was another outward conformer, but as Clarendon observed 'his wife and all his daughters were declared of the Roman religion: and though himself and his sons sometimes went to church, he was never thought to have zeal for it; and his domestic conversation and dependants, with whom only he used entire freedom, were all known catholics, and were believed to be agents for the rest'.[26]

THE SPANISH MATCH

After the outbreak of the Thirty Years War in 1618 the catholic question in England became intertwined with that of foreign policy, as the King clung to his professed solution of restoring harmony to Christendom by means of a marriage between his son, Prince Charles, and the Infanta Maria, daughter of Philip III of Spain. The negotiations for an Anglo-Spanish marriage alliance had been proceeding at a leisurely rate since virtually the beginning of James's reign, but from 1618 onwards the pace increased dramatically. Philip was not a free agent, since he needed a papal dispensation to permit a marriage between his daughter and a protestant, and this would not be issued unless the Pope could be persuaded that such an apparently undesirable match would produce major benefits for the Roman church in the shape of better treatment of the English catholics. James made it plain that there could be no question of repealing the penal laws, since Parliament would never consent to this, but he was prepared to consider using his prerogative powers to moderate or, conceivably, suspend their execution. For the first time since the Treaty of London in 1604 the English catholics could look to Spain for assistance, but this made them over-confident: James told Bacon that they were 'so lifted up in their hopes of what they desire that His Majesty cannot but take a more severe course (as far as by his laws he may) than hitherto he hath done'. James also expressed the belief that greater severity on his part might assist his diplomacy, for 'when they shall see a harder hand carried toward them than hath been accustomed, His Majesty assureth himself they will employ all their means to further the match, in hope of mitigation of that severity when it shall be accomplished'.[27]

By 1621 the international situation had deteriorated to such a point that English involvement in the war seemed a distinct possibility. James therefore summoned Parliament, and in his opening speech he went out of his way to refute the charge that his commitment to the Spanish match had diminished his protestant zeal: 'if I conclude anything therein that shall not be to the glory of God, the good of religion, and honour of this kingdom, let me be reputed unworthy to reign over you'. He reminded members that he had 'both in my word and with my pen, maintained this religion; insomuch that I may say I have been persecuted for it; for Bellarmine wrote against me, and others have spoken bitterly of me for it'. He still believed that the papists should be won over by peaceful persuasion rather than force, but 'if any were emboldened' by reason of the negotiations, and 'shall grow insolent', he would 'cause exemplary punishment to be done upon them'.[28] The Commons responded by calling for an intensification of the penal laws, but James rejected this. Chamberlain reported him as saying that 'there were laws already that only wanted [i.e. lacked] execution, which was no fault of his; besides, it was against his nature to be too rigorous in matters of conscience, and against his course towards other princes, with whom he was a continual mediator for moderation in like cases'.[29] The Commons' initiative was thereby blunted, but anti-papist feeling in the Lower House continued to run high. In the second session, in November, Pym declared that the catholics had taken advantage of James's natural clemency. 'The King may think, by not executing laws against papists, to win their hearts and so procure his own safety', said Pym, but this was a great mistake, for 'the endeavours of that religion are not idle but active, and will admit no mean. For having gotten favour they will expect a toleration; after toleration they will look for equality; after equality, for superiority; and having superiority they will seek the subversion of that religion which is contrary to theirs'.[30]

Following the abrupt end of the 1621 Parliament, James was even more determined to press ahead with the Spanish match, but in order to win the assent of both Spain and the Papacy he had to make concessions to the English catholics. He therefore commanded Lord Keeper Williams to instruct the judges 'to extend his princely favour to all such as they shall find prisoners in the gaols of their circuits for any church recusancy or refusing the oath of supremacy or dispersing of popish books, or any other point of recusancy that shall concern religion only and not matters of state'.[31] The pressure on the King was redoubled in 1623 when his son, Prince Charles, made a dash to Madrid, with the aim of claiming the Infanta as his bride. Charles became a virtual prisoner, for Philip IV let it be understood that he would not be permitted to leave until he had sworn to accept the articles of the marriage treaty. A further condition was that James and his Councillors must do the same. James was reluctant, but he had no choice. In July, therefore, at a ceremony in the royal chapel at Whitehall, the King and Council took a solemn oath to put the articles into operation. The penal laws were to be suspended and not reimposed. Morover, James committed himself to try to persuade Parliament to repeal them altogether. The results of this indulgence soon became apparent, for at the beginning of December Chamberlain reported from London 'that priests and Jesuits swarm here extraordinarily'.[32]

It was fortunate fot James that Parliament was not in session in 1623. When he summoned a new one, in 1624, the Prince was safe at home again and the Spanish marriage policy was on the rocks. There was talk now of war, and in March Sir John Strangways expressed the prevailing mood in the Commons when he declared that since 'we have to do with the most potent prince in the world' it would be prudent 'to secure ourselves at home first'. He urged members therefore 'to begin the maintenance of the war by the popish recusants' forfeitures'.[33] The House followed his lead, and passed a Bill 'for the explanation of a branch of the statute made in the third year of the King's Majesty's reign of England, entitled "An Act for the better discovering and repressing of popish recusants"'.[34] This by itself, however, was insufficient, for there was general agreement that the recusants were spurred on to treacherous courses by the missionary priests. According to Chamberlain, who was writing in April, these 'swarm so thick in every corner that 1,400 friars, Jesuits and priests are certainly discovered in the land, whatsoever there be more'.[35] He referred to reports of a proclamation against them, and this duly appeared, a week later, 'charging all Jesuits, Seminaries, etc., to depart the land'.[36] These measures were a further demonstration of the truism that official policy towards English catholics, secular and religious, was determined by political considerations, both domestic and foreign.

THE ENGLISH MISSION

Chamberlain was no doubt genuine in his belief that several thousand missionary priests were at work in England, yet this figure was grossly exaggerated. At the beginning of James's reign there were some 300 priests on mission, administering to the spiritual needs of some 40,000 English catholics. By 1640 the number of priests had risen to about 750 while their flock had increased to 60,000. This provides justification for the widespread belief among the English protestant majority that catholicism was reviving and expanding, but not for the panic fear that a catholic take-over was imminent. Fear was engendered by ignorance, for nobody knew the true figures, and inflated estimates were common not only among the protestants but also within the catholic community. In May 1614 the newly appointed Spanish ambassador, Count Gondomar, informed Philip III that out of an English population of some 3.5 million, a twelfth (300,000) were committed, non-conforming catholics. Two-twelfths (600,000) were catholic at heart but conformed out of fear and worldly considerations. A further three-twelfths (900,000) were 'favourably inclined' even though they had no religious beliefs and were taken up with the problem of how to live and pass their time in the most agreeable manner. In other words, the total number of catholics and potential catholics was 1,800,000, or half the entire population![37] Gondomar was presumably reporting what his catholic contacts in England had told him, and although they may have deliberately inflated the figures in order to emphasise their import-ance, they were obviously working on estimates which were, in fact, figments of their imagination. Catholics, of course, could take comfort in the thought of their numerical strength, but it is hardly surprising that protestants, presumably working on similar assump-tions, felt that the very foundations of Church and state were under threat.

The great majority of English catholics lived quietly and peace-ably and were only too happy to escape attention. More often than not they were tolerated by their protestant neighbours, for ties of kinship and locality softened the impact of distorted stereotypes. While many English men and women feared the 'catholic menace' in the abstract they found it difficult if not impossible to associate this with particular persons with whom they had long enjoyed friendly relations. But for this degree of *de facto* toleration the cath-olic community would have found if difficult, if not impossible, to survive.

It was unfortunate for English catholics that they were dependent upon foreign seminaries, mainly in Spanish territory, for the provision of priests, since this made them, willy nilly, pawns in the international power struggle. Yet without the priests the English catholic community would have withered and died. It was realisation of this that had led to the creation of the English mission early in Elizabeth's reign, and by the time James came to the throne it was firmly established. It was divided into the seculars and the regulars. The seculars were, so to speak, catholic parish priests, except that they had no parishes and were dependent upon the goodwill of local landowners for the maintenance of their ministry. The regulars were dominated by the Jesuits, who were about half as numerous as the seculars, though the early seventeenth century also witnessed the expansion of the Benedictines, who formally established their English congregation in 1619. The missionary priests, both secular and regular, were almost without exception Englishmen who had gone abroad to receive a catholic education – at St Omer, for instance, or Douai, both of which were in the Spanish Netherlands, or in some cases in Spain itself or in Rome. All the priests risked their lives for the sake of their faith, and they had been specifically trained for their lonely and responsible task. Yet there was a significant difference in attitude between the regulars and the seculars. The Jesuits, in particular, were aware of themselves as part of a movement which embraced – potentially, at any rate – the entire world, and they tended to regard England as a mission field like any other. The seculars were more nationalistic in their approach, and were reluctant to concede that England was no longer a catholic country nor likely to become one.

The Jesuits worked under the direct supervision of their superior, who from 1586 until his arrest and execution for involvement in the Gunpowder Plot was Henry Garnet. By 1623 they were sufficiently numerous to be erected into a separate province, subdivided into twelve districts. Their activities covered the whole country, but their geographical distribution did not match that of the catholic population. There were more priests, both regular and secular, in relation to lay catholics in the south and east than in the north and west, even though the latter areas were those in which catholicism had a mass appeal that it lacked elsewhere. The mission was, to this extent, the prisoner of its own history, for the priests were usually landed on the east coast and were then despatched on a secret trail that led from one magnate or gentry household to another. This was unavoidable, given the fact that priests were illegal immigrants and liable to be arrested if they travelled openly, but because magnate and gentry estates tended to be concentrated in the south-east and south midlands the catholic mission acquired the same bias. The Jesuits, in particular, were inclined to settle down in catholic households. In theory they could have used these as a nucleus around which to extend the range of their activities, but in practice they were usually confined within the existing boundaries of the local catholic community and became little more than family chaplains.

THE RESTORATION OF THE HIERARCHY

By keeping catholic gentry families in touch with Counter-Reformation practices and in tune with its spirituality the Jesuits ensured that English catholicism remained an integral part of the post-Tridentine Roman Church. But many seculars resented the way in which the Jesuits had come to dominate the mission and, in particular, to control the flow of funds from its lay supporters. In the closing years of Elizabeth the seculars had been placed under an Archpriest, appointed by the Pope, but this type of organisation had been developed for use in heathen countries where no Christian substructure existed. The seculars regarded its imposition not only as an insult to English catholic traditions but also as implicit acceptance on the part of the papacy of the Jesuits' belief that deep-rooted heresy would block England's return to the catholic fold for the foreseeable future. The seculars wanted to emphasise the continuity between present and past English catholicism by having the former hierarchy restored. This would have the further advantage from their point of view that a bishop, once appointed, would take charge of the entire mission, direct its funds to where they were most needed, and cut the regulars down to size.

The papacy was unwilling to restore the hierarchy in full or under its old titles. The English catholic community was too small to warrant more than one bishop, and if he were to be nominated to an English see this would offend the King. In 1623, therefore, the Pope appointed one of the more senior of the seculars, William Bishop, as Bishop of Chalcedon, with episcopal jurisdiction over the catholics of England and Scotland. This appointment did not pass unchallenged when Parliament assembled in February 1624. Richard Dyott, member for Stafford, complained of the 'great insolency committed by a popish recusant styling himself Bishop of Calcedon; went abroad not privately but in public . . . had six chaplains, his mitre, and robes'. Christopher Brooke added that 'this titular bishop hath power to make seminary priests in England, and so to defeat the law which maketh it treason for them to come into the land', which prompted the pithy comment by Thomas Wentworth, the

Recorder of Oxford, that all seminary priests were traitors and that 'the land [was] full of traitors and treason'.[38]

William Bishop, who had first been sent on the English mission forty years earlier, was by now an old man. In fact he died in April 1624 having barely had time to establish his position. He was succeeded by Richard Smith, of whom the Jesuit Robert Parsons said 'I never dealt with any man in my life more heady and resolute in his opinions'.[39] After a brief spell on mission in England, Smith had settled in Paris, where he rapidly made a name for himself as a catholic controversialist. He also became a member of Richelieu's household, and helped ensure that when a French marriage treaty was negotiated for Prince Charles it included, like the abortive Spanish one, provisions for the relief of English catholics. Smith took up his duties in April 1625 and soon made it apparent that he intended to exercise his authority to the utmost. In many respects he fulfilled the seculars' highest hopes. He curbed the Jesuits by insisting that they must be licensed by him before they could practise as confessors. He also planned to centralise control of the mission's funds rather than leave their disbursement in the hands of the catholic gentry and their mainly Jesuit chaplains. But the catholic gentry resembled their protestant counterparts in their loathing of clericalism. The mission, or so they believed, existed to serve them, not to rule them, and they put an end to Smith's pretensions by denouncing him to the Privy Council. Charles I responded by issuing a proclamation in December 1628 ordering his arrest, and subsequently offering a reward for his capture. Smith took refuge in the French embassy, and later, after the Pope had declined to support him, returned to exile in France. The seculars were left without a head, and with the conviction that they had been betrayed by the Jesuits and their allies among the catholic gentry.

The failure of Richard Smith to re-establish the catholic hierarchy in England upon a permanent basis was a setback for the seculars, but not for the mission as a whole. The regulars continued to flourish, and by the time the civil war broke out there were some 400 English members of the Society of Jesus, more than a third of whom were actually serving on the mission. The total number of priests, regular and secular, ministering to the needs of the catholic population was proportionately higher in the 1630s than at any time until the mid-nineteenth century, but the over-concentration on the south, at the expense of the west and north, had by now become inbuilt. So too had the link between the mission and the catholic gentry, which was a source both of strength and weakness. Without the support and protection of the gentry the priests would have found it very difficult to carry out their duties, but too many of them were content to be household chaplains, too few were genuine missionaries, keeping the faith alive in the remoter areas of the kingdom and among the less privileged sections of society.

CATHOLICISM AT COURT UNDER CHARLES I

Charles I's marriage to a catholic French princess had an immediate impact upon the adherents of the old faith in England, for despite the formal promise given by Charles that his marriage would involve no concessions to English catholics, a secret clause attached to the marriage treaty had committed him to relax the penal laws. More-over, when Henrietta Maria arrived in England she brought with her an ecclesiastical household presided over by a bishop. Its members, as one observer noted, 'perambulate the palace in their clerical habits, and say mass daily in the little oratory'.[40] Henrietta Maria was not simply a devout catholic. She had also been taught to regard herself as the agent through whom first her husband and then his kingdom would be returned to the papal fold. She was ostentatious in her attendance at catholic services in her own chapel, and made no secret of her contempt for the reformed faith and its adherents. Before leaving Paris she had undergone a course of instruction from Father Bérulle, the founder of the Oratorian order, and as a consequence she brought with her to England the self-confident and assertive attitudes of the Catholic Reformation. She also brought back to London, for the first time since Mary Tudor's reign, the richness of traditional catholic worship, with all its musical and visual splen-dour. This made a particular appeal to courtiers, whose daily life was bound up with pageantry and whose artistic tastes, under the guid-ance of Charles himself and such collectors as Arundel and Buck-ingham, had been focussed upon Italian and Flemish masters who were committedly catholic.

English protestants, especially those of puritan persuasion, never tired of denouncing popish 'superstitions', but while they might be immune from the sensuous appeal of catholic ritual the same was not true of everybody. Catholicism became fashionable at Court, and gained ground rapidly in the 1630s under the impetus of ardent converts such as Olive Porter, a member of the Queen's household. Olive's husband, Endymion, was one of the principal members of

Buckingham's entourage, and after the favourite's death entered the service of Charles I. He was more circumspect than Olive in his behaviour, and outwardly conformed to Anglicanism, but he shared his wife's faith. Olive had been converted by the Scotsman George Con, who in 1636 was chosen by Urban VIII to serve as papal agent at the Queen's court. Con made it his principal aim to build up the strength of the catholic party there, and his activities brought him into collision with William Laud, the Archbishop of Canterbury. The dispute came to a head with the conversion of the Countess of Newport in October 1637. Her husband, who vehemently disapproved, complained to Laud, and at the Archbishop's instigation the King issued a proclamation in December commanding 'all and every person and persons, clerks and lay, that they from henceforth forbear to attempt or endeavour to withdraw any of His Majesty's subjects from religion as it is now professed in the Church of England, or by persuasions or any other means to distract them in the same or to solicit them to adhere to the Church of Rome'.[41] This had no effect, however, and Con continued his activities down to the time of his departure from England in the autumn of 1639.

Although Con was technically accredited to the Queen, the King made him welcome and saw him almost daily. Charles shared his father's hopes for a reunion of the Christian churches and recognised that this could not be achieved without the co-operation of the papacy. Indeed, during his stay in Spain in 1623 Charles had caused some distress to his future subjects by addressing Gregory XV – in a letter sent in reply to one from the Pope – as 'Most Holy Father', assuring him that he did not hate the catholic religion, and professing his desire 'that as we all confess one individual Trinity and one Christ crucified, we may unanimously grow up into one faith'.[42] There were many aspects of catholicism and catholic worship which appealed to Charles. He approved of hierarchy in the Church as in the state, he valued ceremonies as a symbolic means of representing truths, and he had a natural liking for order and ritual in public as in private life. He did not share his people's virulent hatred of popery and all its works – indeed he could hardly have endured his life with a devoutly catholic consort had he done so. In general, Charles turned a blind eye to Court catholicism, and he made no attempt to root out papists and neo-papists from positions in central and local government.

CHARLES I, THE COMMONS AND THE CATHOLIC QUESTION

Charles's relatively unfanatical and tolerant approach to the catholic problem baffled his subjects. Members of Parliament, who wished to assume that his heart was in the right place, acted upon the assumption that he needed their assistance in freeing himself from the grip of popish advisers. Such an assumption – with its implication that Charles was too weak-willed to act for himself – was deeply offensive to the King, but it was the only means by which the Commons could reconcile their loyalty to the crown with their hatred of Rome and all its works. Since the King would not or could not act, they felt obliged to take the initiative. In the first Parliament of his reign they petitioned him for enforcement of the penal laws, but although he gave a favourable response they were not satisfied. Their reservations were voiced by Christopher Sherland, who declared that 'for the answering of our petition for religion, he is as glad of it as any member of the House. But who knoweth what will be the execution of it? Nay, have we not cause to fear the worst?'.[43] Charles provided an answer to this question by issuing a proclamation in August 1625 'for recalling His Majesty's subjects from the seminaries beyond the seas, and putting the laws against Jesuits and popish priests in execution', and in January 1626 he followed this up with another proclamation requiring convicted recusants to stay within five miles of their usual residence.[44]

The Commons were not impressed, for these proclamations had little tangible effect. In 1626, therefore, they called for a clarification and strengthening of the law, and gave consideration to Bills 'for the better discovering and repressing of popish recusants', 'for the better discovery of church papists', and 'to direct the true and real conformity of popish recusants'.[45] They also presented the King with a list of papists and crypto-papists holding official offices, and appealed to him to show his 'wisdom, goodness and piety (whereof they rest assured)' by ordering that 'the parties above-named and all such others . . . be put out of such commissions and places of authority wherein they now are'.[46] However, despite the King's promise to take action, there was no improvement in the situation, for in March 1628 the Commons were once again pressing him to agree 'that no place of authority and command within any of the counties of Your Majesty's kingdom . . . be committed to popish recusants or to non-communicants . . . And that such as have by connivance crept into such places may be by your royal command discharged of the same'.[47]

The contrast between the King's avowed willingness to enforce the laws and his all-too-apparent failure to do so confirmed the Commons in their belief that he was being deliberately misled. They regarded it as their duty to break through the screens that hid the truth from him and to tell him what was really happening in the country over which he nominally ruled. Their suspicions were focussed upon his chief adviser, Buckingham, and members of the Duke's family. In their remonstrance of June 1628 they called Charles's attention to the fact, of which they assumed he was unaware, that 'notwithstanding the many good and wholesome laws and provisions made to prevent the increase of popery within this kingdom, and notwithstanding Your Majesty's most gracious and satisfactory answer to the petition of both Houses in that behalf . . . we find there has followed no good execution nor effect'. On the contrary, 'those of that religion do find extraordinary favours and respect in Court from persons of great quality and power there, unto whom they continually resort, and in particular to the Countess of Buckingham [the Duke's mother], who, herself openly professing that religion, is a known favourer and supporter of them that do the same'.[48]

Charles rejected the Commons' attack upon Buckingham as unfounded, but six weeks later he provided them with further evidence of his good intentions by issuing a proclamation ordering the judges to put 'all . . . our laws in due execution against popish recusants' and to give him 'a true and strict account of their proceedings therein'.[49] By the time the House assembled for the second session, in 1629, Buckingham was dead, but the catholic question had not died with him. Sir Robert Phelips complained that despite 'good and copious charges given to the judges for execution of laws . . . nothing has been done thereon', and proposed the drawing up of a remonstrance to show the King 'his and the state's danger'.[50] The House demonstrated its concern by instructing the committee for religion to consider the 'cessation of execution of laws against popery and papists' and also the 'countenancing of popery and popish persons'.[51]

RECUSANCY FINES AND THE COMMISSIONS FOR COMPOUNDING

The Commons and those they represented would have liked to see the total eradication of catholicism in England, and they were convinced that the only way in which to achieve this was by bringing the full pressure of the law to bear upon the adherents of the old faith. Charles professed the same long-term aim, but did not accept that it could be achieved by driving the catholic community into poverty and despair. In a proclamation issued in February 1627 he emphasised that the campaign against recusancy was 'a work of time [which] cannot at once be begun and perfected'. Indeed, the existing laws, 'if they should all be strictly exacted, are so hard and severe in divers parts that the severe penalties and punishments which they [the recusants] must incur and undergo would utterly disable them and their families in their very subsistence, whereby many of them must become a burden to the place where they live'.[52] Such an outcome, he implied, would be unacceptable to local communities already struggling to meet the demands of poor relief. Furthermore it would do nothing to improve the financial situation of the crown, for impoverished catholics would be unable to pay the fines which were a valuable source of revenue for the royal Treasury. In practice – although Charles did not, of course, spell this out – it made better sense to accept that the English catholics were going to survive, but to make them pay heavily for the privilege. Convicted recusants were liable to have two-thirds of their lands confiscated, but Charles, in his proclamation, announced that those living in the north of his kingdom would in future be allowed to lease them back again – either directly or through friends and relatives. The money so raised would be used to set out six warships for coastal defence.

Charles emphasised that the appointment of commissioners to compound with recusants was not to be taken as an indication that 'our zeal and constancy in our religion were cooled or abated'. There was no intention 'to decline from our first purpose and promise for the due execution of our laws in this case', but merely to 'proceed therein with such moderation as the whole world shall bear witness with us that we seek their conversion and not their ruin'.[53] However, when Parliament met in 1628 it quickly became apparent that members of the Commons did not share the King's confidence in the new plan. Sir Edward Coke declared that 'to speak freely, [it] is a toleration', and he denounced the commission as 'against the law'.[54] Both Houses took up the matter, and in their petition against recusants drawn up in March they called on the King to abandon composition and 'to dissolve the mystery of iniquity, patched up of colourable leases, contracts, preconveyances, being but masks on the one part of fraud to deceive Your Majesty and state; on the other part, for particular men to accomplish their own corrupt ends'.[55] In his reply, the King committed himself to root out 'the deceit and abuses mentioned in this article' and to 'bring the offenders to punishment . . . to the intent that no concealed tolerations may be effected'.[56] But he refrained from making any promise to abandon composition, and no sooner had Parliament ended its session than he announced that 'we have . . . granted and renewed our several commissions to the purposes aforesaid, and have thereby given unto our said commissioners full power and authority, in our name and to our use, to treat and compound with all persons convicted or hereafter to be convicted for recusancy . . . for all debts, arrearages and seizures, without any restraint or limitation of time'.[57]

Members of Parliament might complain about lax enforcement of the penal laws, but partly as a result of their pressure Charles was executing these far more effectively and systematically than his father had done. Some 500 recusants were convicted in London alone during the first four years of his reign, and Exchequer enquiries into recusants' landholdings extended into virtually every county. Indeed, one of the principal motives that persuaded recusants to compound was the desire to be free from harassment. For catholics outside the Court circle, then, Charles's reign was a period of remorseless financial pressure, and they had no reason to regard him with affection. This explains their subdued response to the Queen's appeal for a 'catholic contribution' to assist her husband's campaign against the Scots in 1639. Court catholics were quick to respond, but the total amount raised came to a mere £14,000.

CHARLES AND THE CATHOLICS 1639–1642

Both the Queen and Con took advantage of the Scots' crisis to buttress their argument that the catholics were the natural supporters of monarchy, the only persons on whom the King could, in the last resort, rely. It was the catholic Earl of Nithsdale, working closely with Con, who rallied the Scottish Roman Catholic peers behind the King, while in Ireland the Earl of Antrim, another prominent catholic married to the widow of the Duke of Buckingham, offered to raise an army and put it at the King's disposal. Charles was ready to seek help wherever he could find it, and the Queen and the Court catholics were exploring the possibilities of a papal subsidy and the despatch of troops from the Spanish Netherlands. These projects came to nothing, but in 1640 Charles called on the Roman Catholic Earl of Worcester to raise 2,000 men from Wales, while Strafford persuaded the Irish Parliament to vote funds for an army of 9,000 men to be recruited without regard to their religion.

The Irish troops were designed to strengthen the English forces against the Scots, but the English campaign collapsed so quickly that they never had time to intervene. Charles had to turn for help to Parliament instead, and following Strafford's execution he ordered the disbandment of the Irish army. But he had not abandoned all hope of assistance from that quarter. He instructed Antrim to build up a new army in secret, so that it could be used, at the appropriate moment, to seize Dublin and secure Ireland for him. Antrim and his fellow conspirators, acting in the King's name though not always with his knowledge or approval, made contact with the leaders of the native Irish – who were, of course, catholic – to see if they would pledge their support. The Irish were already planning a rising, and in military terms it would have made sense to link their plans with those of Charles's agents. In the event, however, they chose to act alone, and in October 1641 the Irish Rebellion broke out. Charles condemned it and called for its suppression, but the rebels claimed to be acting on his behalf and with his commission. This claim was almost certainly false, but rumours about Charles's secret negotiations with Antrim and others cast doubt on his reliability and strengthened the hand of his opponents in Parliament.

Nothing did more to weaken Charles's position in 1640–42 than the suspicion that he was not sound on religion. Sir Edward Nicholas, whom he appointed Secretary of State in November 1641, understood this only too well. While Charles was *en route* to Scotland in 1641, Nicholas, who had remained behind in London, wrote to tell him that 'the alarm of popish plots amuse and fright the people here more than anything, and therefore that is the drum that is so frequently beaten upon all occasions; and the noise of an intention to introduce popery was that which first brought into dislike with the people the government both of the Church and commonwealth'.[58] This theme was made explicit in the Grand Remonstrance, which recalled how 'the popish party [had] enjoyed such exemptions from penal laws as amounted to a toleration . . . They had a Secretary of State, Sir Francis Windebank, a powerful agent for speeding all their desires, [and] a Pope's nuncio residing here to act and govern them according to such influence as he received from Rome'. The Remonstrance also complained of the way in which the restoration of the catholic hierarchy had been allowed to take place, leading to the creation of a state within the state, 'independent in government, contrary in interest and affection . . . waiting for an opportunity by force to destroy those whom they could not hope to seduce'.[59]

The anti-catholic clauses of the Grand Remonstrance were more than mere rhetoric. They were a summary of the actions and inactions on the part of the royal government that had created a climate of fear in which rumours of sinister popish plots, centred in the Court, were only too credible. It was this fear that prompted many members of Parliament to support measures with which they would otherwise have had little sympathy. The most obvious example is the Militia Ordinance, which justified itself by referring to 'the bloody counsels of the papists and other ill-affected persons who have already raised a rebellion in the kingdom of Ireland and . . . will proceed not only to stir up the like rebellion and insurrections in this kingdom of England, but also to back them with forces from abroad'.[60] Fear of papists and popery was widespread throughout the country at large. It made possible, indeed it made imperative, the levying of troops, not to attack the King but to defend him. Few people, if any, wanted civil war. The overwhelming desire was for an adequate defence against the popish enemy. Hence the decision of both Houses of Parliament in July 1642 to raise an army 'for the safety of the King's person . . . and preserving of the true religion, the laws, liberty and peace of the kingdom'.[61]

NOTES AND REFERENCES

(*The place of publication is London, unless otherwise stated*)
1. **Letters of King James VI & I** ed. G. P. V. Akrigg (1984), p. 207. (Hereafter James I *Letters*).
2. James I *Letters*, pp. 204–05.
3. **Journals of the House of Commons 1547–1714** (1742). Vol. I, p. 144. (Hereafter *Commons Journals*)
4. **W. B. Patterson** 'King James I's Call for an Ecumenical Council' in G. J. Cuming & Derek Baker (eds.) *Councils and Assemblies* (Cambridge 1971), p. 273. (Hereafter Patterson 'Ecumenical Council')
5. Patterson 'Ecumenical Council', p. 273.

6. **James F. Larkin** & **Paul L. Hughes** (eds.) *Stuart Royal Proclamations.* Vol. I. *Royal Proclamations of King James I* (Oxford 1973), p. 73. (Hereafter Larkin & Hughes *Royal Proclamations*)
7. **J. R. Tanner** (ed.) *Constitutional Documents of the Reign of James I* Cambridge 1930), p. 83–4. (Hereafter Tanner *Constitutional Documents*)
8. **D. H. Willson** *King James VI & I* (1956), p. 222.
9. **Sir Ralph Winwood** *Memorials of Affairs of State in the Reigns of Queen Elizabeth and King James I* (1725). Vol. II, p. 40. (Hereafter Winwood *Memorials*)
10. **W. P. Baildon** (ed.) *Les Reportes del Cases in Camera Stellata 1593–1609* (1894), p. 191. (Hereafter Baildon *Cases in Camera Stellata*)
11. Winwood *Memorials*. Vol. II, p. 48.
12. Winwood *Memorials*. Vol. II, p. 78.
13. Tanner *Constitutional Documents*, p. 90.
14. *The Political Works of James I* ed. C. H. McIlwain (Cambridge, Mass. 1918), p. 71. (Hereafter James I *Political Works*)
15. Tanner Constitutional Documents, p. 91.
16. James I *Political Works*, p. 72.
17. *Commons Journals*. Vol. I, p. 145.
18. James I *Political Works*, p. 127.
19. James I *Political Works*, p. 127.
20. Larkin & Hughes *Royal Proclamations*, pp. 144–45.
21. *The Works of Francis Bacon* ed. James Spedding (1874). Vol. XI, p. 91. (Hereafter Bacon *Works*)
22. **E. R. Foster** (ed.) *Proceedings in Parliament 1610* (New Haven 1966). Vol. I, p. 51.
23. **Wallace Notestein, Frances Helen Relf** & **Hartley Simpson** (eds.) *Commons Debates 1621* (New Haven 1935). Vol. VII, pp. 635–36. (Hereafter *Commons Debates 1621*)
24. **John Rushworth** *Historical Collections* (1682). Vol. I, p. 392. (Hereafter Rushworth *Historical Collections*)
25. Baildon *Cases in Camera Stellata*, p. 190.
26. **Edward, Earl of Clarendon** *The History of the Rebellion and Civil Wars in England* ed. W. Dunn Macray (Oxford 1888). Vol. I, p. 63.
27. Bacon *Works*. Vol. XIII, pp. 301–02.
28. *Commons Debates 1621*. Vol. VI, pp. 367, 368; Vol. II, p. 7. n.11; Vol. V, pp. 426–27.
29. *The Letters of John Chamberlain* ed. N. E. McClure (Philadelphia 1939). Vol. II, p. 345. (Hereafter Chamberlain *Letters*)
30. *Commons Debates 1621*. Vol. II, p. 463.
31. Rushworth *Historical Collections*. Vol. I, p. 63.
32. Chamberlain *Letters*. Vol. II, p. 531.
33. *Commons Journals*. Vol. I, p. 675.
34. *Commons Journals*. Vol. I, p. 678.
35. Chamberlain *Letters*. Vol. II, p. 556.
36. Larkin & Hughes *Royal Proclamations*, p. 591.
37. **'Correspondencia Oficial de Don Diego Sarmiento de Acuña, Conde de Gondomar'** in *Documentos Ineditos para la Historia de España*. Vol. IV. (Madrid 1945), pp. 70–2.
38. *Commons Journals*. Vol. I, p. 674.

39. *Dictionary of National Biography* sub Smith.
40. 'The MSS of H. D. Skrine Esq.' in Historical Manuscripts Commission *Eleventh Report* (1887). Appendix. Part I, p. 25.
41. James F. Larkin (ed.) *Stuart Royal Proclamations*. Vol. II. *Royal Proclamations of King Charles I 1625–1646* (Oxford 1983), pp. 581–82. (Hereafter Larkin *Proclamations of Charles I*)
42. Rushworth *Historical Collections*. Vol. I, pp. 82–3.
43. S. R. Gardiner (ed.) *Debates in the House of Commons in 1625* Camden Society (1873), p. 149.
44. Larkin *Proclamations of Charles I*, pp. 75–7.
45. *Commons Journals*. Vol. I, pp. 822, 852, 857.
46. Rushworth *Historical Collections*. Vol. I, p. 396.
47. Robert C. Johnson, Mary Frear Keeler, Maija Jansson Cole & William Bidwell (eds.) *Commons Debates 1628* (New Haven 1977). Vol. II, p. 215. (Hereafter *Commons Debates 1628*)
48. *Commons Debates 1628*. Vol. IV, p. 312.
49. Larkin *Proclamations of Charles I*, p. 205.
50. Wallace Notestein & Frances Relf (eds.) *The Commons' Debates for 1629* (Minneapolis 1921), p. 145.
51. *Commons Journals*. Vol. I, p. 922.
52. Larkin *Proclamations of Charles I*. pp. 128–29.
53. Larkin *Proclamations of Charles I*. p. 130.
54. *Commons Debates 1628*. Vol. II, p. 85.
55. *Commons Debates 1628*. Vol. II, p. 215.
56. *Commons Debates 1628*. Vol. II, p. 326.
57. Larkin *Proclamations of Charles I*. p. 200.
58. Caroline M. Hibbard *Charles I and the Popish Plot* (Chapel Hill 1983), pp. 211–12
59. S. R. Gardiner (ed.) *The Constitutional Documents of the Puritan Revolution 1625–1660* (Oxford 1906), p. 219. (Hereafter Gardiner *Constitutional Documents*)
60. Gardiner *Constitutional Documents*, p. 245.
61. Gardiner *Constitutional Documents*, p. 261.

CHAPTER THIRTEEN
Charles I and the Church of England

CHARLES AND THE ARMINIANS

With the accession of Charles I in 1625 the high-church or Arminian party came into its own. The Arminians were distinguished from the low-church or puritan majority in a number of ways. In their theology they took more account of the grace of God freely available to all men and played down predestination. They emphasised the significance of the sacrament of holy communion, and made the altar rather than the pulpit the fulcrum around which the worship of the Church revolved. More generally they believed in strengthening the authority of the clergy and ecclesiastical hierarchy and in restoring the Church to a central role in the life of the state. They valued order and decency in services and wished to bring back some of the 'beauty of holiness' which they felt had been lost since the Reformation. They were not crypto-catholics, as many of their opponents believed, but they rejected the virulent hatred of popery which characterised the mass of the population. They accepted the Roman church as a true church, albeit corrupt, and they stressed the elements of continuity between the English protestant church and its Roman Catholic predecessor.

Charles's natural love of order and ceremony predisposed him in favour of the Arminians, but not until his journey to Spain in 1623 did he give clear signs of the way in which he was moving. The two chaplains he took with him were both Arminians, and when one of them, Matthew Wren, returned home he reported to the heads of the Arminian party – Andrewes, Neile and Laud – that the Prince's judgment was 'very right'; that he was more to be relied on than his father, who had displayed 'much inconstancy in some particular

307

cases'; and that he would undoubtedly uphold 'the doctrine and discipline of the Church of England'.[1] This proved to be an accurate forecast, as Charles showed soon after his accession when he removed the Arminian controversialist, Richard Montagu, from the grasp of the Commons by appointing him a royal chaplain. In July 1628 he went further and nominated Montagu for election to the see of Chichester. By this time Parliament had been prorogued, but members of the Commons had already demonstrated their anxiety about what they regarded as a threat to the established Church. Sir Humphrey May tried to allay their fears. 'The King's heart', he told them, 'is right set. Assure yourselves no man shall be preferred by him that is a papist or an Arminian. He hates them both, and you shall find he hates them'.[2] May was presumably speaking what he thought to be the truth, but the evidence pointed in the opposite direction, and Charles's commitment to the Arminians proved to be a major stumbling block in the way of good relations between him and his subjects.

There was no clearly defined body of doctrines or assumptions which distinguished Arminians from non-Arminians, nor did all those who were regarded as Arminians hold identical views. Nevertheless, they constituted a powerful pressure group within the Church, and because they realised that their opponents dominated Parliament they tended to exalt the royal authority. This meant that Charles found himself in sympathy not only with their religious beliefs but also with their political attitudes. However, it also meant that he was increasingly identified in the public consciousness with the stereotype of Arminianism as crypto-catholic and neo-absolutist.

In the eyes of their opponents the Arminians were potentially more dangerous than the catholics because they operated as a fifth column within the protestant community. Recusants made themselves known by refusing to conform to the law, but Arminians claimed the protection of it. Papists denied the validity of the Church of England, but Arminians professed their adherence to the Thirty-Nine Articles which defined its doctrines. Indeed, they went further and accused their critics of being the odd men out. This infuriated all those low-church men and women who regarded themselves as the true guardians of the Anglican tradition. Their anger was reflected in the parliamentary attack on Richard Montagu, who was accused of 'casting the odious and scandalous name of puritans upon such His Majesty's loving subjects as conform themselves to the doctrine and ceremony of the Church of England'.[3]

Montagu was not the only cleric to attract the attention of Parliament. Robert Sibthorpe and Roger Mainwaring were two others singled out for criticism. Sibthorpe preached in favour of the Forced Loan in 1627, and argued that 'if princes command anything which subjects may not perform, because it is against the laws of God, or of nature, or impossible, yet subjects are bound to undergo the punishment without either resistance or railing and reviling, and so to yield a passive obedience where they cannot exhibit an active one'.[4] Mainwaring, preaching before Charles in July 1627, maintained that parliamentary assent was not essential before taxation could be levied, and that the King's demands did 'so far bind the conscience of the subjects of this kingdom that they could not refuse the payment without peril of damnation'.[5] Sibthorpe presented his sermon to Charles, who sent it to Archbishop Abbot to be licensed for publication. Abbot refused to license ·what he later described as 'Dr Sibthorpe's contemptible treatise',[6] but the only consequence of this was that Abbot was suspended from his functions while the book was licensed by the more pliant Bishop of London, an Arminian sympathiser. Mainwaring's sermons were also printed, ostensibly 'by command of the King', although it was later claimed that Laud had in fact been responsible.

The Commons immediately took up the question of Mainwaring when they met in 1628. It was recommended that he should be dealt with by a Bill of attainder, but Sir Dudley Digges argued that 'there is more in this man and this book than can be punished by the Bill. A great many churchmen are gone too far in this kind. The damnable danger of this man is such that I would have him transmitted to the Lords'.[7] The House followed Digges's advice, and Mainwaring was duly impeached. The Lords sentenced him to fine and imprisonment, and barred him from holding any secular or ecclesiastical office. Moreover, the King, at their request, issued a proclamation suppressing the sermons. 'Although the grounds thereof were rightly laid', it said, 'to persuade obedience from the subjects to their sovereign, and that for conscience sake', Mainwaring had trespassed into fields about which he knew nothing, namely 'the laws of this land and proceedings of parliaments' and therefore deserved his punishment.[8] Nevertheless, only a few weeks later Charles presented Mainwaring to a living and subsequently issued a formal pardon to him. Other pardons were drawn up for Montagu and Sibthorpe. Mainwaring and Sibthorpe do not appear to have been Arminian in their theology, but Richard Neile, Bishop of Durham and one of the leading Arminians, was instrumental in procuring their pardons, and the term was coming to be used to describe all

those churchmen who exalted the royal authority – and, by implication, diminished the liberties of the subject. As Sir Nathaniel Rich
reminded the Commons in March 1628, 'we see now those men that
profess these [Arminian] opinions are advanced and preferred . . .
and will preach we have no property'.[9]

In 1626 Charles followed his father's example and tried to dampen
down controversy by ordering an end to public discussion of
disputed topics and warning of 'his utter dislike to all those who
. . . shall adventure to stir or move any new opinions not only
contrary but differing from the sound and orthodoxal grounds of
the true religion sincerely professed and happily established in the
Church of England'.[10] This was widely assumed to be a rebuff to
the Arminians, but it rapidly became clear that the inhibition applied
far less to them than to their critics. Controversy therefore
continued, and indeed was fuelled by genuine uncertainty about
what were the 'orthodoxal grounds of the true religion' as expressed
in the Church of England. The Commons were convinced that
Montagu was heterodox, but in a letter to Buckingham written in
August 1625 three bishops – Richard Neile, John Howson and
William Laud, all of them Arminians – gave their judgment that
'the opinions which at this time trouble many men in the late book
of Mr Montagu are some of them such as are expressedly the
resolved doctrine of the Church of England'.[11]

Pressure from the anti-Arminians led Buckingham to call a
conference at his London home, York House, in February 1626, at
which Montagu's opinions were subjected to expert scrutiny by the
puritan divine John Preston and others. Montagu himself took part,
and the audience – which, with the exception of Sir John Coke,
consisted entirely of peers – included puritans such as Pembroke,
Warwick, and Saye and Sele. It may be that the latter were hoping
for a condemnation of Montagu, but if so they were disappointed.
The conference ended without any formal statement of its
conclusions, but it had become obvious during the proceedings that
Buckingham was inclined to the side of the Arminians. There was
no reason to suppose that his attitude differed from that of Charles,
and the puritan peers had to accept the unpalatable fact that any
further definition of the Church's position made by its supreme
governor was almost certain to be along lines of which they
disapproved.

One of the consequences of the York House Conference was the
impeachment of Buckingham, in which the puritan peers worked
in close co-operation with their allies in the Commons. The attempt

to remove the Duke from the King's counsels was frustrated by Charles himself, but even if it had succeeded it would not have provided more than a momentary check to the progress of the Arminians, for they had the King behind them. Charles had shown this when he appointed Laud to preach at the opening of Parliament in 1625 and 1626. He had also chosen Laud to draw up the form of service for his coronation in February 1626, and in October of that year he promised him the succession to Canterbury after Abbot's death. Laud and his fellow high-churchmen also played a major part, with the King's full support, in securing the election of Buckingham as Chancellor of Cambridge University in 1626, which was followed by the proscription of Calvinist teachings there. Pym condemned Buckingham's election as part of a 'conspiracy to bring in Arminianism',[12] which indeed it was, but although the Commons expressed their anger there was nothing they could do to remedy the situation.

THE ALTAR CONTROVERSY

It was a growing sense of frustration that led the Commons in 1629 to take the more positive step of defining what were in their view the doctrines of the Church of England (see p. 348). Their definition had no force in law, of course, and in the absence of Parliament after March 1629 there was no institution which could challenge the crown's interpretation of disputed issues. The Arminians' claim that they were the true defenders of tradition had some validity, for the Articles and 'public acts' of the Church were open to differing interpretations. This was shown in the controversy over the placing of the communion table which came out into the open during the Personal Rule. The Arminians referred to the table as an altar – a name which, to their opponents, was redolent with popish connotations of sacrifice and transubstantiation – and insisted that it should be set at the east end of the chancel, pointing north–south, as the former altars had done, and railed off to protect it from the sacreligious attentions of local parishioners and their dogs. Laud gave voice to the Arminian view in 1637 when he declared that 'the altar is the greatest place of God's residence upon earth. I say the greatest. Yea, greater than the pulpit, for there 'tis *Hoc est corpus meum*, "This is my body", but in the pulpit 'tis at most but *Hoc est verbum meum*. "This is my word"'.[13]

The Elizabethan Injunctions of 1559 had laid down that 'the holy

table in every church' was to be 'set in the place where the altar stood
. . . and so to stand, saving when the communion of the sacrament
is to be distributed; at which time the same shall be so placed within
the chancel as whereby the minister may be more conveniently heard
. . . and the communicants also more conveniently and in more
number communicate . . . And after the communion done, . . . the
same holy table to be placed where it stood before'.[14] The Canons
of 1604 had made no significant change in the provisions and clearly
assumed that the table would be moved when in use and then
restored to its original position. This was highly inconvenient,
however, and in practice most parishes left the holy table permanently set either in the middle of the chancel or in the body of the
church. This was the situation at Gloucester cathedral, when Laud
arrived there shortly after his appointment as dean in 1616, but he
ordered its immediate transference to the east end of the chancel,
despite protests from the bishop and outraged members of the
congregation. Neile did the same when he took over as Bishop of
Durham in 1617. It is hardly surprising, therefore, that after
Laud's appointment as Archbishop of Canterbury in 1633, there was
pressure on all parishes to adopt a uniform practice by placing the
communion tables where the altar had originally stood.

Many parishes resisted this pressure. One of them was St
Gregory's, which lay in the shadow of St Paul's in London but
refused to follow the example set by the cathedral. The case was
debated before the Privy Council in November 1633, and Charles,
who was present, declared that the positioning of the communion
table was not to be 'left to the discretion of the parish, much less
to the particular fancy of any humorous person' but was to be
determined by the practice of the 'cathedral mother-church, by
which all other churches depending thereon ought to be guided'.[15]
A similar rebuff was administered by the ecclesiastical Court of
Arches to the parishioners of Beckington in Somerset who in 1636
challenged the right of their diocesan to make them move their table,
on the grounds that he was acting against the authority of 'all the
orthodox bishops and governors of the Church' from the time of
the Reformation onwards.[16]

Although Laud and Neile – who became Archbishop of York in
1632 – insisted upon the need for uniformity in siting the
communion table, they did not have the unanimous support of their
fellow bishops. John Williams of Lincoln went so far as to publish
The Holy Table, Name and Thing in 1637, in which he argued that
the correct interpretation of the Elizabethan injunction was that the

table should stand lengthways in the chancel and be moved for the administration of communion. There was opposition too from laymen, on grounds both of principle and of cost, for removing (and often remaking) the table and railing it in were expensive items, particularly for a small parish. Clarendon noted that 'the opinion that there was no necessity of doing anything, and the complaint that there was too much done, brought the power and jurisdiction to impose the doing of it to be called in question',[17] and it was presumably for this reason that the Canons drawn up in 1640 required all churches to 'conform themselves in this particular to the example of the cathedral or mother-churches'. In an attempt to allay disquiet, however, they insisted 'that this situation of the Holy Table doth not imply that it is or ought to be esteemed a true and proper altar, whereon Christ is again really sacrificed, but it is and may be called an altar by us in that sense in which the primitive church called it an altar, and no other'.[18]

LAUD AND THE ENFORCEMENT OF ECCLESIASTICAL DISCIPLINE

Clarendon, who described Laud's insistence upon the removal and railing-off of the communion table as being welcome to 'grave and intelligent persons who loved order and decency', criticised him nevertheless for acting too hastily. The Archbishop, Clarendon felt, did not take sufficient account of the 'long intermission and discontinuance' of what was now defined as orthodox practice, and he 'prosecuted this affair more passionately than was fit for the season'.[19] In 1633, when he was appointed Archbishop, Laud reached sixty, and he was aware that time was running out. Abbot had been primate for more than twenty-two years, and during that period, as Laud saw it, the ecclesiastical discipline imposed by Whitgift and Bancroft had been relaxed to such an extent that the Church was now in danger of dissolution through internal dissension, and this at a time when the threat from a revived and self-confident Roman Catholicism was daily increasing. Laud intended, with the King's approval, to reimpose discipline and to restore the clergy to what he regarded as their natural position as the guides and counsellors of the lay community. This clericalism ran counter to the post-Reformation tradition in England. Indeed it offended basic assumptions about the social superiority conferred by birth and status, for it was noted with disapproval that many if not most of the Arminians were men of low birth: Laud himself was the son of a clothier, Matthew Wren – Bishop successively of Norwich and Ely – of a mercer, and Neile of a tallow-chandler. Such men could hardly be expected to appreciate the inherited rights of property-owners or show the appropriate respect for rank and dignity. In 1628 the Commons had given three readings to a measure designed to exclude clergy from the Commission of the Peace, but Laud took the opposite view and encouraged the appointment of parish priests as Justices. He was himself an active member of the Privy Council and sat regularly in the Star Chamber, for, in his own words, 'a bishop may preach the gospel more publicly, and to far greater edification, in a court of judicature or at a Council table . . . than many preachers in their several charges can'.[20]

Laud's belief that the bishops were the buttresses of the Church, without whom it would surely fall, made him particularly severe on all those who called episcopal authority into question. Three major offenders in this respect were the lawyer William Prynne, the physician John Bastwick, and the clergyman Henry Burton, who were brought before Star Chamber in 1637. All three men had originally accepted episcopacy as a valid means of governing the Church and looked to the bishops to lead the fight against the popish enemy. It was the growing conviction that the bishops, far from fighting popery, were actually in league with it, that turned them into violent opponents. Burton, in two published sermons, accused the bishops of bringing in popish innovations such as altars, crucifixes, and bowing to the east. Prynne, in *News from Ipswich*, attacked Bishop Wren as an innovator and charged him and his fellow bishops with suppressing preaching in order to prepare the ground for popery. Bastwick, in his first English work, *The Litany*, developed a scurrilous polemic on the lines of the Elizabethan *Marprelate Letters* and declared that 'such a multitude of trumperies and grollish ceremonies are brought in by the prelates as all the substance of religion is thrust out'.[21] All three men were sentenced to lose their ears, pay heavy fines, and spend the rest of their lives in prison. Clarendon records the shock felt at the imposition of mutilation upon persons who were not merely gentlemen by birth but also members of the learned elite. 'Every profession', he noted, 'with anger and indignation enough, thought their education and degrees and quality would have secured them from such infamous judgments, and treasured up wrath for the time to come'.[22]

Laud took the opportunity of the trial to refute the charge of innovation and throw it back on his critics, whom he accused of 'being the greatest innovators that the Christian world hath almost ever known'. What they really objected to, he claimed, was his 'care of this Church, the reducing of it into order, the upholding of the external worship of God in it, and the settling of it to the rules of its first reformation'.[23] Laud's passionate desire to purify the Church and make its clergy worthy of their high calling paralleled that of the puritans; but whereas they saw the initiative coming from below, from the body of the faithful, Laud was determined to impose it from above. It was in pursuit of this objective that Laud curbed those elements within the Church which were quasi-autonomous. In 1629, while he was still only Bishop of London, he persuaded the King to issue instructions designed to limit the freedom enjoyed by lecturers, who tended to be puritan in their sympathies. They were now required to wear a surplice and hood and read the Prayer-Book service before delivering their sermons; moreover, future appointments of lecturers in corporate towns were limited to those who were prepared to accept livings and thereby place themselves under the direct control of the diocesan bishop. Four years later Laud took action against the puritan Feoffees for Impropriations, who had established a fund with which to buy up impropriate tithes and use them to supplement the stipends of worthy ministers, lecturers and schoolmasters. 'Worthiness' was defined by puritan criteria, and Laud regarded the whole scheme as an attempt to circumvent the bishops and introduce puritanism by the back door. At his instigation the Feoffees were summoned before the Court of the Exchequer, charged with erecting an illegal corporation. The court ordered their suppression and the transfer of their endowments and patronage into the hands of the crown.

ARMINIANS AND PURITANS

The suppression of the Feoffees and similar actions did not make Laud popular with the puritans and their sympathisers. Yet it should not be assumed that the policies of the Arminians were universally disliked. Clarendon, for instance, strongly approved of their insistence on maintaining the fabric of ecclesiastical buildings. 'The people took so little care of the churches,' he recalled, 'and the parsons as little of the chancels, that instead of beautifying or adorning them in any degree they rarely provided for their stability and against the very falling of very many of their churches, and suffered them, at least, to be kept so indecently and slovenly that they would not have endured it in the ordinary offices of their own houses'.[24] It was not only parish churches which had been allowed to decay; St Paul's Cathedral was also in a tumbledown state, brought about, according to an official report in 1631, by 'the neglect and sufferance of the dean and chapter in times past'.[25] Laud set up a commission, including himself, Neile, and representatives of the City of London, and set about raising funds with his customary energy. Some puritans were of the opinion 'that it was more agreeable to the rules of piety to demolish such old monuments of superstition and idolatry than to keep them standing',[26] and outside London and the Court circle there was no evidence of great willingness to contribute. But the King set an example by promising £500 a year, and others followed suit. The work of reconstruction began in 1633; and Inigo Jones, at the King's expense, provided a classical portico for the west end which was in marked contrast to the gothic of the old building.

The Arminians did not share the puritans' distrust of popular sports and entertainments, nor their belief that the sabbath should be devoted solely to church-going and Bible-reading. Laud took great exception to Sir Thomas Richardson, Chief Justice of King's Bench, for upholding the decision of the Somerset magistrates to suppress the 'wakes' or Sunday revels which were traditional in that county. Richardson was ordered to appear before the Privy Council, where Laud berated him so severely that he complained of being 'choked with the Archbishop's lawn sleeves'.[27] Shortly after this, Charles reissued the *Declaration of Sports* originally promulgated by James I in 1618. James had found 'that his subjects were debarred from lawful recreations upon Sundays after evening prayers ended, and upon holy days, and he prudently considered that if these times were taken from them, the meaner sort who labour hard all the week should have no recreations at all to refresh their spirits'. He therefore decreed that 'after the end of divine service, our good people be not disturbed, letted or discouraged from any lawful recreation'. By re-issuing this *Declaration* Charles was giving specific sanction to such pastimes as 'dancing, either men or women; archery for men; leaping, vaulting or any other such harmless recreation . . . May games, Whitsun ales and Morris dances and the setting-up of maypoles'.[28]

The *Declaration of Sports* created great resentment among puritans, particularly those of the 'middling sort' who had come to occupy the lesser positions of authority in many communities and were actively imposing their own discipline upon the potentially unruly population. It seemed to them that the royal government, which ought to be foremost in upholding order, was instead undermining it. The same was true of other changes which they attributed to the Arminians. In many parish churches, for instance, the size of individual pews reflected the importance of the families which used them, but bishops such as Matthew Wren had no time for such secular considerations, particularly when the pews blocked the view eastwards. Wren and a number of other bishops insisted that pews should be reduced to a uniform height. They had logic on their side, but they affronted and alienated the leaders of the local communities. It may well be that Arminianism was more acceptable to those elements in society below the 'middling' level, but it would be wrong to assume that puritan attitudes were confined to the upwardly mobile. In Cambridgeshire, for example, in the 1630s, many humble parishioners were willing to part with their hard-earned and far from plentiful money in order to pay a lecturer's stipend, or to move out of their parish altogether rather than endure what they regarded as popish practices from their incumbent.[29] And even if some aspects of Arminianism enjoyed popular support, this would have been of limited political advantage, given the fact that power and influence in early Stuart England depended upon property. What became apparent in the 1640s was that while the Prayer Book was well liked, and also the pattern of worship which was tied in with seasonal changes and the rhythms of agricultural life, there was limited enthusiasm in society as a whole for the extremes of either puritanism or Arminianism.

Laud, of course, regarded himself as an orthodox Anglican (though he would never have used this term), and at his trial he insisted that he had 'nothing to do to defend Arminianism, no man having yet charged me with the abetting any point of it'.[30] Although he rejected the puritan concept of the elect as being intolerably narrow, he declined to commit himself to an opposite position. Indeed, when asked about his view of predestination in 1630 he replied that 'I am yet where I was, that something about these controversies is unmasterable in this life'.[31] This led him to oppose public discussion of disputed issues, 'lest while pretending zeal for truth we should offend against religion and charity'.[32] His rise to power in the late 1620s coincided with an apparent attempt to heal divisions rather than exacerbate them. Following the prorogation of Parliament in 1628 the King ordered the Thirty-Nine Articles to be reprinted with a prefatory declaration in which he commanded 'that all further curious search be laid aside and these disputes shut up in God's promises as they be generally set forth to us in the Holy Scriptures and the general meaning of the Articles of the Church of England according to them'.[33] At about the same time Richard Montagu wrote to Archbishop Abbot – newly restored to favour – disclaiming any intention of upholding Arminianism, and a royal proclamation of January 1629 ordered the suppression of his *Appello Caesarem* on the grounds that it 'was the first cause of those disputes and differences which have sithence much troubled the quiet of the Church'.[34]

Had the 1629 session of Parliament been more harmonious it is possible that this even-handed policy might have continued. As it was, the absence of Parliament during the Personal Rule left the initiative in the hands of the Arminians, but even so Laud was careful to remain within the existing law and canons. He insisted, for instance, on bowing at the name of Jesus, since this was a canonical requirement, but he left to individual choice the practice of bowing to the east upon entering a church, which he personally favoured. He showed the same scrupulousness in his treatment of Oxford University after his election as Chancellor in April 1630. He rigidly enforced the proclamation forbidding controversy against Arminians and non-Arminians alike, and he was quite willing to co-operate with those whose opinions differed from his own as long as they shared his commitment to the restoration and maintenance of order and discipline within the university.[35] Nevertheless, Laud was deeply unpopular with a large section, almost certainly a majority, of the political nation, and especially with those low-churchmen whom he affronted by calling them puritans – by which he meant that they were not really members of the Church of England. The 'godly' gentry insisted on the validity of their puritan Anglicanism by giving their protection to anti-Arminians and fomenting opposition to 'innovations': indeed, the Bishop of Chichester told Laud in 1640 that his diocese was far more troubled by puritan magistrates than by puritan ministers.[36] 'Puritanism', as defined by the Arminians, implied separation from the Church. The puritans in fact had no desire to separate, but as time passed and the influence of the Arminians grew ever more apparent, they were forced to consider whether the Church was any longer one to which they could in conscience belong. A considerable number of puritan ministers resolved this problem by emigrating to the New World, where they hoped to be out of the effective range of Laudian episcopacy, and their lay brethren were contemplating the same solution. Sir

Simonds D'Ewes was one, and recorded how he began 'to consider that a higher providence might ere long call me to suffer for His name and gospel, or might prepare a way for my passage to America'.[37] The Providence Island Company, founded in 1630 to establish an English protestant settlement in the Caribbean, brought together prominent puritan aristocrats and gentlemen, including the Earl of Warwick, Lord Saye and Sele, John Pym and Sir Benjamin Rudyerd. They originally planned to promote the emigration of other people, rather than their own, but as the 1630s wore on and the state of religion, as they saw it, steadily deteriorated, a number of them decided to cut their links with England. The decision was an agonising one, for landowners, unlike the majority of ministers, had a great deal to lose, and the very fact that they should have considered such a drastic course is evidence of the role played in their lives by religion. There were some puritans, however, who regarded emigration as equivalent to deserting God's cause at home. This was the case with Sir Robert Harley, the leading Herefordshire puritan, who in 1634 begged the new incumbent of his living of Brampton Bryan to 'do what you can for us, that we be not driven to leave our native country and friends, and, which is more, the stage of Europe, where we are all to act our parts in the destruction of the Great Whore'.[38]

THE SCOTTISH CRISIS AND THE DESTRUCTION OF ARMINIANISM IN ENGLAND

By the time Harley made his plea, events had been set in motion which were to render emigration unnecessary. In 1633 Laud accompanied the King on a state visit to Scotland, and was shocked to find the churches there devoid of ornament and more like preaching barns than places of worship. There were Arminians in Scotland, such as William Forbes, shortly to be made bishop of the newly founded see of Edinburgh, but they were few in number and looked for support from England. Forbes, when he preached before the King, advocated a common liturgy for the English and Scots churches. Charles had already been considering this and had instructed Laud to consult with his Scottish colleagues. Laud, like Charles, was initially in favour of imposing the English form of service on the Scots Church but they were eventually persuaded by the Scottish bishops that a new form should be devised, albeit modelled on that of England, since 'this would relish better with their countrymen'.[39] Laud worked closely with his Scottish brethren in drawing up the new Prayer Book of 1637, which justified itself on the grounds of unity. The preface stated:

It were to be wished that the whole church of Christ were one, as well in form of public worship as in doctrine, and that as it hath but one Lord and one faith, so it had but one heart and one mouth. This would prevent many schisms and divisions, and serve much to the preserving of unity. But since that cannot be hoped for in the whole catholic, Christian church, yet at least in the churches that are under the protection of one sovereign Prince, the same ought to be endeavoured.[40]

Laud gave his opinion that there was 'no one thing in that Book which may not stand with the conscience of a right good protestant',[41] but the Scots thought otherwise. A petition drawn up in October 1637 condemned it for sowing 'the seeds of divers superstitions, idolatry and false doctrine, contrary to the true religion established within this realm',[42] and as resistance mounted among the population as a whole, many thousands subscribed to the National Covenant, which bound them to maintain the true faith as embodied in the Kirk of Scotland against the 'innovations and evils [which] have no warrant of the Word of God . . . and do sensibly tend to the re-establishing of the popish religion and tyranny, and to the subversion and ruin of the true reformed religion, and of our liberties, laws, and estates'.[43] Charles, faced with rebellion in his northern kingdom, determined to suppress it, but the 'Bishops' Wars', as they were called, were deeply unpopular in England, and the King's raw levies proved no match for the Scottish troops, many of whom had learnt their trade fighting as mercenaries on the Continent. The only consequence of the attempt to extend religious uniformity to Scotland was the collapse of the Personal Rule which was followed by the destruction of Laudianism in England.

Even at this late stage Laud was pressing on with his plans to restore discipline within the Anglican church. The Convocation which assembled at the same time as the Short Parliament, and which was permitted by Charles to continue its meetings even after Parliament had been dissolved, drew up a set of canons designed to confirm and ratify the changes that had taken place since the last codification of Church law in 1604. The Canons were prefaced by a defence of the rites and ceremonies enforced by the bishops. These had been unjustly regarded as 'not only contrary to our laws, but also introductive unto popish superstitions', whereas in fact they were Edwardian in origin and 'again taken up' under Elizabeth. Only within living memory had they been discontinued, and it was this which had allowed 'other foreign and unfitting usages by little and little to creep in'.[44] Specific canons prescribed the siting of the communion table at the east end of the chancel, where it was to be railed off, and recommended genuflexion upon entering and leaving church, 'according to the most ancient custom of the primitive Church in the purest times'.[45]

The 1640 Canons also dealt with the duty owed by subjects to their sovereign, and the statement that 'tribute and custom and aid and subsidy and all manner of necessary support and supply be respectively due to kings from their subjects by the law of God, nature and nations, for the public defence, care and protection of them'[46] had distinct echoes of earlier assertions by Mainwaring and Sibthorpe. However, the canon which caused most contention was the sixth, requiring all clergy to swear that they approved the doctrine and discipline of the Church of England as it was now established, and that they would never consent 'to alter the government of this Church by archbishops, bishops, deans and archdeacons, etc.'.[47] It was the vagueness of the final 'etc.' which caused alarm, for it committed the swearers to uphold an open-ended system, which might well be extended to include elements of which they disapproved. The 'Etcetera Oath', therefore, like the Canons as a whole, fuelled controversy rather than extinguishing it.

In December 1640 the Commons resolved that the Canons were illegal, and as they held Laud primarily responsible for them – he was, in the words of one member, 'the root and ground of all our miseries'[48] – they impeached him of treason. The Lords ordered the Archbishop's immediate confinement, and he was subsequently sent prisoner to the Tower, where he remained until his trial and execution three years later. In March 1641 the Upper House also took steps to remove some of the more obnoxious of Laudian 'innovations', by directing that the communion table should 'stand decently in the ancient place where it ought to do by the law, and as it hath done for the greater part of these three-score years past'.[49] In September the Commons resolved that all communion tables should be removed from the east end of churches and the hated rails taken down. They also voted for the removal of 'all crucifixes, scandalous pictures of one or more persons of the Trinity, and all images of the Virgin Mary', along with 'all tapers, candlesticks and basins'. There was to be no more 'corporal bowing at the name of Jesus or towards the east end of the church', nor were such unholy activities as dancing and sports to be allowed to sully the Lord's Day.[50] The

Upper House, however, was not prepared to accept such wholesale changes, especially as there was talk of altering or even abolishing the Prayer Book. Many peers feared that the Commons were opening the way to anarchy in the Church, which would, in turn, lead to the overthrow of the existing social structure. The Lords therefore issued an order 'that the divine service be performed as it is appointed by the Acts of Parliament of this realm, and that all such as shall disturb that wholesome order shall be severely punished'.[51]

The division between the two Houses reflected divisions within them, for now that Laud and a number of his close associates had been removed from the scene it was possible for supporters of the 'traditional' or non-Arminian Church of England to band together and show their strength. They were helped by the fact that Charles made no attempt to intervene on Laud's behalf, and in effect distanced himself from the entire ecclesiastical policy with which he had been associated in the 1630s. Many people, in Parliament as in the country as a whole, had been carried away by disgust at the activities of Arminian prelates into a hatred of episcopacy as such. Others, however, drew a careful distinction between the institution, of which they approved, and the excesses committed by some of its officers. They wanted to reform the Church, not abolish it; to turn it back to the purity of its Elizabethan and Jacobean heyday rather than create in its place some version of Presbyterianism or congregationalism.

This division between conservatives and radicals over religion paralleled that over constitutional issues, and although conservatism in the one might accompany radicalism in the other, there was, generally speaking, a considerable degree of overlap between religious and secular attitudes. What religion provided was the element of passion, of refusal to compromise, which raised the political temperature to the point where civil war became not only possible but inevitable. By a combination of good judgment, good advice (not always listened to) and good luck, Charles was able to transform himself in the eyes of some half of his subjects from an Arminian despot into the upholder of traditional values in Church and state. In turning his back, albeit late in the day, on 'innovation' he revealed the enduring strength of the early Stuart monarchy when it was identified with defence of the established Church and operated by consensus rather than confrontation.

NOTES AND REFERENCES

(The place of publication is London, unless otherwise stated)

1. **Lord Dacre** (H. R. Trevor-Roper) 'Matthew Wren' *Pembroke College Cambridge Society Annual Gazette.* No. 60 1986, p. 18
2. **Robert C. Johnson, Mary Frear Keeler, Maija Jansson Cole & William Bidwell** (eds.) *Commons Debates 1628* (new Haven 1977). Vol. IV, p. 243. (Hereafter *Commons Debates 1628*)
3. **John Rushworth** *Historical Collections* (1682). Vol. I, p. 211. (Hereafter Rushworth *Historical Collections*)
4. *Dictionary of National Biography* sub Sibthorpe.
5. *Dictionary of National Biography* sub Mainwaring.
6. Rushworth *Historical Collections.* Vol. I, p. 444.
7. *Commons Debates 1628.* Vol. III, p. 405.
8. **James F. Larkin** (ed.) *Stuart Royal Proclamations.* Vol. II. *Royal Proclamations of King Charles I 1625–1646* (Oxford 1983), pp. 197–98. (Hereafter Larkin *Proclamations of Charles I*)
9. *Commons Debates 1628.* Vol. II, p. 85
10. Larkin *Proclamations of Charles I*, p. 91.
11. *Cabala sive Scrinia Sacra* (1691), p. 105.
12. **Roger Lockyer** *Buckingham: The Life and Political Career of George Villiers, First Duke of Buckingham 1592–1628* (1981), p. 325. (Hereafter Lockyer *Buckingham*)
13. **Nicholas Tyacke** *Anti-Calvinists. The Rise of English Arminianism c. 1590–1640* (Oxford 1987), p. 202. (Hereafter Tyacke *Anti-Calvinists*)
14. **G. W. Prothero** (ed.) *Select Statutes and other Constitutional Document illustrative of the Reigns of Elizabeth and James I* (Oxford 1913), p. 190.
15. **S. R. Gardiner** (ed.) *The Constitutional Documents of the Puritan Revolution 1625–1660* (Oxford 1906), p. 104. (Hereafter Gardiner *Constitutional Documents*)
16. Tyacke *Anti-Calvinists*, p. 204.
17. **Edward, Earl of Clarendon** *The History of the Rebellion and Civil Wars in England* ed. W. Dunn Macray (Oxford 1888). Vol. I, p. 199. (Hereafter Clarendon *History of the Rebellion*)
18. **J. P. Kenyon** (ed.) *The Stuart Constitution 1603–1688* 2nd edn (Cambridge 1986), p. 153. (Hereafter Kenyon *Stuart Constitution*)
19. Clarendon *History of the Rebellion.* Vol. I, p. 200.
20. **H. R. Trevor-Roper** *Archbishop Laud 1573–1645* 2nd edn (1962), p. 5. (Hereafter Trevor-Roper *Laud*)
21. **S. R. Gardiner** *History of England from the Accession of James I to the Outbreak of the Civil War 1603–1642* (1884). Vol. VIII, pp. 227–28. (Hereafter Gardiner *History of England*)
22. Clarendon *History of the Rebellion.* Vol. I, p. 197.
23. Rushworth *Historical Collections.* Vol. II, p. 383.
24. Clarendon *History of the Rebellion.* Vol. I, p. 198.
25. Trevor-Roper *Laud*, p. 123.
26. Trevor-Roper *Laud*, p. 124.
27. *Dictonary of National Biography* sub Laud.
28. Gardiner *Constitutional Documents*, p. 101.

29. **Margaret Spufford** *Contrasting Communities: English Villagers in the Sixteenth and Seventeenth Centuries* (Cambridge 1974), p. 237.
30. **Peter White** 'The Rise of Arminianism Reconsidered' *Past & Present* No. 101. 1983, p. 53. (Hereafter White 'Arminianism Reconsidered')
31. White 'Arminianism Reconsidered', p. 53.
32. Tyacke *Anti-Calvinists*, p. 85.
33. Gardiner *Constitutional Documents*, p. 76.
34. Larkin *Proclamations of Charles I*, p. 219.
35. **Kevin Sharpe** 'Archbishop Laud and the University of Oxford' in Hugh Lloyd-Jones, Valerie Pearl & Blair Worden (eds.) *History and Imagination* (1981).
36. **J. T. Cliffe** *The Puritan Gentry: The Great Puritan Families of Early Stuart England* (1984), p. 200. (Hereafter Cliffe *Puritan Gentry*)
37. Cliffe *Puritan Gentry*, p. 203.
38. Cliffe *Puritan Gentry*, p. 201.
39. ***The Works of the Most Reverend Father in God, William Laud D. D.*** ed. W. Scott & J. Bliss. Vol. III. *Devotions, Diary and History* (Oxford 1853), pp. 426–29. (Hereafter Laud *Works*)
40. Tyacke *Anti-Calvinists*, pp. 233–34.
41. Laud *Works*. Vol. III, pp. 426–29.
42. Rushworth *Historical Collections*. Vol. II, p. 406.
43. Gardiner *Constitutional Documents*, p. 132.
44. Tyacke *Anti-Calvinists*, p. 238.
45. Tyacke *Anti-Calvinists*, p. 238.
46. Kenyon *Stuart Constitution*, p. 151.
47. Kenyon *Stuart Constitution*, p. 152.
48. Gardiner *History of England*. Vol. IX, p. 249.
49. Gardiner *History of England*. Vol. IX, p. 298.
50.· Gardiner *Constitutional Documents*, p. 198.
51. Gardiner *History of England*. Vol. X, p. 16.

CHAPTER FOURTEEN

The Early Parliaments of Charles I 1625–1629

1625. THE WESTMINSTER SESSION

James I had promised his last Parliament, which he opened in February 1624, that he would hold a second session in the autumn and a third in the following spring. However, the difficulties involved in arranging the French marriage, and the concessions which he had to make on the catholic question, were such that James was anxious to avoid further parliamentary scrutiny. He therefore extended the prorogation, and when that Parliament was brought to an automatic close by his death in March 1625, it was still lacking its second session. Charles I summoned a new Parliament to meet in May, but twice prorogued it in order to await the arrival of his bride, Henrietta Maria. The Queen entered London on 16 June, and two days later the King opened Parliament. By this time the plague had struck, and members were increasingly alarmed for their own safety. They were also in a bad mood, complaining, as Chamberlain reported, that they had been 'kept here with so much danger and expense, to so little purpose, for there is no likelihood they can sit here long, if at all'.[1] What Charles had in mind was a short session focussed upon supply: as long as the members were prepared to 'bestow this meeting upon him and this action' he promised them another, later in the year, at which they could deal with 'domestical business'.[2] The 'action' in question was war, for although no formal declaration of hostilities had been issued, English troops had already been provided for Mansfeld's expedition to the Palatinate, and the King, in the Lord Keeper's words, was preparing 'an invincible navy' with which 'to scatter the forces of his opposites in the circumference of their own dominions'.[3] Spain was not mentioned by name, but there could be little doubt that she would be the object of the assault.

The Lord Keeper had called for a swift response to the King's request for assistance – 'a supply too late is none'[4] – but he gave no indication of the amount that was required, nor was there any guidance on this point from other Councillors. In fact it was not until three weeks later that the Houses were given a detailed account of the King's needs. Charles was presumably working on the assumption that there was such a harmony of interest between him and the representatives of his people that no guidance was necessary. It has to be remembered that the two parliaments of which he had had direct experience – those of 1621 and 1624 – had both urged the King to take the sword in his hands. James had been reluctant to do so, but Charles's commitment to war, and that of his chief adviser, Buckingham, could not be doubted. The Parliament of 1624 had willed the end; surely its successor would provide the means? As Charles reminded the two Houses in his opening speech, they had 'by a liberal declaration engaged ourselves; so that it would be a dishonour to him and to us not to perfect it by yielding such supply as the greatness of the work . . . did require'.[5] Given this unity of purpose, there seemed little need for conciliar initiatives, backstairs bargaining, and the various other measures to which governments habitually resorted when a Parliament was in prospect. In any case, Buckingham, who had co-ordinated these tactics in 1624, was not available for a repeat performance; his attendance on the Queen kept him out of London until the session was about to open.

There is no reason to doubt that the members of the 1625 Parliament felt well disposed towards their new sovereign, but this did not mean that they necessarily approved of either his ministers or his policies. There was widespread fear and distrust of Buckingham, and also of the French marriage. Mansfeld's expedition had consumed men and money with nothing to show for it, and since Buckingham was still in charge of strategic planning there could be no guarantee that any further sums which were voted would be used to better effect. Despite James's solemn promise in 1624, no account had been rendered of the way in which the three subsidies then granted had been spent, and there was a suspicion – which, as it happened, was justified – that they had been used in part for Mansfeld's expedition, even though this did not explicitly fall within the four objectives outlined in the Subsidy Act. The Commons assumed that the 1624 grant had been more than sufficient for the crown's requirements, and that any further grant should be limited in extent, particularly since the economy was still in recession. There was recognition of the need to make some positive response to the King's appeal, but since no specific amount had been mentioned the way was open for Sir Francis Seymour to propose one subsidy. Sir Benjamin Rudyerd, who was at this time the nearest thing to a government spokesman in the Commons, objected that this would be 'too little, both in respect of want and of his [the King's] reputation',[6] but he gave no indication of what would be acceptable. Members therefore followed Sir Robert Phelips's suggestion, made in the debate on 30 June, that they should vote two subsidies. This, he assured them, 'will express the affections of the subjects more than the value . . . They diminish the King that think money can give him reputation'.[7]

These two subsidies eventually brought in £127,000, but this, as Sir John Coke explained on 8 July, would be far from sufficient. The supply voted in 1624 had all been spent – 'For Ireland, to confirm the peace of that kingdom . . . For the navy (the preparation for the enterprise now in hand not computed) . . . [For] the office of the ordnance and forts . . . For the support of the regiments in the Low Countries . . . [and for] the charge of Mansfeld's army' – and a further £150,000 was needed at once.[8] Moreover Charles had promised to pay his uncle and ally, the King of Denmark, £30,000 a month as long as he kept his armies in the field, and Mansfeld £20,000 a month for the same purpose. He was also engaged in preparatory work on the setting out of the 'invincible navy', which would be brought to a halt unless substantial sums were provided.[9] Coke, when he pressed for additional supply, did not specify how much, but in fact the King would have needed something like ten subsidies with their accompanying fifteenths and tenths in order to meet his commitments for the next twelve months.

Sir John Coke's account of the crown's finances had been delivered as part of Buckingham's strategy to persuade the Commons to reconsider their grant. But it was most unusual (though not unprecedented) to vote subsidies twice in one session and the Commons were in no mood to do so. Their numbers had shrunk as members left London to escape the plague, and the sixty or so who remained included many 'dissidents'. They distrusted Buckingham and they accepted no responsibility for funding what they regarded as his, rather than the King's, ill-conceived policies. They also believed that the royal finances were not in so desperate a state as was pretended. It was obvious that they had been weakened by James I's open-handedness, of which Buckingham had been the main beneficiary, but what one King had given, another could take back.

There was the further consideration, which affected their attitude, that when Parliament had voted money on previous occasions it appeared to have been misapplied. This was the case – or so they were convinced – with Tonnage and Poundage, of which James, like his predecessors, had received a life grant. Tonnage and Poundage, as the Act declared, was provided for 'the keeping and safeguard of the seas for the intercourse of merchandise',[10] but the 1620s had seen an increase in the activities of Sallee pirates from North Africa, who cruised off the west coast of England and preyed on shipping. Buckingham, as Lord Admiral, was responsible for keeping the seas clear, and his failure to do so was regarded as yet another indication of incompetence and malversation. It was against this background of distrust and suspicion that the Commons considered the framing of a new Tonnage and Poundage Act. Since the Customs duties formed so large a part of the crown's ordinary revenue, Charles had been collecting them from the moment of his accession, as his father had done. He assumed that these levies would swiftly be authorised by statute, but his confidence proved to be ill founded. Some members of the Commons wanted an assurance that Tonnage and Poundage would be used for the purposes for which it was voted (which meant, in their view, replacing Buckingham as Lord Admiral). Some argued that it would be impolitic to grant the King statutory duties on trade unless and until he abandoned his claim to prerogative levies such as Impositions. The passage of twenty years had done nothing to diminish the Commons' simmering resentment against these levies, which they still regarded as illegal, and further fuel was added to the fire by the economic recession, for Impositions caused merchants to raise their prices and thereby (or so it was argued) inhibited trade.

It was this resentment that explains the extraordinary contrast between the assessments of the current situation given at the beginning of Charles's reign. The Lord Keeper, in opening the 1625 Parliament, had referred to its predecessor as 'justly accounted happy. It made a kind of reconciliation betwixt the King and his subjects . . . There passed then more flowers of the crown, more Bills of grace, than in Magna Carta'.[11] Yet Sir Robert Phelips painted a different picture. 'Never King found a state so out of order [as Charles I]', he declared. 'The privileges of the kingdom, the privileges of this House, have been so broken, such burdens laid upon the people, that no time can come into comparison with this'.[12] Phelips was not thinking solely of Impositions, of course, but they did as much as any single issue to poison the atmosphere at the outset of Charles's reign. The new sovereign was anticipating a honeymoon with his subjects, but instead they called him to account for the sins of his father.

One reason for the Commons' concern to clarify the status of duties on trade before they made any formal grant was Charles's age. The new King was not yet twenty-five and might well live and reign for another forty years, by the end of which time Impositions would have acquired the legitimacy conferred by long usage. The same was true of the royal finances in general: if they were not thoroughly reformed now, they might never be. Yet in a short session, over-shadowed by plague, the Commons would not have the time or the inclination to deal with long-term measures. They therefore passed a Bill granting Tonnage and Poundage for one year only. This would give them the opportunity to reconsider the matter, at greater leisure, in a later session, and they chose to ignore the warning from Sir Robert Heath, the Solicitor General, that such a breach with precedent 'might be distasteful to the King'.[13] They apparently took the co-operation of the Lords for granted, but the Upper House was unwilling to countenance innovation and threw out the Bill. This meant that Charles I, at the outset of his reign and with a major war in prospect, was deprived of the statutory right to some fifty per cent of his ordinary revenue. It was perhaps hardly surprising that he had recourse to the plea of necessity and ordered the collection of Tonnage and Poundage to continue until such time as Parliament should pass the appropriate legislation. Instead of diminishing the range of prerogative taxation, the Commons had inadvertently extended it.

1625. THE OXFORD SESSION

The King and Buckingham had not abandoned their intention of obtaining further supply, and although Charles adjourned Parliament on 11 July he gave notice that he would reconvene it, at Oxford, on the first day of August. Oxford had the advantage of being free of the plague – so far, at any rate – but members would have preferred to stay in the relative safety of their own homes until such time as the epidemic had died down. They also resented the fact that they were being summoned to this second meeting in order to vote additional supply when they had already made plain their unwillingness to do so. It was not at all clear to them what the King hoped to achieve by such a manoeuvre, and some of them came to the conclusion that it was a face-saving trick on Buckingham's part. The naval expedition on which he was pinning his hopes was, they persuaded themselves, so far from ready that it could not possibly sail before the winter storms set in. Rather than acknowledge his own incapacity, Buckingham would call upon Parliament for supply and then, when it refused, hold it responsible for the abandonment of the expedition. As Sir Francis Seymour put it, this meeting 'is a way to breed jealousy betwixt the King and his subjects, a device of those who, knowing their own faults, seek occasions to lay the blame upon us'.[14]

Charles must have been informed of this rumour, for when he opened the Oxford meeting he declared that though 'the great preparations he had made . . . had cost him great sums of money, yet it were better half the ships should perish in the sea than that the fleet should not now go out'.[15] The King was followed by his Secretary of State, Lord Conway, and Sir John Coke, Buckingham's right-hand man in naval affairs, who gave details of the King's commitments. 'The fleet is now at the sea', said Coke, 'going to the rendezvous at Plymouth where there lie 10,000 men at pay, for which action His Majesty is deeply engaged in respect of his own honour, the cause of religion, and support of his allies'.[16] He revealed that no less than £400,000 had so far been spent and that the King's coffers were empty, but he gave no indication of the amount that was still needed. The only mention of a specific figure came from Conway, when he said that the immediate requirement was for £30,000–40,000. In the debate that followed, the Chancellor of the Exchequer, Sir Richard Weston, called for a grant of two subsidies and two fifteenths, which might have yielded £160,000, but Sir John Eliot was probably reflecting the House's opinion when he commented that 'this perhaps was but to hasten the denial the sooner by enlarging the demand'.[17]

If indeed Parliament had been reconvened, at great inconvenience to members, merely to vote the paltry sum of £40,000, then it was a time-wasting exercise. It is more likely that the government was hoping for an additional subsidy or two, not simply to fill its coffers but also as a gesture of confidence that would encourage financiers to advance substantial loans. If it had specified an amount it would have risked a rebuff, and this would have been bad for its public image. It therefore merely made known its wants and left it to the Commons to make an appropriate response. This strategy backfired, however, for it served only to increase members' suspicions and to provide ammunition for the attack on Buckingham which was rapidly gathering momentum. Sir Edward Coke declared that 'multiplicity of offices to be held by one man is a great prejudice to the merit of honour and His Majesty's well-deserving subjects' and that the Lord Admiral's place 'requireth a man of great experience and judgment'.[18] Sir Robert Phelips gave his opinion that 'in the government there hath wanted good advice; counsels and power have been monopolised', and he called on the Commons to 'look into the estate and government, and finding that which is amiss, make this Parliament the reformer of the commonwealth'.[19]

Buckingham decided that the best way in which to head off this attack was by making a public defence of his policies and actions, and with Charles's approval he addressed a meeting of both Houses in Christ Church hall. He began by announcing that the King had accepted the Commons' request that the laws against popish recusants should be strictly enforced. This was intended as a demonstration of Charles's orthodoxy in religious matters and proof that the marriage treaty with France had not (as was widely believed) entailed concessions to the English catholics. It was also meant, of course, to put members in a favourable state of mind for Buckingham's address, and merits Eliot's description of the manoeuvre as 'like to pills that have some sweetness over them to make their reception the more easy'.[20] Buckingham had nothing new to say. Indeed the whole thrust of his argument was that nothing had changed since the Parliament of 1624, 'that was so happy to me that I had the honour to be applauded by you. Now, having the same heart to speak with and the same cause to speak in . . . I doubt not but to have the same success and approbation'.[21] It was true that no war had as yet been declared, but this was only because the King was waiting for assurances of support from Parliament. 'Make the fleet ready to go', said Buckingham, and 'my master gave me command to bid you name the enemy yourselves. Put the sword into his hands and he will maintain the war'.[22]

Buckingham had concentrated upon the naval expedition, which implied hostilities against Spain. This was the sort of war that the Commons had been calling for since 1621, and by reminding them of his own commitment to it he was bidding for their support. It was left to the Lord Treasurer, who foilowed Buckingham, to remind the Houses of the King's continuing obligations to his foreign allies. When the Commons returned to their own chamber and began debating the issue, the Privy Councillors pressed for an immediate decision on supply. They were calculating, as Eliot recalled, that Buckingham's 'overtures had captiv'd all men's judgments and levelled them to the pleasure of the Court',[23] and Weston assured them that if they met the King's request for 'a present despatch of the supply', Charles would give them 'that royal word which he had never yet broken, nor given cause to mistrust, that you shall meet again in the winter in a more seasonable time and stay together until you may bring to maturity those things which were propounded'.[24] Opinion remained divided, however, and powerful voices, among them those of Sir Robert Phelips and Sir Francis Seymour, urged that 'the estate of the commonwealth' should first be looked into.[25] Since there was no consensus, the matter was not put to the question, and the Commons drifted into the state of *de facto* paralysis of which James had frequently complained. Charles therefore decided to cut his losses and dissolve Parliament. The Commons just had time to present him with a resolution assuring him that they would 'ever continue most loyal and obedient subjects' and that they would be ready 'in convenient time, and in a parliamentary way . . . to discover and reform the abuses and grievances of the realm and state, and in like sort to afford all necessary supply to His most excellent Majesty'.[26]

1626. THE IMPEACHMENT OF BUCKINGHAM

Two months after the dissolution of Parliament, the Cadiz expedition at last set sail, but the time and money lavished on it were all in vain, for it accomplished nothing (see p. 25). Charles could at this stage have pulled England out of the war, but his objectives, which included the recovery of the Palatinate and, more generally, the containment of Habsburg power, remained unchanged, as did his belief that they were in the best interests of his country. The most appropriate response to failure was, in Charles's view at any rate, a renewed commitment to the war, but this required, as always, the co-operation of his subjects. Charles therefore summoned another Parliament to meet in February 1626.

Before it did so, however, Buckingham held a conference at his London home, York House, to try to resolve the disputes over religion which were an increasing obstacle in the way of harmony between the King and the political nation. The Commons in the last Parliament had renewed their attack on Richard Montagu, who had only been saved by Charles's decision to appoint him a royal chaplain. Buckingham had links with Montagu and was widely assumed to be an Arminian sympathiser, even though he had numbered the puritan divine, John Preston, among his clients. At the York House conference, Buckingham was given the opportunity to dissociate himself from the Arminians, but he preferred to follow the lead given by Charles and made it plain that he regarded the criticism of them as unjustified. This served to stoke up the anger against Buckingham that had been refuelled by the ignominy of the Cadiz expedition, and strengthened the determination of his critics – who included some of his fellow-Councillors, such as the Lord Chamberlain, the Earl of Pembroke – to call him to account and thereby forcibly remove him from the King's counsels.

Charles had chosen to believe that the failure of the 1625 Parliament had been due to a few malignant spirits, and he excluded these from the 1626 assembly by pricking them as sheriffs and thereby obliging them to remain in their counties. Sir Edward Coke, Sir Thomas Wentworth, Sir Robert Phelips and Sir Francis Seymour were all conspicuously absent from the Commons, but this had the unintended effect of increasing the influence of members such as Sir John Eliot who were even more 'fiery', in the sense that they were liable to be carried away by the strength of their feelings. Eliot had previously been a client of Buckingham, and had hoped to play the key role in naval affairs which had gone instead to his rival, Sir John Coke. A powerful combination of personal jealousy, frustrated ambition, and anger over the Cadiz fiasco, led Eliot to call for a Commons' investigation into the ills affecting the kingdom. This led to the setting up of the Committee for Evils, Causes and Remedies which acted as a clearing-house for information and complaints.

Acting on a suggestion of Eliot, the Committee for Evils initiated an enquiry into the expenditure of the subsidies voted in 1624, and the Speaker thereupon summoned the members of the Council of War to appear before the House. The King acknowledged that under the terms of the Subsidy Act the Commons had a right to know how the monies had been spent, but he would not allow the Councillors to reveal what discussions had taken place about strategy or what advice they had given him. Charles told one of the Councillors that 'it is not you that they aim at, but it is me upon whom they make inquisition', and when it was pointed out that the Commons might react by refusing to vote supply, he made the revealing comment that 'gold may be bought too dear'.[27]

The Chancellor of the Exchequer, acting on Charles's orders, tried to turn the House away from confrontation by reminding it of the King's pressing needs: Charles, he said, must know 'without further delaying of time, what supply you will give him for these his present occasions, that he may accordingly frame his course and counsel'.[28] The Commons, in reply, assured the King that they intended to assist him 'in such a way and in so ample a measure as may make you safe at home and feared abroad', but that they first wished to reveal to him the causes of 'these great evils which have occasioned Your Majesty's wants and your people's grief'.[29] Charles warned them not to call into question 'such as are of eminent place and near unto me' and stressed that Buckingham had not 'done anything concerning the public or commonwealth but by special directions and appointment, and as my servant'.[30] When the Commons ignored this warning and pressed on with their investigations into the Duke's conduct, Charles made another attempt to head them off. At a joint meeting of both Houses, he reminded members that it was with their full support that he had persuaded his father to break off negotiations with Spain, and again with their support that he had embarked upon war. 'Now that you have all things according to your wishes', he added, 'and that I am so far engaged that you think there is no retreat, now you begin to set the dice and make your own game. But I pray you be not deceived. It is not a parliamentary way, nor is it not a way to deal with a King'. In case his meaning should still be unclear, he spelt it out. If Parliament co-operated with him by financing the war, then he would regard it as a partner and summon it frequently. If not, it would be of no further use to him. 'Remember that parliaments are altogether in my power for their calling, sitting and dissolution. Therefore, as I find the fruits of them good or evil, they are to continue or not to be'.[31]

It quickly became evident that nothing would deflect the Commons from their pursuit of Buckingham, for the majority of members were convinced that he was not simply the cause of past failures but a guarantee of future ones. The House therefore drew up a list of charges against him and on 8 May presented these to the Lords. At the same time they made the formal announcement that

for the speedy redress of great evils and mischiefs . . . which this kingdom of England now grievously suffereth . . . the Commons in this present Parliament . . . do by this bill show and declare against George, Duke, Marquis and Earl of Buckingham . . . the misdemeanours, misprisions, offences, crimes and other matters comprised in the articles following; and him, the said Duke, do accuse and impeach of the said misdemeanours, misprisions, offences and crimes.[32]

Buckingham took his time framing his reply to the Commons' charges, but a month later he presented a detailed rebuttal of them to the Lords. In his statement he acknowledged that he had made mistakes, but denied that he had in any way been guilty of criminal behaviour. Such a defence might have carried considerable weight with the Lords in normal circumstances, but the Duke had a number of powerful enemies there. Pembroke, acting behind the scenes, was deeply involved in the attack upon Buckingham, for both personal and political reasons, and he could count on the support of his long-time ally, Archbishop Abbot. Viscount Saye and Sele was another of the Duke's critics, for his puritan leanings made him suspicious of Buckingham's supposed Arminian preferences. The Earl of Arundel was also numbered among the Duke's opponents, for as the self-appointed spokesman of the 'old' aristocracy he resented the predominance of the *parvenu* favourite. Charles had tried to cow Arundel by sequestering him from the House and imprisoning him in the Tower – nominally for allowing his son to marry a royal ward without the King's permission – but this had proved counter-productive, for the Lords were so outraged at what they interpreted as an attack upon their privileges that they went on strike and refused to consider any business until Arundel was restored to them. The King eventually yielded, but he could be sure that if it came to a vote, Arundel would give his voice against Buckingham. In other words, Charles could not rely upon the Lords to throw out the impeachment, yet he was determined neither to part with his chief minister nor to allow him to be found guilty of 'crimes' which in Charles's eyes were nothing of the sort.

Charles was considering bringing the session to a close. He had been so angered by the speeches of Sir Dudley Digges and Sir John Eliot when they presented the charges against Buckingham to the Lords that he had despatched them to the Tower. This was an apparent infringement of the Commons' privilege of freedom from arrest, and the Lower House, like the Upper, declined to do any business until its members were restored to it. Charles therefore ordered their release, but he could not remove the suspicions aroused by his precipitate action. The Commons drew up a Bill to protect their privileges, and gave it two readings. They also prepared articles of impeachment against Richard Montagu (see p. 308). Neither of these measures was calculated to win the King's approval, but the Commons had already decided, in principle, to vote the crown supply, and from the King's point of view it made sense to postpone a dissolution until the subsidy Bill had completed its progress through both Houses. There was the further consideration that a second abrupt dissolution, following the pattern set in his first Parliament, would not only diminish Charles's reputation abroad but make it yet more difficult to win the goodwill of his subjects at home – which was still his hope, if no longer his expectation.

The Commons had protested their willingness to aid the King, but their grant of three subsidies and three fifteenths had been made conditional upon redress of grievances. Charles found this deeply offensive. Not only was the sum insufficient – far from making him 'safe at home and feared abroad', as the Commons had professed, it would expose him, he said, 'both to danger and disesteem' – but the conditional nature of the grant was 'in itself very dishonourable and full of distrust'.[33] Charles had tried to insist that further supply should be voted, and that it should be unconditional, a genuine gesture of trust and confidence in him. He was forced to accept, however, that no such gesture would be forthcoming. The Commons would not even pass their original subsidy Bill until Buckingham was 'removed from intermeddling with the great affairs of state', for they feared that any money they gave would, 'through his misemployment, be turned rather to the hurt and prejudice of this your kingdom than otherwise'.[34] In these circumstances Charles at last took the decision which had long been expected, and on 15 June he ordered the dissolution of his second Parliament.

1628. THE PETITION OF RIGHT

Charles's third Parliament, which assembled in 1628, met under the twin shadows of the defeat at Ré (see p. 29) and the Five Knights' Case (see p. 224). The King opened it with what was by now almost a ritual statement of the need for swift action: 'the only intention of calling this assembly is for present supply; and this way of Parliament is the most ancient way and the way I like best. Wherein if you do use such speedy resolution as the business requireth . . . I shall be glad to take occasion thereby to call you oftener together'.[35] His plea was echoed in the House of Commons by Sir Benjamin Rudyerd, who, through his connexion with the Lord Chamberlain, the Earl of Pembroke, represented a Court viewpoint. 'This is the crisis of parliaments', said Rudyerd. 'By this we shall know whether parliaments will live or die'. He called on the Commons, not for the first time, to take account of the King's feelings and to make concessions in form so that they could obtain the substance of their desires. 'It is comely and mannerly', he reminded them, 'that princes in all fair appearance should have the better of their subjects. Let us . . . give the King a way that he may come off like himself . . . by trusting the King, thereby to breed a trust in him towards us, for without a mutual confidence a good success is not to be expected'. There was, he added, no hope for a satisfactory outcome unless harmony was re-established: 'if we pursue (the King to draw one way and the Parliament another) the commonwealth must sink in the midst'.[36]

The King had spoken in general terms of the need for speed. It was left to Sir John Coke, now a Secretary of State, to flesh out the details. Ships were needed to guard the English coasts from invasion, to send aid to the Huguenot stronghold of La Rochelle, under siege by the French king, and to assist the hard-pressed King of Denmark by blocking the entrance to the Elbe and restricting trade into and out of the Sound. More troops had also to be raised for offensive operations overseas and to strengthen Danish forces. It was not simply a question of 'the King's interest or pleasure', Coke reminded the House, but of 'the defence of us all. Every day we run into more danger'.[37] An immediate response to this came from Edward Kirton. 'We are told of dangers abroad', he observed, but 'we have as great at home'. He was supported by Sir Robert Phelips, who declared that 'I cast not off fear of foreign dangers, but let not these fears so work on us as to weaken our resolutions against our fears at home'.[38]

This insistence upon the overriding need for grievances to be redressed might have presaged another stormy, unharmonious and ultimately abortive session, but there were indicators pointing in a different direction (see p. 227). It seems likely that even before Parliament opened the leading critics of government policy had agreed not to invite an immediate dissolution by renewing the attack upon Buckingham. This removed one obvious obstacle to harmony. Another was removed when Sir John Coke, speaking on behalf of the King, admitted that 'illegal courses have been taken' and that 'the redress must be by laws and punishment'. What became plain was that some sort of bargain was on offer, and that there was a general inclination to accept it. As long as Charles was reassured by a generous vote of supply, he would put an end to the abuses that had been committed. The King had been driven to such courses by necessity, said Coke, and he reminded the House that 'necessity hath no law. You must habilitate the state to do what you do by petition require'.[39]

The Commons showed their readiness to go along with Coke and meet the King half way by appointing a single committee to deal with the two major issues confronting them, namely 'the liberty of the subject in his person and in his goods' and 'His Majesty's supply'.[40] This did not produce immediate results, for in practice the House was reluctant to consider supply until it had dealt with other matters, including the perennial one of catholic recusants. On the last day of March it presented a petition on this subject to the King, who received it graciously but took the occasion to remind members that 'if we do not make provision speedily, we shall not be able to put one ship to sea this year'.[41] This spurred the Commons to action. A few days later the second reading was given to a Bill granting the King Tonnage and Poundage, and then, on 4 April, the House, sitting as a grand committee, decided 'to give the King five subsidies in a parliamentary way. And there was not one negative voice'.[42]

Charles assumed that the grant of supply was unconditional and would be swiftly translated into an Act. But in fact the Commons were determined not to go beyond a declaration of intent until they had secured their liberties. Sir John Coke had already assured them that if they thought fit to do this 'by way of Bill or otherwise' the King would 'give way unto it' so long as it was framed 'with due respect of his honour and the public good'.[43] The House had taken the first step in this direction on 1 April, when it resolved 'that no free man ought to be committed, detained in prison, or otherwise constrained by command of the King or Privy Council or any other unless some cause of the commitment, restraint or detainer be expressed'.[44] A resolution of the House was not binding in law, however, and the Commons therefore sought a conference with the Lords in order to clear the ground for a Bill.

The Commons insisted that they were asking for nothing new, merely a clarification of the existing law, but there was little doubt that in the past the crown had exercised the right to imprison without showing cause in cases where the security of the state was at issue, and the Lords were extremely reluctant to break with precedent in this respect. They therefore proposed that the King should be asked to declare 'that the good old law called Magna Carta, and the six statutes conceived to be explanations and declarations of that law, do still stand in force'. As for his prerogative rights, these were 'intrinsical to his sovereignty and betrusted him withal from God'. The King could not legally be deprived of them, nor even constrained in their use, but he could be requested to 'resolve not to use or divert the same to the prejudice of any of his loyal people in the propriety of their goods or liberty of their persons'.[45]

Charles was prepared to accept a compromise solution along these lines. The Commons, however, who had seen basic liberties trampled under foot by the Forced Loan and its aftermath, were determined to put their trust only in the law, which was less liable to human fallibility than mortal rulers. They therefore drew up a draft Bill 'for the better securing of every free man touching the propriety of his goods and liberty of his person',[46] which included a provision that no imprisonment in the King's name should be valid unless the cause was expressed. Sir Dudley Digges had doubts about the wisdom of this provision – 'it ties the King too much, and makes him say that that never King said before'[47] – but Sir Edward Coke reminded the House that 'it is not now without occasions that we insist upon this. Were there ever such violations offered? Were there ever such commissions and oaths?'.[48] Coke was supported by another lawyer and future Attorney General, William Noy, who began by professing that 'were kings immortal I should be content with His Majesty's royal word' but then asked 'who knows the disposition of the next succeeding King?' It was his opinion that since the Commons were concerned not only with the present but also with the future, they must 'pass a law for posterity'.[49]

These views were challenged by, among others, the Solicitor General, Sir Richard Shelton, who argued that a future ruler who was determined to violate his subjects' liberties would not be deterred by any statutory limitation upon his authority. This point was driven home by Sir John Coke, who affirmed that no legislation could deprive the King and his ministers of their right, indeed their duty, to imprison without showing cause where the safety of the state should require it. 'Do not think that by . . . debate we can make that not to be law which in experience we every day find necessary. Make what law you will. If I discharge the place I bear [as Secretary of State] I must commit men and must not discover the cause to any jailer or judge . . . Government is a solid thing, and must be supported for our good'.[50] The case against legislation was summed up by a more obscure member, Mr Browne. 'We have laws enough', he emphasised. 'It is the execution of them that is their life, and it is the King that gives life and execution . . . If we get the King on our side we have power. Let us tell him we do rely on his word'.[51] However, Browne and those who thought like him were in the minority. The majority agreed with Sir Thomas Wentworth that after a 'public violation' of the subjects' liberties nothing less than 'a public amends' was required, and that this could only be made by Bill.[52] Sir Edward Coke put the case for legislation with uncustomary succinctness: 'my heart goes with a Bill. Though I trust the King as a private man, the King speaks but by record'.[53]

The Commons requested an audience of the King, at which they asked his leave to proceed by Bill, on the clear understanding that they had no intention 'any ways to encroach upon your sovereignty or prerogative' nor 'the least thought of straining or enlarging the former laws in any sort by any new interpretations or additions'.[54] Charles made the pertinent comment that if, as they protested, they were 'full of trust and confidence' in his royal word, then they had no need to legislate, but he agreed to accept a Bill confirming Magna Carta and related statutes 'so as it may be without additions, paraphrases, or explanations'.[55] However, in the subsequent debate it became apparent that many members of the Commons felt the need to go beyond a mere confirmation of existing laws. Their doubts about the wisdom of relying solely upon the King's word were strengthened by their parallel consideration of the case of Roger Mainwaring (see p. 309), whose sermons on the duty of subjects to contribute to the relief of the King's necessities had been printed in late 1627, by royal command. This added to the general fear that while Charles himself might be committed to 'constitutional' government, the same was not necessarily true of those around him. Legislation was therefore essential not in order to bind the King but to strengthen his position against the evil designs of some of his advisers.

The Commons, then, wanted to go beyond mere confirmation of the existing laws, even though they insisted, and seem genuinely to have believed, that they were asking for nothing new. Yet they were uncertain how to proceed, in view of Charles's statement that he would not accept any Bill that contained explanatory or other additional material. They still had the offer of the King's word on which they could rely, but as Sir Edward Coke repeatedly emphasised, 'the King must speak by a record, and in particulars, and not in general'. It was the law itself that was unclear and needed clarifying in such a way that the liberties of the subject would be put beyond doubt or legal cavil. 'Let us have a conference with the Lords', said Sir Edward, 'and join in a petition of right to the King for our particular grievances'.[56]

A petition of right was a traditional means whereby the subject could call upon the sovereign for justice. The King was above the law in the sense that he could not be sued, nor could the actions of his ministers be challenged in any court except the High Court of

Parliament. Where the royal government had acted legally but unfairly, the King could be petitioned to show grace; but where it had gone beyond the limits of law he could be asked to disavow the actions of his servants and to respect the rights of his subjects. A petition of right, in other words, if it was accepted, implied an acknowledgment that the King had done wrong – not personally, of course, but through his deputies – and wished to offer redress. Usually petitions of right and of grace were presented to the King on behalf of individual complainants, but when the actions of the royal government had affected *all* individuals equally, then it was appropriate for Parliament to make such a presentation on their behalf. This was the course of action which Sir Edward Coke now proposed. Since a petition of right was not a statute, its use would circumvent the restriction which the King had imposed on procedure by Bill. Yet if the petition was passed by both Houses and given the royal assent, it would have the force of statute and be binding on the judges.

The principal drawback of a petition of right was that it could deal solely with defined and specified grievances. It did not have the capacity of statute to legislate in general terms. However, as far as members of the Commons were concerned, this was not a serious handicap, for they, like their constituents, had been preoccupied with particular issues, such as the billeting of troops on householders, the issuing of commissions of martial law which undermined the authority of Justices of the Peace, the levying of forced loans, and the imprisonment, without cause shown, of those who refused to contribute to them. These were now listed in the draft Petition of Right which the Commons presented to the Lords on 8 May. The key provision was that which affected the King's authority to imprison, and Charles warned the Lords against attempting to restrict this. 'We find it still insisted upon', he told them, 'that in no case whatsoever (though they should never so nearly concern matters of state and government) we or our Privy Council have power to commit any man without the cause shown; whereas it often happens that should the cause be shown the service itself would thereby be destroyed and defeated'. He did not regard as satisfactory the provision that it should be left to the judges to decide whether the reason given for imprisonment was valid, for in 'cases of that transcendent nature' they might well have 'no capacity of judicature, nor rules of law to direct or guide their judgment'. In short, if the Commons' proposal was accepted unaltered it would lead to the 'intermitting of the constant rule of government for so many ages within this kingdom practised', and this in turn 'would soon dissolve the very foundation and frame of our monarchy'.[57]

Charles was aware, of course, that by using his prerogative powers to punish opponents of the Forced Loan he had weakened his case. He therefore made a formal written promise, contained in a letter to the Lords, 'that neither we nor our Privy Council shall or will at any time hereafter commit or command to prison, or otherwise restrain, the persons of any for not lending money to us, or for any other cause which in our conscience does not concern the state, the public good, and safety of us and our people'. If in any future case this safeguard appeared to have been infringed, Charles gave an assurance that 'upon the humble petition of the party or address of the judges unto us' he would 'readily and really express the true cause of their commitment'. Finally, he promised 'that in all causes criminal of ordinary jurisdictions, our judges shall proceed to the deliverance or bailment of the prisoner according to the known and ordinary rules of the laws of this land, and according to the statutes of Magna Carta and those other six statutes insisted upon, which we do take knowledge stand in full force, and which we intend not to abrogate or weaken'.[58] What Charles was offering the two Houses, in effect, was the kernel of the Commons' demands without the legislative shell. As long as the royal prerogative remained nominally intact he was prepared to accept a voluntary limitation upon his use of it. The Lords regarded this as a major concession and they asked the Commons to accept the King's letter as a formal record which would be binding upon him. But the Commons were not willing to abandon the Petition. They followed the lead of Sir Thomas Wentworth, who insisted that the King's letter was 'not in a parliamentary way. I doubt not but it is a letter of grace, but the people will only like of that which is done in a parliamentary way'.[59]

The Lords were poised, somewhat unhappily, between the Commons' determination to outlaw the prerogative power to imprison without showing cause and the King's insistence that it must be preserved. They now put forward a compromise, by way of an addition to the Petition of Right which specifically acknowledged the King's prerogative, though in order to avoid rousing passions by the use of this emotive term they rechristened it 'sovereign power'. The wording of their proposed amendment was as follows: 'We present this our humble Petition to Your Majesty not only with a care of preserving our own liberties but with a due regard to leave entire that sovereign power wherewith Your Majesty is trusted for the protection, safety and happiness of your people'.[60] The Commons debated the Lords' proposal but it was evident from the beginning that they would not accept it. Sir Edward Coke gave a clear and forceful exposition of their attitude. 'I know the prerogative is part of the law', he declared, 'but *sovereign power* is no Parliament word in my opinion. It weakens Magna Carta and all other statutes, for they are absolute without any saving of *sovereign power*, and shall we now add it we shall weaken the foundations of law, and then the building must needs fall'.[61]

Since the Commons refused to budge, the Lords were left with the alternatives of either refusing to join with them or accepting the Petition as it stood. Had they chosen not to co-operate they would have undermined the whole purpose of the Commons' action, which was to clarify and strengthen the law, for as Lord Saye commented, 'if we petition by ourselves and they by themselves the Petition will be of no strength'.[62] In the end the Lords decided to support the Commons' initiative but at the same time to inform the King 'that our intention is not to lessen or impeach anything which by the oath of supremacy we have sworn to assist and defend'.[63] The Lords' decision was an indication of the extent to which Charles had lost the confidence of the Upper as well as the Lower House, and it is hardly surprising that Sir Edward Coke, when he announced the decision to the Commons, declared that he was 'almost dead for joy'.[64] There was now no further obstacle in the way of the Petition, and in late May it was presented to the King. Charles took several days to frame his answer, for he needed to consult the judges about the legal status of a petition of right (see p. 135), and he was still determined to preserve his prerogative. On 2 June, therefore, he gave a carefully worded response: 'the King wills that right be done according to the laws and customs of the realm, and that the statutes be put in due execution, that the subject may have no just cause of complaint of any wrong or oppression contrary to their just rights and liberties; to the preservation whereof he holds himself in conscience as well obliged as of his just prerogative'.[65]

This reply did not satisfy the Commons. For one thing it linked the subjects' rights with the preservation of the prerogative, which they regarded as a threat to such rights. And, for another, it committed the King to observance of existing laws but not specifically to the interpretation of them contained in the Petition. However, the major weakness of the reply was its *ad hoc* nature. The customary response to a petition of right was an old-French formula, *Soit droit fait comme est désiré* ('Let right be done as is requested'), and this operated for petitions in much the same way as the royal assent, *Le roy le veult* ('The King wishes it') did for Bills. In other words, if the King had made the traditional reply to the Petition it would have acquired the force of law and been virtually indistinguishable from a statute. By giving it a specially constructed answer he had left it in an uncertain state, neither fish, flesh, nor good red herring.

The Commons believed that this unsatisfactory situation was a further indication of Buckingham's pernicious influence, and no sooner were they back in their chamber than Sir John Eliot renewed the attack upon him. He was supported by Sir Edward Coke, who declared that 'the Duke of Buckingham is the cause of all our miseries' – 'whereupon', according to one account, 'they all cried "It is he!" "It is he!"'.[66] The House decided to draw up a remonstrance against the Duke, and when the King sent a message reminding them that the session was almost at an end and that they should therefore refrain from entering into any new business 'which may spend much time, or lay scandal or aspersions on the state, government, or ministers thereof',[67] they gave vent to their emotions in what one witness described as 'such a spectacle of passions as the like had seldom been seen in such an assembly – some weeping, some expostulating, some prophesying of the fatal ruin of our kingdom'.[68]

Charles was contemplating an immediate dissolution, but the vote of supply which had been agreed in principle at the beginning of the session had not yet been transformed into a Bill, and the King desperately needed the money. He was also presumably concerned to have a harmonious ending to this session, in contrast to those of 1625 and 1626. On 7 June, therefore, he summoned the two Houses before him once again, and instructed the clerk to give the conventional response to the Petition of Right. One of the members present described the effect of this second answer: 'it is not possible for me to express . . . with what joy this was heard, nor what joy it does now cause in all this city, where at this hour they are making bonfires at every door, such as was never seen but upon His Majesty's return from Spain'.[69] The Commons now pushed ahead with the subsidy Bill, but on 12 June, when they gave it a third reading, they also voted to name Buckingham in their remonstrance. They presented this document to Charles a few days later, but it met with a cool reception. 'When I gave answer to your Petition', said the King, 'I did it so fully that I little looked for such a remonstrance . . . I must tell you now that you do not understand so much as I thought you had done'.[70]

Although the subsidy Bill had completed its passage through the Lords, Charles did not bring the session to an immediate close. He may have been hoping that the Commons, by way of showing their gratitude for his acceptance of the Petition of Right, would fulfil what he regarded as their moral obligation to make him a life grant of Tonnage and Poundage. The Commons had at various times considered a Bill for this purpose, but they had not yet agreed on its provisions, nor did they feel able to do so in the closing days of the session. As Sir Edward Coke put it, 'we cannot now, in this short time, make a Book of Rates. We can do nothing'. He was supported by Sir Dudley Digges, who added that 'this difficulty to us comes by prorogation of the Parliament. If it were not a session, there might be somewhat done by commission this summer. Let us petition His Majesty, and show our right, and desire only a recess'.[71]

The Commons followed Digges's lead and drew up a remonstrance in which they stated that while they had 'taken into especial care the preparing of a Bill for the granting of Your Majesty such a subsidy of Tonnage and Poundage as might uphold your profit and revenue in as ample a manner as their just care, and respect of trade . . . would permit . . . they find it not possible to be accomplished at this time'. The implication was that in due course they would make the necessary provision. Meanwhile they requested Charles to refrain from levying these duties, on the grounds that 'the receiving of Tonnage and Poundage and other impositions not granted by Parliament is a breach of the fundamental liberties of this kingdom and contrary to Your Majesty's royal answer to the said Petition of Right'.[72] This stung Charles into action. On 26 June, speaking from the throne, he told the assembled members 'that a second remonstrance is preparing for me, to take away my profit of Tonnage and Poundage (one of the chief maintenances of the crown) . . . This is so prejudicial unto me that I am forced to end this session some few hours before I meant it, being not willing to receive any more remonstrances to which I must give a harsh answer'.[73]

1629. ARMINIANISM AND TONNAGE AND POUNDAGE

Two months after the end of the first session of Charles I's third Parliament, Buckingham was assassinated. This removed one of the major obstacles to harmonious relations between the King and the representatives of his people. It also weakened the war party at Court, and created the possibility of a more peaceful foreign policy, which would relieve the pressure not merely on Charles's finances but also upon the institutions of government and conventions of the constitution, which were breaking under the strain. In the short run, however, Charles needed money, and although there was little chance of obtaining a further vote of supply in a second session, he still hoped to receive a formal grant of Tonnage and Poundage, which would obviate the need for prerogative collection. Even if all went well, Charles would not be any better off in financial terms. The fact that he summoned a second session shows that he was still committed to the 'parliamentary way', still striving to win the affections of his subjects and regain the goodwill which he had been accorded as Prince but had inexplicably lost the moment he ascended the throne. Even before the end of the first session he had mended his fences with the Lords by welcoming to Court those peers whom he had earlier ostracised because of their opposition to his policies, and he informed the Upper House that nothing had been more acceptable to him 'all the time of this Parliament, than this dutiful and discreet proceeding of your lordships'.[74]

Charles did not abandon his patronage of the Arminian wing of the Church of England which so angered and alarmed the Commons: Richard Montagu was made Bishop of Chichester, William Laud was translated from Bath to London, and both Laud and Neile were appointed to the Privy Council. There were indications of a less partisan attitude, however, including the restoration to favour of Archbishop Abbot, who represented the Calvinist majority among the clergy. Charles presumably hoped that this and other actions on his part (see pp. 317–18) would go a long way towards removing Arminianism as a cause of disharmony between him and the Commons, but in fact it had become, and was to remain, a major obstacle. This had been demonstrated in the Commons' remonstrance against Buckingham in 1628, which referred to the 'daily growth and spreading of the factions of the Arminians', and implied a link between 'the undermining of religion and these things tending to an apparent change of government'.[75] A number of members, of whom the most important were John Pym and Sir Nathaniel Rich, put Arminianism at the top of their agenda. Others, like Sir John Eliot and John Selden, were more concerned with the privileges of the Commons and the liberties of the subject (which they regarded as two sides of the same coin). For many people, however, there was no clear-cut distinction between religious and political issues, for the sermons of Mainwaring and Sibthorpe, as well as the actions of Neile and Laud, had convinced them that the Arminians were enemies of both Parliament and the ancient constitution.

The second session of Charles's third Parliament opened in January 1629, and the Commons immediately took up the question of the Petition of Right. The King had agreed that it should not only be included in the Parliament Roll, along with the statutes, but also printed, and this was done before the close of the first session. The printed version ended with the King's second and formal answer, but no sooner had Parliament been adjourned than orders were given in the King's name to withdraw this version and replace it with another. The new version added Charles's first answer, his speech of 7 June in which he stressed that 'you neither mean nor can hurt my prerogative', and his speech at the end of the session which asserted unequivocally that the Petition's outlawing of 'any gift, loan, benevolence, tax, or such like charge without common consent by Act of Parliament' did not affect his right to Tonnage and Poundage.[76] The effect of this new version was to dilute the impact of the Petition. It also ran counter to the Commons' claim in their second remonstrance that the collection of Tonnage and Poundage without their consent was in breach of the Petition. Furthermore, from the Commons' point of view, insult had been added to injury by the action of the Customs' officers in seizing the goods of a number of merchants who refused to pay Tonnage and Poundage, for one of these merchants, John Rolle, happened to be a member of the Lower House.

Shortly after the opening of the session, Charles had made a conciliatory address in which he declared that he was taking Tonnage and Poundage only out of necessity, and that 'it ever was, and still is, my meaning by the gift of my people to enjoy it'.[77] The Commons, in their remonstrance at the end of the first session, had given lack of time as an excuse for not making the grant. They now had another opportunity, and in order to speed them on their way Sir John Coke, on the King's behalf, put forward the draft of a Tonnage and Poundage Bill, and called on the House to give this matter precedence over all other considerations. His appeal was not heeded, however, for the Commons were more concerned with religion. Sir Benjamin Rudyerd, who was by no means a radical, expressed the fear that Arminianism had 'lately crept in and crept up into high places' and that the House should therefore 'consider of the articles of our faith . . . to express what those were, and to advance against all that shall vary from those'.[78] He was supported by Sir Robert Harley, who made the valid point that they needed to know 'what our religion is' and proposed that they should answer this question by making 'an unanimous profession' of their faith.[79] This was done a few days later, when the Commons resolved to 'avow for truth . . . that sense of the Articles of Religion' expounded by 'the public acts of the Church of England and by the general and current expositions of the writers of our Church' and to reject 'the sense of the Jesuits, Arminians, and of all other wherein they differ from it'.[80]

The Commons had now taken it upon themselves to define the religious faith of England – a *de facto* extension of their sphere of competence which was paralleled by an assertion of their right to interpret the law even against the judges. Rolle and a number of other merchants who had had their goods seized for refusing to pay duties on them tried to recover them by a legal process known as *replevin*, but the Court of the Exchequer decided that this was not appropriate for claims against the King. The Commons were dissatisfied with this decision. They insisted, for one thing, that the King was not involved, since the duties in question were Tonnage and Poundage, which had never been granted by Parliament and therefore did not belong to him. They also argued that as the collection of the duties had been leased to the Customs farmers, the officers who had seized the merchants' goods had been acting in a private, not an official, capacity.

John Selden, one of the most distinguished lawyers in the Commons, proposed that they should 'send . . . to the judges of the Exchequer to acquaint them that the parties . . . do affirm that they meant Tonnage and Poundage, which we conceive to be mistaken [i.e. wrongly taken] duties; and therefore to move them to call the said parties before them again . . . [so that] then they may alter their decree; and he doubts not but they will'.[81] The House duly followed Selden's advice, but the Exchequer judges replied that they had not been concerned with the legal status of Tonnage and Poundage. They had merely inhibited 'such suits in other courts as were brought by the owners for *replevin*' on the grounds that this process was 'contrary to the legal prerogative of the King'.[82] Selden was unwilling to accept this explanation of the Exchequer Barons' conduct, and accused them of breaking with precedent. The House agreed with him and adopted his proposal that a committee should be set up 'to examine whether it appear by the records and constant course of that court that what the Court of Exchequer hath done in this business be according to the course of the same'.[83]

While the Commons were asserting a right to judge the judges, they were also pursuing the Customs officers ('Customers') who had actually seized the merchants' goods. These were summoned to the bar of the House and told to account for their action. When they replied that they had been acting 'only as the King's officer[s] and for the King's behalf',[84] Sir Humphrey May, the Chancellor of the Duchy, urged the House to let the matter rest. 'If the Customers shall justify themselves on the King's command', he said, 'and then be punished as delinquents for doing it, then the King . . . might think *actum est de imperio* [i.e. his royal authority is at stake (*lit.* 'it is all up with power')], that he should be no more obeyed'.[85] But the Commons had ceased to defer to the wishes of the Privy Councillors, and looked for guidance to their own spokesmen. In the first session these had included politicians of great ability such as Sir Edward Coke and Sir Thomas Wentworth, who had played a key role in bringing into being the Petition of Right. But old age had at last ended Sir Edward's parliamentary career, while Wentworth had achieved his ambition of entering the King's service and was now not only Lord President of the Council of the North but also a member of the House of Lords. The vacuum left by these figures was filled in large part by Sir John Eliot, who was strong on rhetoric but weak on constructive ideas. It was Eliot who insisted that the Customers had acted on their own responsibility and that the House had a duty to proceed against them. 'He hath heard it [said] here and elsewhere that we should take heed how we proceed', stated Eliot, 'lest we fall on a rock and that there should be a breach of the Parliament'. But he dismissed these warnings as ill grounded, and pronounced 'a curse . . . on those that shall take occasion by this our due proceedings to make or prosecute a breach'.[86]

Eliot insisted that the Customers, despite their denials, had been acting on their own authority, not the King's, but the basis of his position was undermined when Sir John Coke announced that the King had instructed him to state 'that what those men have done they have done by his command' and that 'he will not have us proceed against them, for that he conceiveth it doth highly concern him in point of government'.[87] The Commons were now forced to confront the truth that their quarrel was with the King and not with individuals falsely claiming to be acting in his name. Sir Robert Phelips called for an end to all business for the day, so that they could consider what to do. 'The essential and fundamental liberties of this House is now before us', he declared, and another member added that it was 'not only the privilege of this House [that was] in question, but that the fate of the kingdom is also in the balance'.[88] Any action on the part of the House was pre-empted by Charles, who ordered a five-day adjournment, hoping that tempers would cool. He had by now abandoned hope of receiving a grant of Tonnage and Poundage, and was also aware that the Commons' committee on religion had drawn up resolutions calling for firm measures against the Arminians, which they proposed should be submitted to him. Such resolutions would be far from welcome to Charles and he came to the conclusion that it would be better to put an end to the session rather than let it drag on in a negative and hostile fashion.

When the Commons reassembled on 2 March, the Speaker therefore announced a further adjournment. This had been anticipated by Eliot and his close associates, who had guessed that the adjournment would be followed by a dissolution, giving them no further chance to air their views. They therefore decided to take advantage of a technicality. Whereas the Upper House simply obeyed the royal command to adjourn, the Commons were accustomed to vote their own adjournment, and Eliot intended proposing that on this occasion they should decline to do so until they had passed a number of resolutions setting out their attitude. The Speaker, no doubt forewarned, determined to thwart any such manoeuvre by rising from his chair, thereby putting an end to debate. As he tried to do so, however, he was pushed back by Denzil Holles and Benjamin Valentine. The Privy Councillors came to his aid and an unseemly brawl ensued, in which the Speaker broke free but was again forced back into his chair and held there while Holles recited three resolutions. The first declared that 'whosoever shall bring in innovation of religion, or by favour or countenance seek to extend or introduce popery or Arminianism or other opinion disagreeing from the true and orthodox Church, shall be reputed a capital enemy to the kingdom and commonwealth'. The second condemned anyone who should 'counsel or advise the taking and levying of the subsidies of Tonnage and Poundage, not being granted by Parliament' as a 'capital enemy' and also 'an innovator in the government'; while the third denounced 'any merchant or person whatsoever [that] shall voluntarily yield or pay the said subsidies' as 'a betrayer of the liberties of England and an enemy to the same'.[89]

While Holles was speaking, the King's messenger, Black Rod, was hammering on the doors of the House. They were kept closed against him, however, for the House was still technically in session. It remained so until Holles finished reciting the resolutions and put them to the question. The House responded with shouts of 'Aye', 'Aye', and then, at last, voted to adjourn. When the doors were opened it was not to let Black Rod in but the members out. Eleven years were to pass before they returned.

NOTES AND REFERENCES

(*The place of publication is London, unless otherwise stated*)
1. **The Letters of John Chamberlain** ed. N. E. McClure (Philadelphia 1939). Vol. II, p. 623.
2. **S. R. Gardiner** (ed) *Debates in the House of Commons in 1625* Camden Society (1873), p. 2. (Hereafter Gardiner *1625 Debates*)
3. Gardiner *1625 Debates*, p. 2.
4. Gardiner *1625 Debates*, p. 2.
5. Gardiner *1625 Debates*, p. 1.
6. Gardiner *1625 Debates*, p. 30.
7. Gardiner *1625 Debates*, p. 31.
8. Gardiner *1625 Debates*, p. 56.
9. Gardiner *1625 Debates*, p. 57.
10. **G. W. Prothero** (ed.) *Select Statutes and other Constitutional Documents illustrative of the Reigns of Elizabeth and James I* (Oxford 1913), p. 26.
11. Gardiner *1625 Debates*, p. 3.
12. Gardiner *1625 Debates*, p. 31.
13. Gardiner *1625 Debates*, p. 44.
14. Gardiner *1625 Debates*, p. 78.
15. Gardiner *1625 Debates*, p. 73.
16. Gardiner *1625 Debates*, p. 76.
17. **Sir John Eliot** *An Apology for Socrates and Negotium Posterorum* ed. A. B. Grosart (1881). Vol. II, p. 38. (Hereafter *Negotium Posterorum*)
18. Gardiner *1625 Debates*, p. 131.
19. Gardiner *1625 Debates*, pp. 81–2.
20. *Negotium Posterorum*. Vol. II, p. 56.
21. Gardiner *1625 Debates*, p. 95.
22. Gardiner *1625 Debates*, p. 103.
23. *Negotium Posterorum*. Vol. II, p. 75.
24. Gardiner *1625 Debates*, pp. 106–07.
25. Gardiner *1625 Debates*, p. 109.
26. **John Rushworth** *Historical Collections* (1682). Vol. I, p. 190. (Hereafter Rushworth *Historical Collections*)
27. **Roger Lockyer** *Buckingham: The Life and Political Career of George Villiers, First Duke of Buckingham 1592–1628* (1981), p. 311. (Hereafter Lockyer *Buckingham*)
28. Rushworth *Historical Collections*. Vol. I, p. 215.
29. Lockyer *Buckingham*, p. 313.
30. Lockyer *Buckingham*, p. 313.
31. Lockyer *Buckingham*, p. 316.

32. Lockyer *Buckingham*, p. 321.
33. Rushworth *Historical Collections*. Vol. I, p. 224.
34. Rushworth *Historical Collections*. Vol. I, p. 405.
35. **Robert C. Johnson, Mary Frear Keeler, Maija Jansson Cole &
    William Bidwell** (eds.) *Commons Debates 1628* (New Haven 1977).
    Vol. II, p. 8. (Hereafter *Commons Debates 1628*)
36. *Commons Debates 1628*. Vol. II, p. 59.
37. *Commons Debates 1628*. Vol. II, p. 121.
38. *Commons Debates 1628*. Vol. II, p. 122.
39. *Commons Debates 1628*. Vol. II, p. 65.
40. *Commons Debates 1628*. Vol. II, p. 98.
41. *Commons Debates 1628*. Vol. II, p. 216.
42. *Commons Debates 1628*. Vol. II, p. 302.
43. *Commons Debates 1628*. Vol. II, p. 297.
44. *Commons Debates 1628*. Vol. II, p. 231.
45. *Commons Debates 1628*. Vol. III, pp. 74–5.
46. *Commons Debates 1628*. Vol. III, p. 149.
47. *Commons Debates 1628*. Vol. III, p. 153.
48. *Commons Debates 1628*. Vol. III, p. 150.
49. *Commons Debates 1628*. Vol. III, p. 173.
50. *Commons Debates 1628*. Vol. III, p. 189.
51. *Commons Debates 1628*. Vol. III, p. 211.
52. *Commons Debates 1628*. Vol. III, p. 211.
53. *Commons Debates 1628*. Vol. III, p. 221.
54. *Commons Debates 1628*. Vol. III, p. 254.
55. *Commons Debates 1628*. Vol. III, p. 254.
56. *Commons Debates 1628*. Vol. III, p. 272.
57. *Commons Debates 1628*. Vol. III, p. 372.
58. *Commons Debates 1628*. Vol. III, pp. 372–73.
59. *Commons Debates 1628*. Vol. III, p. 406.
60. *Commons Debates 1628*. Vol. III, p. 452.
61. *Commons Debates 1628*. Vol. III, p. 495.
62. **Mary Frear Keeler, Maija Jansson Cole &** William B. Bidwell
    (eds.) *Lords Proceedings 1628* (New Haven 1983), p. 524. (Hereafter *Lords
    Proceedings 1628*)
63. *Lords Proceedings 1628*, p. 532.
64. *Commons Debates 1628*. Vol. III, p. 614.
65. *Commons Debates 1628*. Vol. IV, p. 52.
66. *Commons Debates 1628*. Vol. IV, p. 115.
67. *Commons Debates 1628*. Vol. IV, p. 118.
68. Lockyer *Buckingham*, p. 439.
69. *Commons Debates 1628*. Vol. IV, p. 182 n.29.
70. *Commons Debates 1628*. Vol. IV, p. 352.
71. *Commons Debates 1628*. Vol. IV, pp. 448–49.
72. Rushworth *Historical Collections*. Vol. I, pp. 629–30.
73. Lockyer *Buckingham*, p. 443.
74. Lockyer *Buckingham*, p. 440.
75. *Commons Debates 1628*. Vol. IV, pp. 313, 315.
76. **E. R. Foster** 'Printing the Petition of Right' *Huntington Library Quart-
    erly*. Vol. 38. 1974–75.

77. **S. R. Gardiner** *History of England from the Accession of James I to the Outbreak of the Civil War 1603–1642* (1884). Vol. VII, p. 33.
78. **Wallace Notestein** & **Frances Relf** (eds.) *The Commons' Debates for 1629* (Minneapolis 1921), p. 116. (Hereafter *1629 Debates*)
79. *1629 Debates*, p. 116. note f.
80. *Journals of the House of Commons 1547–1714* (1742). Vol. I, p. 924.
81. *1629 Debates*, p. 143.
82. *1629 Debates*, p. 147.
83. *1629 Debates*, p. 147.
84. *1629 Debates*, p. 156.
85. *1629 Debates*, p. 158.
86. *1629 Debates*, p. 167.
87. *1629 Debates*, p. 168.
88. *1629 Debates*, pp. 168–69.
89. **S. R. Gardiner** (ed.) *The Constitutional Documents of the Puritan Revolution 1625–1660* (Oxford 1906), pp. 82–3.

CHAPTER FIFTEEN

The Later Parliaments of Charles I 1640–1642

THE SHORT PARLIAMENT

It is hardly surprising, given the manner in which his third Parliament had ended, that Charles was in no haste to summon a fourth. In a proclamation issued shortly after the dissolution he made his feelings plain: 'howsoever we have showed by our frequent meeting with our people our love to the use of parliaments, yet the late abuse having for the present driven us unwillingly out of that course, we shall account it presumption for any to prescribe any time unto us for parliaments, the calling, continuing and dissolving of which is always in our own power'.[1] The Personal Rule showed that it was perfectly possible for Charles to rule without Parliament, and he might have done so indefinitely but for the crisis brought about by the revolt in Scotland and the ensuing Bishops' War. By the beginning of 1640 he was in need of substantial sums of money to prosecute the war, with no obvious means of raising it except through Parliament. As in the opening years of his reign, he was dependent upon the goodwill of his subjects, and when the Houses assembled in April 1640 he called on the members to 'lay aside all other debates' so that they could 'pass an Act for such and so many subsidies as you in your hearty affections to His Majesty and to the common good shall think fit and convenient for so great an action'.[2] If they did so, they could rest assured that he 'would give [them] free scope to present unto him all [their] just grievances, and would hear and give a gracious answer unto them, and himself assist in the redress of them'.[3]

In the subsequent debates the speakers covered ground that was already familiar from earlier parliaments. Sir Benjamin Rudyerd urged the Commons to win the King's confidence – 'trust him, that he may trust us'[4] – while the Lord Keeper reminded the peers that the King's 'honour was at the stake, which was as dear to him as his life, and that he thought that in all civility, as well as necessity, he was first to be trusted'.[5] The Lords responded to this appeal and agreed that supply should have precedence, but the Commons were concerned first of all to put an end to prerogative taxation, and in particular to Ship Money: as Sir Francis Seymour observed, they could not supply the King until they knew what was theirs to give. Yet Seymour added that 'if he had satisfaction for Ship Money he should trust the King with the rest',[6] and this became the basis for a bargain that was made explicit when Sir Henry Vane, Secretary of State, 'brought a declaration from His Majesty, whereby the King promised, upon twelve subsidies presently passed, to be graciously pleased to part with Ship Money, in regard that he perceived that to be the main stop in our passage to his supply'.[7]

However, Ship Money raised just the same problem as Impositions had done in 1610; as one member put it, 'if Ship Money were legal, we were much bound to His Majesty for his gracious offer. But if illegal, he knew no reason to buy it out'.[8] Ship Money, again like Impositions, had a judicial verdict in its favour, but the Commons had long since decided that in these constitutional issues the judges were not to be trusted. Pym described the verdict in Hampden's case as 'judgment without any colour at all of law',[9] and another member pointed out that some of the judges had declared Ship Money to be part of the inalienable prerogative of the crown, so that 'even if there were a thousand Acts of Parliament against [it] they were all void'.[10]

Ship Money was not, of course, the only cause of dissatisfaction. There were also the other financial expedients to which the government had resorted during the previous eleven years, of which the most resented were Distraint of Knighthood and the arbitrary extension of the nominal boundaries of the royal forests (see p. 267). In addition, there were older grievances which were still a source of simmering discontent. Impositions were a running sore, as was Tonnage and Poundage, and the Commons also complained of the 'great inundation of monopolies . . . that lay and leave a burden upon all things in our kingdom'.[11] Moreover, there were continuing fears for the safety of the established Church, given the Arminian inclinations of Charles and Archbishop Laud. Pym complained of 'the introduction of popish ceremonies', not those long-established ones which had been part of the Church of England's post-

Reformation inheritance, but 'the superstitions and infirm ceremonies of the most decrepit age of popery' which had been recently introduced. These included 'the setting up of altars, bowing to them, and the like' as well as 'bowing at the name of Jesus' and 'rising up at the *Gloria Patri*'.[12] Under Pym's guidance the Commons drew up a list of religious grievances, for presentation to the Lords. They were obviously unwilling to rest upon the King's assurance that 'none should be more careful in matters of innovation in religion than himself, and that he would speak to his bishops about it'.[13]

It was almost certainly Pym's reservations about the King's religious inclinations that led him to oppose Charles's attempts to rally popular opinion behind the crown, against the Scots. Pym argued that 'this war with Scotland was of dangerous consequence, and since we were not obliged to maintain a war, he thought as yet we had not proofs enough to engage ourselves and the country'.[14] Pym was already in touch with the leaders of the Scottish rebellion, and hoped to persuade the Commons to give a sympathetic hearing to their claim that they were merely defending the established protestant religion against attempts, on the part of the royal government, to transform it. Pym and his supporters were at work on a petition which Parliament would be asked to approve and which would press the King to acknowledge the validity of the grievances complained of by the Scottish rebels, and to come to terms with them. Charles was unwilling to receive any such petition. He was also unwilling to give the Commons more time to consider the voting of supply, for fear that if he did so they would use it to increase the pressure upon him to make concessions. Some of his advisers, including Thomas Wentworth, now Earl of Strafford, urged him not to take any hasty action, but Charles, with the unhappy experience of his early Parliaments to guide him, feared that delay would merely worsen matters. On 5 May, therefore, he dissolved the Short Parliament after a session that had lasted only three weeks.

THE LONG PARLIAMENT

Edward Hyde – who, as Earl of Clarendon, was to become the historian of the Great Rebellion – had been a member of the Commons and felt deeply depressed that 'in such a time of confusion, so wise a Parliament, which could only have found a remedy for it, was so unseasonably dismissed'. Yet another member, Oliver

St John, 'who had naturally a great cloud in his face and very seldom was known to smile', was unaccustomedly cheerful. When Hyde asked him the reason, St John replied 'that all was well; and that it must be worse before it could be better; and that this Parliament could never have done what was necessary to be done'.[15] St John and those who felt like him had not long to wait for another opportunity, for the ensuing six months demonstrated that if Charles could not rule with Parliament, neither, in the circumstances created by the Scottish invasion of England and occupation of the northern counties, could he rule without it. In November 1640 he was driven to summon the fifth – and, as it turned out, the last – Parliament of his reign. By the time it met there was a general feeling that this was indeed the crisis of parliaments, the final chance to prove that traditional ways of doing things could still work. In the words of Sir Benjamin Rudyerd, 'I have often thought and said that it must be some great extremity that would recover and rectify this state, and when that extremity did come, it would be a great hazard whether it might prove a remedy or ruin. We are now . . . upon that vertical turning point'.[16]

Charles had summoned Parliament because he needed money. He seems to have been hoping, even at this late stage, that his subjects would close ranks behind him and provide the funds which would enable him to drive out the invading Scots. He was soon disillusioned, however, for although attitudes towards the Scots varied, there was no enthusiasm for the 'Bishops' Wars'. Yet if members were not willing to vote subsidies for hostilities, they were obliged, by force of circumstances, to provide sufficient sums to pay both the English and Scottish armies. Charles did not insist, as he had done on earlier occasions, that supply should precede redress of grievances, for defeat in the field had deprived him of any trump cards. The Lower House showed its habitual reluctance to vote supply on a realistic scale. In December it agreed on a grant of two subsidies, but later changed its mind and added another two. Even this was not enough, and in May 1641 the total was brought up to six, which the Speaker presented to the King as 'the tribute due to justice and sovereignty' and as 'the earnests of our vast desires, which take their rise from our due regards for the safety of your throne and of your posterity'.[17] It was estimated that this 'tribute' would yield £300,000, or a mere £50,000 per subsidy – a clear indication of the extent to which the value of the subsidy was continuing to decline.

Although the early Stuart period had seen a steady erosion of the influence of the Privy Councillors over the Commons, the attempts of ministers to focus the attention of members upon specific issues, particularly finance, had helped define the agenda of the House, even if only by way of reaction. In 1640–41, however, the crown was on the defensive, and the direction of events came increasingly from the Lords, where a nucleus of dissident peers, most notably Essex and Saye, concerted strategy along with their relatives, clients and well-wishers in the Commons. John Pym was their principal agent, but he could never take his leadership of the Lower House for granted; this depended on his skill in maintaining a precarious balance between a number of conflicting factions.

Pym was among the minority of members who recognised that the fiscal expedients to which the crown had been driven ever since the closing years of Elizabeth were in large part the consequence of fundamental weaknesses in the royal finances, and that the negative steps of outlawing Ship Money, Impositions, monopolies, etc., would have to be accompanied by more positive measures of recon-struction. His difficulty consisted in persuading the House that this was so. It is significant in this context that Pym was not a county member. He sat for Tavistock, by courtesy of his patron, the Earl of Bedford, but he had none of those deep roots in landed property and provincial society which shaped the beliefs of the majority of his fellow members. They shared his hatred of Roman Catholicism and his antagonism towards the Arminians, whom he regarded as neo-papists; they also shared his determination to rid the King of those 'evil counsellors' who had done so much to undermine the protestant religion and English liberties. But whereas Pym wanted office in order to steer the ship of state on to its rightful course, they had a typically 'Country' distrust of power and those who sought it: in the words of Sir Roger Twysden, who had represented Kent in the Short Parliament, 'what was it to me whether the Earl of Strafford or Mr Pym sat at the helm of government, if their commands carried equal pressure?'.[18]

Sir Thomas Wentworth was a former dissident member of the Commons who had achieved his ambition to attain office and had spent the 1630s ruling Ireland for Charles I. He did this very ef-ficiently, crushing opposition, turning the Irish Parliament into an instrument of government, and building up a reputation for himself as a champion of the royal prerogative. Charles called Wentworth home in late 1639, in order to deal with the Scottish crisis, and subsequently made him Earl of Strafford and a Knight of the Garter. Although it was only at this late stage that Wentworth became the

King's chief minister, he had already inspired fear and hatred among the opponents of prerogative rule, and one of the first actions of the Commons in November 1640 was to impeach him. It was Pym who carried up the impeachment to the Lords and persuaded them to order Strafford's arrest. This formidable figure, who had been planning to take similar action against Pym and his associates, was thereby removed from Charles's counsels, and remained a passive observer of the political scene until his trial in Westminster Hall in March 1641.

Strafford was charged with treason, but this was difficult to substantiate since treason was an offence against the King, and Strafford had been acting not only in the King's name but with his entire approval. Pym therefore developed the theory of 'constructive treason', basing his claim upon the argument that while none of Strafford's actions was treasonable in itself they added up to this heinous offence. 'Other treasons', said Pym, 'are against the rule of the law. This is against the being of the law. It is the law that unites the King and his people, and the author of this treason hath endeavoured to dissolve that union, even to break the mutual, irreversible, indissoluble bond of protection and allegiance whereby they are, and I hope ever will be, bound together'.[19]

Strafford, who conducted his own defence, challenged the whole concept of constructive treason. 'How can that be treason in the whole which is not in any of the parts?', he demanded, and he warned the Lords that if they supported this novel doctrine they would be opening the way to their own destruction.

These gentlemen tell me they speak in defence of the commonweal against my arbitrary laws. Give me leave to say that I speak in defence of the commonweal against their arbitrary treason. For if this latitude be admitted, what prejudice shall follow to the King, to the country, if you and your posterity be disabled by the same from the great affairs of the kingdom? . . . Let me be a Pharos to keep you from shipwreck, and do not put such rocks in your own way.[20]

This appeal was not without its effect. Many peers were worried about the failure of the Commons to prove the charges they had brought against Strafford. While they were willing to condemn him on political grounds, they were not prepared to subvert the law by finding him guilty of 'crimes' which either he had not committed or were not crimes at all. In fact the impeachment proceedings might have ended in Strafford's acquittal had not the Commons decided to drop them and to proceed instead by Act of attainder. This was not Pym's idea – indeed, he initially opposed it – but since there was no other way of ensuring Strafford's removal from the scene he went along with it. The advantage of an Act of attainder was that it declared the guilt of the accused without requiring formal trial; in other words it was more a political than a legal process. Absenteeism had by now reduced the Lower House to about half its nominal membership, and it seems probable that many of those who stayed away were sympathetic to Strafford. In the end, just over 200 members voted in favour of the Bill, fifty-nine against. It then went to the Lords, likewise reduced by absenteeism, where it was passed by twenty-six votes to nineteen. All that was now required was the royal assent, which Charles gave with extreme reluctance and foreboding. On 12 May Strafford was executed on Tower Hill, the first of Charles's ministers to fall before a parliamentary assault.

Strafford's death put an end to whatever possibility there had been of resolving the political crisis by appointments designed to bridge the gap between the King and the 'popular' spokesmen in Parliament. In January 1641 there were reports that the Earl of Bedford, Pym's patron, was to become Lord Treasurer, while Pym himself was to be appointed Chancellor of the Exchequer. They would then be in charge of the King's finances and therefore well placed to carry out a programme of fundamental reform. Other posts in the government, it was said, were to be offered to Lord Saye and Sele, the Earl of Essex and Oliver St John. Some credence was given to these rumours by the appointment of St John as Solicitor General in January, and the admission of Bedford, Essex, Saye and other dissident peers to the Privy Council in February. The bargain, however, if such it was, never came into effect, probably because the King demanded, as a minimum condition, the saving of Strafford's life. This was something that Bedford and Pym could never concede, for had they done so they would have lost their influence in their respective Houses. Essex gave voice to the prevailing mood when he told Edward Hyde, who had suggested punishing Strafford by a heavy fine or a long term of imprisonment, that 'stone dead hath no fellow'.[21] St John expressed the same sentiment when he observed that 'it was never accounted either cruelty or foul play to knock foxes and wolves on the head . . . because they be beasts of prey'.[22] Against such powerful emotions rational calculations were impotent. In any case, the King did not trust his critics and feared that the effect of their policies, whether or not they intended it, would be the overthrow of his monarchy. He was prepared to give Bedford a measure of his confidence, but the last hope of bridging the gap at this stage disappeared with Bedford's death (from natural causes) a few days before Strafford's execution.

Strafford was not the only Councillor of whom the King was deprived. In December 1640 his Secretary of State, Sir Francis Windebank, fled abroad rather than answer Commons' charges that he had shown favour to recusants. Lord Keeper Finch displayed more courage by appearing before the House (where he had sat as Speaker in the turbulent session of 1629) and defending his conduct as one of the principal judges in Hampden's Case. When the Commons voted to impeach him, however, he followed Windebank's example and escaped overseas. The Commons also impeached Archbishop Laud, whom one member described as 'the root and ground of all our miseries'.[23] Laud was committed to the Tower, and the attack upon the policies with which he had been identified was signalled by the presentation to the Commons of a London petition calling not simply for fundamental reform of the Church but also the abolition of episcopacy, 'with all its dependencies, roots and branches'.[24] This was followed by similar petitions from Essex, Kent and elsewhere, and the reaction against Laudianism was expressed more violently in various parts of the country by the pulling-down of altar rails, the removal of communion tables from the chancel to the nave of churches, and the interruption of Prayer-Book services.

The King, fearing for the safety of the Church which he governed, sent for both Houses to attend him in January 1641 and warned them against 'petitions given in, in the names of divers counties, against the present established government, and of the great threatenings against the bishops – that they will make them to be but ciphers, or at least their voices [in Parliament] taken away'. He was not averse to reform, he insisted; indeed, he was prepared to limit the temporal authority of bishops where it was 'inconvenient to the state, and not so necessary for the government of the Church'. But under no circumstances would he 'consent that their voices in Parliament should be taken away. For in all the times of my predecessors, since the Conquest and before, they have enjoyed it, and I am bound to maintain them in it as one of the fundamental constitutions of this kingdom'.[25]

When the Commons debated this question the first signs of a split appeared, between the defenders of episcopacy and those who wished to abolish it. In order to prevent the split from widening, the anti-episcopalians changed their tactics and concentrated on aspects of the bishops' power which were generally unpopular. As a consequence, and in spite of Charles's warning, the Commons passed a Bill banning clergy from secular offices and excluding bishops from the Lords. This created considerable resentment in the Upper House, which saw no reason why the Lower should determine its composition, and the Bill was therefore thrown out. Now it was the turn of the Commons to show resentment, and they gave two readings to a Root and Branch Bill which would have abolished episcopacy. The fact that this was introduced by a moderate, Sir Edward Dering, suggests that many members regarded it merely as a device to browbeat the Lords into accepting the Exclusion Bill, and were not in favour of its primary provisions. Even so, the vote on the second reading was a close one – a further sign of polarisation of opinion within the Commons.

Yet if religion tended to divide the House, there was a consensus on the need to keep parliaments in being and to block any possibility of a return to prerogative rule. William Strode gave expression to a typically 'Country' attitude when he proposed, in December 1640, that the executive power should be restrained by annual parliaments. This was subsequently transformed into the Triennial Bill, which began by asserting that according to 'the laws and statutes of this realm the Parliament ought to be held at least once every year for redress of grievances', and then laid down detailed procedures for ensuring that not more than three years should pass without a Parliament either being summoned or assembling automatically.[26] Charles had always insisted that the summoning and dissolving of Parliament was something that concerned him alone, but he was not prepared to take a stand on this issue, particularly at the moment when Strafford's fate was in the balance. He therefore gave the royal assent in February 1641, and the Triennial Act became law. Perhaps Charles thought it would be of limited duration, for in the course of the next few months he became involved in shadowy dealings with discontented army officers both in London and the north of England who plotted to use force against Parliament. The extent of Charles's involvement is uncertain, but as he surveyed the mobs who swirled round the Palace of Westminster calling for Strafford's death he may well have persuaded himself that the resort to violence had already begun. The so-called Army Plot came to nothing, but rumours about it created an atmosphere of panic in which the two Houses passed a Bill forbidding the dissolution of the existing Parliament without its own consent. This was presented to Charles at the same time as the Bill of attainder against Strafford, and like that Bill, and for the same reasons, it received the royal assent.

Charles was too isolated, at this stage, too much the prisoner of events, to have any viable alternative.

It was awareness of his isolation which induced Charles to accept further limitations upon his prerogative. In June 1641, sixteen years after his accession to the throne, he at last received a parliamentary grant of Tonnage and Poundage, but it was limited to a few months instead of his lifetime, and the Act laid down, contrary to Charles's previous assertions, that 'no subsidy, custom, impost, or any other charge whatsoever ought or may be laid or imposed upon any merchandise exported or imported . . . without common consent in Parliament'.[27] This was followed, a month later, by Acts abolishing High Commission, Star Chamber and the other prerogative courts. In August came Acts declaring Ship Money to be illegal, restoring the boundaries of royal forests to their traditional limits, and prohibiting Distraint of Knighthood. The effect of this legislation was to abolish the absolute prerogative and confirm that England was a limited monarchy in which the King shared power with Parliament and ruled within the guidelines laid down by the common law.

The two Houses had not confined themselves to defining and restating the constitution. They had also dealt with short-term issues, of which the most important was the disbandment of both the English and Scottish armies. The money required to pay off the soldiers was to be raised by a poll tax, estimated to bring in a quarter of a million pounds, and it was hoped that the restoration of internal peace would be accomplished by the autumn. Charles had already announced his intention of paying a visit to his northern kingdom, and he planned to leave London in early August. No doubt he wanted a break from the hothouse atmosphere of Westminster, but he may also have been hoping to win over the Scots and use them, as well as loyal elements within the English army, to strengthen his position. Members of Parliament were alarmed by the implications of the King's journey north. In the Ten Propositions, drawn up by the Commons in June 1641, they urged him to delay his departure until 'some of the business of importance concerning the peace of the kingdom, depending in Parliament, may be despatched'.[28] They also called on the King not only to dismiss evil advisers from his service but to replace them with 'such officers and counsellors as his people and Parliament may have just cause to confide in'. As for the Lord Lieutenants and their deputies, who controlled the military forces of the county communities, they should be 'such as may be faithful and trusty and careful of the peace of the kingdom'.[29]

These Propositions were never formally presented to Charles but their importance consists in the way in which they extended the restraints upon his freedom of action. Ever since he came to the throne, the King had been appealing to the Commons to show their trust in him and depend upon his royal word. It had now become plain that a substantial number of members were deeply distrustful of him and believed it essential that Parliament should nominate, or at least approve, those persons who advised the King and carried out his orders. Only by this means could the theory of unfettered royal rule be made to co-exist with the practice of constitutional government. There were medieval precedents for such restraints – as in the Provisions of Oxford of 1258 – but it could hardly be denied that in more recent times the sovereign had exercised an unchallenged right to choose his own advisers and, through his appointment of Lord Lieutenants, to control the county militias, the only armed forces within the kingdom. If Parliament insisted on removing such a right from Charles, it would lay itself open to the charge of innovation. To date it could claim, with some justification, to have been defending the ancient constitution, but distrust of Charles was now pushing some members into going beyond this, for fear that if they did not do so they would leave it open for the King, at some subsequent stage, to revert to arbitrary rule.

Pym and his associates were among the most committed of these members, but they needed to carry the House with them, and a body consisting for the greater part of conservative country gentlemen was not easy to carry, particularly in the direction of innovation. In this respect the religious issue was of great importance, for it was one which united men whose political attitudes were at variance. Charles's commitment to the Arminians and his soft-line attitude towards the Roman Catholics had alienated many potential supporters, and in May 1641, during the great fear created by rumours of the Army Plot, the Commons had drawn up a Protestation, to be taken by all members, binding each one 'to maintain and defend, as far as lawfully I may, with my life, power and estate, the true reformed religion, expressed in the doctrine of the Church of England, against all popery and popish innovation within this realm'.[30] The Protestation had been Pym's brainchild, and he encouraged its extension to the adult nation as a whole. His fear of Arminianism and popery was long-established and genuine, but he also recognised the value of such a manoeuvre in strengthening his political position both inside and outside Parliament. Indeed, the Protestation provided him with the basis for a much broader appeal to the nation, a Grand Remonstrance listing all the misdeeds for which the royal government had been responsible and calling for further limitations upon the King's freedom of action to ensure that they could never recur.

Pym was at work upon the Grand Remonstrance as the King left London in August 1641. He was also acting as chairman of the committee appointed by the Commons to deal with public business during the parliamentary recess which began in early September. Before members departed from Westminster they appointed a committee for defence, with instructions 'to take into consideration what power will be fit to be placed, and in what persons, for commanding of the trained bands . . . of the kingdom'.[31] This was an implicit claim to control of the militia, already foreshadowed in the Ten Propositions; and it so happened that a means of enforcing it, even against the King's will, was provided by another measure, appointing parliamentary commissioners to keep an eye on the King's activities in Scotland. The Lord Keeper refused to pass this measure under the great seal without specific instructions from Charles, but the King was by now out of London, on his way north. In order to prevent delay, therefore, the Commons decided to accept the assurance of a lawyer member and antiquarian, Simonds D'Ewes, that both Houses, acting together, had the right to issue ordinances which were as valid as statutes. The Lords went along with this, and in late August the first parliamentary ordinance was issued. Before the end of the month three more had been promulgated. The two Houses were quickly becoming accustomed to legislating without either asking or receiving the King's assent.

While fear of Arminianism was a source of support to Pym and his associates, fear of religious anarchy worked in the opposite direction, and the Church seemed to be heading for anarchy as episcopal administration collapsed. Charles had at last realised that his identification with the high-churchmen had alienated the hearts of his subjects. During his stay in Edinburgh he appointed Laud's enemy, John Williams, to be Archbishop of York, and filled a number of vacant bishoprics with middle-of-the-road clergy. At the same time he wrote to the peers, assuring them 'that I am constant to the discipline and doctrine of the Church of England established by Queen Elizabeth and my father, and that I resolve, by the grace of God, to die in the maintenance of it'.[32] This was music in the ears of many members of Parliament, and not simply in the Upper House, for a royalist faction was emerging in the Commons. Pym and his supporters were still determined to press ahead with further reform in both Church and state, and planned to use the Grand Remonstrance to win over parliamentary and public opinion, but their success might have been problematical had it not been for the news which reached London at the beginning of November 1641 that a rebellion had broken out in Ireland, where the catholics were slaughtering the protestants. This seemed to confirm everything that Pym had ever said about popish plots, and he was quick to call attention to the rebels' claim – almost certainly unjustified (see p. 303) – that they were acting on Charles's behalf. As Edward Hyde, a leading member of the royalist faction in the House, later recalled, the popular leaders 'took all occasions . . . to insinuate into the minds of the people that this rebellion in Ireland was contrived or fomented by the King, or at least by the Queen, for the advancement of popery'. This insinuation, he observed, 'made more impression upon the minds of sober and moderate men (and who till then had much more disliked the passionate proceedings of the Parliament) than could be then imagined'.[33]

The two Houses resolved that troops should be sent over from England and Scotland to suppress the Irish rebellion, but this brought to the fore the question of trust, for government was still the King's responsibility, and he had shown himself reluctant to take firm action against catholics during the Personal Rule. Pym had no confidence in Charles, and regarded it as essential to impose further limitations upon his authority. But Pym, as always, had to swing majority opinion in the Commons behind him, and he could only do this by a massive exercise in persuasion. The Grand Remonstrance was his instrument, and in its 204 clauses he built up a formidable indictment of Charles's rule. This provided the justification for the demand that the King should only 'employ such Councillors . . . and. other ministers in managing his business . . . as the Parliament may have cause to confide in'.[34] There was no specific mention of the militia, even though command of the armed forces was a controversial and highly pertinent issue, nor was there any commitment to Root and Branch reform in the Church. The bishops were to be deprived of the 'exorbitant power' which they had 'assumed unto themselves', but the Remonstrance disclaimed any intention 'to let loose the golden reins of discipline and government in the Church' or 'to leave private persons or particular congregations to take up what form of divine service they please'. The future shape of the Church was to be determined by Parliament, but only after the whole question had been examined by 'a general synod of the most grave, pious, learned and judicious divines'.[35]

The Grand Remonstrance, then, was strong on rhetoric but weak on specific proposals, for Pym calculated that this was the best way in which to win over moderates and waverers. Those who opposed the Remonstrance did so because it implied much more than it stated.

There were many members of the Commons who had welcomed the action taken by Parliament during its first ten months, for this had removed what they regarded as the cancerous growths of Arminianism in the Church and arbitrary government in the state, but now that the old order had been restored they wanted no further change. They might have reservations about Charles's trustworthiness, but he had accepted the legislation which outlawed his former actions and they worked on the assumption that this would prevent him from ruling in an unacceptable fashion in future even if he wanted to do so. Whatever the dangers of trusting him, they were infinitely less, in their eyes, than those of innovation.

The debates on the Grand Remonstrance, which began at noon on 22 November 1641 and lasted until the early hours of the following morning, pitted 'conservatives' against 'radicals', those who believed (in Wentworth's phrase) in 'running in the worn, wonted channels' and 'treading the ancient bounds'[36] now that these had been restored, against those who were convinced of the need to go beyond the old boundaries in order to ensure that their restoration was permanent. Had Charles been suddenly removed from the scene the number of radicals would no doubt have diminished considerably. As it was, the radicals consisted essentially of those who were not prepared to trust him. In the event the radicals won, for the Remonstrance was carried by 159 votes to 148, a majority of eleven, but the closeness of the result showed that the House of Commons, like the country as a whole, was split down the middle.

Up to this point, Charles had been a relatively isolated figure, with few supporters. Now, however, by distancing himself from innovation and emerging as the defender of the constitution, 'the keystone' (again in Wentworth's phrase) 'which closeth up the arch of order and government [and] contains each part in due relation to the whole',[37] he had won back the allegiance of many of his subjects. Charles's self-confidence had been restored by the warmth of his welcome as he journeyed from London to Scotland and back again, and by his triumphal re-entry into the capital in late November 1641. On the first day of the new year he attempted to bridge the gap between him and his critics by offering the Chancellorship of the Exchequer to Pym, and when that initiative failed he gave the post to the moderate Sir John Colepeper. Another moderate, Lord Falkland, a close friend of Hyde, was made Secretary of State.

Charles's confidence was reinforced by the strengthening of his position in the House of Lords. Secretary Nicholas had been active in building up a 'royalist' group of lay peers which, in concert with the 26 bishops, exerted a powerful and sometimes dominant influence. The dissident peers had reacted by prompting their allies in the Commons to renew their demand for the bishops to be excluded from Parliament, and a Bill to this effect had passed the Lower House in October 1641. The Lords delayed consideration of it, but later that year they came under pressure from the mob swirling around Westminster. The bishops, who were at greatest risk, kept away from the Lords, but twelve of them signed a protest denying the validity of any legislation passed during their enforced absence. Pym persuaded the Commons to impeach the signatories, and the Lords ordered them to be imprisoned. These developments threatened to undermine the entire royalist position in the Upper House, and Charles determined on a pre-emptive counter-strike. On 3 January 1642 his Attorney General appeared before the Lords and accused one peer (Mandeville) and five members of the Commons (Pym, Hampden, Hazelrig, Holles and Strode) of treason. He demanded their immediate arrest, but the Lords declined to comply. On the next day, therefore, Charles went in person to the Commons, accompanied by some four hundred men, many of them armed. Taking his stand before the Speaker's chair he declared once again that 'no King that ever was in England shall be more careful of your privileges . . . than I shall be', but added that 'in cases of treason no person hath a privilege'.[38] He called for the accused members to be handed over, but they had already made their escape to the City, where the radicals had just come to power (see p. 10). Charles's attempted *coup* had failed, and a week later he left London for good.

Civil war was not inevitable, even now. As the King made his way north to York he was clearly contemplating resistance to the demand for further concessions, but although the gentry who turned out to welcome him professed their loyalty, they were thinking in terms of a peaceful settlement, not recourse to arms. The same message came in the petitions that flooded into Parliament from all over the country. These showed how well the Grand Remonstrance had done its task, for they called for the removal of evil counsellors, the reform of the Church, and the suppression of popery. They also showed a concern for strengthening the defences of the country, but there was no indication that this was directed against the King. Charles's subjects were still loyal to him. It was the idea of a 'popish plot' to subvert the English Church and English liberties that appalled and frightened them. Parliament voted to put the kingdom 'in a posture of defence' against this menace, and passed an ordinance appointing new Lord Lieutenants with authority to use the militia 'for the suppression of all rebellions, insurrections and invasions'.[39] Charles was not intransigent. He accepted the Bill excluding bishops from the Lords, in spite of his declared determination not to do so, and he offered to share control of the militia with the two Houses for a twelvemonth period. He would not, however, abandon his rights altogether, and since Parliament refused to withdraw the Militia Ordinance he countered it by sending Commissions of Array to named persons in every county, authorising them to organise and control the trained bands.

If Charles had stayed in London he could have kept in close touch with his supporters in both Houses and recovered much of the ground he had lost by his precipitate action over the Five Members. In his absence, the initiative was seized by the parliamentary leaders, and it was they who, in June 1642, announced their terms for settlement, the Nineteen Propositions. This was an uncompromising document, drawn up on the assumption that public opinion was so strongly set against Charles that he would have no option but to give way. Although government was to remain nominally the King's, in practice it was to be carried out by Privy Councillors appointed by and responsible to Parliament. The militia was to be under parliamentary control, as were, in effect, the judges, and Charles was asked to agree 'that such a reformation be made of the Church government and liturgy as both Houses of Parliament shall advise'.[40]

In his reply to the Nineteen Propositions, which was drafted by Falkland and Colepeper, Charles insisted that 'in this kingdom the laws are jointly made by a King, by a House of Peers, and by a House of Commons chosen by the people'. The three elements of monarchy, aristocracy and democracy, so skilfully balanced one against another, provided the only certain guarantee of order and liberty. The Propositions, he declared, amounted to 'a total subversion of the fundamental laws and that excellent constitution of this kingdom which hath made this nation so many years both famous and happy'. If he were to accept them he would open the way to anarchy, for once monarchical authority was overthrown, the common people would 'set up for themselves' and swiftly 'devour that estate which had devoured the rest'. All property rights, all

The Early Stuarts

'distinctions of families and merit' would be consumed in mob violence, and the present 'splendid and excellently distinguished form of government' would come to an end 'in a dark, equal chaos of confusion, and the long line of our many noble ancestors in a Jack Cade or a Wat Tyler'.[41]

It was a powerful reply, but it was aimed at the nation in general rather than the two Houses, for the Nineteen Propositions had confirmed Charles in his belief that Parliament was now controlled by men who were out to destroy not him alone but the monarchy and the constitution. The only way to prevent this happening was by meeting force with force. On 22 August 1642, therefore, Charles raised his standard on the top of Castle Hill in Nottingham.

NOTES AND REFERENCES

(The place of publication is London, unless otherwise stated)
1. **James F. Larkin** (ed.) *Stuart Royal Proclamations.* Vol. II. *Royal Proclamations of King Charles I 1625–1646* (Oxford 1983), p. 227–28.
2. **Esther S. Cope** & **Willson H. Coates** (eds.) *Proceedings of the Short Parliament of 1640.* Royal Historical Society (1977), p. 120. (Hereafter *Short Parliament*)
3. *Short Parliament*, p. 165.
4. *Short Parliament*, p. 170.
5. *Short Parliament*, p. 176.
6. *Short Parliament*, p. 189.
7. *Short Parliament*, p. 193.
8. *Short Parliament*, p. 194.
9. *Short Parliament*, p. 153.
10. *Short Parliament*, p. 196.
11. *Short Parliament*, p. 153.
12. *Short Parliament*, p. 151.
13. *Short Parliament*, p. 177.
14. *Short Parliament*, p. 190.
15. **Edward, Earl of Clarendon** *The History of the Rebellion and Civil Wars in England* ed. W. Dunn Macray (Oxford 1888). Vol. II, p. 79. (Hereafter Clarendon *History of the Rebellion*)
16. **John Rushworth** *Historical Collections* (1682). Vol. IV, p. 25. (Hereafter Rushworth *Historical Collections*)
17. Rushworth *Historical Collections*. Vol. IV, p. 274.
18. **Anthony Fletcher** *The Outbreak of the English Civil War* (1981), p. 40.
19. **J. P. Kenyon** (ed.) *The Stuart Constitution 1602–1688* 2nd edn (Cambridge 1986), p. 192. (Hereafter Kenyon *Stuart Constitution*)
20. Kenyon *Stuart Constitution*, pp. 194–95.
21. Clarendon *History of the Rebellion*. Vol. I, p. 320.

370

22. **C. V. Wedgwood** *Thomas Wentworth, First Earl of Strafford 1593–1641: A Revaluation* (1962), p. 370.
23. **S. R. Gardiner** *History of England from the Accession of James I to the Outbreak of the Civil War 1603–1642* (1884). Vol. IX, p. 249. (Hereafter Gardiner *History of England*)
24. **S. R. Gardiner** (ed.) *The Constitutional Documents of the Puritan Revolution 1625–1660* (Oxford 1906), p. 138. (Hereafter Gardiner *Constitutional Documents*)
25. Rushworth *Historical Collections*. Vol. IV, p. 155.
26. Kenyon *Stuart Constitution*, p. 197.
27. Gardiner *Constitutional Documents*, p. 160.
28. Gardiner *Constitutional Documents*, p. 163.
29. Gardiner *Constitutional Documents*, p. 164–65.
30. Kenyon *Stuart Constitution*, p. 200.
31. Gardiner *History of England*. Vol. X, p. 2.
32. Gardiner *History of England*. Vol. X, p. 39.
33. Clarendon *History of the Rebellion*. Vol. IV, p. 31.
34. Gardiner *Constitutional Documents*, p. 231.
35. Gardiner *Constitutional Documents*, p. 229.
36. Kenyon *Stuart Constitution*, p. 16.
37. Kenyon *Stuart Constitution*, p. 16.
38. Gardiner *History of England*. Vol. X, p. 139.
39. Gardiner *History of England*. Vol. X, p. 171.
40. Kenyon *Stuart Constitution*, p. 224.
41. Kenyon *Stuart Constitution*, pp. 18–20.

Appendix: Lists of Principal Office-holders

LORD CHANCELLORS AND KEEPERS OF THE GREAT SEAL

1603. Sir Thomas Egerton, Baron Ellesmere (1603), Viscount Brackley (1616). First appointed Lord Keeper by Elizabeth I in 1596. Reappointed by James I. Created Lord Chancellor July 1603.

1617. Sir Francis Bacon, Baron Verulam (1618), Viscount St. Alban (1621). Lord Keeper. Created Lord Chancellor January 1618.

1621. John Williams, Bishop of Lincoln 1621–41, Archbishop of York 1641–50. Lord Keeper. Reappointed by Charles I at his accession.

1625. Sir Thomas Coventry, Baron Coventry (1628). Lord Keeper.

1640. Sir John Finch, Baron Finch (1640). Lord Keeper.

1641. Sir Edward Littleton, Baron Littleton (1641). Lord Keeper.

KEEPERS OF THE PRIVY SEAL

1603. Sir Robert Cecil, Baron Cecil (1603), Viscount Cranborne (1604), Earl of Salisbury (1605).

1608. Henry Howard, Earl of Northampton (1604).

1614. Robert Carr, Viscount Rochester (1611), Earl of Somerset (1613).

1616. Edward Somerset, ninth Earl of Worcester.

1628 (March). Sir John Coke.

1628 (May). Sir Robert Naunton.

1628 (July).   Sir Henry Montagu, Viscount Mandeville (1620), Earl of Manchester (1626).

LORD TREASURERS

1603.   Sir Thomas Sackville, Baron Buckhurst (1567), Earl of Dorset (1604). First appointed by Elizabeth I in 1599. Reappointed by James I.

1608.   Sir Robert Cecil, Baron Cecil (1603), Viscount Cranborne (1604), Earl of Salisbury (1605).

1612.   In commission.

1614.   Sir Thomas Howard, Lord Howard de Walden (1597), Earl of Suffolk (1603).

1618.   In commission.

1620.   Sir Henry Montagu, Viscount Mandeville (1620), Earl of Manchester (1626).

1621.   Sir Lionel Cranfield, Baron Cranfield (1621), Earl of Middlesex (1622).

1624.   Sir James Ley, Baron Ley (1624), Earl of Marlborough (1626).

1628.   Sir Richard Weston, Baron Weston (1628), Earl of Portland (1633).

1635.   In commission.

1636.   William Juxon, Bishop of London (1633–60), Archbishop of Canterbury (1660–1663).

1641.   In commission.

CHANCELLORS OF THE EXCHEQUER

1603.   Sir George Home, Baron Home (1604), Earl of Dunbar (1605).

1606.   Sir Julius Caesar.

1614.   Sir Fulke Greville, Baron Brooke (1621).

1621.   Sir Richard Weston, Baron Weston (1628), Earl of Portland (1633).

1628.   Sir Edward Barrett, Lord Barrett of Newburgh (1627).

1629.   Sir Francis Cottington, Baron Cottington (1631).

1642.   Sir John Colepeper, Baron Colepeper (1644).

SECRETARIES OF STATE

1603. Sir Robert Cecil, Baron Cecil (1603), Viscount Cranborne (1604), Earl of Salisbury (1605). First appointed by Elizabeth I in 1596. Reappointed by James I.

1612. Robert Carr, Viscount Rochester (1611), Earl of Somerset (1613).

1614. Sir Ralph Winwood.

1618. Sir Robert Naunton.

1623. Sir Edward Conway, Baron Conway (1625), Viscount Conway (1627).

1628. Sir Dudley Carleton, Baron Carleton (1626), Viscount Dorchester (1628).

1632. Sir Francis Windebanke.

1641. Sir Edward Nicholas.

1603. Sir John Herbert. First appointed by Elizabeth I in 1600. Reappointed by James I.

1616. Sir Thomas Lake.

1619. Sir George Calvert, Baron Baltimore (1625).

1625 (Feb) Sir Albertus Morton.
1625 (Sept) Sir John Coke.

1640. Sir Henry Vane the elder.

1642. Lucius Carey, second Viscount Falkland.

CHANCELLORS OF THE DUCHY OF LANCASTER

1603. Sir John Fortescue. First appointed by Elizabeth I in 1601. Reappointed by James I.
1607. Sir Thomas Parry.

1616.   Sir John Dacombe.
1618.   Sir Humphrey May.
1629.   Sir Edward Barrett, Lord Barrett of Newburgh (1627).

TREASURERS OF THE HOUSEHOLD

1603.   Sir William Knollys, Baron Knollys (1603), Viscount Wall-
        ingford (1616), Earl of Banbury (1626). First appointed by
        Elizabeth I in 1600. Reappointed by James I.
1616.   Sir Edward Wotton, Baron Wotton (1603).
1618.   Sir Thomas Edmondes.
1639.   Sir Henry Vane the elder.
1641.   Sir Thomas Savile, Viscount Savile (1628), Earl of Sussex
        (1644).

ATTORNEY GENERALS

1603.   Sir Edward Coke. First appointed by Elizabeth I in 1593.
        Reappointed by James I.
1606.   Sir Henry Hobart.
1613.   Sir Francis Bacon.
1617.   Sir Henry Yelverton.
1621.   Sir Thomas Coventry.
1625.   Sir Robert Heath.
1631.   William Noy.
1634.   Sir John Bankes.
1641.   Sir Edward Herbert.

SOLICITOR GENERALS

1603.   Sir Thomas Fleming. First appointed by Elizabeth I in 1595.
        Reappointed by James I.
1604.   Sir John Doddridge.
1607.   Sir Francis Bacon.
1613.   Sir Henry Yelverton.
1617.   Sir Thomas Coventry.

1621. Sir Robert Heath.
1625. Sir Richard Shelton.
1634. Sir Edward Littleton.
1640. Sir Edward Herbert.
1641. ·Oliver St. John.

CHIEF JUSTICES OF THE KING'S BENCH

1603. Sir John Popham. First appointed by Elizabeth I in 1592. Reappointed by James I.
1607. Sir Thomas Fleming.
1613. Sir Edward Coke.
1616. Sir Henry Montagu.
1622. Sir James Ley.
1625. Sir Ranulphe Crewe. Removed from office November 1626.
1626. (Sir John Davies. Died before taking up office).
1627. Sir Nicholas Hyde.
1631. Sir Thomas Richardson.
1635. Sir John Bramston.
1642. Sir Robert Heath.

CHIEF JUSTICES OF THE COMMON PLEAS

1603. Sir Edmund Anderson. First appointed by Elizabeth I in 1582. Reappointed by James I.
1605. Sir Francis Gawdy.
1606. Sir Edward Coke.
1613. Sir Henry Hobart.
1626. Sir Thomas Richardson.
1631. Sir Robert Heath.
1634. Sir John Finch.
1640. Sir Edward Littleton.
1641. Sir John Bankes.

CHIEF BARONS OF THE EXCHEQUER

1603. Sir William Peryam. First appointed by Elizabeth I in 1593.
       Reappointed by James I.
1604. Sir Thomas Fleming.
1607. Sir Lawrence Tanfield.
1625. Sir John Walter. Suspended from office October 1630.
1631. Sir Humphrey Davenport.

Further Reading

The suggestions for further reading made below refer only to secondary works. Primary sources are listed in the Notes to each chapter. The place of publication is London, unless otherwise stated.

The best general guide to published work on this period is MARY FREAR KEELER (ed.) *Bibliography of British History. Stuart Period, 1603–1714* 2nd edn (Oxford 1970). A more recent guide, shorter but very useful, is J. S. ̓MORRILL *Seventeenth-Century Britain* (Folkestone 1980).

J. R. TANNER (ed.) *Constitutional Documents of the Reign of James I* (Cambridge 1930), is still valuable, though increasingly outdated. Two other collections of documents, though without commentary, are G. W. PROTHERO (ed.) *Select Statutes and other Constitutional Documents illustrative of the Reigns of Elizabeth and James I* (Oxford 1913) and S. R. GARDINER (ed.) *The Constitutional Documents of the Puritan Revolution 1625–1660* (Oxford 1906). The best modern collection, with a commentary, is J. P. KENYON (ed.) *The Stuart Constitution 1603–1688* 2nd edn (Cambridge 1986). The earlier volume in this series, G. R. ELTON (ed.) *The Tudor Constitution* 2nd edn (Cambridge 1982), also contains much of relevance in its commentary.

S. R. GARDINER's majestic ten-volume *History of England from the Accession of James I to the Outbreak of the Civil War 1603–1642* (1884) is still indispensable. Of more recent, smaller-scale works, BARRY COWARD *The Stuart Age* (1980) is particularly good.

THE ECONOMIC BACKGROUND

There are a number of general accounts of the English economy during the early modern period. These include D. C. COLEMAN *The Economy of England 1450–1750* (Oxford 1977); CHARLES WILSON *England's Apprenticeship 1603–1763* (2nd edn 1984); and C. G. A. CLAY *Economic Expansion and Social Change: England 1500–1700* (Cambridge 1984). Among those which focus on specific topics are D. C. COLEMAN *Industry in Tudor and Stuart England* (1975); RALPH DAVIS *English Overseas Trade 1500–1700* (1973); G. D. RAMSAY *The English Woollen Industry 1500–1750* (1982); JOAN THIRSK *Economic Policy and Projects: The Development of a Consumer Society* (Oxford 1978); and B. E. SUPPLE *Commercial Crisis and Change in England 1600–1642* (Cambridge 1959). BRIAN DIETZ 'England's Overseas Trade in the Reign of James I' in ALAN G.R. SMITH (ed.) *The Reign of James VI and I* (1973) is a useful summary.

The best account of English agriculture during this period is given in *The Agrarian History of England and Wales* Vol. IV. *1500–1640* (Cambridge 1967) edited by JOAN THIRSK. A useful supplement is JOAN THIRSK *England's Agricultural Regions and Agrarian History 1500–1750* (1987). Rural unrest is dealt with in E. F. GAY 'The Midland Revolt and the Inquisitions of Depopulation of 1607' *Transactions of the Royal Historical Society* new series Vol. 18 (1904); D. G. C. ALLAN 'The Rising in the West 1628–1631' *Economic History Review* 2nd series Vol. 5 (1952); BUCHANAN SHARP *In Contempt of All Authority: Rural Artisans and Riot in the West of England 1586–1660* (Berkeley 1980); KEITH LINDLEY *Fenland Riots and the English Revolution* (1982); and DAVID UNDERDOWN *Revel, Riot and Rebellion: Popular Politics and Culture in England 1603–1660* (Oxford 1985).

The standard work on English demography is now E. A. WRIGLEY & R. S. SCHOFIELD *The Population History of England 1541–1871. A Reconstruction* (1981).

N. G. BRETT-JAMES *The Growth of Stuart London* (1935) is still valuable. Among many more recent works is A. K. BEIER & ROGER FINLAY *London 1500–1700. The Making of the Metropolis* (1986). Four important articles are F. J. FISHER 'The Development of London as a Centre of Conspicuous Consumption in the Sixteenth and Seventeenth Centuries' *Transactions of the Royal Historical Society* 4th series Vol. 30 (1948); ROBERT BRENNER 'The Civil War Politics of London's Merchant Community' *Past & Present* No. 58 (1973); R. G. LANG 'Social Origins and Social Aspirations of Jacobean London Merchants' *Economic History Review* 2nd series Vol. 27 (1974); and

VALERIE PEARL 'Social Policy in Early Modern London' in HUGH LLOYD-JONES, VALERIE PEARL & BLAIR WORDEN (eds.) *History and Imagination* (1981). Relations between the City and the royal government are scrutinised in VALERIE PEARL *London on the Outbreak of the Puritan Revolution: City Government and National Politics 1625–1643* (1961) and ROBERT ASHTON *The City and the Court 1603–1642* (Cambridge 1979). A great deal of information about aristocratic property developers is to be found in two books by LAWRENCE STONE: *The Crisis of the Aristocracy 1558–1641* (Oxford 1965) and *Family and Fortune: Studies in Aristocratic Finance in the Sixteenth and Seventeenth Centuries* (Oxford 1973).

FOREIGN POLICY

There is no satisfactory single-volume study of English foreign policy under the early Stuarts. In many ways the best source on this as on so many other topics is still S. R. GARDINER's *History* (see above).

A useful antidote to the popular belief that James I was an unwitting tool of the Spaniards is C. H. CARTER 'Gondomar: Ambassador to James I' *Historical Journal* Vol. 7 (1964).

Anglo-French relations in the early years of James I's reign are dealt with by MAURICE LEE in *James I and Henri IV: An Essay in English Foreign Policy 1603–10* (Urbana 1970). Subsequent developments are analysed in SIMON ADAMS 'The Road to La Rochelle: English Foreign Policy and the Huguenots 1610–1629' *Proceedings of the Huguenot Society of London* Vol. XXII (1975); ROGER LOCKYER *Buckingham: The Life and Political Career of George Villiers, First Duke of Buckingham 1592–1628* (1981); and R. M. SMUTS 'The Puritan Followers of Henrietta Maria in the 1630s' *English Historical Review* Vol. 93 (1978). Also relevant is ALBERT J. LOOMIE 'The Spanish Faction at the Court of Charles I 1630–38' *Bulletin of the Institute of Historical Research* Vol. 59 (1986).

Three useful studies of parliamentary attitudes towards foreign policy are SIMON ADAMS 'Foreign Policy and the Parliaments of 1621 and 1624' in KEVIN SHARPE (ed.) *Faction and Parliament* (Oxford 1978); R. E. RUIGH *The Parliament of 1624: Politics and Foreign Policy* (Cambridge, Mass. 1971); and THOMAS COGSWELL 'Foreign Policy and Parliament: the Case of La Rochelle 1625–1626' *English Historical Review* Vol. 99 (1984). SIMON ADAMS 'Spain or the Netherlands? The

Dilemmas of Early Stuart Foreign Policy' in HOWARD TOMLINSON (ed.) *Before the Civil War* (1983) is a good introduction to a major but neglected theme.

CONSTITUTIONAL IDEAS AND ASSUMPTIONS

Three indispensable studies of constitutional ideas during this period are F. D. WORMUTH *The Royal Prerogative 1603–1649* (1939); M. A. JUDSON *The Crisis of the Constitution: An Essay in Constitutional and Political Thought 1603–1645* (New Brunswick 1949); and J. G. A. POCOCK *The Ancient Constitution and the Feudal Law* (Cambridge 1957). There is much to be gleaned also from FAITH THOMPSON *Magna Carta: Its Role in the Making of the English Constitution 1300–1629* (Oxford 1948). An important recent study is J. P. SOMER-VILLE *Politics and Ideology in England 1603–1640* (1986). ALAN G. R. SMITH'S 'Constitutional Ideas and Parliamentary Developments in England 1603–25' in the volume of essays edited by him, *The Reign of James VI and I* (1973), is a good introduction to the subject.

DAVID WOOTTON (ed.) *Divine Right and Democracy* (1986) is a useful anthology of political writing in Stuart England.

The best general account of political thinking in the early modern period is now QUENTIN SKINNER *The Foundations of Modern Political Thought*. Vol. 2. *The Age of Reformation* (Cambridge 1978).

W. J. JONES *Politics and the Bench* (1971) considers the political role of the judges. He also has an essay on 'The Crown and the Courts in England 1603–25' in ALAN G. R. SMITH (ed.) *The Reign of James VI and I* (1973). The judges' administrative functions are dealt with in J. S. COCKBURN *A History of English Assizes 1558–1714* (Cambridge 1972). One particular judge is the subject of L. A. KNAFLA *Law and Politics in Jacobean England: The Tracts of Lord Chancellor Ellesmere* (Cambridge 1977) and of W. J. JONES 'Ellesmere and Politics 1603–17' in HOWARD S. REINMUTH (ed.) *Early Stuart Studies* (Minneapolis 1970). There is no adequate biography of Sir Edward Coke, but the Selden Society lecture by S. E. THORNE *Sir Edward Coke 1552–1952* (1957) is an illuminating sketch. More substantial is C. GRAY 'Reason, Authority and Imagination' in P. ZAGORIN (ed.) *Culture and Revolution* (Berkeley 1980). ROLAND G. USHER 'James I and Sir Edward Coke' *English Historical Review* Vol. 18 (1903) is still of interest. STEPHEN D. WHITE *Sir Edward Coke and the Grievances of the Commonwealth* (Manchester 1979) is mainly concerned with Coke's role in Parliament. Relations between Coke and Ellesmere are the subject of J. P. DAWSON 'Coke and Ellesmere Disinterred: The Attack on the Chancery in 1616' *Illinois Law Review* Vol. 36 (1941). Also relevant are WILLIAM EPSTEIN 'Issues of Principle in the Controversy over Prohibitions to Ecclesiastical Courts in England' *Journal of Legal History* Vol. I (1980), and G. W. THOMAS 'James I, Equity and Lord Keeper John Williams' *English Historical Review* Vol. 91 (1976).

Studies of English law in this period include R. J. TERRILL 'William Lambarde: Elizabethan Humanist and Legal Historian', and C. P. RODGERS 'Humanism, History and the Common Law', both in *Journal of Legal History* Vol. 6 (1985). The relationship between law and the constitution is considered in C. H. MCILWAIN 'The English Common Law, Barrier against Absolutism' *American Historical Review* Vol. 49 (1944); CHRISTOPHER BROOKS & KEVIN SHARPE 'History, English Law and the Renaissance' *Past & Present* No. 72 (1976); HANS S. PAWLISCH 'Sir John Davies, the Ancient Constitution, and Civil Law' *Historical Journal* Vol. 13 (1980); MARTYN P. THOMPSON 'The History of Fundamental Law' *American Historical Review* Vol. 91 (1986) and David S. Berkowitz 'Reason of State in England and the Petition of Right' in Roman Schnur (ed.) *Staatsrason; Studien zur Geschichte eines politischen Begriffs* (Berlin 1980). RICHARD TUCK *Natural Rights Theories* (Cambridge 1979) has much of interest to say about Selden, as does his article '"The Ancient Law of Freedom": John Selden and the Civil War' in JOHN MORRILL (ed.) *Reactions to the English Civil War 1642–1649* (1982).

The meaning of 'absolutism' is considered in two articles by JAMES DALY: 'The Idea of Absolute Monarchy in Seventeenth-Century England' *Historical Journal* Vol. 21 (1970) and 'Cosmic Harmony and Political Thinking in Early Stuart England' *Transactions of the American Philosophical Society* Vol. 69, Part 7 (Philadelphia 1979). S. B. CHRIMES discusses 'The Constitutional Ideas of Dr John Cowell' in *English Historical Review* Vol. 64 (1949), while ROLAND USHER summarises the importance of 'Nicholas Fuller: A Forgotten Exponent of English Liberty' in *American Historical Review* Vol. 12 (1906–07). 'Impositions and the Courts 1554–1606' is the theme of G. D. H. HALL in *Law Quarterly Review* Vol. 69 (1953). The most comprehensive study of Jacobean proclamations is R. W. HEINZE 'Proclamations and Parliamentary Protest 1539–1610' in DELLOYD J. GUTH & J. W. MCKENNA (eds.) *Tudor Rule and Revolution* (Cambridge 1983).

The contrast between the English experience and that of other countries is considered in J. P. COOPER 'Differences between English

and Continental Governments in the early Seventeenth Century' in
J. S. BROMLEY & E. H. KOSSMANN (eds.) *Britain and the Netherlands*
(1960); J. H. ELLIOTT 'England and Europe: A Common Malady?' in
CONRAD RUSSELL (ed.) *The Origins of the English Civil War* (1973); and
CONRAD RUSSELL 'Monarchies, Wars and Estates in England, France
and Spain c. 1580–c. 1640' in *Legislative Studies Quarterly* Vol. 7
(1982).

Star Chamber in this period still awaits a full-scale treatment, but
there are three valuable articles by T. G. BARNES: 'Due Process and
Slow Process in the late-Elizabethan and early-Stuart Star Chamber'
American Journal of Legal History Vol. 6 (1962); 'A Cheshire Seduc-
tress, Precedent, and a "Sore Blow" to Star Chamber' in MORRIS S.
ARNOLD (ed.) *On the Laws and Customs of England* (Chapel Hill 1981);
and 'Star Chamber Litigants and their Counsel 1596–1641' in J. H.
BAKER (ed.) *Legal Records and the Historian* (Royal Historical Society
1978). Also relevant is H. E. I PHILLIPS 'The Last Years of the Court
of Star Chamber' *Transactions of the Royal Historical Society* 4th series
Vol. 21 (1939). PENRY WILLIAMS discusses another prerogative court
in 'The Activity of the Council in the Marches under the Early
Stuarts' *Welsh History Review* Vol. I (1961).

There is little or nothing available on the Church courts, but B. P.
LEVACK *The Civil Lawyers in England 1603–1641: A Political Study*
(Oxford 1973) is relevant. Common lawyers are dealt with in
WILFRID R. PREST (ed.) *Lawyers in Early Modern Europe and America*
(New York 1981); WILFRID R. PREST *The Rise of the Barristers: A Social
History of the English Bar 1590–1640* (Oxford 1986); and C. W.
BROOKS *Pettyfoggers and Vipers of the Commonwealth: The 'Lower
Branch' of the Legal Profession in Early Modern England* (Cambridge
1986).

THE ROYAL FINANCES

The basic work is still F. C. DIETZ *English Public Finance 1485–1641*
Vol. II. *English Public Finance 1558–1641* (New York 1932).

For James's reign MENNA PRESTWICH *Cranfield: Politics and Profits
under the Early Stuarts* (Oxford 1966), is invaluable. So, for Charles's
reign as well, is ROBERT ASHTON *The Crown and the Money Market
1603–1640* (Oxford 1960). There are also two important articles by
ASHTON: 'Revenue Farming under the Early Stuarts' *Economic History
Review* 2nd series Vol. 8 (1956) and 'Deficit Finance in the Reign of

James I' *Economic History Review* 2nd series Vol. 10 (1957). Loan operations are the subject of another article by ASHTON: 'The Disbursing Official under the Early Stuarts: the Cases of Sir William Russell and Philip Burlamachi' *Bulletin of the Institute of Historical Research* Vol. 30 (1957). A. P. NEWTON 'The Establishment of the Great Farm of the English Customs' *Transactions of the Royal Historical Society* 4th series Vol. I (1918) is still of interest. DAVID THOMAS 'Financial and Administrative Developments' in HOWARD TOMLINSON (ed.) *Before the Civil War* (1983) is a useful brief survey.

Any discussion of James's extravagance should take into account the figures for Household expenditure given in P. R. SEDDON 'Household Reforms in the Reign in James I' *Bulletin of the Institute of Historical Research* Vol. 53 (1980). Wardship is dealt with in H. E. BELL *An Introduction to the History and Records of the Courts of Wards and Liveries* (Cambridge 1953) and PAULINE CROFT 'Wardship in the Parliament of 1604' *Parliamentary History* Vol. 2 (1983). For Impositions, see PAULINE CROFT 'Fresh Light on Bate's Case' *Historical Journal* Vol. 30 (1987). Attitudes towards parliamentary supply are analysed in G. L. HARRISS 'Medieval Doctrines in the Debates on Supply 1610–1629' in KEVIN SHARPE (ed.) *Faction and Parliament* (Oxford 1978).

Charles I's finances are the subject of two articles by CONRAD RUSSELL: 'Parliament and the King's Finances' in CONRAD RUSSELL (ed.) *The Origins of the English Civil War* (1973) and 'Charles I's Financial Estimates for 1642' *Bulletin of the Institute of Historical Research* Vol. 58 (1985). There are a number of relevant biographies: MICHEAL VAN CLEAVE ALEXANDER *Charles I's Lord Treasurer. Sir Richard Weston, Earl of Portland 1577–1635* (1975); THOMAS A. MASON *Serving God and Mammon. William Juxon 1582–1663* (1985); and MARTIN J. HAVRAN *Caroline Courtier. The Life of Lord Cottington* (1973).

RELIGION

CLAIRE CROSS *Church and People 1450–1660* (1976) is a good general introduction to the religious history of early modern England. The best account of the Jacobean Church is given in PATRICK COLLINSON *The Religion of Protestants: The Church in English Society 1559–1625* (Oxford 1982). ROLAND G. USHER *The Reconstruction of the English Church* (1910) is still valuable.

The Hampton Court conference has given rise to a number of

important articles: MARK CURTIS 'The Hampton Court Conference and its Aftermath' *History* Vol. 46 (1961); FREDERICK SHRIVER 'Hampton Court Revisited: James I and the Puritans' *Journal of Ecclesiastical History* Vol. 33 (1982); and PATRICK COLLINSON 'The Jacobean Religious Settlement: The Hampton Court Conference' in HOWARD TOMLINSON *Before the Civil War* (1983). It is also scrutinised in NICHOLAS TYACKE *Anti-Calvinists. The Rise of English Arminianism c. 1590–1640* (Oxford 1987), which offers, in addition, an illuminating discussion of the meaning of the term 'puritan'. Also relevant in this context are PATRICK COLLINSON *English Puritanism* (Historical Association 1983); R. T. KENDALL *Calvin and English Calvinism to 1649* (Oxford 1980) and PETER LAKE 'Calvinism and the English Church 1570–1635' *Past & Present* No. 114 (1987). PATRICK COLLINSON 'Lectures by Combination: Structures and Characteristics of Church Life in Seventeenth-Century England' *Bulletin of the Institute of Historical Research* Vol. 48 (1975) examines a 'puritan' aspect of the Church of England. Another aspect is surveyed in W. J. SHEILS *The Puritans in the Diocese of Peterborough 1558–1610* (Northamptonshire Record Society 1979). Separatism and semi-separatism are the theme of MURRAY TOLMIE *The Triumph of the Saints: The Separate Churches of London 1616–1649* (Cambridge 1977). The important (and relatively unresearched) phenomenon of lay puritanism is analysed in J. T. CLIFFE *The Puritan Gentry: The Great Puritan Families of Early Stuart England* (1984).

James I's attitude towards the puritans is discussed in B. W. QUINTRELL 'The Royal Hunt and the Puritans 1604–05, *Journal of Ecclesiastical History* Vol. 31 (1980). Also relevant is STUART BABBAGE *Puritanism and Richard Bancroft* (1962). The development of James's attitude is analysed in KENNETH FINCHAM and PETER LAKE 'The Ecclesiastical Policy of King James I' *Journal of British Studies* Vol. 24 (1985). Episcopal views of James's headship of the Church are discussed in J. P. SOMERVILLE 'The Royal Supremacy and Episcopacy "Jure Divino" 1603–40' *Journal of Ecclesiastical History* Vol. 34 (1983).

CHRISTOPHER HILL *Economic Problems of the Church, from Archbishop Whitgift to the Long Parliament* (Oxford 1956) is still indispensable. A useful summary of improvements in the quality of the clergy is ROSEMARY O'DAY 'The Reformation of the Ministry 1558–1642' in ROSEMARY O'DAY and FELICITY HEAL (eds.) *Continuity and Change: Personnel and Administration of the Church of England 1500–1642* (1976). Also relevant is IAN GREEN 'Career Prospects and Clerical Conformity in the Early Stuart Church' *Past & Present* No. 90 (1981).

NICHOLAS TYACKE's pioneering study of 'Puritanism, Arminianism and Counter-Revolution' in CONRAD RUSSELL *The Origins of the English Civil War* (1973) has now been superseded by his *Anti-Calvinists. The Rise of English Arminianism c. 1590–1640* (Oxford 1987). Tyacke's views have been challenged by PETER WHITE in 'The Rise of Arminianism Reconsidered' *Past & Present* No. 101 (1983), and a debate between the two is printed in *Past & Present* No. 115 (1987). A leading Arminian is studied in ANDREW FOSTER 'The Function of a Bishop: the Career of Richard Neile, 1562–1640' in ROSEMARY O'DAY and FELICITY HEAL (eds.) *Continuity and Change: Personnel and Administration of the Church of England 1500–1642* (1976). An illuminating discussion of Arminianism is G. J. HOENDERDAAL 'The Debate about Arminius outside the Netherlands' in T. H. LUNSINGH SCHEURLEER (ed.) *Leyden University in the Seventeenth Century* (Leyden 1975).

James I's attitude towards Arminianism in Holland is analysed in CHRISTOPHER GRAYSON 'James I and the Religious Crisis in the United Provinces 1613–19' and JOHN PLATT 'Eirenical Anglicans at the Synod of Dort', both in DEREK BAKER (ed.) *Reform and Reformation: England and the Continent c. 1500–c.1750* (1979). Charles I's inclinations in religion are scrutinised by LORD DACRE (H. R. TREVOR-ROPER) in 'Matthew Wren' *Pembroke College Cambridge Society Annual Gazette* No. 60 (1986).

The best life of Laud is still that by H. R. TREVOR-ROPER *Archbishop Laud 1573–1645* (2nd edn 1962). One aspect of his career is considered in Kevin Sharpe 'Archbishop Laud and the University of Oxford' in HUGH LLOYD- JONES, VALERIE PEARL & BLAIR WORDEN (eds.) *History and Imagination* (1981). Laud's opponents feature in STEPHEN FOSTER *Notes from the Caroline Underground: Alexander Leighton, the Puritan Triumvirate, and the Laudian Reaction to Nonconformity* (1978) and ISABEL M. CALDER 'A Seventeenth-Century Attempt to Purify the Anglican Church' [The Feoffees for Impropriations] *American Historical Review* Vol. 53 (1948).

The relationship between religious and political opposition to Charles I is discussed in P. G. LAKE 'Constitutional Consensus and Puritan Opposition in the 1620s: Thomas Scott and the Spanish Match' *Historical Journal* Vol. 25 (1982) and in two articles by JOHN MORRILL: 'Sir William Brereton and England's Wars of Religion' *Journal of British Studies* Vol. 24 (1985), and 'The Religious Context of the English Civil War' *Transactions of the Royal Historical Society* 5th series Vol. 34 (1984). MORRILL's essay on 'The Church in England 1642–49' in the volume edited by him *Reactions to the English Civil*

War 1642–1649 (1982) also throws light on pre-war attitudes. Also relevant is S. P. SALT 'The Origins of Sir Edward Dering's Attack on the Ecclesiastical Hierarchy' *Historical Journal* Vol. 30 (1987).

The standard works on English catholicism in this period are J. C. H AVELING *The Handle and the Axe: the Catholic Recusants in England from Reformation to Emancipation* (1977) and JOHN BOSSY *The English Catholic Community 1570–1850* (1976). The best short account is ALAN DURES *English Catholicism 1558–1642* (1983).

A summary of changing interpretations of early modern English catholicism is given in CAROLINE HIBBARD 'Early Stuart Catholicism: Revisions and Re-Revisions' *Journal of Modern History* Vol. 52 (1980). The effectiveness of the mission is considered by CHRISTOPHER HAIGH in 'The Continuity of Catholicism in the English Reformation' *Past & Present* No. 93 (1981) and 'From Monopoly to Minority: Catholicism in Early Modern England' *Transactions of the Royal Historical Society* 5th series Vol. 31 (1981).

The background of the Gunpowder Plot is analysed in JOHN BOSSY 'The English Catholic Community 1603–1625' in ALAN G. R. SMITH (ed.) *The Reign of James VI and I* (1973) and JENNY WORMALD 'Gunpowder, Treason, and Scots' *Journal of British Studies* Vol. 24 (1985).

Anti-catholic paranoia is the theme of CAROL Z. WIENER 'The Beleagured Isle: a Study of Elizabethan and early Jacobean Anti-Catholicism' *Past & Present* No. 51 (1971); ROBIN CLIFTON 'Fear of Popery' in CONRAD RUSSELL (ed.) *The Origins of the English Civil War* (1973); and PETER LAKE 'The Significance of the Elizabethan Identification of the Pope as Anti-Christ' *Journal of Ecclesiastical History* Vol. 31 (1980). Also relevant are RICHARD CUST and PETER LAKE 'Sir Richard Grosvenor and the rhetoric of Godly Magistracy' *Bulletin of the Institute of Historical Research* Vol. 54 (1981) and PETER LAKE 'Constitutional Consensus and Puritan Opposition in the 1620s: Thomas Scott and the Spanish Match' *Historical Journal* Vol. 25 (1982).

The treatment of recusants under Charles I is discussed in MARTIN J. HAVRAN *The Catholics in Caroline England* (1962); K. J. LINDLEY 'Lay Catholics in England in the Reign of Charles I' *Journal of Ecclesiastical History* Vol. 22 (1971) and T. S. SMITH 'The Persecution of Staffordshire Roman Catholic Recusants 1625–60' *Journal of Ecclesiastical History* Vol. 30 (1979). By far the best analysis of Court catholicism and its political impact is given in CAROLINE M. HIBBARD *Charles I and the Popish Plot* (Chapel Hill 1983).

GOVERNMENT AND SOCIETY

Two good recent studies of English society during the early modern period are KEITH WRIGHTSON *English Society 1580–1680* (1982) and J. A. SHARPE *Early Modern England: A Social History 1550–1760* (1987). The early Stuart Court is analysed in NEIL CUDDY 'The Revival of the Entourage: the Bedchamber of James I, 1603–1625' and KEVIN SHARPE 'The Image of Virtue: the Court and Household of Charles I, 1625–1642', both in DAVID STARKEY (ed.) *The English Court: from the Wars of the Roses to the Civil War* (1987). Patronage is discussed by LINDA LEVY PECK in: *Northampton: Patronage and Policy at the Court of James I* (1982); 'Problems in Jacobean Administration: Was Henry Howard, Earl of Northampton, a Reformer?' *Historical Journal* Vol. 19 (1976); 'Corruption at the Court of James I: the Undermining of Legitimacy' in B. MALAMENT (ed.) *After the Reformation* (Manchester 1980); and 'Court Patronage and Government Policy: the Jacobean Dilemma' in GUY FITCH LYTLE & STEPHEN ORGEL (eds.) *Patronage in the Renaissance* (Princeton 1981). This volume also has R. MALCOLM SMUTS's essay on 'The Political Failure of Stuart Cultural Patronage' which adumbrates a number of themes developed in his *Court Culture and the Origins of a Royalist Tradition in Early Stuart England* (Philadelphia 1987). An individual case of patronage is examined by JOHN H. BARCROFT 'Carleton and Buckingham: The Quest for Office' in HOWARD S. REINMUTH (ed.) *Early Stuart Studies* (Minneapolis 1970). A broader treatment is in ROGER LOCKYER *Buckingham: The Life and Political Career of George Villiers, First Duke of Buckingham 1592–1628* (1981). Faction is the theme of KEVIN SHARPE 'Faction at the Early Stuart Court' *History Today* Vol. 33 (October 1983), and he examines one particular group in 'The Earl of Arundel, His Circle and the Opposition to the Duke of Buckingham, 1618–1628' in the volume of essays edited by him *Faction and Parliament* (Oxford 1978). Later factions are discussed in R. M. SMUTS 'The Puritan Followers of Henrietta Maria in the 1630s' *English Historical Review* Vol. 93 (1978) and ALBERT J. LOOMIE 'The Spanish Faction at the Court of Charles I, 1630–8' *Bulletin of the Institute of Historical Research* Vol. 59 (1986).

The staffing and functions of the central administration are analysed in G. E. AYLMER *The King's Servants: the Civil Service of Charles I* (1961). There is nothing specifically on the Privy Council, though D. H. WILLSON deals with *The Privy Councillors in the House of Commons 1604–29* (Minneapolis 1940). The problems of formulating and executing policy are considered in G. E. AYLMER 'Attempts at Administrative Reform 1625–1640' *English Historical Review* Vol. 72 (1957) and KEVIN SHARPE 'The Personal Rule of Charles I' in HOWARD TOMLINSON (ed.) *Before the English Civil War* (1983). RICHARD CUST examines the role of the Council in *The Forced Loan and English Politics 1626–28* (Oxford 1987) and 'Charles I, the Privy Council, and the Forced Loan' *Journal of British Studies* Vol. 24 (1985).

The relationship between the central government and the local communities is analysed in depth in ANTHONY FLETCHER *Reform in the Provinces: The Government of Stuart England* (1986). A valuable case study is B. W. QUINTRELL 'Government in Perspective: Lancashire and the Privy Council 1570–1640' *Transactions of the Historic Society of Lancashire and Cheshire* (1982). The difficulties involved in implementing government policy are considered in DEREK HIRST 'The Privy Council and Problems of Enforcement in the 1620s' *Journal of British Studies* Vol. 18 (1978) and KEVIN SHARPE 'Crown, Parliament and Locality: Government and Communication in Early Stuart England' *English Historical Review* Vol. 101 (1986).

The significance of the Book of Orders is discussed in B. W. QUINTRELL 'The Making of Charles I's Book of Orders' *English Historical Review* Vol. 95 (1980), PAUL SLACK 'Books of Orders: The Making of English Social Policy 1577–1631' *Transactions of the Royal Historical Society* 5th series Vol. 30 (1980), and R. B. OUTHWAITE 'Dearth and Government Intervention in English Grain Markets 1590–1700' *Economic History Review* Vol. 34 (1981).

Ship Money is the theme of R. J. W. SWALES 'The Ship Money Levy of 1628' *Bulletin of the Institute of Historical Research* Vol. 50 (1977); M. D. GORDON 'The Collection of Ship Money in the Reign of Charles I' *Transactions of the Royal Historical Society* 3rd series Vol. 4 (1910); E. MARCOTTE 'Shrieval Administration of Ship Money in Cheshire, 1637: Limitations of Early Stuart Governance' *Bulletin of the John Rylands University Library of Manchester* Vol. 58 (1976); N. P. BARD 'The Ship Money Case of William Fiennes, Viscount Saye and Sele' *Bulletin of the Institute of Historical Research* Vol. 50 (1977); P. LAKE 'The Collection of Ship Money in Cheshire during the 1630s: a Case Study of Relations between Central and Local Government' *Northern History* Vol. 17 (1981); and KENNETH FINCHAM 'The Judges' Decision on Ship Money in February 1637: the Reaction of Kent' *Bulletin of the Institute of Historical Research* Vol. 57 (1984).

Other government initiatives are discussed in G. HAMMERSLEY 'The Revival of the Forest Laws under Charles I' *History* Vol. 45 (1960); P. A. J. PETTIT 'Charles I and the Revival of Forest Law in Northamptonshire' *Northamptonshire Past & Present* Vol. 3 (1961);

H. H. LEONARD 'Distraint of Knighthood: The Last Phase, 1625–41' *History* Vol. 63 (1978); and B. W. QUINTRELL 'Oliver Cromwell and Distraint of Knighthood' *Bulletin of the Institute of Historical Research* Vol. 57 (1984).

The basic work on the militia is LINDSAY BOYNTON *The Elizabethan Militia* (1967). Relevant articles include G. P. HIGGINS 'The Militia in Early Stuart Cheshire' *Journal of the Chester Archaeological Society* Vol. 61 (1978) and A. HASSELL SMITH 'Militia Rates and Militia Statutes 1558–1663' in PETER CLARK, ALAN G. R. SMITH & NICHOLAS TYACKE (eds.) *The English Commonwealth 1547–1640* (Leicester 1979). Also relevant is LINDSAY BOYNTON 'Martial Law and the Petition of Right' *English Historical Review* Vol. 79 (1964).

The structure of administration in the localities is examined in G. C. F. FORSTER 'The English Local Community and Local Government' in ALAN.G. R. SMITH (ed.) *The Reign of James VI and I* (1973) and L. M. HILL 'County Government in Caroline England 1625–1640' in CONRAD RUSSELL (ed.) *The Origins of the English Civil War* (1973). G. P. HIGGINS examines 'The Government of Early Stuart Cheshire' in *Northern History* Vol. 12 (1976). The administrative functions of the assize judges are considered in J. S. COCKBURN *A History of English Assizes 1558–1714* (Cambridge 1972). The role of the magistrates is assessed in G. C. F. FORSTER *The East Riding Justices of the Peace in the Seventeenth Century* (East Yorkshire Local History Society 1973) and the same author's 'The North Riding Justices and Their Sessions 1603–25' *Northern History* Vol. 10 (1975). Also relevant is J. H. GLEASON *The Justices of the Peace in England 1558–1640* (Oxford 1973).

The standard work on the constable is now JOAN R. KENT *The English Village Constable 1580–1642* (Oxford 1986). A useful summary is the same author's 'The English Village Constable, 1580–1642: The Nature and Dilemmas of the Offices' *Journal of British Studies* Vol. 20 (1981). Attitudes towards the law and its enforcement are the theme of CYNTHIA B. HERRUP *The Common Peace: Participation and the Criminal Law in Seventeenth-century England* (Cambridge 1987); J. A. SHARPE 'Enforcing the Law in a Seventeenth-Century English Village' in V. A. C. GATRELL, BRUCE LENMAN & GEOFFREY PARKER (eds.) *Crime and the Law* (1980); and KEITH WRIGHTSON 'Two Concepts of Order: Justices, Constables and Jurymen in Seventeenth-Century England' in JOHN BREWER & JOHN STYLES (eds.) *An Ungovernable People: The English and Their Law in the Seventeenth and Eighteenth Centuries* (New Brunswick 1980).

The best single book on poverty and vagrancy is now A. L. BEIER *Masterless Men: The Vagrancy Problem in England 1560–1640* (1985).

PARLIAMENT

The role of Parliament in early Stuart England has become in recent years the subject of reassessment. The process began with an article by CONRAD RUSSELL 'Parliamentary History in Perspective 1604–1629' *History* Vol. 61 (1976) and was further stimulated by the same author's *Parliaments and English Politics 1621–1629* (Oxford 1979). A useful summary of RUSSELL's views is his essay 'The Nature of a Parliament in Early Stuart England' in HOWARD TOMLINSON (ed.) *Before the English Civil War* (1983). Criticism of revisionist views associated with Russell is to be found in three articles in *Past & Present* No. 92 (1981): CHRISTOPHER HILL 'Parliament and People in Seventeenth-Century England'; DEREK HIRST 'Revisionism Revised: The Place of Principle'; and THEODORE K. RABB 'Revisionism Revised: The Role of the Commons'.

Elections and the expansion of the electorate are the theme of J. H. PLUMB 'The Growth of the Electorate in England from 1600 to 1715' *Past & Present* No. 45 (1969); DEREK HIRST *The Representative of the People? Voters and Voting in England under the Early Stuarts* (Cambridge 1975); and MARK KISHLANSKY *Parliamentary Selection: Social and Political Choice in Early Modern England* (Cambridge 1986). The Commons' role in disputed elections is examined in DEREK HIRST 'Elections and the Privileges of the House of Commons in the early Seventeenth Century: Confrontation or Compromise?' *Historical Journal* Vol. 18 (1975). The Buckinghamshire election dispute of 1604 is scrutinised in R. C. MUNDEN 'The Defeat of Sir John Fortescue: Court versus Country at the Hustings?' *English Historical Review* Vol. 93 (1978) and LINDA LEVY PECK 'Goodwin v Fortescue: The Local Context of Parliamentary Controversy' *Parliamentary History* Vol. 3 (1984).

Parliamentary procedure is the theme of SHEILA LAMBERT 'Procedure in the House of Commons in the Early Stuart Period' *English Historical Review* Vol. 95 (1980) and E. R. FOSTER *The House of Lords 1603–1649* (Chapel Hill 1983). The latter volume is also concerned with the revival of parliamentary judicature, which is the theme of COLIN G. C. TITE *Impeachment and Parliamentary Judicature in Early Stuart England* (1984) and of J. STODDART FLEMION 'Slow Process, Due Process, and the High Court of Parliament: A Re-interpretation of the Revival of Judicature in the House of Lords, 1621' *Historical Journal* Vol. 17 (1974). Also relevant is E. R. FOSTER 'The Procedure of the House of Commons against Patents and Monopolies 1621–24' in W. AIKEN & B. HENNING (eds.) *Conflict in Stuart England* (1960).

James I's attitude towards Parliament is analysed in R. C. Munden 'James I and "the growth of Mutual Distrust": King, Commons, and Reform, 1603–1604' in KEVIN SHARPE (ed.) *Faction and Parliament* (Oxford 1978) and, most illuminatingly, in JENNY WORMALD 'James VI & I: Two Kings or One?' *History* Vol. 68 (1983). The Commons' view of their role is considered in J. H. HEXTER 'The Apology' in RICHARD OLLARD & PAMELA TUDOR-CRAIG (eds.) *For Veronica Wedgwood These* (1986) and PAULINE CROFT 'Annual Parliaments and the Long Parliament' *Bulletin of the Institute of Historical Research* Vol. 59 (1986).

The proposed Union of James's two kingdoms is discussed in D. H. WILLSON 'King James I and Anglo-Scottish Unity' in W. AIKEN & B. HENNING (eds.) *Conflict in Stuart England* (1960); JOEL J. EPSTEIN 'Francis Bacon and the Issue of Union 1603–08' *Huntington Library Quarterly* Vol. 33 (1969–70); BRUCE GALLOWAY *The Union of England and Scotland 1603–08* (Edinburgh 1986); in two articles by BRIAN P. LEVACK: 'Toward A More Perfect Union: England, Scotland and the Constitution' in BARBARA MALAMENT (ed.) *After the Reformation* (Manchester 1980); and the same author's 'English Law, Scots Law, and the Union' in ALAN HARDING (ed.) *Law-Making and Law-Makers in British History* (Royal Historical Society 1980); and in the same author's *The Formation of the British State: England, Scotland, and the Union 1603–1707* (1987).

The role of Councillors in the Lower House is analysed in D. H. WILLSON *The Privy Councillors in the House of Commons 1604–29* (Minneapolis 1940). Also relevant is the same author's 'The Earl of Salisbury and the "Court" Party in Parliament 1604–10' *American Historical Review* (1931). Two 'tribunes of the people' are scrutinised in ROLAND G. USHER 'Nicholas Fuller: A Forgotten Exponent of English Liberty' *American Historical Review* Vol. 12 (1906–07) and ROBERT ZALLER 'Edward Alford and the Making of Country Radicalism' *Journal of British Studies* Vol. 22 (1983).

The first Parliament of James I is dissected in WALLACE NOTESTEIN *The House of Commons 1604–1610* (1971); the second in T. L. MOIR *The Addled Parliament of 1614* (Oxford 1958); the third in ROBERT ZALLER *The Parliament of 1621: A Study in Constitutional Conflict* (Berkeley 1971); and the last in ROBERT E. RUIGH *The Parliament of 1624: Politics and Foreign Policy* (Cambridge, Mass. 1971).

Purveyance is the theme of ALLEGRA WOODWORTH 'Purveyance for the Royal Household in the Reign of Queen Elizabeth' *Transactions of the American Philosophical Society* Vol. 35. Part 1 (1945) and J. J.N. MCGURK 'Royal Purveyance in the Shire of Kent 1590–1614' *Bulletin of the Institute of Historical Research* Vol. 50 (1977). Wardship is discussed in NICHOLAS TYACKE 'Wroth, Cecil and the Parliamentary Session of 1604' *Bulletin of the Institute of Historical Research* Vol. 50 (1977); PAULINE CROFT 'Wardship in the Parliament of 1604' *Parliamentary History* Vol. 2 (1983); and ERIC LINDQUIST 'The Failure of the Great Contract' *Journal of Modern History* Vol. 57 (1985). An illuminating article on Impositions is PAULINE CROFT 'Fresh Light on Bate's Case' *Historical Journal* Vol. 30 (1987).

G. L. HARRISS analyses the significance of 'Medieval Doctrines in the Debates on Supply 1610–1629' in KEVIN SHARPE (ed.) *Faction and Parliament* (Oxford 1978). Other relevant essays in this collection are SIMON ADAMS 'Foreign Policy and the Parliaments of 1621 and 1624'; J. N. BALL 'Sir John Eliot and Parliament 1624–1629'; and CHRISTOPHER THOMPSON 'The Divided Leadership of the House of Commons in 1629'. Another valuable article by CHRISTOPHER THOMPSON is 'The Origins of the Politics of the Parliamentary Middle Group 1625–29' *Transactions of the Royal Historical Society* 5th series Vol. 22 (1972).

The first Parliament of Charles I is discussed in G. A. HARRISON 'Innovation and Precedent: a Procedural Reappraisal of the 1625 Parliament' *English Historical Review* Vol. 102 (1987). CONRAD RUSSELL examines 'The Parliamentary Career of John Pym, 1621–9' in PETER CLARK, ALAN G. R. SMITH & NICHOLAS TYACKE (eds.) *The English Commonwealth 1547–1640* (Leicester 1979). Various aspects of the Petition of Right are surveyed in two articles by E. R. FOSTER: 'Petitions and the Petition of Right' *Journal of British Studies* Vol. 14 (1974) and 'Printing the Petition of Right' *Huntington Library Quarterly* Vol. 38 (1974–75); and also in J. A. GUY 'The Origins of the Petition of Right Reconsidered' *Historical Journal* Vol. 25 (1982).

The Short Parliament is the theme of JOHN K. GRUENFELDER 'The Election to the Short Parliament' in HOWARD S. REINMUTH (ed.) *Early Stuart Studies* (Minneapolis 1970) and ESTHER S. COPE 'Compromise in Early Stuart Parliaments: the Case of the Short Parliament of 1640' *Albion* Vol. 9 (1977). CONRAD RUSSELL answers the question 'Why did Charles I call the Long Parliament?' in *History* Vol. 69 (1984) and SHEILA LAMBERT discusses 'The Opening of the Long Parliament' in *Historical Journal* Vol. 27 (1984). Attempts at compromise are the theme of CLAYTON ROBERTS 'The Earl of Bedford and the Coming of the English Revolution' *Journal of Modern History* Vol. 49 (1977). The role of the peers is the theme of an important essay by J. S. A. ADAMSON, 'The House of Lords and Parliamentary Management, 1640–49' in CLYVE JONES (ed.) *A Pillar of the Constitution: The House of Lords in British Politics 1603–1784* (1988). This volume also includes

ESTHER S. COPE 'The Bishops and Parliamentary Politics in Early Stuart England'.

Strafford is the subject of a biography by C. V. WEDGWOOD *Thomas Wentworth, First Earl of Strafford: A Revaluation* (1961). Articles on him include J. P. COOPER 'The Fortunes of Thomas Wentworth, Earl of Strafford' *Economic History Review* 2nd series Vol. 2 (1958); PEREZ ZAGORIN 'Did Strafford change sides?' *English Historical Review* Vol. 101 (1986); CONRAD RUSSELL 'The Theory of Treason in the Trial of Strafford' *English Historical Review* Vol. 80 (1965); JOHN H. TIMMIS III 'Evidence and 1 Eliz. I. Cap. 6: The Basis of the Lords' Decision in the Trial of Strafford' *Historical Journal* Vol. 21 (1978); and PAUL CHRISTIANSON 'The "Obliterated" Portions of the House of Lords Journals dealing with the Attainder of Strafford, 1641' *English Historical Review* Vol. 95 (1980). Strafford's principal opponent is the subject of J. H. HEXTER *The Reign of King Pym* (Cambridge, Mass. 1941) and of CONRAD RUSSELL 'The Parliamentary Career of John Pym, 1621–9' in PETER CLARK, ALAN G. R. SMITH & NICHOLAS TYACKE (eds.) *The English Commonwealth 1547–1640* (Leicester 1979).

The best single-volume study of the events of 1640–42 is now ANTHONY FLETCHER *The Outbreak of the English Civil War* (1981).

MAPS

Map 1   Europe in the early seventeenth century

Map 2   England *c.* 1603

Map 3   Diocesan boundaries in the early seventeenth century

Index